D0086935

ESSAYS IN APPRECIATION

ESSAYS IN APPRECIATION

CHRISTOPHER RICKS

CLARENDON PRESS · OXFORD
1996

Oxford University Press, Walton Street, Oxford OX2 6DP
Oxford New York
Athens Auckland Bangkok Bombay
Calcutta Cape Town Dar es Salaam Delhi
Florence Hong Kong Istanbul Karachi
Kuala Lumpur Madras Madrid Melbourne
Mexico City Nairobi Paris Singapore
Taipei Tokyo Toronto
and associated companies in
Berlin Ibadan

Oxford is a trade mark of Oxford University Press

Published in the United States
by Oxford University Press Inc., New York

© Christopher Ricks 1996

All rights reserved. No part of this publication may be reproduced,
stored in a retrieval system, or transmitted, in any form or by any means,
without the prior permission in writing of Oxford University Press.
Within the UK, exceptions are allowed in respect of any fair dealing for the
purpose of research or private study, or criticism or review, as permitted
under the Copyright, Designs and Patents Act, 1988, or in the case of
reprographic reproduction in accordance with the terms of the licences
issued by the Copyright Licensing Agency. Enquiries concerning
reproduction outside these terms and in other countries should be
sent to the Rights Department, Oxford University Press,
at the address above

British Library Cataloguing in Publication Data
Data available

Library of Congress Cataloging in Publication Data
Ricks, Christopher B.
Essays in appreciation / Christopher Ricks.
p. cm.
Includes index.
1. English literature—History and criticism. 2. American
literature—History and criticism. I. Title.
PR99.R49   1995   820.9—dc20   95-25050
ISBN 0-19-818344-5

1 3 5 7 9 10 8 6 4 2

Typeset by Graphicraft Typesetters Ltd., Hong Kong
Printed in Great Britain
on acid-free paper by
Bookcraft Ltd.,
Midsomer Norton, Bath

PR
99
.R49
1996

121696-3633 K8

CONTENTS

DOCTOR FAUSTUS AND HELL
ON EARTH

One context for Marlowe's *Doctor Faustus* is so obvious as to have become largely invisible. A sense of it may do something to meet the complaint by Wilbur Sanders that the play is 'chronically over-explicit', and even to meet Sanders's further predicament: 'It is a nagging sense that there is some more broadly-based and more humanly intelligible way of looking at the Faustian predicament . . . that makes me reluctant to call *Doctor Faustus* a great play.'[1]

William Empson often sought the more broadly-based and more humanly intelligible way of looking at works of literature by suggesting that, far from our being faced by the 'over-explicit', there was something about the plot which had become obscured. 'I think the point was obvious at the time, so obvious that it did not get stated in the text,' Empson says of his suggestion that in *The Spanish Tragedy* 'Andrea had been murdered for love'.[2] Similarly, of Joyce's *Ulysses* Empson posits the offering of Molly by Bloom to Stephen, and then is sweetly reasonable about the substantiation: 'Last of the list, the textual evidence for the Bloom Offer should now be given. There is none to give, as Bloom feels that plain words would put Stephen off, or give him an excuse for a refusal; but I could not think that this upsets the theory.' *Ulysses* is then one kind of extreme case of something's being importantly unstated, since the Bloom Offer is both obvious and a secret: 'Why then does the book make a secret of it? Because the procedure which it regards as an innocent act of charity is heavily penalised by the law. A sexual act performed by two people in the presence of a third one, whatever their sexes, counts as "gross indecency". Prosecutions are seldom mounted, as any eye-witness confesses to the offence automatically.'[3] 'Mounted' has its glint.

The plot of *Doctor Faustus*, too, made Empson think. Mephistophilis says of the trapped Faustus:

[1] *The Dramatist and the Received Idea* (1968), pp. 205, 251.
[2] '*The Spanish Tragedy*' (1956); *Essays on Renaissance Literature*, ii. *The Drama*, ed. John Haffenden (1994), p. 17.
[3] *Using Biography* (1984), pp. 246, 253.

> his labouring brain
> Begets a world of idle fantasies
> To overreach the devil; but all in vain.
>
> (xix 13–15)[4]

The rhyme is grimly conclusive. Empson, asking himself how it could be that an unstupid Faustus could have made so stupid a bargain, set his own labouring brain to beget a world of not-idle fantasies as to how and why Faustus might ever have supposed that he could overreach the devil. Empson even engaged in one supreme kind of practical criticism, the writing of a passage of verse which, interpolated in the text, would make cogent his, Empson's, inter-pretation of the play. In a letter to me in 1976 (which I quote with the kind permission of Lady Empson), Empson said:

I have written a bit more [all? *added above*] for the chorus introducing Act II, usually starting with the soliloquy *Now Faustus must thou needs be damned*:

> Faustus would overreach the Devil now
> And work the spirits yet not pay in Hell.
> He fancies they are doubledealing him
> Claiming Hell's grandeur for a fantasy—
> Not making much of Mephistophilis
> Thinks him a spirit of the elements,
> Until he sees the face of Lucifer.
> He offers murder, but in words alone,
> As meet to flatter Mephistophilis;
> Not after he has seen great Lucifer.

Then the meeting with the other magicians, and the start of the soliloquy after they have gone, are in prose, resuming at 'Despair in God'. I hope my Faust gets performed, but writing the jolly scene in the Sultan's harem will be delayed as long as possible.

'*Usually* starting with the soliloquy' is deliciously cool. But this too is a different type of the extreme case, Empson being obliged to write a passage (of extraordinary ageless non-pastiche, it must be said) without which his thesis about the play will not be credited. The new lines don't just give the argument a leg up, they give it a leg to stand on.

Such suppositions about a plot within a work are usually more vulnerable than suppositions about what presses upon a work from

---

[4] Quotations are from the Revels Plays edition, ed. John D. Jump (1962).

without. Recent critical theory, with its 'margins', might have its own ways of exfoliating Empson's point about *The Ancient Mariner*, for instance; a point not about the poem's plot but about its contemporary context. Empson argued, among other things, that the slave-trade impinges upon the poem.[5] What great guilt so preoccupied Coleridge during those years? What is the great guilt that attaches to the heroic maritime expansions? For the slave-trade may be one of the three or four monstrosities so great as to make any direct contemplation and realization in art unthinkable (hideously rivalled by the death-camps and by atomic devastation). The best poem that deals with the slave-trade (perhaps the only good poem?) would then not be about it; rather, the slave-trade would be about the poem. For Empson would not have wished to speak of the slave-trade as the subject of *The Ancient Mariner*, but nor would he have wished to square it as a mere frame. It is rather one of the poem's elements. It is in the air.

What was in the air for the early audiences of *Doctor Faustus* was the plague.

F. W. Bateson saw that 'with *Piers Plowman*, *Troilus and Criseyde*, the *Canterbury Tales*, and *Sir Gawain and the Green Knight*, English literature suddenly came of age': 'It cannot be a coincidence that this literature all belongs to the generation immediately succeeding the bubonic pandemic of 1348–49 that is now known as the Black Death . . . A society that loses one third of its population in some fifteen months must adjust itself violently if it is to survive.'[6] The plague was to be endemic in England after the Black Death. Everyone knows about the plague in Marlowe's London, but apparently no one chooses to bring it into substantial relation to *Doctor Faustus*; not even F. P. Wilson, author of *The Plague in Shakespeare's London* and of *Marlowe and the Early Shakespeare*, and editor of Dekker's Plague Pamphlets. The pressure of the plague upon the play strikes me as obvious and yet ignored. A *cordon sanitaire* has been left between *Doctor Faustus* and even the biographical facts or likelihoods. Plague was so rife then that the less likely choice, for the play's composition, of 1588–9 rather than 1592–3 would not much matter. Still, 1592–3—the last year of Marlowe's life—has more to be said for it. W. W. Greg noted that the play 'was performed, presumably on

---

[5] (1964); *Argufying*, ed. John Haffenden (1987), pp. 297–319.
[6] *A Guide to English Literature* (1965), p. 26.

the London stage, by some unidentified company, no doubt before the plague of 1592–4 reached its height and put a stop to all acting'. In May 1593, Marlowe was at Thomas Walsingham's country house, 'having perhaps taken refuge there from the plague which was raging in London'.[7]

Marlowe's personal involvement with the plague would matter less than everyone's involvement with it. Even to speak of a 'context' is to understate what is at issue. Keith Thomas's title for the Prologue to *Religion and the Decline of Magic* is 'The Environment', and he at once gives the plague a hideous pride of place:

Most dreaded of all was the bubonic plague, which was endemic until the last quarter of the seventeenth century ... In the hundred and fifty years before the great visitation of 1665 there were only a dozen years when London was free from plague. Some people were thought to have died of it every year and periodically there were massive outbreaks ... In 1563 some 20,000 Londoners are thought to have died; in 1593, 15,000 ... The plague terrified by its suddenness, its virulence and its social effects.[8]

Even the words 'The Environment', though far less abstract and academic than my speaking of a 'context', have here too much equanimity. The plague horrifyingly environs you, but then—even worse—you environ it.

The plague then pressed everywhere in the city, as the plague-orders will evidence (perhaps first printed 1574; an important collection in 1583; 1592 ...). But the plague pressed notoriously upon the theatre. F. P. Wilson devotes a separate section to this: 'The Elizabethan theatres suffered heavily from the many epidemics of the sixteenth and seventeenth centuries.'[9] The City wrote to the Privy Council (*c.*1584): 'To play in plague-time is to increase the plague by infection: to play out of plague-time is to draw the plague by offendings of God upon occasion of such plays.' *Play* tolls with *plague* (guilt by association and infection), in a way which must have left French preachers envious (*la peste* having no such tolling against French plays); and so it does again in a sermon of 1577: 'the cause of plagues is sinne, if you looke to it well: and the cause of sinne are plays: therefore the cause of plagues are playes'. 'The reward of sin is death.'

[7] Jump (ed.), pp. xxx–xxxi, xxii.   [8] (1971), pp. 7–8.
[9] *The Plague in Shakespeare's London* (1927), pp. 50–3.

Even those who did not think that the plague was God's wrath against plays must still have conceded that, for other reasons, the authorities were right to close the theatres, as they so often did from 1564 on. Wilson quotes the Court of Aldermen in 1583 on the danger of 'the assembly of people to plays . . . and many infected with sores running on them . . . perilous for contagion . . . the terrible occasion of God's wrath and heavy striking with plagues.' The assembly of people to church-services was a shifty matter: 'The authorities', Wilson notes drily, 'for the most part held that it was impossible to take the infection during the act of worship, but their regulations do not tally with their convictions.' Some of the fierceness with which churchmen attacked the theatres is likely to be an unease at such odious comparisons. By the time there appeared, in 1604, 'the earliest edition of the play of which a copy has survived', a huge and hideous failure to survive had supervened: the plague of 1603, *The Wonderfull yeare* in the title of Dekker's lacerating account, when 36,000 died, over a sixth of the inhabitants of London. Three years later, and not without memories of *Doctor Faustus*, Dekker gave to the world *The Seven Deadly Sinnes of London, Drawn in seven severall coaches, through the seven severall Gates of the Citie, Bringing the Plague with them* (1606). Edward Arber's nineteenth-century reprint, prefacing the work with 'The Scheme of the Triumphs of the Seven Deadly Sins of London', produced a sentence which has its aptness to *Doctor Faustus* as I see it: 'The Plague is threatened, but not described; having been so recently experienced.'

It is doubtful whether an audience at any play performed in 1594 and soon thereafter could extirpate the consciousness that plague was in the air. Plague was even to put in bizarre appearances in *Volpone* and *The Alchemist*. But in any case Marlowe, with decisiveness and tact, immediately intimates the plague's importance without letting it become the subject of the play (it is the play's element, not its subject). For what is Faustus's triumph as a doctor, there in the twenty-first line of the play's first scene?

> Are not thy bills hung up as monuments,
> Whereby whole cities have escap'd the plague?

—with *plague* given the salience of rhythmical conclusion, and yet (here is the tact) not left there—not pressed, but touched:

> Whereby whole cities have escap'd the plague
> And thousand desperate maladies been cur'd?

Cur'd is exactly stationed against *the plague*; you escape the plague, or you don't—cures are something else. An audience in these years, in a theatre of all places, would not have taken lightly a reference, twenty lines into a play, to medicine's mastery as that 'Whereby whole cities have escap'd the plague'. Nor would they have taken lightly (as we do, when we say that we avoid something like the plague, or talk of being pestered) that oath which recurs in *Doctor Faustus*: 'A plague on her'; 'A plague take you' (four times, this last or a form of it). The centre of the play is visited by these curses; the beginning and end of the play speak of the visitation of the plague itself, which thereby swathes the play. First, the literal plague of the first scene; last, the eternal plague that is Hell. Faustus had cursed his enemies ('And hell shall after plague their treachery'), and at the very end, twelve lines before his last words, he contemplates his undying soul: 'But mine must live still to be plagu'd in hell'. Let us at least think of what it was to live in terror of the plague, and in terror of Hell; and let us (later) think too of their likeness and unlikeness.

But first it must be stressed not only that the world of Marlowe and of the theatre was alive to plague but that so is *The History of Doctor Faustus* (translated 1592, and either Marlowe's source or— less likely—derived from a source shared with Marlowe). Three of the *History*'s chapters refer literally to plague, and two others have the extended sense ('as plagues unto men', 'plaguing us'). Faustus had powers of prediction for which in Marlowe's England men would have given much: 'If anything wonderful were at hand, as death, famine, plague, or wars, he would set the time and place in true and just order, when it should come to pass' (ch. 17). Not, again, that there is anything surprising about this connection, which would rather have about it a tacit obviousness amounting to inevitability. For the Devil was intimate with plague. In *The Hour of Our Death*, Philippe Ariès has a section on (a happy conjunction) 'The Influence of the Missionaries and of the Plague'; and in 'The Visit to the Cemetery' he expatiates on the plague as 'the work of the devil'; 'For the devil extends his power in time of plague . . . The plague, the devil, and the cemetery form a kind of unholy trinity of influence'.[10] In the plague-ridden London of Marlowe's day, people knew

---

[10] (1981), pp. 123, 477. Also *Religion and the Decline of Magic*, p. 472: 'The Puritan, Henry Holland, attributed the plague to evil spirits.'

just how diabolical was the notorious longing for company felt by the damned. When Faustus elicits from Mephistophilis the reason why the devils crave to enlarge their kingdom—*Solamen miseris socios habuisse doloris* (To the unhappy, it is a comfort to have had companions in misfortune)—the thought would have struck with particular force upon those who knew one diabolical horror of the plague: that, as Defoe was later to say in *A Journal of the Plague Year*, 'there was a seeming propensity or a wicked inclination in those that were infected to infect others.'

To feel the pressure of the plague upon the play is to gain a different sense of much about Faustus's bargain and about the exercises of power which follow it—or rather, about how both of these matters would have been likely to strike the contemporary audience. There is a long tradition of mere disparagement of Faustus's bargain, a tradition which gravitates naturally from a sense that Faustus demeans himself to a sense that *Doctor Faustus* demeans itself. Francis Jeffrey spoke of Faustus's selling his soul 'for the ordinary price of sensual pleasure';[11] L. C. Knights, of 'the perverse and infantile desire for enormous power and immediate gratifications'. In his Revels edition, John Jump exhibits this conventional wisdom, which of course has a lot of truth in it: 'Faustus, then, concludes an infamous bargain in order to enjoy the knowledge, the pleasure, and above all the power for which he craves.' But to say only this is to ignore the greatest and most fundamental thing which Faustus buys with his soul, so great and fundamental as to go unnoticed if we are not careful: the guarantee that he will live for another twenty-four years. Such a guarantee would never be nugatory (and critics are oddly blithe who write as if it would be), but it must come with particular force in times of, say, war and—even more—in time of plague. In the midst of life we are in death: this was monstrously manifest in a society haunted by plague. Faustus, in buying those years (a span of years which would at his age take him up to about the life-expectancy of Elizabethan England—a great many young adults died in their prime between 20 and 50), could not but be a manifestation of a guarantee which even the most devout must sometimes crave and which all, in those years, might especially crave.

[11] Here and elsewhere I profit from John Jump's *Doctor Faustus* in the Casebook series (1969).

When Wilbur Sanders says that 'Faustus's condemnation is . . . writ large (too large, as I see it) in the opening scene', I should want to stay a little with the word 'condemnation', and relate it to the pressure then of being condemned to sudden death. Faustus is plainly condemned by the play; but we make this too easy for ourselves, too untaxing, if we abstract Faustus's decision from a world which would at least have been more than usually *tempted* (the notion is dramatically and spiritually apt) to condone all such bargains as, in extremis, tried to buy sheer life. G. H. Lewes's words are touched with complacency: 'a legend admirably characteristic of the spirit of those ages in which men, believing in the agency of the devil, would willingly have bartered their future existence for the satisfaction of present desires'. But Faustus, when he mortgages his post-mortal life (*not* barters his future *existence*, exactly), buys with it not just the satisfaction of present desires, but a guarantee of twenty-four years of precisely 'future existence'. Hazlitt may say that, in order to 'realise all the fictions of a lawless imagination', Faustus 'sets at defiance all mortal consequences', but *mortal* consequences are just what Faustus precludes for twenty-four years. It is all very well for Hazlitt to deplore the bargain, but his words 'for a few short years' are unimaginative. How short is short, and how few is few? Hazlitt is not really contemplating sequent death. The point is not that Faustus is shown as under such sentence of sudden death, but that his tragedy was devised for an audience who would inform it with their own sense of such a visitation, and who would therefore not sell short, as being sold 'for a few short years', the fearful impulses with which the play is in touch. Most of us, even young scholars, would not simply or entirely despise a guarantee of twenty-four years of life; the more so, in a society where life-expectancy was markedly less than in ours; and *a fortiori* in a society ravaged by plague. The most thoroughgoing excoriation of Faustus is by James Smith; the essay has all of Smith's fierce clarity and theological edge, and it twice speaks of Faustus as not having 'the shadow of an excuse'. But it is a consequence of Smith's merciless position that he should not ever ask about one shadow which might fall upon the play as first performed ('Whereby whole cities have escap'd the plague'), a shadow which would constitute at least the relevant *temptation* to see an excuse; just as it is a consequence of Smith's position that he should make no mention whatsoever of Faustus's aspirations and achievements in medicine.

For the most important function of the middle scenes of the play is their explicit insistence upon Faustus's being, for his twenty-four years, incapable of dying. My word 'function' carries the traditional reservation about these scenes, which are often unimaginative in conception and feeble in execution. But execution is the word. When the play (in its B text) took over from *The History of Doctor Faustus* the revenge-stories—of the Knight Benvolio with his horns, and of the horse-courser—it took over stories which turn upon the impossibility of killing Faustus. But the play is explicit where the *History* is not, for it is only in the play that Faustus is given this to say, when his head had seemed to be struck from his shoulders:

> Knew you not, traitors, I was limited
> For four-and-twenty years to breathe on earth?
> And had you cut my body with your swords,
> Or hew'd this flesh and bones as small as sand,
> Yet in a minute had my spirit return'd
> And I had breath'd a man made free from harm.
> But wherefore do I dally my revenge?
>
> (xiii 71-6)[12]

It is a mere six lines later that Faustus exults, imprudently and blasphemously, in divine vengeance ('And hell shall after plague their treachery'); and it is this speech—'I was limited / For four-and-twenty years to breathe on earth'—which makes clear how the play takes the pre-eminent contractual item, on Faustus's side of the bargain, which is adapted from the *History*: 'On these conditions following: First, that Faustus may be a spirit in form and substance'. That is, incapable of mortality. 'Yet in a minute had my spirit return'd / And I had breath'd a man made free from harm'.

The divine peripety is such that everything which makes for Faustus makes also against him. The unkillability which is a mercy when he loathes others is a torment when he loathes himself; it is one of the tacitly horrible things about Faustus's impulse to commit suicide that suicide is not his to commit:

> 'Faustus, thou art damn'd!' Then guns and knives,
> Swords, poison, halters, and envenom'd steel
> Are laid before me to dispatch myself;

---

[12] The killing of Faustus receives mention, of various kinds, at for instance xiii 13, 22, 28, and at xv 37.

> And long ere this I should have done the deed
> Had not sweet pleasure conquer'd deep despair.
>
> (vi 21–5)

He speaks too soon. No more than Spenser's Despair could Faustus kill himself.

> Damn'd art thou, Faustus, damn'd; despair and die!
>
> (*Mephistophilis gives him a dagger*)
>
> Hell claims his right and with a roaring voice
> Says, 'Faustus, come; thine hour is almost come';
> And Faustus now will come to do thee right.
>
> (xviii 55–9)

But until his hour is come, Mephistophilis's dagger is cruelly—tantalizingly—absurd; and once his hour is come, no dagger will release him.

Faustus, then, buys not only knowledge and power, but time—half a lifetime of it, and this is to be put before an audience who knew with particular force that a lifetime might now be no time at all. In the words of the *History*, he buys 'certain years to live'; and years certainly to live. Dekker wrote of the plague: 'And albeit, no man at any time is assured of life, yet no man (within the memory of man) was ever so neere death as now.'[13] But Faustus was 'assured of life'. It is just that the premium was damnably steep. My claim is not that our apprehending this will make the play perfect but that it will make much of the play more explicable; the enterprise makes sense. Here I have in mind what I take to be the exemplary demonstration in our day of such a critical argument: the account of *Cymbeline*, and of the pressure put upon the play by King James's statecraft, by Emrys Jones;[14] an account of 'Stuart *Cymbeline*' which scrupulously distinguishes explanation from justification.

T. S. Eliot described Marlowe as 'the most thoughtful, the most blasphemous (and therefore, probably, the most Christian)' of Shakespeare's contemporaries.[15] One dimension of the blasphemy within the play is the hideous perversion, within the Faustian bargain,

---

[13] *A Rod for Run-awayes* (1625); *The Plague Pamphlets of Thomas Dekker*, ed. F. P. Wilson (1925), p. 166.

[14] *Essays in Criticism*, xi (1961), 84–99.

[15] 'Shakespeare and the Stoicism of Seneca' (1927); *Selected Essays* (1932), 1951 edn, p. 133.

of the usual high and holy hope. The hope was that God and goodness would protect you; protect you even against the plague. On
the other hand, mere underlings of the supernatural were likely to
prove inadequate: 'There was seldom any suggestion that a cunning
man could cure a victim of the plague, though he might be able
to give him a charm or amulet which would prevent him from
catching it': Keith Thomas's words might be related to his insistence on the frequency of Faustian stories during the sixteenth and
seventeenth centuries:

> Spirit-raising was a standard magical activity. Spiritual beings were thought
> to offer a short cut to riches, love, knowledge and power of all kinds; and
> the Faustian legend had a literal meaning for its Elizabethan and Jacobean
> audiences.[16]

But if we give a literal meaning to 'power of all kinds', it becomes
clear that one such kind is the ground of all others. The supreme
Faustian bargain could on occasion give a short cut to not being cut
short.

'In times of plague, remarked an Elizabethan theologian, men
"flee for remedy . . . some to certain saints as S. Roch or S. Anthony;
and some to the superstitious arts of witchcraft" ' (Keith Thomas).[17]

> Say he surrenders up to him his soul
> So he will spare him four-and-twenty years,
> Letting him live in all voluptuousness . . .
>
> (iii 92–4)

Spare him, not only as granting him years, but as granting him clemency
in the face of death. The same sense of first-things-first is tacit in
the sequence of the line 'Letting him live in all voluptuousness'.

Doctor Faustus is a play not only about buying time and a guarantee of living to spend it, but about buying them with an eternity
of Hell. Hell eternally vibrates with—to and against—the plague.
For the plague was Hell on earth; it was both more hideously Hell
than this earth had seen, and yet—just because it was on this earth—
it fell hideously short of that eternity, not the less appalling for being

---

[16] *Religion and the Decline of Magic*, pp. 208, 230; also p. 473 on 'Faustian legends',
and p. 637 where 'Faustian dreams' are followed, six lines later, by a mention of
the plague.

[17] Ibid., pp. 638–9.

inconceivable, of suffering. It is not anything so cool as a trope which leads the play to reiterate the conjunction:

> And hell shall after plague their treachery.
>
> (xiii 83)

> But mine must live still to be plagued in hell.
>
> (xix 179)

Still: always. Take the worst suffering the earth has seen; take away from it the one thing which mitigates its terror, that it does end ('All's well that ends', in the happy amputation of Robert Lowell); and you are left with the plague's bitter likeness and ultimate unlikeness to Hell, such as struck more than the usual fear of God into people. 'Ay, we must die an everlasting death' (i 45): a fate worse than death. When Dekker cried out, of the plague, 'What miserie continues ever?',[18] he sought comfort even within the plague. But the plague that is Hell (a plague made manifest in the sores and blains in the art of Bosch and Breughel) is all darkness visible and comfortless. It is the agonizing pincer-jaws of the divine paradox. Faustus 'now must die eternally' (xix 29). 'Impose some end to my incessant pain' (xix 168), he pleads, desperately contradicting himself in the very utterance.

No one can write about the plague as well as Dekker without calling up Hell on earth:

> What an unmatchable torment were it for a man to be bard up every night in a vast silent Charnell-house? hung (to make it more hideous) with lamps dimly & slowly burning, in hollow and glimmering corners: where all the pavement should in stead of greene rushes, be strewde with blasted Rosemary, withered Hyacinthes, fatall Cipresse and Ewe, thickly mingled with heapes of dead mens bones: the bare ribbes of a father that begat him, lying there: here the Chaples hollow scull of a mother that bore him: round about him a thousand Coarses, some standing bolt upright in their knotted winding sheetes: others halfe mouldred in rotten Coffins, that should suddenly yawne wide open, filling his nosthrils with noysome stench, and his eyes with the sight of nothing but crawling wormes . . . were not this an infernall prison? would not the strongest-harted man (beset with such a ghastly horror) looke wilde? and runne madde? and die? And even such a formidable shape did the diseased Citie appear in.[19]

---

[18] *The Wonderfull yeare* (1603); *Plague Pamphlets*, p. 42.

[19] *Plague Pamphlets*, pp. 27, 31.

Here, in *The Wonderfull yeare*, Dekker moves naturally, horribly so, from such an evocation of Hell on earth—'an infernall prison'—to a sermon on sin and mortality; to blasphemy; to tragedy ('the shutting up of this Tragicall Act'); and to the old undying mingling of fascination and exhaustion: 'My spirit grows faint with rowing in this Stygian Ferry', but then at once:

> Imagine then that all this while, Death (like a Spanish Leagar, or rather like stalking *Tamberlaine*) hath pitcht his tents, (being nothing but a heape of winding sheetes tackt together) in the sinfully-polluted Suburbes: the Plague is Muster-maister and Marshall of the field: Burning Feavers, Boyles, Blaines, and Carbuncles . . .

Why, this is hell, nor am I out of it. And yet not so, for this—being within time, which is the mercy of eternity—is a Hell which men and women can die out of.

This knot—of the play and the plague, temporal and eternal—is drawn so tight by Marlowe that the binding strands are less visible than they are in lesser art, for instance that of George Wither's *History of the Pestilence* (1625):

> And harke yee People, harken you, I pray,
> That were wth me preserv'd to see this day:
> And listen you, that shall be brought upon
> This *Stage* of action, when our *Sceane* is done.
> Come harken all, and lett no soule refraine
> To heare; nor lett it heare my words in vayne.
> ffor, from the slaughter house of *Death*, & from
> The habitations of the *Dead*, I come.
> I am escaped from the greedie Iawes
> Of *Hell*.
>
> (i 31–40)

If the plague cannot be conceived of except as a type of Hell (and yet far short), then likewise Hell is brought home as plague. But in *Doctor Faustus* the words 'perpetual' and 'that ne'er can die' are admonitions that hereafter the last twist of the knife is that there will be no last twist of the knife:

> Now, Faustus, let thine eyes with horror stare
> Into that vast perpetual torture-house.
> There are the furies, tossing damned souls
> On burning forks; their bodies boil in lead:

> There are live quarters broiling on the coals,
> That ne'er can die.

(xix 116–21)

Wilbur Sanders deplores this 'obsessive preoccupation with infernal torments': 'It is one of those matters on which his imagination appears to have dwelt with unwholesome insistence.' But the case is altered if the torments are not only infernal and not only imagined.

'No mortal can express the pains of Hell' (xviii 47)—not least because it is immortals who feel them. But the plague can express something, along with the sense of just what the inexpressibility amounts to.

> Inspire us therefore how to tell
> The *Horror* of a *Plague*, the *Hell.*[20]

Inspire has its horrid power here. 'Sicknes was sent to breathe her unwholsome ayres into thy nosthrils.' For if plague was in the air, it was dangerous to breathe a word. Hence the grim comedy of certain of the 'tokens', as Defoe was to acknowledge. 'My friend Dr Heath was of opinion that it might be known by the smell of their breath; but then, as he said, who durst smell to that breath for his information? since, to know it, he must draw the stench of the plague up into his own brain, in order to distinguish the smell!'

John Berryman wrote in one of the Dream Songs (No. 366):

> These Songs are not meant to be understood, you understand.
> They are only meant to terrify & comfort.

Berryman was looking back at one of Dekker's Plague Pamphlets: *London Looke Backe, At That Yeare of Yeares 1625. And Looke Forward, Upon This Yeare, 1630: Written, not to Terrifie, But to Comfort.* Marlowe's *Doctor Faustus* is aligned rather with Berryman's '&' than with Dekker's 'not . . . But'. It is written to terrify and comfort. The sources of the terror are not quite what is sometimes said; it is not 'the possibility of final destruction' (Sanders) which is supremely appalling, but the final possibility that there is no such thing, instead an eternity of damnation, never final. 'Thy fatal time draws to a final end' (xv 22). Not final, but only temporarily finite, and to be succeeded by an infinite eternity of being plagued in Hell. The comfort, consolation

---

[20] *Newes from Graves-ende* (1604); *Plague Pamphlets*, p. 82. Also *The Seven Deadly Sinnes of London.*

even, is that which is characteristic of art, which must not be—in
Frank Kermode's great phrase—'too consolatory to console'. In time
of plague, there can be imagined—even then—something worse: an
eternity of plague. In time of plague, there can be imagined, too,
something better: an eternity without plague. An eternity of Heaven,
perhaps; or at least, not least, of oblivion. If the Christian vision is
not true (Marlowe's great compliment to Christianity is not to believe
it but to entertain it), our souls may be 'chang'd into little water
drops, / And fall into the ocean, ne'er be found' (xix 185–6). Eliot,
who paid Marlowe the compliment of believing him blasphemous,
once argued with A. A. Milne about pacifism:

> I think . . . that writers like Mr. Milne suffer from two prejudices. One is
> that the great thing is to go on living. 'If', he says 'the intelligent man of
> war wishes to know why death is taken so seriously by so many people,
> I will tell him'. After this portentous preparation, Mr. Milne stops for an
> impressive moment (indicated by a new paragraph) and continues: 'The
> reason is this: Death is final . . . Death is the worst thing that can happen,
> because it is the last thing that can happen'. Well, I felicitate Mr. Milne;
> he is haunted neither by the thought of Achilles among the shades, nor
> by the terrors of death that beset the Christian. 'Death is final'. If I thought
> that death was final, it would seem to me a far less serious matter than
> it does. I should still no doubt be afraid of dying (though tired of living,
> as Mr. Paul Robeson sang), but I should not be afraid of death. And life
> would seem to me much less important than it does.[21]

Marlowe's *Doctor Faustus* takes the plague more seriously than might
seem from the plot alone. So does Goethe's *Faust*. Goethe's social
satire against fashionable medicine may seem airy light:

> But above all, learn to handle women!
> Their everlasting moans and groans,
> So multifarious, miscellaneous,
> Are cured at a single point.[22]

But everlasting moans and groans call up another scene. This grim
levity of an impersonating Mephistophilis is reached only after we
have passed through the extraordinary story of the plague. First,
there is the Old Peasant's gratitude to Faust and his father:

---

[21] *Time and Tide*, 12 January 1935.
[22] *Goethe's Faust: Part I*; trans. Randall Jarrell (1976), pp. 96–7, 50–2.

> Many a man stands living here'
> That your father, in the nick of time,
> Snatched from the fever's burning rage
> When he put limits to the plague.
> And you yourself, a young man then,
> Went into every stricken house:
> Many a corpse they took away
> But you, though, came out safe and sound
> And bore up under bitter trials.
> The Helper yonder gave our helper aid.

More bitter, though, is the diabolical truth:

> I thought to extort from the Lord in Heaven
> This ending of that plague. The crowd's applause
> Sounds to me, now, like mockery.
> Oh, if only you could look into my soul:
> How little father and son deserve such fame!

> There was the medicine! The patients died
> And no one asked: But who's recovered?

> And so with hellish electuaries
> Worse, far worse, than the plague itself,
> We raged through these mountains and these valleys.
> I myself have given poison to thousands.
> They withered away—and I must live
> To hear men praise the shameless murderers!

Goethe's Faust is one by whom whole cities have incurred the plague, and thousand desperate maladies been caused.

Again, when Thomas Mann turned to a modern *Doctor Faustus*, it was natural to him to recur repeatedly to the plague. The Devil's insinuating conversation with Adrian Leverkühn turns naturally to a memory of the plague at Cologne, just as witchcraft is here more than once called a pestilence. A modern *Doctor Faustus* inevitably makes explicit the sex-horror (of which D. H. Lawrence wrote so penetratingly) attendant upon that sub-species of the plague which was thought to invite the larger plague: venereal disease. When Mann's Devil invokes 'running sore and plague and worm-eaten nose' (ch. 25), he conjures up a venereal plague. When Leverkühn in his illness is 'pinched and plagued with hot pincers' (ch. 33), these anticipate the plagues of Hell. Such a conjunction had been manifest in Marlowe's understanding of Faust and lust, and in others of the age. John Donne has a hot punitive lust upon him when in a sermon on the plague he relishes the fact of 'men whose lust carried them into the jaws of infection in lewd houses, and seeking one sore perished with another'.[23] Dekker more than once sees the plague as a diseased whore. If we seek a modern counterpart to the plague, we have it, horribly to hand, in the ungrounded panic and the grounded terror of AIDS.

Mann's novel is, too, a reminder of the way in which art—in the face of the greatest horrors (plague, the slave-trade, the death-camps)—may be obliged by indirections to find directions out. For even as the plague is not Marlowe's subject but his environment and element, so the Nazi horror, with its culmination in the death-camps, is Mann's pressure and oppression. 'Yet how strangely the times, these very times in which I write, are linked with the period that forms the frame of this biography!' Those words come two pages after the novel itself has cracked open:

A transatlantic general has forced the population of Weimar to file past the crematories of the neighbouring concentration-camp. He declared that these citizens—who had gone in apparent righteousness about their daily concerns and sought to know nothing, although the wind brought to their noses the stench of burning human flesh—he declared that they too were guilty of the abominations on which he forced them now to turn their eyes. Was that unjust? Let them look, I look with them. In spirit I let myself be shouldered in their dazed or shuddering ranks. Germany had become a thick-walled underground torture-chamber, converted into one by a profligate dictatorship vowed to nihilism from its beginnings on. Now the torture-chamber has been broken open, open lies our shame before the eyes of the world. Foreign commissions inspect those incredible photographs everywhere displayed, and tell their countrymen that what they have seen surpasses in horribleness anything the human imagination can conceive.[24]

Why, this is Hell. It remains the central critical question about Mann's *Doctor Faustus* whether it did achieve a true relation of those horrors to the Faustian legend. 'Needing Hell, we have learned how to build and run it on earth', says George Steiner, musing upon the price we may have paid for 'the loss of Hell': 'The absence of the familiar damned opened a vortex which the modern totalitarian

[23] 15 January 1626; quoted in *The Plague in Shakespeare's London*, p. 155.
[24] (1947); trans. H. T. Lowe-Porter.

state filled.'[25] Some of us, though, think that the presence of the familiar damned did not do much exactly to stanch the Inquisition and its lively work at enacting Hell on earth. Rather a Christian country, Germany.

Let me end, then, with a work which contemplates Hell (and totalitarianism), but with a reversal of the figure and ground as I see them in Marlowe: *The Plague* of Albert Camus. Its essential context, or again element, is not here the subject of the novel: totalitarian evil in general, and Nazi anti-semitism in particular. When Camus first set down notes for the novel, the nightmare consummation of this evil had not yet brought about the death-camps. Yet Camus as early as 1941 saw the association of the plague with anti-semitism; he noted that 'in 1342 . . . at the time of the Black Death, Jews were executed. In 1481, when the plague ravaged southern Spain, the Inquisition blamed the Jews.'[26] When Camus's novel was published in 1947, it could be seen as more truly responsive to the vile genocide than any direct engagement in art had been. The man who jotted down in 1941 the disconcerting words *La Peste libératrice* did not stay in thrall to the perverted religious asseverations of Antonin Artaud, who craved the plague as a great cleanser and was sure that 'the theatre is like the plague'. Yet Artaud's argument, in 'Theatre and the Plague', does rise, in its dementia, to being blasphemy; as Camus's novel, in its sanity, rises to being a work of art which engages with a supreme horror, of Hell on earth and elsewhere, by not allowing the horror to practise the subjections of being the subject—any more than Marlowe had yielded to the pressure of the plague. 'I, too, believe in calling things by their name . . . But what's the name in this case?' 'That I shan't say; and anyhow you wouldn't gain anything by knowing.'[27] But we who hear this conversation in *The Plague* know what is not being said. 'The doctor was still looking out of the window. Beyond it lay the tranquil radiance of a cool spring sky; inside the room a word was echoing still, the word "plague"'. In Marlowe's *Doctor Faustus*, it echoes, but from outside too, though from no tranquil radiance: 'O, it strikes, it strikes!'

[25] *In Bluebeard's Castle* (1971), p. 48.
[26] Herbert Lottman, *Albert Camus* (1979), pp. 256-7.
[27] *The Plague*, Part I, chs. v–vi; trans. Stuart Gilbert.

JOHN DONNE: 'FAREWELL TO LOVE'

Donne's poems, whether or not they are personal memories, record a dislike of having come. Post-coital sadness and revulsion are grimly seized, but what is more grim is that the poems are so often driven to bend this animus upon their own previous act of creative love. The old criticism of Donne was that he did not create whole poems; for me, this takes shape in the recurrent phenomenon of how unhealthily the poems end. Of the half-dozen essential instances, 'Farewell to Love' may be the starting-point, an extremity.

FAREWELL TO LOVE

Whilst yet to prove,
I thought there was some deity in love
So did I reverence, and gave
Worship; as atheists at their dying hour
Call, what they cannot name, an unknown power,
As ignorantly did I crave:
Thus when
Things not yet known are coveted by men,
Our desires give them fashion, and so
As they wax lesser, fall, as they size, grow.

But, from late fair
His highness sitting in a golden chair,
Is not less cared for after three days
By children, than the thing which lovers so
Blindly admire, and with such worship woo;
Being had, enjoying it decays:
And thence,
What before pleased them all, takes but one sense,
And that so lamely, as it leaves behind
A kind of sorrowing dullness to the mind.

Ah cannot we,
As well as cocks and lions jocund be,
After such pleasures? Unless wise
Nature decreed (since each such act, they say,
Diminisheth the length of life a day)
This; as she would man should despise
The sport,

> Because that other curse of being short,
>   And only for a minute made to be
> Eager, desires to raise posterity.
>
>   Since so, my mind
> Shall not desire what no man else can find,
>   I'll no more dote and run
> To pursue things which had endamaged me.
> And when I come where moving beauties be,
>   As men do when the summer's sun
>   Grows great,
> Though I admire their greatness, shun their heat;
>   Each place can afford shadows. If all fail,
> 'Tis but applying worm-seed to the tail.[1]

The poem's ending is an act of revulsion, and in me it then
inspires a revulsion, not only from its repudiation of love and sex
but also from its repudiation of the poem's own deepest
apprehendings. The point is not just that the preceding lines were
more merely beautiful, but that they have a depth, a corporeal and
spiritual grace, worth gaining; the preceding lines are unsentimentally
comfortable in their sexuality, even in the act of imagining the relief
of freedom from it:

> And when I come where moving beauties be,
>   As men do when the summer's sun
>   Grows great,
> Though I admire their greatness, shun their heat;
>   Each place can afford shadows. If all fail,
> 'Tis but applying worm-seed to the tail.

'If the worst comes to the worst, I can always clap an anaphrodisiac
to my penis': is that an ending worthy of the poem's reconciliation
to age's unobtrusively castrative rescindings?

What is at issue is not effectiveness; Donne's ending is entirely
effective, and all the more so because 'applying worm-seed'—as
against the lenitive gloss 'an anaphrodisiac'—so cruelly applies to
the emissions that are sex and death, food for worms and limp as
a worm. So effective is the ending that it usurps entire rights over
the poem, and becomes its point. But the success of the ending is
the failing of the poem, since it demeans.

---

[1] Donne's poems are quoted from *The Complete English Poems*, ed. A. J. Smith
(1971).

The issue is not contrariety of mood, or of thought and feeling, or heterogeneity of ideas, but the incompatibility—for an integrity of response—of the depth of the poem at its best with the shallowness of such final repudiatory bitterness. William Empson's cheery paraphrase—'It tells us never to bother about women, because a man gets bored with a woman as soon as he has enjoyed her'[2]— is a mercy, but the poem is merciless. The poem had contemplated the pincer beliefs that in the short run ('that other curse of being short') sex dulls and revolts you while at the same time lethally affecting your chances of a long run: 'since each such act, they say, / Diminisheth the length of life a day'. It is under the pressure of these double diminishings that Donne is then driven to diminish, to demean, and to endamage his poem.

Arthur F. Marotti, in *John Donne, Coterie Poet*, is given no offence by the poem, which is for him an 'exercise in an established form performed for an audience of sympathetic, knowledgeable males, gentleman-amorists'; the poem is 'mischievous, iconoclastic', and indeed altogether hygienic: 'He demystifies courtly Petrarchan and Neoplatonic amorousness by pointing out that it has no proper object.' Marotti can speak here of 'the familiar Donnean fantasy that love hurts or kills',[3] as if that were a fantasy (has he never noticed that love does hurt and kill?), and as if 'familiar Donnean fantasy' were words of sufficient weight for the poem's centric—uneccentric— gravity.

The professionalizing of literary studies, of which our culture is the victim-beneficiary, has brought with it the price paid for all professionalism: an induration against its own central human imperatives. Doctors become not only more but also less sensitive to suffering than others are; judges, to justice; journalists, to truth; soldiers, to slaughter. And critics to the apprehensions of joy and pain both within a poem and reached by a poem. It suits the professionalized critic to suppose that, contrary to what used to be believed, a poem of any energy not only need have no problem about reconciling gravity with levity but also need not even have any difficulty in doing so. The fierce truths for which T. S. Eliot fought are now bromides. Donne's imperious wit need fear no

[2] 'Donne in the New Edition' (1966); *Essays on Renaissance Literature*, i. *Donne and the New Philosophy*, ed. John Haffenden (1993), p. 148.
[3] *John Donne, Coterie Poet* (1986), pp. 111–13.

challenge from such suppliant criticism; and yet, as 'Love's Alchemy' shows, a poem itself may contain along the way a resistance to the poet's imperiousness, only to be finally overborne.

LOVE'S ALCHEMY

Some that have deeper digged love's mine than I,
Say, where his centric happiness doth lie:
    I have loved, and got, and told,
But should I love, get, tell, till I were old,
I should not find that hidden mystery;
        Oh, 'tis imposture all:
And as no chemic yet the elixir got,
    But glorifies his pregnant pot,
    If by the way to him befall
Some odoriferous thing, or medicinal,
    So, lovers dream a rich and long delight,
    But get a winter-seeming summer's night.

Our ease, our thrift, our honour, and our day,
Shall we, for this vain bubble's shadow pay?
    Ends love in this, that my man,
Can be as happy as I can; if he can
Endure the short scorn of a bridegroom's play?
        That loving wretch that swears,
'Tis not the bodies marry, but the minds,
    Which he in her angelic finds,
    Would swear as justly, that he hears,
In that day's rude hoarse minstrelsy, the spheres.
Hope not for mind in women; at their best
Sweetness and wit, they are but mummy, possessed.

Marotti underestimates the end of the first stanza so that he may overestimate the end of the last. 'Some that have deeper digged love's mine than I': there is to my ears a depth at the end of the first stanza which is lost in Marotti's words, 'the tone of personal disappointment, if not of self-hate':[4]

    So, lovers dream a rich and long delight,
    But get a winter-seeming summer's night.

The lines are hauntedly vacillatory, though not restless or restive, and they are unexpectedly at peace with what can be got, a summer's night that does outlast the words 'winter-seeming'. Is it possible to

---

[4] *John Donne, Coterie Poet*, p. 111.

say the lines with a merely personal worldly disappointment or self-hate?

> So, lovers dream a rich and long delight,
> But get a winter-seeming summer's night.

They have the cool compassion of an angel's gravity. But the poem ends in the scrannel levity of a fallen angel:

> Hope not for mind in women; at their best
> Sweetness and wit, they are but mummy, possessed.

For Marotti, the poem is 'an exercise in outrageous paradox', and he has no difficulty in smilingly swallowing the last lines: 'Donne uses a kind of facile antifeminism (e.g., "Hope not for minde in women") to demythologize the *donna angelicata* of spiritual lovers.' That 'e.g.' is distinctly placating, as is the curbing of the misogyny in question (tailored as 'antifeminism' throughout Marotti) to the half-dozen words 'Hope not for mind in women':

> Hope not for mind in women; at their best
> Sweetness and wit, they are but mummy, possessed.

Helen Gardner's word 'insulting' is to be preferred to 'demythologizing'. Empson speaks of 'a rather nasty brash boyishness'[5] in the poem; but the nastiness is worse than boys', it is *the* boys (those 'gentleman-amorists'). Donne's lines speak of wit, but are they themselves truly witty? They are certainly crushing, especially in that final compacting in 'possessed', but like all brutally crushing retorts, they are inadvertently self-indicting and self-demeaning. 'Ends love in this'? One may even sympathize with Leslie Fiedler's hunger to import something deeper than this routine misogyny into the poem's last words by hearing 'mummy, possessed' as the deeply accredited old oedipality.[6]

Donne is often witty, but he often isn't, and Marotti is altogether too lavish with the word. 'Air and Angels' is rangingly ruminative, wondering and wonderful, about men and women and love, and then what is the upshot?

> Just such disparity
> As is 'twixt air and angels' purity,
> 'Twixt women's love, and men's will ever be.

[5] *Essays on Renaissance Literature*, i 154.   [6] *No! in Thunder* (1960), p. 320.

Tilottama Rajan praises this as 'cleverly epigrammatic';[7] what exactly is clever and epigrammatic, as against flatly brusque, about it? Marotti says that these lines 'engage in some witty antifeminist teasing',[8] but again what exactly is witty about them? And is 'teasing' (a word with which Marotti persistently teases us out of thought) quite the word? 'The teasing antifeminism of the conclusion of this lyric—one more example of Donne's strategy of literary surprise . . .': oh, that's all right, then, for what, these days, could be less assaulting, or insulting, than a strategy? But the end of 'Air and Angels' strikes me as an offence—against women, against men, against love, and against the poem which it wantonly degrades. I appreciate the candour of John Carey: ' "Aire and Angels", in which the girl is spoken of with transfiguring wonder, ends up with a cheap crack about the inferiority of woman's love to man's'[9]—except that I'd rather a critic didn't highly value something he himself calls cheap. Which means appreciating J. E. V. Crofts, who said of women's inferiority to men: 'This doleful notion . . . runs through the poems of Donne like spilt acid, producing the oddest effects of corrosion and distortion, yields, for instance, that quiet insult at the end of "Air and Angels".'[10] But the corrosion and distortion are produced by what for Donne comes to spilt acid: spilt semen. Coleridge's marginal note on 'Air and Angels' said: 'The first Stanza is noble . . . the 2nd I do not understand.'[11] What has to be understood is not just what Donne meant but what he meant by it, by being so de-meaning. For not all agencies of the fashionably supreme prefix *de* should be esteemed; we may, or may not, welcome Rajan's welcoming of all that deconstructs or destabilizes, or Marotti's unqualified pleasure in that which demystifies, deromanticizes, demythologizes, and desentimentalizes; but what of that in Donne's poetry which debases, demeans, and degrades?

The better the best things in his poem, the more Donne is driven to rend it with his ending. So 'The Will', engaged throughout at

---

[7] ' "Nothing Sooner Broke": Donne's *Songs and Sonets* as Self-Consuming Artifacts', *ELH* xlix (1982), 817.

[8] *John Donne, Coterie Poet*, p. 221.

[9] *John Donne: Life, Mind, and Art* (1981), p. 190.

[10] 'John Donne: A Reconsideration', *Essays and Studies* (1937); reprinted in *John Donne*, ed. Helen Gardner (1962), p. 79.

[11] Quotations from Coleridge, except that at n. 59, are from *Marginalia*, ed. George Whalley, ii (1984), 213–338.

no serious level, was in no danger, whereas 'The Curse', just because it is alive with the profoundest acts of Donne's noticing, was
doomed to an upshot that would take it down a peg or two, or—
in the terms of Iago's Donne-like cynicism—'I'll set down the pegs
that make this music.'

THE CURSE

Whoever guesses, thinks, or dreams he knows
Who is my mistress, wither by this curse;
    His only, and only his purse
    May some dull heart to love dispose,
And she yield then to all that are his foes;
    May he be scorned by one, whom all else scorn,
    Forswear to others, what to her he hath sworn,
    With fear of missing, shame of getting, torn:

Madness his sorrow, gout his cramps, may he
Make, by but thinking, who hath made him such:
    And may he feel no touch
    Of conscience, but of fame, and be
Anguished not that 'twas sin, but that 'twas she:
    In early and long scarceness may he rot,
    For land which had been his, if he had not
    Himself incestuously an heir begot:

May he dream treason, and believe, that he
Meant to perform it, and confess, and die,
    And no record tell why:
    His sons, which none of his may be,
Inherit nothing but his infamy:
    Or may he so long parasites have fed,
    That he would fain be theirs, whom he hath bred,
    And at the last be circumcised for bread:

The venom of all stepdames, gamesters' gall,
What tyrants, and their subjects interwish,
    What plants, mines, beasts, fowl, fish,
    Can contribute, all ill which all
Prophets, or poets spake; and all which shall
    Be annexed in schedules unto this by me,
    Fall on that man; for if it be a she
    Nature before hand hath out-cursed me.

The point of the poem turns out to be the old jibe at women,
altogether without wit, since if it is in a way surprising, after all
those curses, that none of them is so bad as the curse of being a

woman, it is surprising only in that a great poet should have thought this adequate even as misogyny. Such an ending manages even to demean misogyny (which is not the same as 'questioning' it); one recalls T. S. Eliot's speaking of Donne's 'scoffing attitude' toward the fickleness of women as perhaps 'hardly more than immature bravado; it comes to me with none of the terrible sincerity of Swift's vituperation of the human race.'[12] The revenge that is the poem's end is not against the tattler of the beginning, a stalking-horse; or really against women, its mere butt; but against sex and against the poem itself, the poem having had the noble effrontery to imagine at a depth that Donne then feared and repudiated. There was the imagining of desire at a depth that rivals Shakespeare's sonnet on lust in action.

> May he be scorned by one, whom all else scorn,
> Forswear to others, what to her he hath sworn,
> With fear of missing, shame of getting, torn.

And there was the imagining of the nightmare world of suspected treason's damnation, at a depth that rivals or outdoes Kafka:

> May he dream treason, and believe, that he
> Meant to perform it, and confess, and die,
> And no record tell why.

How could such apprehensions—lines of lamination that press, with hideous levelness, upon *and* until it is the torture of 'peine forte *et* dure'—not be suffocated by a poem the point of which turns out to be:

> Fall on that man; for if it be a she,
> Nature before hand hath out-cursed me.

The answer is that they couldn't; Donne treats them treasonably, and we are forced to practise our own snatched violation of the poem's integrity, to rescue them, if we would resist Donne's corrosive violation. For what we should have responded to, in the hiding places of the poem's power, is something in an entirely different world from anything that Marotti's unmisgiving words would suggest: 'After wishing an inventively varied series of ills on the hypothetical male . . .'.[13]

---

[12] 'Donne in Our Time', *A Garland for John Donne*, ed. Theodore Spencer (1931), p. 10.

[13] *John Donne, Coterie Poet*, p. 81.

'Woman's Constancy' is an instance of the poet's inconstancy. Coleridge turned the woman addressed into a whore, one way of making the end not inappropriately meretricious. Marotti has the poem addressed by a woman to a man, and licks its boots for being on the other feet. But then he hears merely 'a series of hypothetical excuses',[14] much as Carey observes Donne's 'turning round and disparaging the arguments he has fabricated'.[15]

WOMAN'S CONSTANCY

Now thou hast loved me one whole day,
Tomorrow when thou leav'st, what wilt thou say?
Wilt thou then antedate some new made vow?
　　Or say that now
We are not just those persons, which we were?
Or, that oaths made in reverential fear
Of Love, and his wrath, any may forswear?
Or, as true deaths, true marriages untie,
So lovers' contracts, images of those,
Bind but till sleep, death's image, them unloose?
　　Or, your own end to justify,
For having purposed change, and falsehood, you
Can have no way but falsehood to be true?
Vain lunatic, against these 'scapes I could
　　Dispute, and conquer, if I would,
　　Which I abstain to do,
For by tomorrow, I may think so too.

The trouble is that Donne at times wrote more deeply than he meant, or than he could bear, and what we then engage with is not Carey's 'fabricated arguments' or Marotti's 'hypothetical excuses', but imaginings which—beyond the poet's final digestive powers— the poem is forced to spit out and spit upon. The airy hauteur of the end is a spurning of the poem's previous precious magnanimities:

Or, as true deaths, true marriages untie,
So lovers' contracts, images of those,
Bind but till sleep, death's image, them unloose?

With how true a love knot, even at such a time, does 'unloose' gather the insinuatingly interrogative syntax, plaiting it and plighting it even in the prospect of rupture. This, 'hushed into depths beyond

---

[14] Ibid., p. 74.　　　[15] *John Donne: Life, Mind, and Art*, p. 231.

the watcher's diving' as it contemplates what it is to sleep together
(dissolved in sleep, perhaps to be dissolved by sleep)—this outdoes
even that other great conjunction of death and sleep in Donne, the
hours when 'the condemned man' 'Doth practice dying by a little
sleep.' ('Obsequies to the Lord Harrington')

'Song: Go, and catch a falling star' is likewise quintessential Donne,
something rich and strangely cheapened.

SONG

Go, and catch a falling star,
  Get with child a mandrake root,
Tell me, where all past years are,
  Or who cleft the Devil's foot,
Teach me to hear mermaids singing,
  Or to keep off envy's stinging,
    And find
    What wind
Serves to advance an honest mind.

If thou be'est born to strange sights,
  Things invisible to see,
Ride ten thousand days and nights,
  Till age snow white hairs on thee,
Thou, when thou return'st, wilt tell me
All strange wonders that befell thee,
    And swear
    No where
Lives a woman true, and fair.

If thou find'st one, let me know,
  Such a pilgrimage were sweet,
Yet do not, I would not go,
  Though at next door we might meet,
Though she were true, when you met her,
And last, till you write your letter,
    Yet she
    Will be
False, ere I come, to two, or three.

Empson judged that 'the song had aimed at being gay and flippant
but turned out rather heavy and cross';[16] but though the end may

---

[16] 'There is No Penance Due to Innocence', *New York Review of Books*, 3 December 1981; omitted by Haffenden from Empson's *Essays on Renaissance Literature*, vol.
i, as mostly repeated elsewhere.

be heavy, it is of no weight, being the most attenuated of old jeers. This leaves the field open for Marotti, for whom the poem is a 'sportful literary exercise', to claim that the poem isn't really about love and sex but about 'a topic of more genuine concern to Donne and his Inns readers'[17] (or in-readers): worldly advancement. So Marotti locates the poem's central impulse in the lines—

> Or to keep off envy's stinging
>   And find
>   What wind
> Serves to advance an honest mind.

—lines which I find rhythmically and syntactically inert and sententious in comparison to what is for me the poem's centric happiness of conception:

> If thou be'est born to strange sights,
>   Things invisible to see,
> Ride ten thousand days and nights,
>   Till age snow white hairs on thee.

'Things invisible to see' is at once straightforwardly an unperturbed redundancy and—with the inverted syntax—a miraculous accomplishment; and what follows has been exquisitely praised by Carey: 'Hair, and its greying, are as distinct from our conscious life, and as unknowable, as the weather.'[18] But what, then, of the smart and smarting intrusion of Donne's conscious life, the knowingness beamed at the boys in the poem's unworthy ending?

> Though she were true, when you met her,
> And last, till you write your letter,
>   Yet she
>   Will be
> False, ere I come, to two, or three.

The poem is more false to itself than any of its convenient women could ever be.

Coleridge noted in the margin of his *Donne*:

As late as 10 years ago, I used to seek and find out grand lines and fine stanzas; but my delight has been far greater, since it has consisted more in tracing the leading Thought thro'out the whole. The former is too much

---

[17] *John Donne, Coterie Poet*, pp. 79–80.
[18] *John Donne: Life, Mind, and Art*, p. 140.

like coveting your neighbour's Goods: in the latter you merge yourself in the Author—you *become He*.—

But becoming He (while grammatically superb) is misguided, since without difference and distance there couldn't ever be a meeting of the poet's consciousness and conscience with our own. The nub, on this reading, is not Johnson's complaint that the metaphysicals 'broke every image into fragments'; Johnson's own procedure here in the life of Cowley was to break every metaphysical poem into fragmented images, and not once to attend to a whole poem—even while he turned propitiatingly to the crucial word: 'their whole endeavour'; 'as they were wholly employed'; 'is never wholly lost'. Nor is the nub what is usually meant by 'unevenness', since it is not effectiveness but the nature of the effect, the divisive effect, which is at issue. Coleridge, who is Donne's greatest critic, is so partly because he is authentically provoked by division in Donne, and often provoked to criticize him. It is Coleridge who needs the word 'deep' to get at both Donne's powers and his abuse of them. Of the end of 'The Good Morrow': 'Too good for mere wit. It contains a deep practical truth—this Triplet.' This is itself a deep praise, not least because it is instinct with the warning that elsewhere a deep truth might be too good to be subservient to 'mere wit', especially if the wit were 'concupiscence of wit'. It is Coleridge who speaks of 'a substrate of profound, tho' mislocated, Thinking', and who is unable to resolve his pained perplexity of praise and blame, again in depth. Of 'The Undertaking': 'A grand Poem; and yet the Tone, the *Riddle* character, is painfully below the dignity of the main Thought.' It is Coleridge who points to something damagingly (not delectably) paradoxical about Donne's art; alongside lines 25–8 of 'A Fever', Coleridge wrote:

Just & affecting *as dramatic*, i.e. the out-burst of a transient Feeling, itself the symbol of a deeper Feeling, that would have made *one* Hour, *known* to be *only* one Hour (or even one year) a perfect Hell! All the preceding Verses are detestable. Shakespere has nothing of this. He is never *positively* bad, even in his Sonnets. He *may* be sometimes worthless (N.B.: I don't say, he *is* but no where is He *un*worthy).

When Donne is unworthy, this is—as Coleridge saw—a matter of what violates 'a deeper Feeling'. One may dissent from Helen Gardner's judgements as to what is worthy, but this would be a more limited dissent than is involved when the critical procedure is such as to preclude the whole question of unworthiness or any such judgement as she passes when she says of the variant endings of 'The Good Morrow', 'Neither version provides a close worthy of the poem's opening.'[19] Or there is Hazlitt, who was sensitive to intertextual erotics: 'This is but a lame and impotent conclusion from so delightful a beginning.'[20] Empson once feared that he had gone too far in suspecting an insensitivity in the close of a Donne poem, but he did not exactly retreat: of 'A Valediction: Of Weeping', 'The language itself has become flattened and explanatory: so that he almost seems to be feeling for his hat. But perhaps I am libelling this masterpiece. . . .'[21] Donne himself libels his masterpieces. Empson (it is a fault usually on the right side) is sure that any fault must be the critic's, not the poet's. 'It is true that the words are not explicit. But when such a master has used all his resources to present an astonishing turn in his logic and his story, the usual presumption is that he means something adequate to the occasion he has created.'[22] But the 'usual presumption' may not fit the fiercely unusual Donne, who takes perverse delight in meaning in the end something not only inadequate to, but unworthy of, the occasion he has created.

There survives only one interesting critical statement by Donne about the art of poetry; it furnishes the clinching conclusion to the introduction to Barbara Herrnstein Smith's *Poetic Closure*, and John Carey, who cannot bring himself to ignore it, affects that it makes for his sense of Donne.

And therefore it is easie to observe, that in all Metricall compositions, . . . the force of the whole piece, is for the most part left to the shutting up; the whole frame of the Poem is a beating out of a piece of gold, but the last clause is as the impression of the stamp, and that is it that makes it currant.[23]

Carey gives the thought his audacious setting:

Even when, in a sermon, he discusses metrical composition more generally, he retains a view of poems as unstable processes. 'The whole frame of the Poem,' he asserts, 'is a beating out of a piece of gold, but the last clause is as the impression of the stamp, and that is it that makes it currant.' The

[19] *The Elegies and the Songs and Sonnets* (1965), p. 199.
[20] On 'The Blossom', *Lectures on the Comic Writers* (1819); reprinted in *John Donne: The Critical Heritage*, ed. A. J. Smith (1975), p. 311.
[21] *Seven Types of Ambiguity* (1930), 1947 edn, p. 145.
[22] 'Donne in the New Edition', *Essays on Renaissance Literature*, i 158.
[23] Donne, *Sermons*, ed. George R. Potter and Evelyn Simpson (1953–62), vi 41.

emphasis on the ending looks a bit exaggerated here, especially if applied wholesale to poetry, but it fits in well enough with Donne's own insistent modification and development of his material throughout a poem, and with the sense he gives us that it would be unwise to conclude anything about it until it's concluded.

Or when it's concluded, come to that. For the conflicts of attitude within Donne's poems relate to irresolvable confusions within the human personality.[24]

This is perverse. First, the impression of the stamp is the authoritative termination of any 'unstable processes'. Second, Carey finds the 'emphasis on the ending . . . a bit exaggerated' only because he would prefer Donne's poems to be open-ended since their endings resist Carey's resolute allegiance to unresolvability. And third, though it makes sense to say that Donne's emphasis on the ending fits Donne's not wishing us 'to conclude anything about it until it's concluded', it is a rhetorical sleight to continue: 'Or when it's concluded, come to that.' People may now prefer—to the point of nullifying Johnson's witty stubbornness—conclusions in which nothing is concluded, but the stamp of Donne's conviction is firmly upon the last clause, 'the impression of the stamp, and that is it that makes it currant'. Donne resolves his poems, even when—or rather, especially when—the poem turns on its heels. But Carey is in hock to the idea that conclusions are not last impressions. 'As the final stanza counteracts the rest of the poem, so the rest of the poem counteracts the final stanza, making its briskness seem blustering.'[25] *As . . . so? Seem?* This is a sentimentality of simultaneity and a pretence of equipollence.

Barbara Herrnstein Smith is entirely persuasive on the power, within poems, of 'closural allusion', 'references not to termination, finality, repose, or stability as such, but to events which, in our nonliterary experiences, are associated with these qualities—events such as sleep, death, dusk, night, autumn, winter, descents, falls, leave-takings and home-comings'.[26] And comings, nowhere mentioned by her but no less apt. As with all endings, there is an equivocation as to how final they are; after orgasm, something takes its course, but then after what does it not? 'Allusions to any of the "natural" stopping places of our lives and experiences—sleep, death, winter, and so forth—tend to give closural force when they appear

---

[24] *John Donne: Life, Mind, and Art*, p. 192.
[25] Ibid., p. 196, on 'A Valediction: Of My Name in the Window'.
[26] *Poetic Closure* (1968), pp. 175–6.

as terminal features in a poem.'[27] It is a pity about the cagey quotation-marks round 'naturally', since those stopping-places are indeed natural. Another natural stopping-place is orgasm, perhaps the most serious rival to death, whom it wedded and bedded in the pun on 'die'; death, which is for Smith 'more than sleep, winter, or the permanence of the fixed stars, the most personal and ultimate of ultimates'. It is not wilful of Smith not to mention erotic closure, but it would have provided warrant for her staunch footnote: 'The question . . . is whether or not we can assume a universal psychology of closure—and I can only answer that I do not know, but that I am assuming it anyway.'

Frank Kermode does not make too much of this sense of an ending, but there are erotic energies in the opening chapter of his inaugurative book:

Men, like poets, rush 'into the middest,' *in medias res*, when they are born; they also die *in mediis rebus*, and to make sense of their span they need fictive concords with origins and ends.[28]

For, prior to our being born, there is our origin; there is—as Tristram Shandy knew—an act of rushing into the middest; Sidney, whom Kermode is quoting, went so far as to say 'thrusteth into the middest'—not that 'rush' lacks eroticism, of the white rush and of this:

> Let us not then rush blindly on unto it,
> Like lustful beasts, that only know to do it.[29]

Kermode later speaks of 'biology', saying that 'the End is a fact of life and a fact of the imagination, working out from the middle',[30] where his words are decently open to the vulgarism 'the facts of life', and to the sexuality of the middle, the waist/waste and middle of the night. A reconsideration by Kermode in 1978, 'Sensing Endings', says: 'The rules are culture-specific; as to that, one would expect rules about endings to be culture-specific, though I have no doubt that the interest in them is species-specific, having to do with our understanding that our time is not the time of the world, nor

[27] Ibid., pp. 102, 182, 32.
[28] *The Sense of an Ending* (1967), p. 7.
[29] Ben Jonson, translating Petronius.
[30] *The Sense of an Ending*, p. 58.

is the time of our culture.'[31] Having to do as well with doing, since for any species the one thing necessary is that we (in Donne's words) 'propagate our kind'. Kermode in this essay is respectfully wary of John Kucich's theory of concentration and release: 'Certainly the view that this concentration and release is related to orgasm and to death is intuitively acceptable; Milton's last word is "spent," and the notion of a cathartic discharge is very persistent. But all the evidence is surely against the opinion that it is only to be had at the end. And the notion of orgasmic or cathartic dispersal is not one that I find it easy to hold.' One could easily maintain a scepticism about the general applicability of orgasmic endings (and penultimata) while remaining confident that for Donne, alive to the pun on 'die', a poem's ending is likely to relate to, though it may not reproduce or mimic the timing of, orgasm's affiliation to death. 'Death and conception in mankind is one';[32] and the resurrection— since 'Only in heaven joy's strength is never spent'—is the only consummation devoutly to be wished by Donne, devoutly and wholeheartedly since it will be the consummation to end consummations and though spoken of as the 'last great consummation' will be essentially the first:

> Joy that their last great consummation
> Approaches in the resurrection.

> ('The Second Anniversary:
> Of the Progress of the Soul')

The rhyme of 'consummation' / 'resurrection' is itself both a consummation and a resurrection (a reprise and reprieve for 'We die and rise the same' in 'The Canonization'); and 'Approaches', with its sense of gathering tinglingly for the great consummation, assures that here at last there comes the one orgasm which will not issue in revulsion and disappointment.

'Textual erotics', whether or not prosecuted as in Peter Brooks's *Reading for the Plot* (1984), is clearly not limited to such art as is patently erotic. But textual erotics may gain a warrant from Donne's preoccupations and from his finding it natural to write of poems in relation to 'strange adultery' and to 'concupiscence of wit'. Donne meant his asseveration in Paradox XI, 'I say again, that the body

---

[31] *Nineteenth-Century Fiction*, xxxiii (1978), 153, 155.
[32] Donne, 'Upon the Annunciation and Passion falling upon one day. 1608'.

makes the minde.' A letter on letters invokes ecstasy as the conjunction of that which is supremely erotic with that which supremely
is not:

> I make account that this writing of letters, when it is with any seriousness,
> is a kind of extasie, and a departure and secession and suspension of the
> soul, which doth then communicate it self to two bodies: And as I would
> every day provide for my souls last convoy, though I know not when I shall
> die, and perchance I shall never die; so for these extasies in letters, I often
> times deliver my self over in writing.[33]

But Donne was no more at ease with delivering himself over in
writing than in sex, 'the poor benefit of a bewildering minute'. Donne's
disparagement of his poetry is notorious, and crucial to the arguments of Carey and Marotti. Yet they avert an eye from the extremity of it, assimilating Donne to the usual deprecations, regarding
'his poems as trifles', and wishing to be thought 'a literary amateur'.[34] But it was not just 'the stigma of print' from which he shrank,
and to speak of 'his characteristic aversion to becoming a publishing
poet' is to elide his aversion from having consummated poems at
all. For, as Marotti himself concedes, Donne 'tried to foreclose the
possibility that it [his writing] would travel further by the normal
means of manuscript transcription'. Donne did think it unpardon-
able in himself to have 'descended to print anything in verse',[35] but
this is something of a disguise—not in the usual sense of false modesty
but rather as insufficiently repudiatory. He craved from his friend
'assurance upon the religion of your friendship that no copy shall
be taken for any respect of these or any other my compositions sent
to you'.[36] The coterie insouciance is indeed germane, but is not
Donne's case. Coleridge acknowledged the courtly context—'The
idea of degradation & frivolity which Donne himself attached to the
character of a professed Poet, & which was only not universal in
the reigns of Elizabeth & James'—but Coleridge's terms, 'degradation
and frivolity', suppose a deep entwining, not a social affectation.

---

[33] Letter from Donne to Goodyer; quoted by R. C. Bald, *John Donne: A Life*
(1970), p. 169.

[34] Marotti, *John Donne, Coterie Poet*, pp. x–xi, 341.

[35] Letter from Donne to 'G.G.' (14 April 1612); quoted in *John Donne: The Critical
Heritage*, p. 2.

[36] Letter from Donne, possibly to Wotton (c.1600); quoted in *John Donne: The
Critical Heritage*, p. 3.

The entwining is that of the poetic act and the sexual act. Donne writes about his writings as if they were intimate with the act of love and its issue. Those which he permitted to circulate were called by him, in the decent obscurity of a learned language, 'virgins (save that they have been handled by many)', and those which he kept private were 'so unhappily sterile that no copies of them have been begotten'.[37] Marotti quotes the famous words about the Paradoxes, 'To my satires there belongs some fear and to some elegies, and these perhaps, shame';[38] but where Donne speaks of shame, his critic speaks at once of embarrassment—and of the 'dissemination' of his lyrics without remarking that for Donne both disseminations are an expense of spirit in a waste of shame. *Fear . . . shame.* The pincer-jaws are those which Donne saw sharp in lust: 'With fear of missing, shame of getting, torn.'

For Donne, the expense of spirit in a waste of shame is *love* in action. Contempt for sex, or for poetry (Carey's phrase), is not quite it, for perfect contempt casteth out fear. A double shame moves the poems to suicide; *Biathanatos* admired this forethought consummated, 'As Demosthenes did with poison, çarried in a pen.' Donne wrestled there with the text 'No man hateth his own flesh' (exquisitely equivocal), confident that it did not 'yield an argument against self homicide'. The poems, after love, imagine hating their own flesh, and they turn their revulsion upon the body of the poem, their own flesh. If the body is his book, then the book will be his body. The terms of the sonnet 'To Mr. B. B.' are those of textual erotics pricked by sexual and textual dismay:

> If thou unto thy Muse be married,
>   Embrace her ever, ever multiply,
>   Be far from me that strange adultery
> To tempt thee and procure her widowhead.
> My Muse (for I had one,) because I am cold,
>   Divorced herself: the cause being in me,
>   That I can take no new in bigamy,
> Not my will only but power doth withhold.
> Hence comes it, that these rhymes which never had
>   Mother, want matter, and they only have
>   A little form, the which their father gave;

[37] Letter from Donne to Goodyer (1611); quoted by Marotti, *John Donne, Coterie Poet*, p. 16.
[38] *John Donne, Coterie Poet*, p. 41.

> They are profane, imperfect, oh, too bad
> To be counted children of poetry
> Except confirmed and bishoped by thee.

That last line is wistful beyond belief. Donne, in the days of his sexually unsatisfied Muse (accusing him of frigidity), had often committed his own form of 'strange adultery', unfaithful to his love, his self, and his poem, all at once: 'To invent, and practise this one way, to annihilate all three,' he writes in 'The Will'.

It is not simply that wit may be concupiscent but that wit is concupiscence, and concupiscence wit, each an utterance (and it is men, not women, who disseminate).

> So when thy brain works, ere thou utter it,
> Cross and correct concupiscence of wit.

> ('The Cross')

The younger Donne did not so much cross and correct concupiscence of wit as cross and corrode it. He knew about corrosiveness, and about its being the ingrate's suicidal revenge; in the words of the poem 'To Sir Edward Herbert, at Juliers':

> We do infuse to what he meant for meat,
> Corrosiveness.

No longer meat, and not meet.

The uncorrosive genius is Byron's: T. S. Eliot was exactly right in setting up the Donne/Byron choice (not simply a comparison), and the recovery of Byron since Eliot's heyday has gone with the partial eclipse of Donne. To Eliot, Byron—unlike Donne—offers merely 'the substitution of one mood for a wholly different one': 'Byron's "effective" change here is not only a theatrical effect: it is callowness masquerading as maturity of cynicism; it represents an uninteresting mind, and a disorderly one'.[39] But those who value Byron as the greatest comic poet in the language may retort that it is Donne who is retrospectively cynical, and may urge the praise given to *Don Juan* by Swinburne: 'There is in that great poem an especial and exquisite balance and sustenance of alternate tones.' Thomas Moore told Byron that he always felt about his art 'as the French husband did when he found a man making love to his (the Frenchman's) wife—"Comment, Monsieur,—sans y être obligé!" '

[39] *The Nation and Athenaeum*, 9 June 1923.

Byron (*noblesse oblige*) at once assented and dissented: 'I feel exactly
as you do about our "art," but it comes over me in a kind of rage
every now and then, like ****, and then, if I don't write to empty
my mind, I go mad.'[40] But emptying his mind, and his body, was
for Byron a generous pleasure, even in retrospect. 'Oh pleasure,
you're indeed a pleasant thing,' this Scotsman found it necessary
to insist not to himself but to the English.

That Donne's poems practise some form of self-destruction has
long been recognized. What Hazlitt saw as a wanton dissolution
('The scholastic reason he gives quite dissolves the charm of tender
and touching grace in the sentiment itself'),[41] Carey might see as
a due recognition of life's wantonness ('The poem dissolves itself,'[42]
he therefore says gratefully). These days, critical practice often sounds
like sub-Empson with a cold in the head: subversions of pastoral.
Tilottama Rajan finds the *Songs and Sonnets* of self-consuming interest,
since they are so self-compromising, self-defeating, self-emptying,
and self-reversing. (It is something of a relief when the grizzled
ruffian 'undermining' puts in an appearance.) Rajan says that she
'would argue, without making a value judgment, that all Donne's
lyrics are in a sense evaporations',[43] but her critical allegiances do not
permit of not making value judgements, and in any case it is clear
from every page that she highly values Donne's lyrics exactly as
evaporations. One trouble with Rajan's 'hermeneutics of suspicion'
(which explicitly consigns the rest of us to a limbo of naïfs called the
'hermeneutics of immediacy') is that it is insufficiently suspicious. It
expends so much suspicion on New Critics and other traitorous
clerks that it has none left for Donne. But there is something missing
from any account of Donne which implies that only a buffoon, or
someone suckled in a creed outworn, would ever have been moved
to cry, as an anonymous critic did in 1823, that Donne's poems are
'so completely *irritating* to the imagination, as well as to the taste'.[44]

No doubt there have been traitorous clerks, but Donne is the one
who matters most.

---

[40] Byron to Moore, 2 January 1821; *Letters and Journals*, ed. Leslie A. Marchand,
viii (1978), 55 and n.

[41] On 'The Funeral'; quoted in *John Donne: The Critical Heritage*, p. 311.

[42] *John Donne: Life, Mind, and Art*, p. 181, on 'A Lecture upon the Shadow'.

[43] *ELH* xlix (1982), 828.

[44] *The Retrospective Review* (1823); quoted in *John Donne: The Critical Heritage*,
p. 328.

> But O, self traitor, I do bring
> The spider love, which transubstantiates all,
> And can convert manna to gall.

('Twicknam Garden')

And so he did. It is a shocking blasphemy, and one ought to pay it the compliment of being shocked by it. The poems are not beamed at the self-consumer society; they are tortured into becoming self-traitors. They then mean their contaminating conversions. 'And confess, and die', though *some* record tells why. Their unmistakable power partakes of the venomous irresponsibility which Donne feared:

> for hearing him, I found
> That as burnt venomed lechers do grow sound
> By giving others their sores, I might grow
> Guilty, and he free.

('Satire 4')

This should not be an art conducive to equanimity, and I am mildly shocked by such criticism as is even less than mildly shocked. Rajan makes the love poems amenable not only by the abstractions of deconstruction but also by giving their sores to 'personae'. Carey makes the love poems amenable by having them not really be about love at all but about religion: 'the love poems are a veil for religious perturbations',[45] and Carey himself writes as one quite unperturbed by religion since for him it is nothing but the expression of psychological 'preferences'. Marotti makes the love poems amenable in two ways: either (one more example of the critic's strategy of surprise, surprise) by having them be meta-poems, 'virtually "self-consuming artifacts"', 'virtual meta-poems', 'virtually a meta-poetic statement'[46] (much virtue in that 'virtually'); or by having them be not just the products, but statements, of worldly ambition's socio-economic frustrations. This insistence that the poems are really not about sex but about politics has its calmative side, but it regularly entails a slighting of—among other things—sexual politics.

The poems may be said to be marked by a vengeful infidelity to their own deepest apprehensions; they may also be said to commit the infidel's supreme act, suicide. Donne's inordinate respect for suicide was lifelong. *Biathanatos* was 'A Declaration of that Paradoxe

---

[45] *John Donne: Life, Mind, and Art*, p. 38.
[46] *John Donne, Coterie Poet*, pp. 22, 71, 74.

or Thesis, that Selfe-homicide is not so naturally Sinne, that it may never be otherwise'. One of the Paradoxes had been devoted to the thesis 'That all things kill themselves'. Even plants, with their vegetable love, kill themselves by an expense of spirit in a waste of shamelessness: 'This they spend their Spirits to attaine.' As for men, 'we kill dayly our bodyes with Surfets,' for instance 'Of affections, Lusting our Lust'. This cruel love knot, tightening its lusts and luxuries, twists about the poems. Carey describes 'A Nocturnal Upon St. Lucy's Day' as 'suicidal'—is this its mood or its act? His good jokes about 'Donne's suicidal longings' sharply differ from Donne's mood: 'Suicide drill, like fire drill, reduces the chance of a fatality.' Carey is persuasive on Donne's penchant for valedictions—'His partings are miniature suicides'[47]—but 'miniature' comes across as endearing. The question is less that of Donne's staving off his own suicide ('the kind of poem which helped to keep Donne alive by giving scope to his suicidal fantasies') than of his inciting his poems to commit this act of darkness.

Just as Carey's page on death in the *Songs and Sonnets* never mentions the pun on 'die', so his pages on death *tout court* never mention Donne's recurrence to the fear that every act of sex 'diminisheth the length of life a day'. Marotti keeps his spirits up by being still the coterie votary.

The truth of the remark 'We kill our selves, to propagate our kinde' lies as much in the context of the careerist hampered by 'hostages to fortune,' as in that of the (hardly serious) belief that orgasms shortened one's life span.[48]

'Hardly serious' is too much of a nub to be tucked within those prophylactic brackets. Marotti pooh-poohs 'the flimsy folk belief that every orgasm costs a day of one's life'. Donne's accents, though, are not sportive, or s'pportive:

> For that first marriage was our funeral:
> One woman at one blow, then killed us all,
> And singly, one by one, they kill us now.
> We do delightfully ourselves allow
> To that consumption; and profusely blind,
> We kill ourselves, to propagate our kind.
>
> ('The First Anniversary:
> An Anatomy of the World')

[47] *John Donne: Life, Mind, and Art*, pp. 93, 173, 215–16.
[48] *John Donne, Coterie Poet*, pp. 237, 239.

Wishing for a Donne of sprightliness, Marotti says: 'He cannot resist puns and other comic elements as he points to the self-destructiveness of mankind, jokingly referring to "new diseases" (like syphilis).' But puns are not necessarily comic, and comedy not necessarily joking, and joking not necessarily tousling; venereal disease—again those prophylactic brackets, '(like syphilis)'—is treated by Donne with grim horror, and itself constitutes, as D. H. Lawrence argued, a central impulse in the revulsion from sex in Donne and his age. ('Lust-bred diseases rot thee; and dwell with thee / Itchy desire and no ability.')[49]

> With new diseases on ourselves we war,
> And with new physic, a worse engine far.
>
> ('The First Anniversary')

'New diseases', critick'd to a joke; 'new physic'—ah yes, iatrogenic . . . But Donne was infected by the sinful perversity he so imagined:

> Of nothing he made us, and we strive too,
> To bring ourselves to nothing back.

Donne strove to bring his poems to nothing back, and he warred on them diseasedly.

'Self murder' is not just exploited in the love poems and explored in the religious ones, but is poetically prosecuted. The conviction did not change, and it lethally animates Donne's 'Epitaph on Himself':

> Whilst in our souls sin bred and pampered is,
> Our souls become worm-eaten carcases;
> So we ourselves miraculously destroy.

'Miraculously' is stingingly salty. And if we destroy ourselves, why not those other carcases?:

> Sickly, alas, short-lived, aborted be
> Those carcase verses, whose soul is not she.
>
> ('A Funeral Elegy')

Like Walton, and unlike his modern critics, Donne does not use the word 'aborted' blithely, acclamatorily.

Sex can be, in its quiet incremental way, murderous. Empson speaks with level dismay of Donne's killing his wife by giving her

---

[49] Donne, 'Elegy 11: The Bracelet'.

a baby every year (she died, at 33, just after the birth, the stillbirth, of their twelfth child); but Empson urged, too, a historical mitigation:

> I should warmly agree that he was a bad husband to give his wife so many children, if this is what is at the back of the editor's [Helen Gardner's] mind; but the idea seems to have been unknown at the time, and besides, Donne was becoming more under the influence of the Church throughout his married life; we may be sure that the clergy would have denounced any relief for child-birth, then as later. Donne says nothing in verse about his children because he found them merely a nuisance, but this didn't keep him from being devoted to his wife; I expect Blake and D. H. Lawrence would have felt the same, if they had not been spared.[50]

Donne may have been insufficiently sensitive to this domestic aspect of sex as murderous (though there are in his letters about his wife and children what sound like whinges of guilt), but he was exacerbatedly sensitive to sex as suicidal, killing us daily by 'Lusting our Lust':

> freely on his she friends
> He blood, and spirit, pith and marrow spends,
>   Ill steward of himself, himself in three years ends.
>
> Else might he long have lived;
>
> Yet chooseth he, though none of these he fears,
> Pleasantly three, than straitened twenty years
>   To live, and to increase his race, himself outwears.
>
>   ('The Progress of the Soul')

Carey's dismissal of 'the worn Elizabethan pun on "die" '[51] would be telling only if 'worn' were taken this seriously ('himself outwears'), just as it would be right of him to speak of 'the boring old Elizabethan sexual pun on "die" ' only if he were triplicating 'boring' (Beckett: 'And they talk of stiffs being bored!'). But the pun on 'die' does need its 'substrate of profound, tho' mislocated, Thinking' in the fear that in the sexual act man 'himself outwears'.

> We are tapers too, and at our own cost die.
>
> We can die by it, if not live by love.
>
>   ('The Canonization')

---

[50] *Essays on Renaissance Literature*, i 151.
[51] *John Donne: Life, Mind, and Art*, pp. 43, 176.

The timbre, elsewhere, of the end of Elegy 9, 'The Autumnal', is unique in Donne (as 'Marina' is unique in Eliot) in its quietude of hope, its aspirations disowning all 'panting'. Here the tacit pun on 'die' is muted to an acquiescence which is the opposite of Joyce's panting ahquickyes; is muted to a making friends with the twofold necessity of dying.

> Since such love's natural lation is, may still
>   My love descend, and journey down the hill,
> Not panting after growing beauties, so,
>   I shall ebb out with them, who homeward go.

'I shall ebb out with them, who homeward go': it is Donne's 'Crossing the Bar'; and a coming that is for once a homecoming.

The occasions when Donne conquers the itch to violate his poem are those when the poem suffers no orgasm. The act of love may be still to come—'I shall ebb out . . .' It is so in 'The Dream', which—whatever it may say—prefers this being unsatisfied (escaping 'The greater torment / Of love satisfied'). 'The Dream' ends:

> Thou cam'st to kindle, goest to come; then I
> Will dream that hope again, but else would die.

'That hope again', it had a dying fall. 'The Ecstasy' is all in prospect, nothing in retrospect. Sometimes the love is not just not consummated 'as yet', it is supreme because it never was or will be. 'What miracles we harmless lovers wrought': the poem itself is less harmed than is Donne's wont, for if 'The Relic' had not been the story of two lovers who had escaped the act of love and its ashy fruits, it is likely that the sexual revulsion would not have been the merely distasteful and laboured aside of the first stanza—

> (For graves have learned that woman-head
> To be to more than one a bed)

—but the upshot, the last word. Even in 'The Good Morrow' the terms of undying love are those of unacted desire, for desire after action must 'slacken'. The sense of chastened chastity in 'slacken' ('none do slacken, none can die') is the benign, albeit strict, counterpart to the sardonic further detumescence in 'The Apparition':

> Will, if thou stir, or pinch to wake him, think
>   Thou call'st for more,
> And in false sleep will from thee shrink.

Perhaps the sharpest of the occasions when Donne claims to be making the best of things when actually he is enjoying what is for him the best of things (the *not* enjoying love's fruition), is Elegy 10, 'The Dream'. It gives unforgettable expression to the cruellest of imagination's distempers, the conviction that, whereas joys are imaginary, pain is true; and then it expresses its gratitude for the best of mercies, the smallest one:

> So, if I dream I have you, I have you,
>   For, all our joys are but fantastical.
> And so I 'scape the pain, for pain is true;
>   And sleep which locks up sense, doth lock out all.
>
> After a such fruition I shall wake,
>   And, but the waking, nothing shall repent;
> And shall to love more thankful sonnets make,
>   Than if more honour, tears, and pains were spent.

The thankfulness, the reprieve from repentance, 'after a such fruition', depend upon the flagrant omission from that last line, 'Than if more honour, tears, and pains were spent'. No expense of spirit, no waste of shame; then, I 'nothing shall repent'.

Relatedly, the very beautiful high spirits of Elegy 19, 'To his Mistress Going to Bed', are a consequence of the act of love's being all in prospect; the sadder usual tale would be 'To his Mistress Coming from Bed'. Empson misrepresents the poem in describing its last two lines:

> To teach thee, I am naked first, why then
> What needst thou have more covering than a man.

as 'the jolly remark at the end, after all is won',[52] for it stanches the act of love to suppose that 'all is won' once the lady is in this sense won. This would herald the cult of the simultaneous non-orgasm; in some ways easier but less jolly. Elsewhere Empson, fiercely repudiating the reading in the penultimate couplet 'Here is no penance, much less innocence,' turned to the general question, 'Why is this not simply a dirty poem, please?': 'I think it becomes very dirty if you make the poet jab his contempt into the lady at the crisis of the scene of love.'[53] Empson's fierceness is properly erotic (against a demeaning of the erotic such as jabs contempt into her),

---

[52] *New York Review of Books*, 3 December 1981.
[53] *Essays on Renaissance Literature*, i 133.

and he is right about the poem's being pure of contempt; but in using the words 'at the crisis of the scene of love', he is premature (for some, the praecox trope), since the crisis of the scene of love must be securely off the end of the poem, still to come, and it is exactly this which disarms in Donne the rage to jab his contempt into a poem.

'There is no penance due to innocence': this (the manuscript reading preferred by Empson) is said before the act and may recall the close of Ben Jonson's translation of Petronius, where amorous unconsummation is revered as serenely endless:

> There is no labour, nor no shame in this;
> This hath pleased, doth please, and long will please; never
> Can this decay, but is beginning ever.

In the Bridgewater manuscript, about 1625, an unknown reader wrote beside a line from 'To his Mistress Going to Bed' ('To enter in these bonds, is to be free'): 'Why may not a man write his owne Epithalamion if he can doe it so modestly.'[54] It is a beautiful question because it is not just a rhetorical one. 'All that belongs to love . . . is to desire, and to enjoy; for to desire without fruition is a rage, and to enjoy without desire is a stupidity . . . nothing then can give us satisfaction, but where those two concur, *amare* and *frui*, to love and to enjoy.'[55] But if, in these terms of Donne's, to enjoy without desire is a stupidity, what is it to enjoy without then having enjoyed? 'To desire without fruition is a rage':

> After a such fruition I shall wake,
>   And, but the waking, nothing shall repent.

'If he can do it so modestly': Donne's name—*nomen est omen*—notoriously announced the sibling pun to 'die'. Do and die. Done as consummated. That the other intimate name on which he grounded and ground his puns, that of his wife, More/more,[56] incarnates the opposite impulse to 'done', entrenched his siege of contraries. 'More' is the unsatisfied, perhaps the insatiable ('think / Thou call'st for more'); 'done' ought to be the quietus of satisfaction but is for John

[54] 'Marginalia on the Bridgewater Manuscript'; quoted in *John Donne: The Critical Heritage*, p. 77.

[55] Donne, *Sermons*, i 237; quoted by Marotti, *John Donne, Coterie Poet*, p. 135.

[56] Harry Morris, 'John Donne's Terrifying Pun', *Papers on Language and Literature*, ix (1973), 128–37.

Donne the revulsion from satiety. In the words of Jonson's translation from Petronius,

> Doing, a filthy pleasure is, and short,
> And done, we straight repent us of the sport.

Yet the delivery of himself over in a verse letter to Sir Henry Wotton permitted Donne a final gracious bow of social solicitude, the name pun a firm signature:

> But, Sir, I advise not you, I rather do
> Say o'er those lessons, which I learned of you:
> Whom, free from German schisms, and lightness
> Of France, and fair Italy's faithlessness,
> Having from these sucked all they had of worth,
> And brought home that faith, which you carried forth,
> I throughly love. But if myself, I have won
> To know my rules, I have, and you have
>
>   Donne.

Donne's dear equanimity here comes from his confidence that his love for Wotton is entirely without carnal consequence, so that words which would elsewhere be erotically charged ('faithlessness', 'sucked', 'I throughly love') manifest such a 'white integrity' as to permit the name Donne, for once, both to pun, and not to pun on *sexual* doings. His friends could of course play more blithely with his name. Why did Thomas Pestell write as if the verse letter 'Written by Sir H. G. and J. D. *alternis vicibus*' were written by Goodyer and Donne not—as it clearly was—in alternate stanzas but in alternate lines? Because this permitted Pestell a further flight of textual erotics, since seventeenth-century loins are lines too:

> '*On the Interlinearie poëme begott twixt Sr H. Goo: & Dr Donne*'
> Here two rich ravisht spirrits kisse & twyne;
> Advanc'd, & weddlockt in each others lyne.
> Goode-res rare match with only him was blest,
> Who haes out donne, & quite undonne the rest.[57]

When Donne delivered himself over to Wotton, he and his name— 'have Donne'—could bow; when he delivers himself over to the supreme patron, he and his name kneel:

---

[57] Quoted by Bald, *John Donne: A Life*, p. 168 n.

> Wilt thou forgive that sin where I begun,
>   Which was my sin, though it were done before?
> Wilt thou forgive that sin, through which I run,
>   And do run still: though still I do deplore?
>   When thou hast done, thou hast not done,
>   For, I have more.
>
>   ('A Hymn to God the Father')

Kneeling, this shudders at the primal parental shudder in the loins, for 'that sin where I begun, / Which was my sin, though it were done before' is not only Adam's implicating sin but also the lethal act of love which was to issue in John Donne. 'Death and conception in mankind is one': 'is'—not 'are'—compounds the pun on 'die', and it issues in something deeper than the earlier flat revulsion of

> Think further on thy self, my soul, and think
> How thou at first was made but in a sink.
>
>   ('The Second Anniversary')

Carey says of Donne and bodies, 'We are reminded, yet again, of Lawrence';[58] but Carey is not moved to remind us of what Lawrence said about Donne in 'Introduction to These Paintings': 'Man came to have his own body in horror, especially in its sexual implications . . . Donne, after his exacerbated revulsion-attraction excitement of his earlier poetry, becomes a divine.' 'Pornography is the attempt to insult sex, to do dirt on it.' 'Do dirt on' is, in Lawrence, something more than the dictionary's 'to harm or injure maliciously', partly because the earlier instances lack any preposition (and 'doing dirt to' is next the more usual form); doing dirt on—ugly, unignorable—is excremental. Donne, doing dirt on his poems, insults sex. It was à propos of Donne that Coleridge invoked The Filter: 'To eject is as much a living Power, as to assimilate: to excrete as to absorb. Give therefore honor due to the Filter-poet.'[59] Honour due: how much is that? 'Just so much honour'.

Marotti praises Donne for insulting sex: 'Sex is portrayed in the most imaginatively energetic sections of the piece [Elegy 8, "The Comparison"] as nauseatingly filthy. The perspiration on the antagonist's mistress's brow is "Ranke sweaty froth" "Like spermatique

---

[58] *John Donne: Life, Mind, and Art*, p. 164.

[59] Coleridge, *Notebooks*; quoted in *John Donne: The Critical Heritage*, p. 276.

issue of ripe menstruous boiles." [60] 'Perspiration' there is a touch
decorous. Carey goes the whole hog, praising 'The Comparison' as
'a rich, ingenious and medically informed physical experience—
especially the disgusting parts, such as the description of the other
woman's sweat.'

> Rank sweaty froth thy mistress' brow defiles,
> Like spermatic issue of ripe menstruous boils.

'Here we can see Donne pursuing his interest in the body's excremental secretions, and speculatively blending four of them—sweat,
pus, sperm, and menses—in order to gain something more satisfying than mere sweat.' [61] Even Carey underrates Donne's pursuit of
excremental secretions, for to sweat, pus, sperm, and menses should
be added spittle ('froth'), bile (*defiles / biles*, the rhyme and the manuscript spelling), and—the monstrously spermatic *issue* of the menstruous, and the supreme excremental secretion—a baby. There is
something disconcerting about Carey's being so undisconcerted, as
there is about Marotti's equanimity as to how Donne here uses 'the
aesthetics of disgust'. Do Carey and Marotti bring these lines into
relation to their own bodies, or to anyone's really? 'A Hell for the
other people': [62] that is how Eliot repudiated Pound's 'aesthetics of
disgust'. Honourably, Eliot himself did not publish his most extreme
feats here, such confected and cunning (*con* and *cun*) revulsions as
might have graced 'The Comparison':

> Odours, confected by the cunning French,
> Disguise the good old hearty female stench. [63]

Undisguised disgust, not now to be disguised by the professionalized
antisepsis of 'the aesthetics of disgust': what does it minister to?

---

[60] *John Donne, Coterie Poet*, p. 49.

[61] *John Donne: Life, Mind, and Art*, p. 141. Compare Raymond Briggs, *Fungus the Bogeyman* (1977): 'This John Dung bloke is really bogus* [*bogus: real, genuine, true]—just listen to this—

> "Rank sweaty froth thy mistress' brow defiles,
> Like ███████ issue of ripe ███████ boils,"

Marvellous writing isn't it, drear?' [*Black block*: The words deleted on this page were considered offensive and unsuitable for Surface publication. An unexpurgated edition is available only in Bogeydom.]

[62] *After Strange Gods* (1934), p. 48.

[63] *The Waste Land: A Facsimile and Transcript of the Original Drafts*, ed. Valerie Eliot (1971), p. 39.

It is one of the strengths of Empson's criticism of Donne that he not only conceives of it in moral terms but also concedes that there could be principled moral objections to the poet. Against Carey's unimpeded consciencelessness should be set Empson's acknowledgement: 'Many people, I should say, have at the back of their minds a real moral objection to the earlier Donne love poems because they regard the poet as a cad who boasts of getting girls into trouble.'[64] But even this protects Donne, for 'cad' ('the cad needs taking down a peg or two,'[65] Empson says elsewhere of Donne) and 'getting girls into trouble' come out as too charmingly archaic; anyway it isn't so much that Donne is a cad to women (who may now find the concept of the cad more insulting than the behaviour of such), but that he is corrosively unfaithful to his poems.

Post-coital sadness is something other than revulsion, though the two may make common cause. For Empson, attirelessly resourceful in defence of Donne ('Donne may have invented knickers, as a final obstacle on the overdressed lady'), Donne was decently reluctant: 'He accepted the cynicism of Christianity about love, along with all the rest of its horrors, because he could not otherwise feed his wife and children.'[66] But Donne did not accept, he relished; and with 'profound, tho' mislocated, Thinking' he then fiercely eroticized his revulsion from the erotic. 'Between the excremental jelly that thy body is made of at first, and that jelly which thy body dissolves to at last; there is not so noysome, so putrid a thing in nature.'[67]

Since sperm is men's, not women's, Donne is fleetingly able to imagine a post-coital mood that has less self-revulsion; but this, since it is women's remission not men's, is then another strike against women. Carey writes with beauty, though with exorbitant liberality, about the moment in Problem VII when Donne broods on why the most beautiful women are always the falsest:

Doth the minde so follow the temperature of the body, that because those complexions are aptest to change, the mind is therefore so? Or as Bels of the purest metal retain their tinkling and sound largest; so the memory of the last pleasure lasts longer in these, and disposeth them to the next.

[64] 'Rescuing Donne' (1972); *Essays on Renaissance Literature*, i 176.

[65] *New York Review of Books*, 3 December 1981.

[66] *Essays on Renaissance Literature*, i 152.

[67] Donne, *Sermons*, iii 105; quoted by Carey, *John Donne: Life, Mind, and Art*, p. 135.

Carey has his own resonance when he comments: 'Something within the woman, as Donne imagines it, remains quivering and resonant, like a struck bell, after love-making is over . . . orgasm fills the body like a musical note setting up its lingering whispers.'[68] But the resonance is Carey's own. For Donne's 'tinkling and sound' is less generous than Carey's 'quivering and resonant', 'like a musical note setting up its lingering whispers'; and that this is 'within the woman' breeds its own resentment, so that the use to which Donne puts his momentary concession that orgasm may not always be dismaying is punitive and vengeful; the point, after all, is that women are not only false but also insatiably and lethally demanding, too well remembering their 'last pleasure'.

But it is in the end incumbent on someone who finds that Donne's post-coital malaise degrades the poems' own deepest understandings to give a hostage, a contrastive poem such as deeply imagines something other than a sadness colluding with revulsion. The twentieth-century poet most, and best, influenced by Donne is also his best twentieth-century critic, and Empson's poem 'Camping Out' (thanks to 'Donne the Space Man') has its rocketing climax and then at the end rises above being aggressively *anti*-climax:

CAMPING OUT

And now she cleans her teeth into the lake:
Gives it (God's grace) for her own bounty's sake
What morning's pale and the crisp mist debars:
Its glass of the divine (that Will could break)
Restores, beyond Nature: or lets Heaven take
(Itself being dimmed) her pattern, who half awake
Milks between rocks a straddled sky of stars.

Soap tension the star pattern magnifies.
Smoothly Madonna through-assumes the skies
Whose vaults are opened to achieve the Lord.
No, it is we soaring explore galaxies,
Our bullet boat light's speed by thousands flies.
Who moves so among stars their frame unties;
See where they blur, and die, and are outsoared.

'See where they blur, and die, and are outsoared': this, in its surprising, and gratefully surprised, unenvious awe, shows the achieved possibility of an art of post-coital gladness.

---

[68] *John Donne: Life, Mind, and Art*, p. 139.

THE WIT AND WEIGHT OF
CLARENDON

Roguish Auden put in some words 'in defence of gossip':

And as for books, if you had to choose between the serious study and
the amusing gossip, say, between Clarendon's History of the Rebellion and
John Aubrey's Scandal and Credulities, wouldn't you choose the latter? Of
course you would! Who would rather learn the facts of Augustus' imperial
policy rather than discover that he had spots on his stomach? No one.[1]

Fortunately, in the real world, as against the world of bluff broad-
casting, we do not have to choose between Clarendon and Aubrey.
Yet we must admit that in one respect their very different styles
invite the same question: are we delighting in an inadvertence, a
fluke, rather than in any intended effect? Those who still hold to
the belief that it is possible for a reader to take an unwarrantable
pleasure in a writer's words are not obliged to equate intention with
fully conscious decision; felicities are a coinciding of the happily
unplanned with the deliberated. But Aubrey thrusts upon us the
choice between apprehending his prose as genius or as ingenuousness.
Consider this death sentence from the life of Sir William Davenant:

He was next a servant (as I remember, a Page also) to Sir Fulke Grevil,
Lord Brookes, with whom he lived to his death, which was that a servant
of his (that had long wayted on him, and his Lordship had often told him
that he would doe something for him, but did not, but still putt him off
with delayes) as he was trussing up his Lord's pointes comeing from Stoole
(for then their breeches were fastned to the doubletts with points; then
came in hookes and eies; which not to have fastened was in my boyhood
a great crime) stabbed him.[2]

The flashing naked surprise of those last two words—'stabbed him'—
is a re-enactment of the crime, made the more horrible by the
juxtaposition of a truly great crime with the observations about
tailoring and about the need to adjust one's dress. The world of

---

[1] *The Listener*, 22 December 1937.
[2] *Brief Lives*, ed. Oliver Lawson Dick (1949), pp. 85–6. The paragraph on Aubrey,
I lift from my essay on Gower (*The Force of Poetry*), where I acknowledged that it
would figure here.

daily banality (lavatories and fly-buttons) is one where the moments
of possible social embarrassment (as when eating or making love)
are indeed the moments of great vulnerability, and are monstrously
continuous with murder. Then the three sets of parentheses, which
occupy two-thirds of the sentence and which settle into stubborn
procrastination (from six words to thirty-one and twenty-nine), dilate
with a murderous impatience at the lord's delays, throbbing at once
with a sharp pun on 'wayted on': '(that had long wayted on him,
and his Lordship had often told him that he would doe something
for him, but did not, but still putt him off with delayes)'. What could
more dramatically realize the scene, its unfulfilled promises and its
mounting tensions, than putting the reader off with delays? Yet all
the while the sentence's plot is undisguised even within delay's
swaddlings: 'with whom he lived to his death, which was that a
servant of his . . . stabbed him'. Are the 'points' (tags) both pointed
toward and at odds with 'stabbed him'? Are the breeches alive to
such contrarieties as those in *Macbeth*, where a breach is stabbed
between 'breach' and 'breeched'?

> Here lay *Duncan*,
> His Silver skinne, lac'd with his Golden Blood,
> And his gash'd Stabs, look'd like a Breach in Nature,
> For Ruines wastfull entrance; there the Murtherers,
> Steep'd in the Colours of their Trade; their Daggers
> Unmannerly breech'd with gore.

> (II iii)

Is Aubrey's prose instinct with something of Shakespeare's genius,
or am I imagining all this, transubstantiating clumsiness to felicity?
There were those who thought Aubrey a maggotty-headed credulous fellow, and it is possible that his especial attraction is for those
of us who are maggotty-headed credulous fellows.

Few have suspected Clarendon of being maggotty-headed or
credulous, but his prose too, for all the differences between its high
equanimity and Aubrey's down-to-earth astonishments, must make
any reader who exercises his imagination wonder whether he is
imagining things. Consider the following death sentence about the
Earl of Holland's anger at the Earl of Strafford:

The first could never forget or forgive a sharp sudden saying of his, (for
I cannot call it counsel or advice,) when there had been some difference
a few years before between his lordship and the lord Weston, in the managing
whereof the earl of Holland was confined to his house, 'that the King

should do well to cut off his head:' which had been aggravated (if such an injury were capable of aggravation) by a succession of discountenances mutually performed between them to that time.[3]

What flashes out so directly here is the direct speech of that saying, 'that the King should do well to cut off his head', a phrase all the more cutting and lethal because of the silky, understated suavity of 'should do well' as against the edged and stated indubitability of 'cut off his head'. We are not told at once or suddenly what the 'sharp sudden saying' was, or why 'sharp' will prove glintingly the word; and something of the same frightening imperturbability attaches to the word 'injury', ensconced within those parentheses that play as important a part within Clarendon's prose as within Aubrey's. For although it is questionable whether there could as a remark be anything more injurious than that quoted, the effect of the word 'injury'—as a summing-up of this particular saying—is, first, to sound chillingly flat, and, second, to set disconcertingly before us the fact that, though it might not at first seem possible to inflict a graver injury than cutting off the head, they were at the time all too capable of aggravating even this injury. Hanging, drawing, and quartering, for a start. Then again, what are we to make of 'discountenances', with its woundedness at the slights of incivility? Is the word given a greater gravity, aggravated, a different face put on it, by the succession 'sharp . . . cut off his head . . . injury . . . discountenances', which speaks of a succession of discountenances?

Clarendon's intelligence, though not simply greater than Aubrey's, is so much more deliberative than his, so much more weighed, pondered, and concerned explicitly with what should be credited, as to make it likely that his prose should be credited with these germane provocations. 'The style was not answerable to the provocation': this may sometimes have been true between King and Parliament, but it is not true of their historian. Clarendon's prose, like all great prose, is alive in its tissue, alive, since his subject is civil war, with sadness and reproof at everything that ruptures the tissue and that puts asunder those whom God hath joined: the English people, joined by courtesy not only of the English land but of the English language. So that an apparently innocuous word like 'succession' not only intimates that we should be alive to the succession

---

[3] Quotations from Clarendon's *History of the Rebellion* are from the edition by W. Dunn Macray (6 vols.; 1888). I have followed the convention of giving references in the form: book, paragraph. Here: 1, 101.

of words within such a sentence but also—through its political commitment—asks us to be pained by those successions within the words that realize a nocuous severance. Clarendon writes with his greatest sombre acuteness when the tissue of his prose has to acknowledge a civil war; has to acknowledge, within the very words that constitute its successive life, those misguided energies that cut off life or that cut off one English life from another.

Cut, or dissolve. Clarendon gives salience to the word 'dissolution' in the conviction that it was the ill-judged dissolutions of Parliament that led to the dissolution of the kingdom.[4]

And here I cannot but let myself loose to say, that no man can shew me a source from whence these waters of bitterness we now taste have more probably flowed, than from this unseasonable, unskilful, and precipitate dissolution of Parliaments. (1, 6)

'Dissolution' is fed by the confluence of 'loose', 'source', 'waters', 'flowed', and 'precipitate'; and the bitterness that we taste not only in the political diagnosis but also in the words themselves has as its source this tragic apprehension: that the self-same process, the sequence of words which recalls a flow of events, and which gives depth to the word 'dissolution', is a death-dealing sequence. The word 'unseasonable', which is crucial to Clarendon's sense of things and of the sadness of things, precipitates later in this sentence the words 'at those sad seasons'.

The continuities that are constitutional and a matter of legality and succession are at one with those that constitute a language, and the depth of Clarendon's dismay (not despair) at what he contemplates is felt in how the continuities of his own prose are so often obliged to incarnate discontinuity.

And therefore one day sir Arthur Haslerigge (who, as was said before, was used by that party, like the dove out of the ark, to try what footing there was) preferred a bill 'for the settling the militia of the kingdom, both by sea and land, in such persons as they should nominate;' with all those powers and jurisdictions which have been since granted to the earl of Essex or sir Thomas Fairfax by land, or to the earl of Warwick by sea. (3, 244)

The biblical dove was innocent and peaceful in its enterprise; the acute wresting of Genesis both diagnoses (the more trenchantly

[4] See B. H. G. Wormald, *Clarendon: Politics, Historiography and Religion* (1964), p. 104.

because in passing), and at the same time preserves antisepsis by lodging the witticism within the parenthesis. For this dove is as cunning as a serpent (is a decoy dove), and is in collusion with hawks. The political realities are, first, that the flood, the blood-dimmed tide, has yet to be loosed, rather than being blessedly over; and second, that the footing in question is not the ancient mountain but the modern militia by sea and land. Such are the elements of Clarendon's prose.

The sense of profound travesty is active in Clarendon's lucid perception of collusion, of—for instance—the perfect fit with which man's imperfection can fashion its travesties of what ought to be the case. A civil war is particularly cursed with this fittingness, a monstrous match of breach and observance, as in the vicious circle of honour rooted in dishonour:

And as this breach of the articles was very notorious and inexcusable, so it was made the rise, foundation, and excuse for barbarous injustice of the same kind throughout the greatest part of the war; insomuch as the King's soldiers afterwards, when it was their part to be precise in the observations of agreements, mutinously remembered the violation at Reading, and thereupon exercised the same license; and from thence, either side having somewhat to object to the other, that requisite honesty and justice of observing conditions was mutually, as it were by agreement, for a long time after violated. (7, 37)

Only a great writer, more in sorrow than in anger though in anger, could have effected so pained a movement, first, from the 'inexcusable' to the 'excuse', and then (a heartfelt shaking of the head) from 'the observations of agreements' to the laconically exact 'as it were by agreement'. The true agreements within the prose devote themselves to the doomed falsity of collusive agreement.

What agrees, or what adheres, is bitterly at odds with the ways in which things are at odds:

So aguish and fantastical a thing is the conscience of men who have once departed from the rule of conscience, in hope to be permitted to adhere to it again upon a less pressing occasion. (11, 249)

The aguish and fantastical conscience is perfectly caught in what is at once the perseverance and the perversity of the move from 'departed' to 'adhere' to 'less pressing'. '*More* pressing' would after all have made more sense in terms of adherence. It is the imaginative ingenuity of ingratitude that is sadly acknowledged within a prose to which we feel gratitude for its lacerated equanimity.

A second act of the same day, and the only way they took to return their thanks and acknowledgment to the Queen for her intercession and mediation in the passing those bills, was the opening a letter they intercepted which was directed to her majesty herself. (4, 308)

Clarendon is writing about two other kinds of writing: parliamentary bills and a letter. Each, like all writing, is a 'mediation', and a letter might be thought particularly suited to the 'return' of 'thanks'. The mediations of this prose are vibrantly indignant at the interception, the profound discourtesy; and the word 'intercepted' is given its tone of a just rebuke, of effrontery confronted, by its tingling proximity to and distance from the word 'intercession'. The Earl of Essex

died without being sensible of sickness, in a time when he might have been able to have undone much of the mischieve he had formerly wrought; to which he had great inclinations; and had indignation enough for the indignities himself had received from the ingrateful Parliament. (10, 80)

Clarendon's sound-effects are sound; not jinglings but tinglings. He is repeatedly though diversely drawn to such collocations as 'intercession' / 'intercepted', or 'inclinations' / 'indignation' / 'indignities' / 'ingrateful'. On some occasions, the likeness of sound may intimate a hope (or a fear) that essential likeness may yet win the day, resolving the antagonisms within language (of which too much may be made). But on other occasions, the unlikeness of sound may suggest that a very small breach may yet be unbridgable and may grievously be prised open further by the divisive. The way in which words, like fellow-countrymen, may so easily run with or run against each other: this is caught, with the simplicity of genius within a complicated elucidation, when Clarendon sets *con-* with and against *contra-*. So near and yet so far.

For in religion he [Falkland] thought to carefull and to curious an enquiry could not be made, amongst those whose purity was not questioned, and whose authority was constantly and confidently urged, by men who were furthest from beinge of on minde amongst themselves, and for the mutuall supporte of ther severall opinions, in which they most contradicted each other; and in all those contraversyes, he had so dispassioned a consideration, such a candor in his nature, and so profounde a charity in his conscience, that in those pointes in which he was in his owne judgement most cleere, he never thought the worse, or in any degree declined the familiarity of those who were of another minde.[5]

The aspiration that we should be of one mind has to contemplate the large fact (which daunts smaller men than Falkland in his charity and magnanimity) to which the small prefixes *con-* and *contra-* bear witness: that not only were there 'those who were of another mind' but there were those 'who were furthest from being of one mind amongst themselves'.

Trust and truth must do their best to pinion treachery, but they must not feel confident that they will succeed. Unlike Wilmot, Goring would

without hesitation have broken any trust, or done any act of treachery, to have satisfied an ordinary passion or appetite; and, in truth, wanted nothing but industry (for he had wit and courage and understanding and ambition, uncontrolled by any fear of God or man) to have been as eminent and successful in the highest attempt in wickedness of any man in the age he lived in or before. (8, 169)

'In truth' he was false: within a world so bent upon destruction and self-destruction, it is all too likely that words will turn upon themselves and undo themselves. Fortunately it will sometimes be folly that undoes itself, here where any word may be hoist with its own petard.

And such as were brought in and delivered to the officers, declared such an averseness to the work to which they were designed, and such a peremptory resolution not to fight, that they only increased their numbers, not their strength, and ran away upon the first opportunity. (7, 203)

The words themselves run away upon the first opportunity from their agreed meanings: 'resolution', which should mean firmness and unyielding temper, turns tail and becomes the firm decision not to stand firm ('resolution not to fight'), just as the army's 'strength', which in a proper parlance would mean its numbers, finds itself cut off: 'they only increased their numbers, not their strength.'

The continuities within the prose once more set themselves to advertise and to advise ('that he had advertised the first, and advised the last, to take the same course' (2, 104)), to make real the

---

[5] Clarendon, *Life*; quoted from *Characters from the Histories and Memoirs of the Seventeenth Century*, ed. D. Nichol Smith (1920), pp. 93–4.

discontinuities and hostilities that they contemplate. These exact effects impinge within a prose that does not allow itself to settle into a routine or into any one angle of junction, but which—vigilant through 360 degrees—spins round to catch every tangent of sound and sense. For want of a word, or for want of the ability to distinguish one word from another, a kingdom may be lost.

And it is not here unseasonable, (how merry soever it may seem to be,) as an instance of the incogitancy and inadvertency of those kind of votes and transactions, to remember, that, the first resolution of the power of the militia being grounded upon a supposition of an imminent necessity, the ordinance first sent up from the Commons to the Lords for the execution of the militia expressed an *eminent* necessity; whereupon some lords, who understood the difference of the words, and that an *eminent* necessity might be supplied by the ordinary provision which possibly an *imminent* necessity might not safely attend, desired a conference with the Commons for the amendment; which, I remember, was at last with great difficulty consented to, many (who, I presume, are not yet grown up to conceive the difference) supposing it an unnecessary contention for a word, and so yielding to them for saving of time rather than for the moment of the thing. (5, 151)

It is no unnecessary contention for a word that sets in balance or in imbalance such characteristic Clarendon turns as these, evincing— as Clarendon said of Falkland—'the wit and weight of all he said':

But by the King's interposition, and indeed imposition. (2, 58)

But this was rather modestly insinuated than insisted upon. (2, 71)

. . . the only persons excepted from pardon and exempted from the benefit of that oblivion. (4, 43)

. . . purely to perfecte his conversion by the conversation of those who had the greatest name.[6]

. . . would distress, if not destroy, his whole army. (7, 204)

L. C. Knights, to whom many of us feel special gratitude for having joined Matthew Arnold in bringing home, not to historians but to students of English literature, how great a writer Clarendon is: even Knights underrates the extent to which the movement of Clarendon's prose has its own economy of balance.[7] With some

---

[6] Clarendon, *Life*, in Nichol Smith (ed.), *Characters*, p. 175.

[7] 'Reflections on Clarendon's *History of the Rebellion*' (1948); *Further Explorations* (1965).

writers, you might at small cost drop a short parenthetical bit. But there is a high price to be paid when Knights abbreviates the beginning of Clarendon's sketch of Attorney-General Noy.

The first, upon the great fame of his ability and learning, (and very able and learned he was,) was by great industry and importunity from Court persuaded to accept that place for which all other men laboured, (being the best for profit that profession is capable of,) and so he suffered himself to be made the King's Attorney-general. (2, 157)

Knights effects a false economy by dropping the second parenthesis, '(being the best for profit that profession is capable of)'. This is unprofitable, because it removes, first, the characteristically telling antithesis of the two parentheses: the honest admission of Noy's abilities—'(and very able and learned he was)'—against the admission that the opportunities for the dishonest or the self-serving were strong within the office—'(being the best for profit)'. Second, the excision removes the alert prefix and its magnetism: 'for profit that profession', which is not only taut in itself but is tautened against the play of 'industry and importunity'. Third, it removes the word 'capable', which might seem relatively unimportant but which gathers so much around it, as in that other parenthesis, '(if such an injury were capable of aggravation)'. Most of Clarendon's capabilities are exerted upon what men are capable of, what can and cannot be effected. Clarendon raises political history to the art of the possible. He is drawn therefore, naturally and unobsessively, to the suffix -ible or -able. Within a mere four pages in Knights's excellent excerpting, the eye falls on these:

Mr Jermin, who still valued himself upon the impossible faculty to please all and displease none. (7, 189)

... a weak judgment, and a little vanity, and as much of pride, will hurry a man into as unwarrantable and as violent attempts as the greatest and most unlimited and insatiable ambition will do. (6, 402)

... very few men of so great parts are, upon all occasions, more counsellable than he ... nor is he uninclinable in his nature to such an entire communication in all things which he conceives to be difficult. (4, 128)

And the temper and composition of his mind was so admirable, that he was always more pleased and delighted that he had advanced so far, which he imputed to his virtue and conduct, than broken or dejected that his success was not answerable, which he still charged upon second causes, for which he could not be accountable. (9, 126)

So that to remove that parenthesis, '(being the best for profit that profession is capable of)', is to 'save' ten words that ought to be saved.

This sketch of Noy itself ends:

In a word, he was an unanswerable instance how necessary a good education and knowledge of men is to make a wise man, at least a man fit for business. (1, 157)

'Unanswerable': in a word, and this is the right word for Clarendon's succinct sentencing. Often when he is moved to this calm decisive introduction of his climax, the word in question then incorporates his valued suffix. There is wit in moving from 'In a word' to 'unanswerable', of all words. There is authority in moving from 'in a word' to 'despicable' ('In a word, he became the most despicable to all men' (6, 403)). Supremely, in the end, in the penultimate paragraph of the great work, at the Restoration, there is a high gratitude with a high modesty in the movement from 'In a word' to the word 'unexpressible':

On Monday he went to Rochester, and the next day, being the 29th of May and his birthday, he entered London, all the ways from Dover thither being so full of people and exclamations as if the whole kingdom had been gathered. About or above Greenwitch the Lord Mayor and aldermen met him, with all those protestations of joy which can hardly be imagined; and the concourse so great that the King rode in a crowd from the bridge to Temple Bar. All the companies of the city stood in order on both sides, giving loud thanks for his majesty's presence. And he no sooner came to Whitehall but the two Houses of Parliament solemnly cast themselves at his feet, with all the vows of affection and fidelity to the world's end. In a word, the joy was so unexpressible and so universal, that his majesty said smilingly to some about him, that he doubted [feared] it had been his own fault that he had been absent so long, for he saw nobody that did not protest he had ever wished for this return. (16, 246)

There is ground for gratitude, at last, in that succession of *all*'s: 'all the ways', 'all those protestations', 'all the companies', 'all the vows'.[8] Then the conclusion of this great paragraph takes up the earlier awe of 'all those protestations of joy which can hardly be imagined'; takes it up, goes beyond it, and 'in a word' finds the perfect word, the one that admits the insufficiency of words especially at such a

---

[8] These *alls* contrast with the poignant reiteration of 'all' in the account of the captivity of Charles I (11, 157).

moment: 'In a word, the joy was so unexpressible.' At which, with a true balance of alternate tones, the sentence moves at once from the unexpressible to something that was ne'er so well expressed: the King's salty, salutary expression of benign wit, that he feared 'it had been his own fault that he had been absent so long, for he saw nobody that did not protest he had ever wished for this return.' The King, unlike some of those who welcome him, does not protest too much.

The art of the possible is one that has to acknowledge both what proves impossible even to art, the unexpressible, and what proves impossible even to prosperous politics. Even the miracles of God have their sacred limits, as the penultimate sentence of the entire history shortly insists:

Yet did the merciful hand of God in one month bind up all these wounds, and even made the scars as undiscernible as in respect of their deepness was possible. (16, 247)

One reason why Clarendon's style is answerable, in both senses, to the provocations of the civil war is that, in this civil war, fighting was continuous with writing. More than usual force attaches here to such a phrase as 'the authors of a civil war'; to 'paper combat' and 'paper skirmishes'; to 'sovereignty of language' and 'that new license of words'; to the wresting of words like 'law' and 'liberty', 'words of precious esteem in their just signification'; and to the sturdy old phrases with which Clarendon opposes the new 'hard words': 'in plain terms', and 'in plain English'. Charles Whibley said of Clarendon:

He did not set the persons of his drama against any background, natural or artificial. His world has not houses, nor courts, nor fields. The person-ages of his drama seem to move hither and thither, in vast, vacant spaces.[9]

But whatever he may or may not have seen, Clarendon always heard the persons of his drama against the background of—or rather, as brought into this breathing world by—the English language, and filling like air every cubic inch of his vast unvacant space.

Fills it, some have thought, a shade too full. Matthew Arnold, who honoured Clarendon for honouring Falkland, was careful not to be excessive in his praise:

[9] *Political Portraits* (1917), p. 60.

Clarendon's style is here a little excessive, a little Asiatic. And perhaps a something Asiatic is not wholly absent, either, from that famous passage,— the best known, probably, in all the *History of the Rebellion*,—that famous passage which describes Lord Falkland's longing for peace.

> Sitting among his friends, often, after a deep silence and frequent sighs, he would with a shrill and sad accent ingeminate the word *Peace, Peace*; and would passionately profess that the very agony of the war, and the view of the calamities and desolation the kingdom did and must endure, took his sleep from him, and would shortly break his heart.

Clarendon's touch, where in his memoirs he speaks of Falkland, is simpler than in the *History*. But we will not carp at this great writer and faithful friend. Falkland's life was an uneventful one, and but a few points in it are known to us. To Clarendon he owes it that each of those points is a picture.[10]

But it is better to carp if the alternative is to condescend. The passage of Clarendon, indeed the best known in the *History*, is supremely well judged. The strong sighing repetition of *Peace, Peace* finds both strength and sadness in its assonance with 'deep' and 'sleep' ('Silence, you troubl'd waves, and thou Deep, peace' (*Paradise Lost*, vii 216)); the singular word—'the word *Peace, Peace*', instead of the words, exactly captures what it is to double the one word; and, linguistically unique in the passage, 'ingeminate' is a double touch of genius. It was a much less unusual word in Clarendon's day than in Arnold's, and *a fortiori* than in ours; and in Clarendon it is informed by much of its current life, so that it can stand as an unaffected and (*pace* Arnold—*pace, pace*) unexcessive, albeit striking, complement to the profound simplicity of *Peace, Peace*.

Ingeminate: 1. to utter (a sound) twice or oftener; to repeat, reiterate (a word, statement, etc.), usually for the purpose of being emphatic or

---

[10] 'Falkland' (1877); in *Mixed Essays* (1879). Arnold changed the balance and spirit of Clarendon's passage for the worse by beginning at 'Sitting'; Clarendon had written:

> When there was any overture or hope of peace he would be more erect and vigorous, and exceedingly solicitous to press any thing which he thought might promote it; and sitting amongst his friends, often, after a deep silence and frequent sighs, would, with a shrill and sad accent, ingeminate the word *Peace, Peace*. (7, 233)

For an exact and penetrating account of some important reservations about Clarendon's style, see George Watson, 'The Reader in Clarendon's *History of the Rebellion*', *RES*, NS, xxv (1974), 396–409.

impressive . . . (Freq. in 17th c.; now chiefly used in echoes of quot. 1647 [Clarendon].) (*OED*)

It is important not to hold against Clarendon his very success in having so imprinted his greatness forever upon, and via, the word; there is some happy irony in those later 'echoes' of him, since ingemination is itself an echoing, and one of the *OED* instances before Clarendon is from Sandys's translation of Ovid, where it is Echo itself who 'yet ingeminates'.

Falkland (and hence Clarendon) is himself echoing or ingeminating. 'They have healed also the hurt of the daughter of my people slightly, saying, Peace, peace; when there is no peace.' The verse of Jeremiah (6: 14) is itself, moreover, repeated verbatim, ingeminated (as 8: 11), and it is the double fact—that there may be no healing of the hurt of his people, and that the completion of the cadence remains unspoken but all too acknowledged ('saying, Peace, peace; when there is no peace')—which gives such heart-breaking depth to the sad accents of Falkland and of Clarendon.

We should accept it as evidence of Clarendon's strength that journalists have been incited to artificial ingemination: 'Thus our Canon ingeminates peace (*OED*, 1887).' With a pun on *cannon*, presumably. 'Here comes Mr. Balfour with his olive branch, ingeminating peace (*OED*, 1892).' Like the dove out of the ark, to try what footing there was. For one of the things that we might ask of our great writers is their giving occasion for happy wit, such as that recorded by Horace Walpole, Walpole who elsewhere wrote of Clarendon: 'His majesty and eloquence, his power of painting characters, his knowledge of his subject, rank him in the first class of writers—yet he has both great and little faults. . . . Perhaps even his favourite character of Lord Falkland takes too considerable a share in the history':[11]

T'other night at Brooks' the conversation turned on Lord Falkland; Fitzpatrick said he was a very weak man and owed his fame to Lord Clarendon's partiality. Charles Fox was sitting in a deep reverie, with his knife in his hand. 'There,' continued Fitzpatrick, 'I might describe Charles meditating on the ruin of his country, ingeminating the words, Peace! Peace! and ready to plunge the knife in his own bosom.'—'Yes,' rejoined Hare in the same ironic dolorous tone, 'and he would have done so, but hap-

[11] *A Catalogue of the Royal and Noble Authors of England* (1758).

pening to look on the handle of the knife, he saw it was silver, and put it in his pocket.'[12]

How different (and not just because the dolorous tone is here ironic) is 'ingeminating the words Peace! Peace!' from 'the word, *Peace, Peace*'. Yet it is not just the ingeminating peace, peace, but that 'deep' reverie that shows how deeply Clarendon's words etch themselves, even for those light-fingered and light-hearted wags who merely pocket the silver sentence.

To repeat a cry—Peace, Peace (no exclamation marks in Clarendon, not incidentally, any more than in Jeremiah)—may be both to acknowledge a fact and to resist it. Geoffrey Hill has drawn attention to the 'stubborn reiterative outcry' in the poems of John Crowe Ransom and has remarked that 'the particular significance of the reiterated cry' may be 'in its power to transform pure spontaneous reflex into an act of will'.[13] Then again, 'ingeminate' is happily suited to the unhappy fact of civil war, the deep kinship of twinship at war with itself. Moreover, the word had often figured within the evocation of the saviour, the prince of peace who came not to bring peace but a sword. The *OED* cites such instances from 1616, 1637, and 1658: 'This ingeminated zeal of Christ for his people's unity and love.' Likewise the ingeminated zeal of Falkland for his people's unity and love, at a time of disunity and hate ingeminating the word *Peace, Peace*. The *OED*'s 'for the purpose of being emphatic or impressive' sadly sells short the possibilities and the actualities of such a repetition.

'In a word': and there was one word that incarnated Clarendon's zeal for unity and love. *Composition* is the word—'The temper and composition of his mind was so admirable'—and is so at one with his temper as to move naturally into 'was' not 'were'. Almost all of the senses given in the *OED* could be illustrated from Clarendon, and many are at the heart of his lifelong endeavour.

OED 3. The putting [of things] into proper position, order, or relation to other things.

---

[12] Walpole to William Mason, 7 February 1782; *The Yale Edition of Horace Walpole's Correspondence*, ed. W. S. Lewis, xxix (1955), 179.

[13] 'What Devil Has Got into John Ransom?' (1980, 1983); *The Lords of Limit* (1984), pp. 133–4.

6b. The due arrangement of words into sentences, and of sentences into periods; the art of constructing sentences and of writing prose or verse.

7. The composing of anything for oral delivery, or to be read; the practice or art of literary production.

11. The composing or settling (of differences etc.).

12. The settling of a debt, liability, or claim by some mutual arrangement.

16b. Mental constitution, or constitution of mind and body in combination; the combination of personal qualities that make any one what he is.

17. Artistic manner, style; the mode or style in which words or sentences are put together.

22. A mutual agreement or arrangement between two parties, a contract.

23. An agreement for the settlement of political differences; a treaty etc. (b) A mutual agreement for cessation of hostilities, a truce; an agreement for submission or surrender on particular terms.

24. An agreement or arrangement involving surrender or sacrifice of some kind on one side or on both; a compromise.

25. An agreement by which a creditor accepts a certain proportion of a debt, in satisfaction, for an insolvent debtor. 'The fines paid by Royalists under the Commonwealth were called *Compositions of Delinquents*.'

That which makes up an individual or a society, a sentence or a style or a work of art; that which makes up terms, treaties, settlements, and compromises: nature, art, and society meet in the word, and it is the word for which Clarendon reserves the highest praise and for which he himself deserves the highest praise:

He was a person of so rare a composition by nature and by art, (for nature alone could never have reached to it,) that he was so far from being ever dismayed upon any misfortune, (and greater variety of misfortunes never befell any man,) that he quickly recollected himself so vigorously, that he did really believe his condition to be improved by that ill accident, and that he had an opportunity thereby to gain a new stock of reputation and honour. (10, 13)

Just such a stock of reputation and honour as Clarendon himself gained.

In her moving and challenging book on history and the novel, *The Story-Teller Retrieves the Past*, Mary Lascelles has said:

Though civil war is the most tragic of all conflicts yet it allows the belief that something might be said on either side. There can be no two thoughts

about an invading army; about King and Parliament there may be—
afterwards; seldom at the time.[14]

Seldom, not never, since there may be a person—someone who
retrieves the present and, thereby, centuries later retrieves the past—
of so rare a composition by nature and by art.

[14] (1980), pp. 61–2.

GEORGE CRABBE'S THOUGHTS OF CONFINEMENT

George Crabbe left a few riddles. To all but one of them, he appended the answer. *Modesty. Sovereign.* And—a word which, when moved from its place in Suffolk, has a riddling element—*Quanting*:

> My Station I keep when I move from my Place,
> And my Station I leave in my Place when I stand.
> I get nothing forward, tho' running a Race,
> And move in the Water by pressing the Land.[1]

Crabbe's superb editor, Norma Dalrymple-Champneys, has a note: '*Quanting*: a term used by bargemen on the East coast for propelling a boat or punt with a "quant" or pole.' The stationing is perfect for Crabbe, who is always in his element when water meets land (Peter Grimes and many another); who has a feeling for what 'pressing' truly is; and whose couplets manifest a disconcerting relation of movement to staying in the same place. They observe gait, their own and others'.

> 'At times there is upon her features seen,
> What moves suspicion—she is too serene.
> Such is the motion of a drunken man,
> Who steps sedately, just to show he can.'[2]

The line steps sedately, just to show what an oddly self-conscious motion this is. For how, given what 'sedate' seatedly is, can a man *step sedately*? At any moment a drunken man may suddenly sit down. 'My Station I keep when I move from my Place'.

It is fitting that Crabbe then was moved to another version of his riddle, thereby enforcing a sense that what he was doing even now was keeping his station when he moved from his place, getting forward and yet not:

> I walked as it were in a Race,
> Yet nothing I gained by my Speed,

---

[1] *The Complete Poetical Works*, ed. Norma Dalrymple-Champneys and Arthur Pollard (Oxford English Texts; 1988), iii 366–7, 422. Crabbe's poems are quoted from this exemplary edition.

[2] *Tales of the Hall* (1819) VIII, 'The Sisters', 793–6.

> But had I sat still in my Place,
> I then had gone forward indeed.

The riddle (of September 1817) to which he did not append the answer is this:

> When I'm held in my first, as my betters may be,
> As nothing prevents it! I call myself free!
> If held by my second, how vain is your Strife,
> If he has you for once, Sir, He has you for Life!

Editor: 'The answer is perhaps "Bondage" '. No solution, no dissolution.

Crabbe is the poet of bondage, of age, and of bonds, the valued bonds of responsibility or tradition, the dour ones that are chains or habits or acquiescences, the artistic and technical ones that are rhymes or couplets. We all, like 'the fond Girl' rawly away at boarding-school, have to learn to be schooled. She

> Nauseates her Food, and wonders who can sleep
> On such mean Beds, where she can only weep:
> She scorns Condolence—but to all she hates
> Slowly at length her Mind accommodates;
> Then looks on Bondage with the same concern
> As others felt, and finds that she must learn
> As others learn'd—the common Lot to share,
> To search for Comfort and submit to Care.[3]

To rhyme upon 'accommodates' is to make the adjustment to what one 'hates': 'such mean Beds', such demeaning accommodation. A rhyme is, in ample yet narrow ways (like the couplet), an accommodation.

To rhyme upon 'free', as Crabbe does in the riddle, is to put freedom in its place, to hold *free* to its responsibilities as a word with a bond, to insist that there is no simply floating free. Milton, 'Sonnet XII':

> That bawle for freedom in their senceless mood,
> And still revolt when truth would set them free.
> Licence they mean when they cry libertie.

---

[3] *The Borough* (1810), Letter XXIV, 'Schools', 156–63.

For liberty comprehends its affiliations: it rhymes (and with 'free', moreover),[4] whereas 'licence' not only is not rhymed by Milton (though it grates against 'senceless'), it is sullen about rhyming at all.

Crabbe understood that even the fight for freedom could turn to an enslavement; a man to whom the poet gave his own Christian name understood as much:

> George loved the cause of freedom, but reproved
> All who with wild and boyish ardour loved;
> Those who believed they never could be free,
> Except when fighting for their liberty.[5]

His son said of his proud parent: 'he ever had an ardent passion for personal liberty, inconsistent with enjoyment under the constraint of ceremony.'[6] Yet this has its tension, for Crabbe constituted his art as an enjoyment under the constraint of ceremony. The heroic couplet is such a constraint, paired in propriety. Crabbe never really was 'Pope in worsted stockings', but even less was he Pope bare-legged or in dishabille—Pope, who wrote of 'thoughts just warm from the brain, without any polishing or dress, the very dishabille of the understanding'.[7]

> This shrubby belt that runs the land around
> Shuts freedom out! what being likes a bound?[8]

A poet, for one, especially a poet who is in two minds about freedom but not about rhyming.

Crabbe's rhymes are bounds, proprieties and bonds. As in 'The Learned Boy', where Stephen is taken aback by the modern fine couples:

> Soon he observ'd, with terror and alarm,
> His friend enlock'd within a lady's arm,
> And freely talking—'But it is,' said he,
> 'A near relation, and that makes him free.'[9]

---

[4] Bob Dylan, 'Abandoned Love': 'I march in the parade of liberty / But as long as I love you I'm not free'.
[5] *Tales of the Hall* I, 'The Hall', 146–9.
[6] *Life of the Rev. George Crabbe*, by George Crabbe (1834), p. 115.
[7] 5 December 1712; *Works* (1737), v 188.
[8] *Posthumous Tales* X, 'The Ancient Mansion', 130–1.
[9] *Tales* (1812), XXI 255–8.

The rhyme on 'free' is itself one form of the responsibly and re-sponsively 'enlock'd', yet the word *free* freely adapts the earlier word 'freely' as well. But then for a strolling man to take these social freedoms with a woman, he being so relaxed or lax, may witness to no true freedom. How corporeally, then, the rhyme for 'alarm' turns out not just to be 'arm', but the more expansive gesture: 'within *a lady's arm*' (*a l . . . arm*). There's an enlocking. A near relation.

Terror and alarm at the prospect of being enlocked, incarcer-ated, are what urged the most urgent letter that Crabbe ever wrote (it is the first in the *Selected Letters and Journals of George Crabbe*),[10] that to Edmund Burke, in February–March 1781, when Crabbe was 26.

Sir

I am sensible that I need even your Talents to apologise for the Freedom I now take but I have a Plea which however simply urged will with a Mind like yours Sir procure me Pardon; I am one of those outcasts on the World who are without a Friend without Employment & without Bread.

The freedom that Crabbe took was the only means by which he could stop his freedom from being taken. For his poems, or rather the misconduct of the printer and the tardiness of the subscribers' payments, had brought Crabbe to the gates of prison:

In April last I came to London with 5 £ & flatter'd myself it was sufficient to supply me with the common Necessaries of Life, til such of my Abillities shou'd procure me more; of these I had the highest Opinion & a poetical Vanity contributed to my Delusion; I knew little of the World & had read Books only; I wrote & fancied Perfection in my Compositions, when I wanted Bread they promised me Affluence, & sooth'd me with Dreams of Reputation, whilst my Appearance subjected me to Contempt.

Time, Reflection, & Want, have shown me my Mistake; I see my Trifles in that which I think the true Light, & whilst I deem them such, have yet the Opinion that holds them Superior to the ordinary run of Poetical Productions.

About Ten Days since I was compell'd to give a Note for 7 £ to avoid an Arrest for about double that Sum, which I owe; I wrote to every Friend I had but my Friends are poor likewise; the time of Payment approach'd & I ventured to represent my Case to Lord Rochford; I begg'd to be credited for this Sum til I received it of my Subscribers which I believe

---

[10] Ed. Thomas C. Faulkner, with the assistance of Rhonda L. Blair (1985), pp. 3–5. The letter appears in the *Life*, pp. 90–3.

will be within one Month; to this Letter I had no Reply & I have probably offended by my Importunity. Having used every honest Means in vain, I Yesterday confess'd my Inabillity & obtain'd with much entreaty & as the greatest Favor a Week's forbearance, when I am positively told that I must pay the Money or prepare for a Prison. You will guess the purpose of so long an Introduction: I appeal to You Sir as a good & let me add a great Man; I have no other Pretensions to your Favor than that I am an unhappy one. It is not easy to support the Thoughts of Confinement; & I am Coward enough to dread such an End to my Suspense.

I will call upon You Sir tomorrow & if I have not the Happiness to obtain Credit with You, I will submit to my Fate.

Crabbe's dignity met at once the dignity of Burke, who saved him, secured him and his art.

Crabbe never forgot Burke's magnanimity, and he never forgot what it would be to prepare for a prison. 'It is not easy to support the Thoughts of Confinement.' He did not like the thoughts but he liked the word *confine* and its cognates, and he liked to make it enact its meaning by calling upon it as a rhyme, an end to one's suspense. And then a new beginning:

> At first his care was to himself confin'd;
> Himself assur'd, he gave it to mankind:
> His zeal grew active—honest, earnest zeal,
> And comfort dealt to him, he long'd to deal.[11]

Confinement may mean an escapable self-attention. Or a new birth. Or a long day's dying.

The Borough in Letter XXIII enters 'Prisons'. In the preface, Crabbe emitted a deeply equivocal 'Alas!' for those who suppose themselves too refinedly liable to wince:

Alas! sufferings real, evident, continually before us, have not effects very serious or lasting, even in the minds of the more reflecting and compassionate; nor indeed does it seem right that the pain caused by sympathy should serve for more than a stimulus to benevolence. If then the strength and solidity of truth placed before our eyes have effect so feeble and transitory, I need not be very apprehensive that my representations of Poor-houses and Prisons, of wants and sufferings, however faithfully taken, will excite any feelings which can be seriously lamented.

---

[11] *Tales* (1812), 'Advice; or, The 'Squire and the Priest', 108–111.

The feelings that Crabbe excited in Hazlitt were harsh, and yet in Hazlitt's exacerbation, his craving to speak hurtfully, there can be felt an acknowledgement of Crabbe's power, the power to confine Hazlitt where he does not want to be.

The world is one vast infirmary; the hill of Parnassus is a penitentiary, of which our author is the overseer: to read him is a penance, yet we read on! Mr. Crabbe, it must be confessed, is a repulsive writer.[12]

After 'penance' (itself coming after 'penitentiary'), the phrase 'it must be confessed' is on its knees, signalling one of the most authentic of tributes, the grudging one. 'The hill of Parnassus is a penitentiary': this sees how Sisyphean a place Crabbe's world is.

Hazlitt judged that not only Crabbe's subjects but Crabbe's readers were patients and prisoners. 'By degrees we submit, and are reconciled to our fate, like patients to the physician, or prisoners in the condemned cell.' He judged the art a revenge for the life, again an imprisoning:

The situation of a country clergyman is not necessarily favourable to the cultivation of the Muse. He is set down, perhaps, as he thinks, in a small curacy for life, and he takes his revenge by imprisoning the reader's imagination in luckless verse. Shut out from social converse. . . .

Shut out from social converse, what can you effect but unsociable verse? But what saves Crabbe's verse from being luckless is its level gratitude for the luck that is a rhyme. A debtor is in prison, as the poet so nearly had been and for his poems too, but the poet is now in debt to a provident or providential rhyme:

> And there sits one, improvident but kind,
> Bound for a Friend, whom Honour could not bind.[13]

There, 'but kind' gets contracted to 'bind', constrained by the rhyme and by the rotating of 'Bound'. The lines are inexorable in what they catch, but central to what they catch is the indestructible honour of the act of kindness which has brought the man to this pass.

For there are good debts as well as bad debts. The poet may be in debt to a serious pun, one which he honours:

---

[12] *The Spirit of the Age* (1825). Revised by Hazlitt from: 'Mr. Crabbe is a *fascinating* writer'. (*London Magazine*, May 1821, iii 484–90; I owe my knowledge of this to Jonathan Bean.)

[13] 'Prisons', 96–7.

'Oft I perceiv'd my Fate, and then would say,
"I'll think to-morrow, I must live to-day:"
So am I here—I own the Laws are just—
And here, where Thought is painful, think I must:
But Speech is pleasant, this Discourse with thee
Brings to my Mind the sweets of Liberty,
Breaks on the sameness of the place, and gives
The doubtful Heart Conviction that it lives.'

The rhyme of 'Liberty' with 'thee' is itself both painful and pleasant (would that 'Liberty' rhymed here with *me*). 'Breaks on', too, is both pleasant and painful, for this conversation breaks on the sameness of the place as day or daylight begins to shine (*OED* 41a, 'break on'), and yet the conversation is bound before long to break on, be broken by, the sameness of the place. And 'Conviction' is at once the pleasant convincedness—'gives / The doubtful Heart Conviction that it lives'—and the painful acknowledgement that he is in the place because he has been convicted.

Like the other masters of the heroic couplet, Crabbe—in his life, his character, and his art—is contrarious. Open to contrarieties, especially those which engage what it is to be open or to be shut in. The prison unhappily shuts in; the louring landscape is for Crabbe happily oppressive, though he is open to the fact that this is not the usual sensation or sensibility:

I envied your wet Journey to the Boggy Ground of Friskney & will remember it, as one of the Places I purpose to visit. People speak with Raptures of fine Prospects, clear Skies, Lawns, Parks & the blended Beauties of Art and Nature, but give me a wild, wide Fen, in a foggy Day; with quaking Boggy Ground and trembling Hillocks in a putrid Soil: Shut in by the Closeness of the Atmosphere, all about is like a new Creation & every Botanist an Adam who explores and names the Creatures he meets with.—[14]

Friskney sounds far from frisky, and is all the more to Crabbe's liking. He was a remarkable botanist; the botanist, like the poet and like Adam, explores and names the creatures he meets with, there in a new creation—a creation made possible by what might have seemed to preclude it: 'Shut in by the Closeness of the Atmosphere'.

The couplet shuts in close, especially when as end-stopped as Crabbe's couplets often are. The atmosphere of his couplets is notoriously close. Pent to the point of Pentonville. Atmosphere can

[14] To Edmund Cartwright, 1 October 1792; *Selected Letters*, pp. 51-2.

be oppressive in him. So there is a strange play of mind in what is perhaps Crabbe's most famous critical remark, when, defending his art in the preface to *Tales*, he speaks of his predecessors:

And, to bring forward one other example, it will be found that *Pope* himself has no small portion of this actuality of relation, this nudity of description, and poetry without an atmosphere; the lines beginning, '*In the worst inn's worst room*,' are an example.

Poetry without an atmosphere: I had not realized till I read the notes in the Oxford edition[15] that Crabbe was taking up the challenge of a phrase from Grant's review of *The Borough* in 1810: 'He lives, if we may be allowed the expression, without an atmosphere.' Crabbe makes much of this, much that is extraordinary. For one thing, though you scent what he senses when he calls Pope's particular lines 'poetry without an atmosphere', the phrase has an air of appropriate perversity.

> In the worst inn's worst room, with mat half-hung,
> The floors of plaister, and the walls of dung,
> On once a flock-bed, but repair'd with straw,
> With tape-ty'd curtains, never meant to draw,
> The George and Garter dangling from that bed
> Where tawdry yellow strove with dirty red,
> Great Villiers lies—alas how chang'd from him,
> That life of pleasure, and that soul of whim![16]

Poetry without an atmosphere, yes, and yet a room not with a view but with an atmosphere. To be cut with a knife. True, the dung of which the walls are made will long have dried out, but that room in that inn, that bed, that dirt: this squalid setting of a life is thick with atmosphere.[17] 'No small portion of this actuality of relation . . . this poetry without an atmosphere'?—no, a grimly small portion, this small room, all that was in the end left to Villiers of his great portion.[18] 'Shut in by the Closeness of the Atmosphere', Pope, like Crabbe, effects 'a new Creation', poetry both with and without an atmosphere.

---

[15] *Complete Poetical Works*, ii 694.   [16] 'Epistle to Bathurst', 299–306.

[17] Hazlitt, incited by 'Peter Grimes' which he quoted extendedly, said of 'the whole of Mr. Crabbe's *Borough*' that it has 'a strong local scent of tar and bulge-water'.

[18] Compare *The Parish Register* (1807), ii 53: 'That be thy Portion, my ungrateful Spouse!'

Then again there is Crabbe's change, inspired (the breathing word), of his reviewer's sentence, 'He lives, if we may be allowed the expression, without an atmosphere', to 'poetry without an atmosphere'. To live without an atmosphere is impossible to a man though not to a poem.

Crabbe's father used occasionally to read poetry to his family, Milton and Young being particularly named,[19] and Crabbe alluded to Young's *Love of Fame the Universal Passion*,[20] so perhaps he would have felt with Young's pained couplet in Satire V:

> Like cats in airpumps, to subsist we strive
> On joys too thin to keep the soul alive.[21]

But what in Young is allowed the breathing space of simile ('Like cats in airpumps . . .') is in Crabbe the experiment itself, with sensibility and science coupled:

> The kind old Student, to oblige the Maid,
> The Tricks of Science with its Pride display'd:
> The Captive Mouse, half-dead for want of Air,
> Had Freedom granted at the Virgin's prayer,
> Who had no pleasure in th' exhausted House
> To view the panting of the captive Mouse.[22]

The tricks of science are realized by the more than tricks of art. How airy, the rhyme of 'Air' and 'prayer', prayer needing air for the Virgin's utterance.[23] And 'for want of Air' has a feeling for callousness, in the range of 'want'—not just for *lack* of air. 'The

---

[19] *Life*, p. 12.

[20] *The Parish Register*, i 91–2; *Complete Poetical Works*, i 215, 695. Crabbe's lines on Young, 'Midnight', 82–5 (i 61), praise *Night Thoughts*, but 'Reproof' was also the forte of *Love of Fame*.

> Young, Thought's Œconomist, who wove Reproof
> Her glomiest Vest, and yet a Vest that shone:
> Whose Invitation was Assault: he found
> The World asleep and rent its drowsy Ear.

[21] Used, with ominous wit, as the title-page epigraph to William Empson's *The Gathering Storm* (1940).

[22] 'Tracy' (1813), 781–6; *Complete Poetical Works*, ii 827.

[23] Compare Hopkins, 'The Blessed Virgin compared to the Air we Breathe', the penultimate rhyme of the poem: 'O live air, / Of patience, penance, prayer'. Atmosphere had just been called upon: 'Be thou then, O thou dear / Mother, my atmosphere'.

captive Mouse', first at the head of one couplet, is displayed to conclude the next couplet, berimed like an Irish rat. Exhausted its house may be (a flatly suffocating term, 'th' exhausted House', for the experimental cage of airlessness), but the resources of the couplet are far from exhausted.

The technical feeling for the couplet's grasp and gasp is at one with a larger sense of tradition and convention: was the heroic couplet by Crabbe's late time an exhausted house, a narrow and suffocating form? ('That which I have used is probably the most common measure in our language.'[24]) To these suggestions of Crabbe's art should be added the actualities of his life. His son records Crabbe's hearing the venerable John Wesley on one of his last peregrinations: 'The chapel was crowded to suffocation.'[25] Perhaps this is no more than an exhausted figure of speech. Perhaps it is only a coincidence that when Crabbe exclaims in botanical pleasure, 'I found my Trifolium out before Sr Joseph [Banks] was so kind as to inform me', there should be a note telling us just what *my* Trifolium here was:

GC's trefoil is the species *Trifolium suffocatum* L., so called because the flower heads are sessile, numerous, and confluent. The common name 'Suffocated Clover' is quite descriptive.[26]

It may even be a coincidence that one of the moments when life is most manifestly breathed into Crabbe's sermons is inspired by Ezekiel 37. 'Come from the four winds, O breath, and breathe upon these slain that they may live.'[27] It is certainly a coincidence that Crabbe spent so many of his years in Suffolk, of which he became uniquely the poet, knowing, as others have, what it feels like to be 'suffolkated'.

But what is not a coincidence is the closeness of the two most terrifying experiences of Crabbe's life to a terror much realized in his poems: suffocation. 'He lives, if we may be allowed the expression, without an atmosphere.' No, in that case he dies.

In his early childhood (his son does not know the year, but writes as if Crabbe were younger than 11), he was sent away to school:

Soon after his arrival he had a very narrow escape. He and several of his schoolfellows were punished for playing at soldiers, by being put into

[24] Preface to *Tales of the Hall.*   [25] *Life*, p. 148.
[26] To Edmund Cartwright, 3 January 1795; *Selected Letters*, p. 62.
[27] Sermon XV, *Posthumous Sermons* (1850), pp. 162–3.

a large dog-kennel, known by the terrible name of 'the black hole.' George was the first that entered; and, the place being crammed full with offenders, the atmosphere soon became pestilentially close. The poor boy in vain shrieked that he was about to be suffocated. At last, in despair, he bit the lad next to him violently in the hand. 'Crabbe is dying—Crabbe is dying,' roared the sufferer; and the sentinel at length opened the door, and allowed the boys to rush out into the air. My father said, 'A minute more, and I must have died.'[28]

Suffocated . . . he bit . . . the sufferer: Crabbe's son inherited a feeling for words and their mordant pressure. (And had the acumen to profit from Lockhart's kindly editorial pressure.)[29] 'The atmosphere soon became pestilentially close': this is the black hole of which Crabbe's dark fen-love is the benign version, 'Shut in by the Closeness of the Atmosphere, all about is like a new Creation'.

The Black Hole of Calcutta darkened England when Crabbe was a baby. It was to take its hold not only on his schoolboy imagination but on his adult imaginings, and especially on what he felt to be the constraints of a responsible imagination.

Elizabeth Charter . . . supplied him with the 'Story of the locked-up Bride' which he tried to use but found too harrowing. 'The Great Difficulty lies in this, that such Incident must be the principal one and yet the Mind must not be left with lacerated feelings. Who c^d make a Story from the "Black Hole at Calcutta"?' (1 May 1816).[30]

Nevertheless Crabbe could make a story, or made an episode within a story, from a later grim occasion when he might again have said, 'A minute more, and I must have died.' His son, telling of how his father, not yet married, nearly drowned (which would have meant this narrator's losing his life too), incorporates Crabbe's verses within the telling:

In one of these visits to Beccles, my father was in the most imminent danger of losing his life. Having, on a sultry summer's day, rowed his Sarah to a favourite fishing spot on the river Waveney, he left her busy with the rod and line, and withdrew to a retired place about a quarter of a mile off, to bathe. Not being a swimmer, nor calculating his depth, he plunged at once into danger; for his foot slid on the soft mud towards the centre of the stream. He made a rush for the bank, lost his footing, and

---

[28] *Life*, pp. 16–17.   [29] See *Complete Poetical Works*, iii 375–6.
[30] Ibid., ii 848.

the flood boiled over his head: he struggled, but in vain; and his own words paint his situation:—

> 'An undefined sensation stopp'd my breath;
> Disorder'd views and threat'ning signs of death
> Met in one moment, and a terror gave
> —I cannot paint it—to the moving grave:
> My thoughts were all distressing, hurried, mix'd,
> On all things fixing, not a moment fix'd.
> Brother, I have not—man has not the power
> To paint the horrors of that life-long hour;
> Hour!—but of time I knew not—when I found
> Hope, youth, life, love, and all they promised, drown'd.'

(Tales of the Hall)

My father could never clearly remember how he was saved. He at last found himself grasping some weeds, and by their aid reached the bank.[31]

Grasping and gasping. Crabbe is among the many poets who notoriously live upon drowning, the stifling of breath and speech.

Crabbe realizes gasps. Sometimes resolution can overcome them, as when a proposal of marriage is found unthinkable:

> She gasp'd for breath—then sat as one resolved
> On some high act, and then the means revolved.
> 'It cannot be . . .'[32]

Sometimes the gasp, locked within the couplet's constraints and the tight syntax, strains in its movement, from 'fast lock'd' to 'at last' (*internal* rhymes may show the workings of the breath):

> The arm, fast lock'd in mine, his fear betray'd,
> And when he spoke not, his designs convey'd;
> He oft-times gasp'd for breath, he tried to speak,
> And studying words, at last had words to seek.[33]

Sometimes Crabbe's lines exhale what Hazlitt sniffed at as malodorous. 'His poetry has an official and professional air. He is called in to cases of difficult births.' How bitterly 'air' is called in to 'difficult births', in the spirit—such again is Hazlitt's reluctant admission—of the dark contrast in Crabbe (the poet as man-midwife) when 'Air' proceeds to the 'abortive':

---

[31] *Life*, pp. 37–8.   [32] *Tales of the Hall* XVI, 'Lady Barbara', 340–2.
[33] *Tales of the Hall* XI, 'The Maid's Story', 994–7.

That feeble Sob, unlike the new-born Note,
Which came with vigour from the op'ning Throat;
When Air and Light first rush'd on Lungs and Eyes,
And there was Life and Spirit in the Cries;
Now an abortive, faint attempt to weep,
Is all we hear; Sensation is asleep.[34]

Crabbe, who had known terror of suffocation and of drowning, was one whose apprehension gravitated naturally from the room narrowly without air to the ocean so widely without it, from (one stanza to the next) 'Pale Weavers sat, of Air bereav'd', to 'Men dropt into the rav'nous tide'.[35] And from the cell to the sea: in *The Borough*, the felon condemned to death—Crabbe never forgot his visit to one such—has a dream of a happy seascape, so equable ('Ships softly sinking in the sleepy Sea'), and then suddenly wrenched into a dream of a terrifying wave.[36]

Yet Crabbe is in his obdurate way a comic writer too, glinting in his flintiness, which is one reason for something that Hazlitt remarked: 'many of his verses read like serious burlesque, and the parodies which have been made upon them are hardly so quaint as the originals.' The popular term 'the vital air', at once scientific and poetical, flows into a stream—but is not left to drown there:

The vital Air, a pure and subtle Stream,
Serves a Foundation for an airy Scheme,
Assists the Doctor, and supports his Scheme.[37]

Not only airy but supported on air, the triplet.

So the poet who imagined airlessness felt his own exhilaration whenever he could catch these tricks of thin air.

His person all that charms a vacant Eye;
His Air what vacant Minds are fetter'd by;
His Song enchanting, and his manners free;
A dangerous youth in Village Wakes was he![38]

The move from 'Eye' to 'Mind' is hardly a heightening, since the particular minds are no less vacant than the eyes. For only a very

---

[34] *The Borough*, Letter VII, 'Physic', 207–12.
[35] 'The Insanity of Ambitious Love', 242, 247; *Complete Poetical Works*, ii 671.
[36] Letter XXIII, 'Prisons', 285–332. Compare the dream of drowning, and then of the fate worse than death, in 'Tracy', 320–47, *Complete Poetical Works*, ii 815–16.
[37] *The Library* (1808), 394–6.
[38] 'Susan', 5–8; *Complete Poetical Works*, ii 827.

vacant mind could be *fetter'd* by an *Air*.[39] And then 'his Air' immediately turns to a musical air before our very ears (doubly so: 'His
Song enchanting'). The freedom of such a young man's manners—
with 'free' rhyming away for all it is worth, which is not much with
these people—is evidence neither of his true freedom nor of their
freedom who are attracted by him (enthralling and enthralled). And
the 'Village Wakes' turn 'dangerous', darkened into something
funereal as against merry.[40]

Crabbe is not a poet of the larger air, but one whose metres have
a barometer's hermetic keenness to the pressures of the gathering
storm. Again and again his faithful word is not the flattering but
the flattening one.

> And I was thankful for the moral sight,
> That soberized the vast and wild delight.[41]

What I as a reader am thankful for, here in the concluding couplet
of this Tale, is the unexpectedly gratifying word *soberized*, for all the
world as if the verb to sober were not sufficiently flat.

In a word, such flatness can put afflatus in its place.

> She praised her lucky stars, that in her place
> She never found neglect, nor felt disgrace;
> To do her duty was her soul's delight,
> This her inferiors would to theirs excite,
> This her superiors notice and requite;
> To either class she gave the praises due,
> And still more grateful as more favour'd grew:
> Her lord and lady were of peerless worth,
> In power unmatch'd, in glory and in birth;
> And such the virtue of the noble race,
> It reach'd the meanest servant in the place;

[39] Compare Marvell, 'The Fair Singer':

> But how should I avoid to be her slave,
> Whose subtle art invisibly can wreathe
> My fetters of the very air I breathe?

[40] Crabbe's editor sometimes has the air of darkly joking, as when, annotating
Crabbe's lines on the 'scandalous and degrading state of the prisons', she says of
the Gaol Distemper Act of 1774, which required that prisons should be cleaned
and well ventilated: 'But the Act remained virtually a dead letter' (*Complete Poetical
Works*, iii 382).

[41] *Tales of the Hall* VI, 'Richard's Adventures Concluded', 386–7.

All, from the chief attendant on my lord
To the groom's helper, had her civil word;
From Miss Montregor, who the ladies taught,
To the rude lad who in the garden wrought;
From the first favourite to the meanest drudge,
Were no such women, heaven should be her judge;
Whatever stains were theirs, let them reside
In that pure place, and they were mundified;
The sun of favour on their vileness shone,
And all their faults like morning mists were gone.[42]

From 'in her place', through 'in the place', to 'In that pure place'. Heaven should be her judge, but in the mean time Crabbe will be her judge, judging even her goodness, and not credulous about her accommodating credulities. It is 'mundified', unique in its register (of language and parish), that shows what it is for Crabbe to notice and requite.[43]

What 'soberized' and 'mundified' have in common, apart from their flat-tongued relish, is that Crabbe probably met them in Richardson's *Clarissa*. The *OED* citation that immediately precedes Crabbe's 'mundified' is Richardson's 'Mundified or purified from my past iniquities', and a citation that precedes Crabbe's 'soberized' is Richardson's 'The instant I beheld her I was soberized into awe and reverence'. What Crabbe does is both soberize and mundify the world of Richardson's high swelling drama. *Clarissa* furnished an epigraph for *The Borough*, Letter XV, which then introduced its charmer:

But then came one, the *Lovelace* of his Day,
Rich, proud, and crafty, handsome, brave, and gay.

(55–6)

Crabbe's poems are intrigued by the cavalier villain Lovelace.[44] As to the Cavalier hero Lovelace: Crabbe took leave to doubt that stone walls do not a prison make nor iron bars a cage.

[42] *Tales of the Hall* XIX, 'William Bailey', 240–60.
[43] '*mundified*: cleansed or purified (*OED* 1 *obs.*)'; *Complete Poetical Works*, ii 730.
[44] Lovelace appears by name elsewhere (*The Parish Register*, ii 269); and *Clarissa* in *Posthumous Tales* XV, 'Belinda Waters', 65–76. There is a dry turn in *Posthumous Tales* I, 'The Family of Love', 364–5, when Crabbe, who not only loved reading novels but wrote some, imagines a pious reader for whom it is not the seducer but the heroine or the novel that is found seductive:

To read a novel was a kind of sin—
Albeit once Clarissa took her in.

Perhaps the greatest of these felicities of Crabbe's (felicities characteristically cross-hatched with unhappiness) is one which it is strange
to mouth, haply or happily:

> 'But here we land, and haply now may choose
> Companions home—our way, too, we may lose:
> In these drear, dark, inosculating lanes,
> The very native of his doubt complains;
> No wonder then that in such lonely ways
> A stranger, heedless of the country, strays.'[45]

The Oxford edition glosses 'inosculating' as 'meeting or running
together', which is right so far as it goes but does not remind us
(for a full pleasure in the couplets' ways) where one of the word's
lanes goes: to a mouth. So darkly delectable, the word 'inosculating',
oddly palatable while not rinsing away anything of the drear or
dark. Notice how the rhyme-words' dismay is not allowed to slide
into despair; for 'lose' will not be lost, since its way follows from
'choose', and 'complains' has its 'lanes' to follow, and 'strays' is still
in earshot of its 'ways'.

Alive to rhyme as metaphor, Crabbe lets his rhymes be themselves: he controls with 'control', he restrains with 'restrain', he bonds
with 'bond', and he binds with 'bind'. He is helped by his rhymes
to say what he thinks:

> 'Art thou too thrown upon the Waves to'—sink
> He meant to say, but was content to think,
> Then left me pacing on that wintry Shore,
> Our parting Scene: for him I saw no more—[46]

An adverse review of *The Borough*, in failing to appreciate what is
truly binding, fails to rise to Crabbe's art of sinking in poetry:

To talk of binding down poetry to dry representations of the world as it
is, seems idle; because it is precisely in order to escape from the world as
it is, that we fly to poetry.[47]

'Enchain'd' is a natural rhyme for Crabbe,[48] and if—with the smallest
change from that word—'unchain'd' is so too, this is because Crabbe's

---

[45] *Tales of the Hall* VI, 'Richard's Adventures Concluded', 321–6.
[46] 'David Morris', 54–7; *Complete Poetical Works*, iii 190.
[47] Grant; quoted in *Complete Poetical Works*, ii 695.
[48] *Tales of the Hall* VII, 'The Elder Brother', 558.

couplets are there set to trap the wishful wistful folly of supposing
that any such unchaining can be effected:

> 'Then was it time, while yet some Years remain'd,
> To drink untroubled and to think unchain'd,
> And on all Pleasures, which his Purse could give,
> Freely to seize, and, while he liv'd, to live.'[49]

There is no unchaining those external chains, as Abel Keene now
well knows, knowing ill; 'Freely' amounts to enslavedly; and 'To
drink untroubled and to think unchain'd' exposes gullibility about
those rhyming internalities, drinking and thinking.

There is nothing surprising, then (Crabbe sets no great store by
surprise), about his liking to tie a couplet with a rhyme on 'tied'.

> 'Think ere the contract—but, contracted, stand
> No more debating, take the ready hand:
> When hearts are willing, and when fears subside,
> Trust not to time, but let the knot be tied.'[50]

Crafty, though, is his liking to hear in 'tied' the 'tide', the might
of waters, that movement both very large and very small which is
itself tied always to the due although it changes; and is predictable
for all its variations; and measures things levelly even as the couplets
themselves come in as lapsing waves on Crabbe's flat coast. How
better to give a sense of the anchored, or rather of the *seemingly*
anchored, than to stop 'glide' from gliding away by having it tied
to 'tide':

> Then the broad bosom of the Ocean keeps
> An equal motion; swelling as it sleeps,
> Then slowly sinking; curling to the Strand,
> Faint, lazy Waves o'ercreep the ridgy Sand,
> Or tap the tarry Boat with gentle blow,
> And back return in silence, smooth and slow.
> Ships in the Calm seem anchor'd; for they glide
> On the still Sea, urg'd solely by the Tide.[51]

Donald Davie, alertly imaginative about syntax and so much else,
praised Crabbe's epithets as giving his verses their distinction, but
then moved to the part of speech that moves:

[49] *The Borough*, Letter XXI, 'The Poor of the Borough: Abel Keene', 29–32.
[50] *Tales of the Hall* XIII, 'Delay Has Danger', 47–50.
[51] *The Borough*, Letter I, 'General Description', 179–86.

On the other hand it is probably true that in greater poets the imaginative thrust is carried by other parts of the speech. This is true of Crabbe himself at his best, as in a matchless couplet from *The Borough*, about the behaviour of waves in a dead calm:

> That tap the tarry boat with gentle blow,
> And back return in silence smooth and slow.

For here it is the verb 'tap', more than the epithets 'gentle', 'smooth', 'slow', which conveys the menace—the sea that for the moment toys with its victims has inexhaustible reserves of what can destroy them.[52]

When the rhyme of 'tide' and 'glide' returns later in *The Borough*, in 'Peter Grimes', it swells more fully, not only because the rhyme-word takes up 'the Tide's delay', 'the Tides', 'the Tide', and 'Tides' (as inexorably repetitive as the tides), but because it swells the couplet to a triplet—and sets before us the cruel and cruelly suffering figure of Peter Grimes *tied* to his dread monotony of tidescape:

> Thus by himself compell'd to live each day,
> To wait for certain hours the Tide's delay;
> At the same times the same dull views to see,
> The bounding Marsh-bank and the blighted Tree;
> The Water only, when the Tides were high,
> When low, the Mud half-cover'd and half-dry;
> The Sun-burnt Tar that blisters on the Planks,
> And Bank-side Stakes in their uneven ranks;
> Heaps of entangled Weeds that slowly float,
> As the Tide rolls by the impeded Boat.
>
> When Tides were neap, and, in the sultry day,
> Through the tall bounding Mud-banks made their way,
> Which on each side rose swelling, and below
> The dark warm flood ran silently and slow;
> There anchoring, *Peter* chose from Man to hide,
> There hang his Head, and view the lazy Tide
> In its hot slimy Channel slowly glide.[53]

Once again the thought of 'anchoring' fastens upon the rhyming 'Tide'. The verse-paragraph draws towards its end with a complementary play, not on one homophone, 'tied/tide', but on another, 'sound':

---

[52] *Times Literary Supplement*, 30 September–6 October 1988. But Crabbe's word-waves are even better than as given there; not 'That tap', but 'Or tap', which creeps forward from 'o'ercreep' four words earlier.

[53] Letter XXII, 'The Poor of the Borough: Peter Grimes', 171–87.

> Where the small Stream, confin'd in narrow bound,
> Ran with a dull, unvaried, sad'ning sound.

Those who disrelish Crabbe's couplet hear it as itself confined in narrow bound, running with a dull, unvaried, saddening sound. But 'sound', after 'the small Stream', wins pathos from the contrast with the ocean, the sound. Elsewhere in *The Borough*, the waves first imprison the holiday-makers and then are set to drown them:

> They shout once more, and then they turn aside,
> To see how quickly flow'd the coming Tide;
> Between each Cry they find the Waters steal
> On their strange Prison, and new Horrors feel;
> Foot after foot on the contracted Ground
> The Billows fall, and dreadful is the sound.[54]

The sound of the sound.

Crabbe acknowledged his station, coupled with his imaginative restlessness:

for though I have a fixed Habitation and am tyed to a place by Contracts & Duties, yet my Mind does not love to abide there, nor among eight thousand Minds can meet with one that makes this, the favourite Home. When the Duties are done, the Affections or at least the Imagination go forth & we wander (Citizens thus of the World) in search of other Wanderers—[55]

Tyed . . . abide.

'The Affections or at least the Imagination': Crabbe's oddly affectionate imagination is often devoted to the relation between the couplet and a couple. His couplet perfectly shapes the spirit which Crabbe discovered in—and invented for—an imagined marriage in perversity:

> Thus liv'd the Couple, daily to contend,
> And never wish'd their Quarrels at an End.
> They felt no fondness, and no more of hate

---

[54] Letter IX, 'Amusements', 249–54. Compare 'The Lover of Virtue', 37: 'Placed on the Beach he listened to the Sound'; and 66–7:

> I dare not trust me to th'uncertain deep,
> The Sound so thretning and the Bank so steep

> (*Complete Poetical Works*, ii 738–9.)

[55] To Elizabeth Charter, 14 March 1815; *Selected Letters*, p. 169.

> Than gave an Edge and Pleasure to Debate.
> Contentions sprang from themes of every kind
> And wak'd from Sloth to Energy the Mind;
> Quarrels they took, like Bitters, to excite
> And give Exertion to the Appetite.
>   For twice ten years the sprightly Course they try'd;
> When the Strife ended, and the Husband died.[56]

Crabbe, in his wit, may have remembered Pope's moue:

> For *Wit* and *Judgment* often are at strife,
> Tho' meant each other's Aid, like *Man* and *Wife*.[57]

Crabbe knows that not only do we fix attention, and arrest it, we rivet it.[58] The couplets' rhyming is riveting. Hazlitt was paying another of his reluctant tributes when he said of Crabbe that 'he rivets attention by being tedious'. The same goes for Hazlitt's parodic cadence, 'Whatever *is*, he hitches into rhyme', which manages to hitch not only Pope—'One truth is clear, Whatever IS, is RIGHT'— but Crabbe's recurrent variations on that line. As for Hazlitt's judgement that Crabbe's verse 'is not an electric shock to kindle or expand, but acts like the torpedo's touch to deaden or contract', this is in its way admirably admiring, not only because of how much *contract* does in Crabbe ('the contracted Ground', 'Think ere the contract—but, contracted, stand'), but because of where Hazlitt's simile floated in from: Crabbe's note to *The Borough*, Letter IX, 83, the sting of the jellyfish 'resembling that caused by the torpedo'.

One reason Hazlitt gave for the verses reading like 'serious burlesque' was that 'there is so little connection between the subject-matter of Mr. Crabbe's lines and the ornament of rhyme which is tacked to them'. Though 'ornament' is not right (it demeans not only Crabbe's rhymes but rhymes), 'tacked' in many ways is. Tacked. Riveted. I should like to think that Lilian Haddakin was imitating her poet's ways when she described the heroic couplet as 'his staple metre'.[59]

---

[56] 'Tracy', 625–34; *Complete Poetical Works*, ii 823.

[57] *An Essay on Criticism*, 82–3.

[58] When he first saw 'The Lay of the Last Minstrel', 'A few words only riveted his attention, and he read it nearly through while standing at the counter, observing, "a new and great poet has appeared!"' (*Life*, p. 172).

[59] *The Poetry of Crabbe* (1955), p. 147.

The poet wrote of 'hammering out Verses',[60] and his son brought together the hammering out of couplets and the geologist's hammer: 'His note-book was at this time ever with him in his walks, and he would every now and then lay down his hammer to insert a new or amended couplet.'[61] Crabbe's love of geology informed his art, not only as subject-matter but as exemplarily patient. 'He gradually made himself expert in some branches of geological science'[62]—*gradually* is right for geology's sense of time.

> Shell now no more; a gradual Change came on,
> And the thin Shell became the Solid Stone.[63]

Never, after my mother's death, did he return seriously to botany, the favourite study of his earlier life. Fossils were thenceforth to him what weeds and flowers had been: he would spend hours on hours hammer in hand, not much pleased if any one interrupted him.[64]

This is right too, since what weeds and flowers had been is the stuff of fossils. And in the year of his own death: 'You will say, What, then, do you do at Trowbridge? There, you know, I have a number of small and often recurring duties, and I play with my fossils.'[65]

Lockhart recorded that when Crabbe visited Edinburgh and walked out to Salisbury Craigs, 'he appeared to be more interested with the stratification of the rocks about us, than with any other features in the landscape'. But then Crabbe is the poet of stratifications, and his measure, the heroic couplet, keeps its strata geologically alive by equivocating as to whether the stratum is the couplet or the line.

Perhaps by the end of his life, or even by the time of *Tales* and *Tales of the Hall*, the heroic couplet may itself have felt like a fossil for him to play with. The Augustan heroic couplet had, after all and after all those years, started to burgeon in the 1640s of Waller and Denham.

Perhaps his life came to seem to him, as well as to others, to have a geological aspect. He lived on, literally, but literarily?

His 'Parish Register' was published at the interval of *twenty-two years* after 'The Newspaper;' and, from his thirty-first year to his fifty-second, he buried himself completely in the obscurity of domestic and village life, hardly

---

[60] To Walter Scott, 21 December 1812; *Selected Letters*, p. 97.
[61] *Life*, p. 262, of 1817–18.   [62] Ibid., p. 129.
[63] 'Tracy', 849–50; *Complete Poetical Works*, ii 828.   [64] *Life*, p. 259.
[65] Ibid., p. 309.

catching, from time to time, a single glimpse of the brilliant society in which he had for a season been welcomed, and gradually forgotten as a *living* author by the public.[66]

The italics are his son's.

Geology was alive for Crabbe, both as the living rock and as a living discipline. His art partakes of geology's nature. Compacted, contracted, stratified, tied tight, without an atmosphere. He had no respect (though he mildly apologized for such offence as he had given) for instant ageing, 'the imitation of what are called weather-stains on buildings'.[67] Likening lichen?

> Thou may'st thy various Greens and Greys contrive,
> They are not Lichens, nor like aught alive;—
>
> Then may'st thou see how Nature's Work is done,
> How slowly true she lays her Colours on;
> When her least speck upon the hardest Flint
> Has Mark and Form and is a living Tint.[68]

It is flint that strikes sparks for Crabbe, as in Peter Grimes, 'a mind so depraved and flinty': 'and the harder that nature is, and the longer time required to work upon it, so much the more strong and indelible is the impression'.[69] And so to prisons: 'I confess it is not pleasant to be detained so long by subjects so repulsive to the feelings of many, as the sufferings of mankind.' Detained.

'How slowly true', and truly slow. It is characteristic of Crabbe that he should take a previous preservation and intensify it, imprison it again to good effect, as when he played with a fossil from Pope.

> Pretty! in Amber to observe the forms
> Of hairs, or straws, or dirt, or grubs, or worms.[70]

Crabbe:

> And in that rock are shapes of shells, and forms
> Of creatures in old worlds, of nameless worms.[71]

Pope, too, made play with shells:

---

[66] *Life*, p. 131.   [67] Preface to *The Borough*.
[68] *The Borough*, Letter II, 'The Church', 57–8, 63–6.
[69] Preface to *The Borough*.   [70] *Epistle to Dr. Arbuthnot*, 169–70.
[71] *Tales of the Hall* XIII, 'Delay Has Danger', 13–14.

The most recluse, discreetly open'd find
Congenial matter in the Cockle-kind.[72]

Something of a recluse, Crabbe found congenial matter, abutting
on the geological and on the suffocating, in the oyster, 'The food
that feeds, the living luxury'.[73] But, discreet opener, Crabbe was
able to find congenial matter and manner in the fossil kind.

[72] *The Dunciad*, IV 447–8.
[73] *The Borough*, Letter I, 'General Description', 68.

JANE AUSTEN
AND THE BUSINESS OF MOTHERING

And then, by not beginning the business of Mothering quite so early in life, you will be young in Constitution, spirits, figure & countenance, while Mrs Wm Hammond is growing old by confinements & nursing. (To Fanny Knight, 13 March 1817)

It is a half-truth universally acknowledged that Jane Austen disliked babies and didn't blankly like children. The other half-truth—that she sometimes loved babies and often loved children—is clear enough from her family life, where, for every chastening coolness about the little ones, there can be found a heart-warming admission. Katherine Mansfield flourished a rhetorical question: 'Can we picture Jane Austen caring—except in a delightfully wicked way— . . . that people said she was no lady, was not fond of children . . . ?'[1] Well, yes, since you ask, we can. She would have repudiated the idea that she was not fond of children almost as crisply as the idea that she was no lady. The fondness of a fond parent is a travesty of true fondness. 'I saw their little girl, & very small & very pretty she is . . . Harriet's fondness for her seems just what is amiable & natural, & not foolish.'[2] This way of putting it is not so foolish (or unamiable) as to equate the natural with the objective and rational.

'Altogether I remember we liked her greatly as children from her entering into all Games &c', Maria Beckford recollected. 'She was a most kind & enjoyable person *to Children*'; 'her sister Cassandra was very lady-like but *very prim*, but my remembrance of Jane is that of her entering into all Childrens Games & liking her extremely.'[3]

Brigid Brophy has observed that 'some of Jane Austen's funniest sarcasms are against babies. It was a peculiarity of that most rational woman that she held it against babies that they were not rational. More bitterly still, she held it against mothers that they

---

[1] Mary Lascelles, *Jane Austen and Her Art* (1939), p. 119.

[2] To Cassandra Austen, 20 June 1808; *Jane Austen's Letters*, ed. R. W. Chapman, 2nd edn (1962), p. 193.

[3] D. G. Le Faye, *TLS*, 3 May 1985, quoting letters that were tucked inside a copy of Austen-Leigh's *Memoir* of Jane Austen (1870).

showed an irrational adoration of their babies.'[4] Miss Brophy is moved to speculate that, deep down, Jane Austen may have been protesting against the putting-away of her mentally defective brother George. Yet it should be said that Jane Austen was not sarcastic but ironical, and this not about babies but about parental folly and crass flattery, and moreover that, if she held it against mothers that they irrationally doted, she knew perfectly well that even an unsentimental aunt was not—and should not be—immune to the irrationality of family love:

I spent two or three days with your Uncle & Aunt lately, & though the Children are sometimes very noisy & not under such Order as they ought & easily might, I cannot help liking & even loving them, which I hope may be not wholly inexcusable in their & your affectionate Aunt,

J. Austen[5]

Again, if she smiled at parental doting, she did not find it as offensive, as odious, as that travesty of her own unsentimentality which gives animation—and animus—to Aunt Norris. 'She never knew how to be pleasant to children,' says Edmund Bertram, with lethal understatement; and it is, of all people, Mary Crawford who is given one of Jane Austen's most deft slightings of children, a witty perfunctoriness: 'I sat there an hour one morning waiting for Anderson, with only her and a little girl or two in the room, the governess being sick or run away, and the mother in and out every moment with letters of business . . .'[6] A little girl *or two* in the room: the passing drawl is witty and is not to be respected. It is very different from Jane Austen's rueful haplessness in the matter of totting up tots; as in the running joke of arithmetical correction in her letters:

—and I am prevented from setting my black cap at Mr. Maitland by his having a wife & ten children.[7]

Correction in the postscript: 'I scandalized her nephew cruelly; he has but three children instead of Ten.' (So she is that much less prevented—seven children's worth—from setting her cap at him?)

[4] 'Jane Austen and the Stuarts', *Critical Essays on Jane Austen*, ed. B. C. Southam (1968), p. 33.
[5] To Caroline Austen, 23 January 1817; *Letters*, p. 473.
[6] *Mansfield Park*, ch. iii, ch. v.
[7] To Cassandra Austen, 21 May 1801; *Letters*, p. 132.

Or, drawn again to that round number ten, 'It was a mistake of mine, my dear Cassandra, to talk of a tenth child at Hamstall. I had forgot there were but eight already'—where the effect once more ('but three children', 'but eight already') owes a lot to the parody of a determination not to overstate.[8] A huge family—such as the eleven children of her brother Edward—could be a threat not only to family life but to the art of the novel. The youthful work *Edgar & Emma* knows this:

Their Children were too numerous to be particularly described; it is sufficient to say that in general they were virtuously inclined & not given to any wicked ways. Their family being too large to accompany them in every visit, they took nine with them alternately.

And then we are launched upon a particularizing which finally fortunately falters:

'Our children are all extremely well but at present most of them from home. Amy is with my sister Clayton. Sam at Eton. David with his Uncle John. Jem & Will at Winchester. Kitty at Queen's Square. Ned with his Grandmother. Hetty & Patty in a Convent at Brussells. Edgar at college, Peter at Nurse, & all the rest (except the nine here) at home.'[9]

The children at Mansfield Park are not too numerous to be particularly described; those born in Portsmouth to Mrs Price are. And if a novelist can't cope, how could a mother? 'The simple regimen of separate rooms', which Jane Austen would recommend to one fecund couple, has some counterpart within the complex regimen of her novels.[10]

The place of babies and of young children within her novels is teasing and challenging. For, on the face of it, babies and young children are much less important to the novels than one would expect, given that the claim made by the novels—implicitly by their author and explicitly by the best 19th-century critics—is of their so thoroughly dealing with the circumscribed and decorous world that they choose. One might expect 'such pictures of domestic life in country villages as I deal in' to give some prominence or salience to this

[8] 29 May 1811; *Letters*, p. 280.
[9] *The Works of Jane Austen*, vi. *Minor Works*, ed. R. W. Chapman (1954), pp. 31–2.
[10] To Fanny Knight, 20 February 1817; *Letters*, p. 480.

embodiment of domesticity; and '3 or 4 Families in a Country Village' might seem to ask that this central family fact be made central.[11]

Now there are a great many ways of qualifying or resisting such an assertion and of explaining or calming it. It may be said that babies and young children are actually much more important in the novels than they seem at first, or than one's prejudiced or casual memory acknowledges. It may be said that this act of selection is as principled and defensible an exclusion or subordination as any other. It may be said that her inerrancy as to what she could and could not do—her understanding of the powers of her eye and her ear—rightly told her that the language and conduct of young children could not much be accommodated within her plots, her scenes, and her society.

But there does remain a challenge of some sort. For one would expect a very great novelist of family life, as she is, either substantially to accommodate this incarnation of family life (babies and young children), or to decline to do so because of a wisdom, to be shared, about life and about art, and not just because of personal experience or inexperience, temperamental affinity, or craftsmanlike prudence—all of which are proper contingencies but all of which are transcended by the greatest art. Simply: what truth about life, and perhaps about art, is Jane Austen in possession of when she so much subordinates babies and young children? What challenge to our usual feelings, or illusions of feeling, do the novels constitute in this matter? The evidence of her life and of her letters makes it unquestionable that she was greatly interested in children, loved them and was loved by them. Lord David Cecil is moved here to some of the most eloquent and touching pages of his *Portrait of Jane Austen*. So the novels are shaped not by personal limitation but by humane belief and artistic decision; and in a great writer, artistic decision is something more than convenience or canniness.

To some degree, her decision seems to me to constitute her admonishing a world—a society and a literature—which was fast becoming child-fixated, and was to become baby-fixated, to keep a sense of proportion. You might apply to Jane Austen's art, in comparison with countless poems and novels then and since, a form of Dr Johnson's famous commendation of Shakespeare. For Johnson, Shakespeare was great because he did not minister to the over-

[11] To Anna Austen, 9 September 1814; *Letters*, p. 401.

estimation of romantic love. Jane Austen was great because she did not minister to the over-estimation of parental and filial love. To which might be added a different, though not contradictory, admonition; not that such love is less important than we have got into the way of believing or pretending to believe, but that insofar as such love is truly important, it is far less imaginable—less shareable— than we have allowed ourselves to admit. The supreme irrationality and credulity would then not be a parent's love for a child, say, but our supposing that in daily life we can much enter into such feelings in others. This would be a counterpart in the household world to that truth about the great world which she famously expressed à propos of a battle in the Peninsular War: 'How horrible it is to have so many people killed!—And what a blessing that one cares for none of them!'[12] This is an irony, not a sarcasm or a cynicism; it means what it says.

The limits of our daily imagination, even at its most generous, are much more strict than we like to concede. The same goes, to some extent, for the limits of the sympathetic imagination in art. When Milton tells of the pain of a mother seeking her child, the pain which he makes us feel is not that of the mother but that of contemplating her pain; we have the further, albeit lesser, pain of acknowledging our exclusion from these greatest pains;

> Not that faire field
> Of Enna, where Proserpin gathring flours
> Her self a fairer Floure by gloomie Dis
> Was gatherd, which cost Ceres all that pain
> To seek her through the world;
>
> (*Paradise Lost*, iv 268–72)

All that pain, not *this* pain. Such is not a failure to imagine Ceres' pain, but a success in imagining the inevitable failure of even the greatest imaginings in art, in the face of such suffering in life. Jane Austen's comedy, for all its differences from epic, seems to me to share Milton's apprehension, that the greatest art will imagine an authentic acknowledgment of the limits of imagination.

For her, the nub is the profundity of privacy. Miss Lascelles was profoundly respectful of her 'habitual preference for respecting her lovers' privacy':

---

[12] To Cassandra Austen, 31 May 1811; *Letters*, p. 286.

'I shall not dwell minutely on this Part of my Hero's Life', Sarah Fielding says, 'as I have too much Regard for my Readers to make them *third Persons to Lovers.' David Simple* (1744) . . . I think that Jane Austen would have agreed with her unreservedly.'[13]

Indeed, and there are more kinds of lover than romantic or erotic lovers; the idea of lovers' privacy would accommodate the privacy of parent and child, and might value a novelist who had too much regard for us as readers than to make us third persons to these lovers too. The shocked embarrassment with which parental and filial privacy are violated in such a novel as *The Way of All Flesh* or *Sons and Lovers* is the condition of gains and losses as art. We know how fiercely D. H. Lawrence deplored Jane Austen's being so *apart*; the right retort would not be to deny it, but to ask what it is that a writer can see and show by stationing himself or herself apart.

But let me return to some of these tangents on the matter, and illustrate them. First, is it that babies and young children are more important to the novels than they seem at first? They are, for one thing, found very worthy of attention if only as something which people repeatedly and wrongly believe worthy of attention. There is always comedy in Jane Austen's presenting it as laughable of people to find children such a helpful topic of conversation when their doing this is so helpful a topic to the novels. Children thus become a further topic of conversation (the conversation of Jane Austen with her readers) at the very times when the reported conversation within the novels is ludicrous.

Conversation, however, was not wanted, for Sir John was very chatty, and Lady Middleton had taken the wise precaution of bringing with her their eldest child, a fine little boy about six years old, by which means there was one subject always to be recurred to by the ladies in case of extremity; for they had to inquire his name and age, admire his beauty, and ask him questions, which his mother answered for him, while he hung about her and held down his head, to the great surprise of her ladyship, who wondered at his being so shy before company, as he could make noise enough at home. On every formal visit a child ought to be of the party, by way of provision for discourse. In the present case it took up ten minutes to determine whether the boy were most like his father or mother, and in what particular he resembled either; for of course everybody differed, and everybody was astonished at the opinion of the others. (*Sense and Sensibility*, ch. vi)

[13] *Jane Austen and Her Art*, p. 194.

Jane Austen is too self-aware and sly not to relish the comedy of her saying this, since it could so obviously be retorted that in every novel a child ought to be of the party, by way of provision for discourse. The same goes for the later scene, when 'one subject only engaged the ladies till coffee came in, which was the comparative heights of Harry Dashwood and Lady Middleton's second son, William, who were nearly of the same age' (ch. xxxiv). The subsequent argument, all fatuity, adroitness, and smiles, gets much of its magnanimity from Jane Austen's being duly grateful for all the folly; after all, if the subject engaged the ladies, it is now—within the novel—engaging another lady, our author.

This feeling for a happy opportunity (the novelist too as a resourceful social being) is what gives width to a passing return, in *Emma* (ch. liv), to the same basic yet equivocal insistence that babies and young children are overrated as a social subject:

When Mr. Weston joined the party, however, and when the baby was fetched, there was no longer a want of subject or animation, or of courage and opportunity for Frank Churchill to draw near her and say—

For if children are a great convenience to a character like Emma, who has her little plots, the same must be true for the creator of the novel's plot. When Emma is eager to let Harriet and Mr Elton walk on ahead together, providence provides a child who can be most convenient to her plot. Slowly doing up her bootlace would not have been enough;

By the time she judged it reasonable to have done with her boot, she had the comfort of farther delay in her power, being overtaken by a child from the cottage, setting out, according to orders, with her pitcher, to fetch broth from Hartfield. To walk by the side of this child, and talk to and question her, was the most natural thing in the world, or would have been the most natural, had she been acting just then without design; and by this means the others were still able to keep ahead, without any obligation of waiting for her. She gained on them, however, involuntarily: the child's pace was quick, and theirs rather slow; and she was the more concerned at it, from their being evidently in a conversation which interested them. Mr. Elton was speaking with animation, Harriet listening with a very pleased attention; and Emma, having sent the child on, was beginning to think how she might draw back a little more, when they both looked around, and she was obliged to join them. (ch. x)

There is something both winning and chilling in Emma's resourcefulness here; we do not hear a word of the talk between Emma and the child (any more than we hear, or Emma hears, the talk between Harriet and Mr Elton), and there is an unloveable briskness then (the child having finished serving Emma's turn) in the parenthetical 'and Emma, having sent the child on, was . . .' But then the child does serve Jane Austen's turn too.

A child, in its very blankness and unworthiness of serious attention for itself, can be just the thing. How is Emma to make it up with Mr Knightley?

Concession must be out of the question; but it was time to appear to forget that they had ever quarrelled; and she hoped it might rather assist the restoration of friendship, that when he came into the room she had one of the children with her—the youngest, a nice little girl about eight months old, who was now making her first visit to Hartfield, and very happy to be danced about in her aunt's arms. It did assist; for though he began with grave looks and short questions, he was soon led on to talk of them all in the usual way, and to take the child out of her arms with all the unceremoniousness of perfect amity. Emma felt they were friends again; and the conviction giving her at first great satisfaction, and then a little sauciness, she could not help saying, as he was admiring the baby—
'What a comfort it is that we think alike about our nephews and nieces! As to men and women, our opinions are sometimes very different; but with regard to these children, I observe we never disagree.' (ch. xii)

Emma, whom Mr Knightley is soon addressing as 'a pretty young woman and a spoiled child', is felt, strangely and memorably, both to love this nice little girl and not now to be at all attending to her.

A later turn in the plot demands the intervention of children, when Harriet is rescued by Frank Churchill from the obstreperous gipsies. 'A child on the watch came towards them to beg': 'Harriet was soon assailed by half a dozen children, headed by a stout woman, and a great boy.' It is characteristic of Jane Austen that she should bring the chapter to rest with a comic return to those very different children Henry and John:

The gipsies did not wait for the operations of justice; they took themselves off in a hurry. The young ladies of Highbury might have walked again in safety before their panic began, and the whole history dwindled soon into a matter of little importance but to Emma and her nephews: in her imagination it maintained its ground; and Henry and John were still asking every day for the story of Harriet and the gipsies, and still tenaciously setting her right if she varied in the slightest particular from the original recital. (ch. xxxix)

For Jane Austen's recital, though it need not—as to children—be told every day, is as important to her plot as the incident was to Emma and her nephews. Jane Austen is very good on children as nuisances, but partly because their being so is anything but a nuisance to her.

It is *Persuasion*, though, which finds children a supreme convenience, expecially when one of them inconveniences some of the characters. Little Charles's fall may inconvenience his parents, but it greatly conveniences Anne Elliot. It does so by supplying her 'with a pretence for absenting herself' from the social occasions when Captain Wentworth might be present (ch. viii) and by giving her someone actively to love: 'Her usefulness to little Charles would always give some sweetness to the memory of her two months' visit there, but he was gaining strength apace, and she had nothing else to stay for' (ch. xi).

Then again, the convalescing child, in Anne's care, is what makes possible the very moving scene when Captain Wentworth performs his solicitude for Anne by removing the other child, the boisterous 2-year-old, from her neck. There is too a beautifully unforced patterning of little Charles's fall with Louisa's. That Louisa on the steps is behaving like an over-excited child is perfectly caught in the words of her wanting first the fun and then a repeat of it: 'she must be jumped down them by Captain Wentworth. . . . She was safely down, and instantly to shew her enjoyment, ran up the steps to be jumped down again' (ch. xii). Anne, who had nursed little Charles after his fall, is soon nursing Louisa after hers. One of the reasons why there is less than might be expected about children in the novels is that the adults are so often quite sufficiently childish.

The principle of selection, by which a specific attention to a child is relatively rare in a Jane Austen novel, is itself two-edged, since it may substitute for the importance of what is frequent the importance of what is infrequent. Inarticulacy is not at home in her novels, or at least only in its ripest form as garrulity. But the voice of a child, just because it is rare, and the more tellingly when it is reported, can be unforgettable. It is left to Mrs Norris, in her fluent and repugnant self-congratulation, to mimic the speech of someone who is both a child and a social inferior. Mrs Norris is in spate:

'I *am* of some use, I hope, in preventing waste and making the most of things. There should always be one steady head to superintend so many young ones. I forgot to tell Tom of something that happened to me this very day. I had been looking about me in the poultry-yard, and was just coming out, when who should I see but Dick Jackson making up to the servants' hall-door with two bits of deal board in his hand, bringing them to father, you may be sure; mother had chanced to send him of a message to father, and then father had bid him bring up them two bits of board, for he could not nohow do without them. I knew what all this meant, for the servants' dinner-bell was ringing at the very moment over our heads; and as I hate such encroaching people (the Jacksons are very encroaching, I have always said so: just the sort of people to get all they can), I said to the boy directly (a great lubberly fellow of ten years old, you know, who ought to be ashamed of himself), "*I'll* take the boards to your father, Dick, so get you home again as fast as you can." The boy looked very silly, and turned away without offering a word, for I believe I might speak pretty sharp; and I dare say it will cure him of coming marauding about the house for one while. I hate such greediness—so good as your father is to the family, employing the man all the year round!'

Nobody was at the trouble of an answer; the others soon returned; and Edmund found that to have endeavoured to set them right must be his only satisfaction.

Dinner passed heavily. Mrs. Norris related again her triumph over Dick Jackson, but neither play nor preparation were otherwise much talked of, for Edmund's disapprobation was felt even by his brother, though he would not have owned it. (*Mansfield Park*, ch. xv)

The dinner—'Dinner passed heavily'—which is the setting for this sour anecdote about young 'greediness' is not made a meal of by Jane Austen, but she has given Dick Jackson the memorability of a pure victim, there in his muttering that his father 'could not nohow do without them'.

Jane Austen was not so simple as to suppose that children could be seen and not heard. In a letter she could deplore a child's exuberance ('He was almost too happy, his happiness at least made him too talkative'),[14] but it is the spirited child whom she permits to be heard. Mr Knightley quotes the taunting words with which the young Emma accompanied her saucy looks; Susan Price at first startles Fanny with her boldness of speech, but the 'fearless, self-defending tone' is a warrant of a valued independence.[15] What is very unusual is for a child's conversation to be delighted in. Her unpublished writings show both sides of this. On the one hand,

[14] To Cassandra Austen, 15 June 1808; *Letters*, p. 188.
[15] *Mansfield Park*, ch. xxxviii.

there is the genially preposterous opening of *Henry and Eliza*, where an infant (*infans*, unspeaking) is found to fant:

As Sir George and Lady Harcourt were superintending the Labours of their Haymakers, rewarding the industry of some by smiles of approbation, & punishing the idleness of others, by a cudgel, they perceived lying closely concealed beneath the thick foliage of a Haycock, a beautifull little Girl not more than 3 months old.

Touched with the enchanting Graces of her face & delighted with the infantine tho' sprightly answers she returned to their many questions, they resolved to take her home &, having no Children of their own, to educate her with care & cost.[16]

On the other hand, there is the ballroom scene in *The Watsons*, where 10-year-old Charles Blake—longing to dance—is mortified by the broken promise of Miss Osborne but is then rewarded by the kindness of Emma Watson. Touching, because in Jane Austen's world we seldom hear a child say something to stave off tears ('but tho' he contrived to utter with an effort of Boyish Bravery "Oh! I do not mind it"—it was very evident by the unceasing agitation of his features that he minded it as much as ever'); but it is also that here, unusually, Jane Austen found herself delighting in a relationship between a child and an adult and in what they said to each other, ending with Charles's urging her to visit Osborne Castle: 'There is a monstrous curious stuff'd Fox there, & a Badger— anybody would think they were alive. It is a pity you should not see them.'[17] She has been so kind to him that he is moved to issue these sweet manly little kindnesses back.

But Jane Austen's writings mostly do not think it part of their enterprise to show what a dutiful and loving relation between adult and child would be. They expose cruelty here—as elsewhere—with such imaginative cogency as necessarily to recommend kindness, but they do not much show kindness in action. It is certainly a puzzle about this writer so fascinated by education and by what now gets called 'the problematics of pedagogy' that 'thoroughly good training for the young is never directly described' in the novels.[18] The omission is a striking one, and not in itself disabling, but the moments when the novels are importantly *not* persuasive are for me

---

[16] *Minor Works*, p. 33.   [17] Ibid., pp. 330, 333.
[18] Patricia Meyer Spacks, in *Jane Austen in a Social Context*, ed. David Monaghan (1981), p. 161.

related to this omission or abstention. The actual language, for instance, seems to have given up trying to *realize* what it is speaking of, when in *Pride and Prejudice* we are told glidingly that 'The children, two girls of six and eight years old, and two younger boys, were to be left under the particular care of their cousin Jane, who was the general favourite, and whose steady sense and sweetness of temper exactly adapted her for attending to them in every way— teaching them, playing with them, and loving them' (ch. xlii). Jane may be 'attending', but Jane Austen is not, not really. And in *Mansfield Park*, Fanny is permitted a very easy contrast between the domestic turmoil at Portsmouth and the calm order at Mansfield Park.

At Mansfield, no sounds of contention, no raised voice, no abrupt bursts, no tread of violence, was ever heard; all proceeded in a regular course of cheerful orderliness; everybody had their due importance; everybody's feelings were consulted. If tenderness could be ever supposed wanting, good sense and good breeding supplied its place; and as to the little irritations sometimes introduced by aunt Norris, they were short, they were trifling, they were as a drop of water to the ocean, compared with the ceaseless tumult of her present abode. (ch. xxxix)

Jane Austen is not entirely at one with Fanny in this, not only lest we forget that aunt Norris is more energetically appalling than the phrase 'little irritations' might suggest, but because an intelligent and fair-minded ponderer of children would have to try to imagine —as the novel never really does—the way in which small children were, day by day, actually brought up in the house of the Bertrams.

There is for me a related inauthenticity in *Pride and Prejudice*. Nothing could be more authentic than Jane Austen's understanding of spoilt children and their flatterers, notably in *Sense and Sensibility* but also in *Emma, Mansfield Park*, and *Persuasion*. But by the same token, nothing was more dangerously attractive to her than to take this as the short cut. It is a revelation to Elizabeth Bennet when the housekeeper at Pemberley, a woman of good sense, praises Darcy with a directness and experience that carry conviction: 'I have never had a cross word from him in my life, and I have known him ever since he was four years old' (ch. xliii). It is likewise a revelation to Elizabeth Bennet when Darcy brings himself to admit having been spoilt:

'As a child, I was taught what was *right*; but I was not taught to correct my temper. I was given good principles, but left to follow them in pride and conceit. Unfortunately, an only son (for many years an only *child*), I was spoiled by my parents, who, though good themselves (my father particularly, all that was benevolent and amiable), allowed, encouraged, almost taught me to be selfish and overbearing—to care for none beyond my own family circle, to think meanly of all the rest of the world, to *wish* at least to think meanly of their sense and worth compared to my own. Such I was, from eight to eight-and-twenty; and such I might still have been but for you, dearest, loveliest Elizabeth!' (ch. lix)

The trouble is that these two revelations, though they are not exactly contradictory, would need to be rendered compatible or likely. There is a feeling that Elizabeth may have been credulous to believe a housekeeper who may have been lovingly inattentive (if Darcy is to be believed as to his having been spoilt, selfish, and overbearing); or that Elizabeth may be credulous now to believe a self-deceived Darcy, a man grateful for an escape from a spiritual and social state which he wasn't actually ever in. Jane Austen does not attempt the elaborate task of rendering fitting the two things, each separately to Darcy's credit but an implausible and convenient conjunction.

Yet whatever the particular caveats of a reader, Jane Austen's subordination of children is in the service of a social wisdom, and is offered as styptic. She is at her best in this when she allows us to glimpse children without their getting a look-in; at her best here, because the glancing list, say, is naturally a comic form or device. Hence her pleasure (partly a pleasure of ruffling the doters on children) in the felicitously perfunctory transit.

> Their party was small, and the hours passed quietly away. Mrs. Palmer had her child, and Mrs. Jennings her carpet-work; they talked of the friends they had left behind, arranged Lady Middleton's engagements, and wondered whether Mr. Palmer and Colonel Brandon would get farther than Reading that night. (*Sense and Sensibility*, ch. xlii)

It is the timing (the syntax and the punctuation) of these two sentences which is so right, so equably dry. A writer not of genius but of talent would have paused for smiles, with a full-stop, after 'carpet-work' ('Mrs. Palmer had her child, and Mrs. Jennings her carpet-work'); Jane Austen has a semi-colon, and moves on, with leisurely indifference, to 'the friends they had left behind' (the child is being left behind by the sentence), and so into all those names (from Mrs Palmer and Mrs Jennings to Lady Middleton, and on to Mr Palmer and Colonel Brandon), all creating a strong sense of the namelessness and even characterlessness (except to the mother) of Mrs Palmer's child. There is no dislike of the child, but a considerable scepticism about those who would affect to care more for it than for Mrs Jennings's carpet-work. Elsewhere a comma does the work of keeping children in their place. 'She [Emma] did not think it in Harriet's nature to escape being benefited by novelty and variety, by the streets, the shops, and the children' (ch. l). Fanny Price is not much like Emma, but she practises a similar comma'd subordination:

Her own thoughts and reflections were habitually her best companions; and, in observing the appearance of the country, the bearings of the roads, the difference of soil, the state of the harvest, the cottages, the cattle, the children, she found entertainment that could only have been heightened by having Edmund to speak to of what she felt. (*Mansfield Park*, ch. viii)

Such subordination will feel legitimate only if we feel too the active presence of those other, higher, ties to which parental and filial love must mostly yield precedence. What is so striking about the famous panegyric to fraternal love in *Mansfield Park* (as Fanny and William retrace their childhood memories) is its unaffected simplicity of contrast. Shared memory: 'An advantage this, a strengthener of love, in which even the conjugal tie is beneath the fraternal' (ch. xxiv). Parental and filial love are not brought into the comparison. Jane Austen believed (valuably, since there is much to be said for it) that fraternal love is greater than all of its family rivals. There is a fascinating misguidedness about R. F. Brissenden's argument that 'the alliance between Edmund and Fanny has distinctly incestuous overtones. . . . The marriage thus can be seen as fulfilling the forbidden incestuous dream.'[19] For the point of what is said in the first chapter of the novel, and of the relation of Fanny to William too, is that incest is relevant exactly as preposterous. Mr Brissenden seems to me right to suggest that it is meant to come to mind ('My Fanny— my only sister—my only comfort now'), but only so that it may be sent packing.

Jane Austen is seldom willing to grant that one's children constitute the highest tie; and when she deplores someone who wrongly sets higher store by something else, she has usually intimated that this extravagance is an extension of his family extravagance of feeling. Of Mr Parker in *Sanditon* it is said 'Sanditon was a second Wife & 4 Children to him—hardly less Dear—& certainly more engrossing.—

[19] *Jane Austen: Bicentenary Essays*, ed. John Halperin (1975), pp. 165–6.

He could talk of it for ever' (ch. ii). (And not being a person, it could not talk back or remonstrate.) It is a fatuous charmer who brandishes Scott's verses:

'Had he written nothing more, he w^d have been Immortal. And then again, that unequalled, unrivalled address to Parental affection—

> "Some feelings are to Mortals given
> With less of Earth in them than Heaven" &c' (ch. vii)

It is this resistance to any easy acquiescence in granting supreme priority to filial and parental love which constitutes one of the novels' challenges. But it does not absolve us from the difficult task of deciding whether an imperceptiveness hereabouts is that of the character or the novelist. When the character is as lucidly self-aware as Anne Elliot and the novelist as lucidly self-aware as Jane Austen, the judgment can be a difficult one. But it has to be made because it greatly affects our sense of just what we are apprehending. One of the greatest and most famous conversations in Jane Austen, and one of the most moving scenes, is the good-natured passionate disagreement between Anne Elliot and Captain Harville about men's feelings and women's. From a distrust of books and of bias, the conversation moves to an exclamation:

'Ah!' cried Captain Harville, in a tone of strong feeling, 'if I could but make you comprehend what a man suffers when he takes a last look at his wife and children, and watches the boat that he has sent them off in, as long as it is in sight, and then turns away and says, "God knows whether we ever meet again!" And then, if I could convey to you the glow of his soul when he does see them again; when, coming back after a twelvemonth's absence, perhaps, and obliged to put into another port, he calculates how soon it be possible to get them there, pretending to deceive himself, and saying, "They cannot be here till such a day," but all the while hoping for them twelve hours sooner, and seeing them arrive at last, as if Heaven had given them wings, by many hours sooner still! If I could explain to you all this, and all that a man can bear and do, and glories to do, for the sake of these treasures of his existence! I speak, you know, only of such men as have hearts!' pressing his own with emotion.

'Oh!' cried Anne eagerly, 'I hope I do justice to all that is felt by you, and by those who resemble you. God forbid that I should undervalue the warm and faithful feelings of any of my fellow-creatures! I should deserve utter contempt if I dared to suppose that true attachment and constancy were known only by woman. No, I believe you capable of everything great and good in your married lives. I believe you equal to every important exertion, and to every domestic forbearance, so long as—if I may be allowed the expression, so long as you have an object. I mean while the woman you love lives, and lives for you. All the privilege I claim for my own sex (it is not a very enviable one: you need not covet it), is that of loving longest, when existence or when hope is gone!' (*Persuasion*, ch. xxiii)

It is a famously moving exchange; but this is not to say that its readers are all moved by the same things about it. To me, its profound poignancy comes from the combination in it of a true meeting between the speakers with their being profoundly at cross-purposes, their so painfully *not* meeting. I don't mean their not agreeing; rather, something like the profound misapprehension in Malcolm's conversation with Macduff about the murder of his family. For Captain Harville's impassioned speech has at its heart the words 'wife and children', which then becomes the insistent 'them' as he asks Anne to imagine his imaginings: 'and watches the boat that he has sent them off in . . . when he does see them again . . . possible to get them there. . . . They cannot be here till such a day . . . hoping for them . . . seeing them arrive at last, as if Heaven had given them wings . . .' And what is so sad in Anne Elliot's entirely honourable reply is its entire inability to engage with that part of what is being said, with 'wife *and children*'. She speaks with great feeling, and she grants that a good man is capable of everything great and good in his married life; but, in the urgency of her love for Wentworth, she can think only in terms of *one* object: 'I believe you equal to every important exertion, and to every domestic forbearance, so long as—if I may be allowed the expression, so long as you have an object. I mean while the woman you love lives, and lives for you.' It is so different from anything that Captain Harville was speaking of as to make it unignorable that even the most generous and just of people may *need* not fully to attend. It is Anne Elliot, and not Jane Austen, who for the best of reasons—sheer survival—is not able fully to attend to what Captain Harville said. For Jane Austen has brought Captain Harville particularly alive to us as a lover of children.

One point at issue is whether an aunt may not make the best mother. Jane Austen has a vested interest in believing such a thing, but this has no bearing on whether she is right. The novels bear eloquent witness to such a belief. That a surrogate mother may well be the best mother is touched upon in Knightley's confidence that Mrs Weston is excellently placed to comprehend Frank Churchill justly: 'standing in a mother's place, but without a mother's affection to blind her' (*Emma*, ch. xviii). Anne Elliot 'was always on friendly terms with her brother-in-law; and in the children, who loved her nearly as well, and respected her a great deal more than their mother, she had an object of interest, amusement, and wholesome exertion' (*Persuasion*, ch. vi). Anne is therefore the best person to care for little Charles after his fall, and not his mother Mary, who says 'You, who have not a mother's feelings, are a great deal the properest person' (ch. vii). 'She knew herself to be of the first utility to the child': and the challenge of Jane Austen is in her really concurring with Anne, and meaning *first*.

One way of bringing these various consideration into focus might be to look at a summing-up by Lord David Cecil and at a feminist alternative to it. Lord David has a characteristically lucid and humane evocation, ending:

Here it was that she differed from most women. The creative impulse which in them fulfilled itself as wife and mother in her fulfilled itself as an artist.[20]

In the same year in which those words appeared in *A Portrait of Jane Austen*—1978—there appeared in a feminist journal, *Woman and Literature*, an article by Nina Auerbach, called 'Artists and Mothers: A False Alliance'.[21]

Like a lot of feminist criticism, it offers some grounded grievances and much perversity of argument. It is implacably opposed to the parallel between children of the imagination and children of the womb. It has no difficulty in showing that such a parallel can be tactlessly, complacently or patronizingly used. But it has many other difficulties, among them the fact that both of the novelists whom it considers, Jane Austen and George Eliot, made explicit use of the parallel—or rather, metaphor.

Professor Auerbach maintains that the feminist biographers and psychiatrists who have speculated upon the relation between creativity and childlessness (she has not noticed that she is herself positing a very strong relation, that of active dissociation) have been colluding

---

[20] *A Portrait of Jane Austen* (1978), p. 141.

[21] Collected in Nina Auerbach, *Romantic Imprisonment* (1986), pp. 171–83. As Rachel Brownstein has pointed out, 'It is well known that many male authors have also spoken of their literary creations in terms borrowed from biological maternity' (*Becoming a Heroine*, 1982, p. 319). And in terms borrowed from biological paternity.

with a male falsity, and that Jane Austen and George Eliot unfortunately colluded with it too:

The honorary motherhood bestowed on woman artists, in the nineteenth
century as today, seems to have created a nagging confusion in the self-
perception of two of the century's greatest and most determinedly childless
novelists: Jane Austen and George Eliot.

The nagging confusion seems to me not theirs.

The essay is fiercely provocative, and well worth reading. But it
is marred. First, by a refusal to consider the conjunction as a metaphor
rather than as an analogy. (Of course a metaphor must have some
element of analogy, but in a valuable metaphor the analogy or likeness is not the end of the matter—the illumination is in the relation
of likeness to unlikeness.) Second, the argument is marred by its
tacking back and forth between two very different positions: one is
that writing novels has nothing to do with wombs, child-bearing or
childlessness ('Artists and Mothers: A *False* Alliance'); the other is
to say, what do you mean the one has nothing to do with the
other?—the great thing about a woman's creating a novel is that
it frees her from the false compulsion to believe that creating babies
is woman's complete and only fulfilment. ('*Determinedly* childless novelists'.) Now there is something to be said for both of these positions,
but they are at odds, and though each may sometimes hold sway,
they cannot both do so at once.

The essay opens with a question inviting the answer *no*: 'Do our
wombs silently dictate when we write?' But half of Nina Auerbach's
argument cannot afford to scorn the possibility, since if Jane Austen
and George Eliot did 'produce art that allowed them a freer, finer,
more expansive world than the suppressions of nineteenth-century
motherhood allowed', the art—in so *escaping* motherhood—is as determined by motherhood as any bad man could wish. 'In the popular
image of the creative process, creativity and childbirth are often
entangled': a bad thing, apparently, though in Nina Auerbach's
own argument the two are inexorably bound. Psychiatrists are
deplored for their 'difficulty in perceiving an adult woman without
reference to children'; but it is impossible to see what could *more*
perceive an adult woman with reference to children than to insist,
as Nina Auerbach does, that 'Far from endowing Austen with second-
hand motherhood, her identity as an artist represented an escape
from confinement into a child-free world with space for mind and

spirit, time for change, and privacy for growth'. You cannot be 'perceived' as '*child-free*' 'without reference to children'.

The third respect in which the argument is perverse is in its averting its eyes from the fact that the childlessness of men writers has as often been the subject of comment and critical speculation. In our century alone, D. H. Lawrence, T. S. Eliot, and Samuel Beckett are writers whose childlessness has been discussed, often responsibly, tentatively and directly. There is, as often in feminism, a sexism in this refusal to grant that such formulations are not visited upon one sex only.

Nina Auerbach turns to a famous or infamous moment in one of Jane Austen's letters:

Her seemingly callous, unapologetic distaste for childbearing has shocked generations of critics, perhaps because their stereotypes become dislodged when a woman novelist lashes out against parturition. Her most widely-quoted description of motherhood is a Gothic comedy of marriage's abortion and biology's grotesque invasion: 'Mrs. Hall, of Sherbourne, was brought to bed yesterday of a dead child, some weeks before she expected, owing to a fright. I suppose she happened unawares to look at her husband.'[22] Considering this ruthless vision of misadventure, it seems unlikely that Jane Austen's novels represent sighs over lost fulfillment.

The discussion of this flash in the letters has indeed preoccupied people at least since E. M. Forster deplored her offering such a thing as 'a jolly joke': 'Did Cassandra laugh? Probably, but all that we catch at this distance is the whinnying of harpies.'[23] R. W. Chapman tactically granted that it was 'naughty' of Jane Austen, and then brought deftly into play (as a rebuttal of Forster's squeamishness— 'no doubt distressing to a sensitive middle-aged bachelor') the healthy instincts of others: 'I once ventured to put this test case to an audience of young women. It was received, not with the pained silence I was prepared for, but with a shout of merriment.'[24] Mrs Leavis, who was nothing if not robust, did not need to test the case, and savoured the moment all the more for its having 'pained Mr. Forster'.[25]

Jane Austen's words there do seem to me amazingly fierce. One suggested explanation has been offered in another essay by Nina

---

[22] To Cassandra Austen, 27 October 1798; *Letters*, p. 24.

[23] (1932), *Abinger Harvest* (1936), p. 160.

[24] *Jane Austen; Facts and Problems* (1948), pp. 106–7.

[25] *Scrutiny*, xii (1944), 106.

Auerbach, which brings Jane Austen's babies explicitly into the vicinity of *Rosemary's Baby*, and which says of this moment in the letters that Jane Austen reveals 'a penchant for Romantic abortions': 'This unappealing tableau is as far from Wordsworth as it is from the Jane Austen many people want to see, but if we think of Romantic fiction, with its demon marriages that become claustrophobic bondages to the unnatural, its penchant for monstrous and aborted births, we can locate even Austen's seeming aberrations in the proclivities and fears of her time.'[26]

I should myself fetch an explanation less far, and suggest not a cultural but a corporeal speculation for the fierceness about Mrs Hall, her dead baby and her ugly husband. We should not avert our eyes from the occasion when Mrs Hall did not avert herself from her ugly husband, and the baby—now dead—was begotten. Jane Austen is elsewhere drawn (perfectly naturally but disconcertingly) to remark upon a husband's ugliness or age when she sees a pregnant woman; as in this profession about Mrs Warren:

Mrs. Warren, I was constrained to think a very fine young woman, which I much regret. She has got rid of some part of her child, & danced away with great activity, looking by no means very large.—Her husband is ugly enough; uglier even than his cousin John; but he does not look so *very* old.[27]

But in any case the fact is that if Nina Auerbach were to put the paragraph about Mrs Hall and the dead baby back into the context of the whole letter, she would find it resisted her argument. For the letter (27 October 1798) is full, not only of Gothic comedy about dead babies, but of sweet affection and salutary teasing for little George:

My dear itty Dordy's remembrance of me is very pleasing to me—foolishly pleasing, because I know it will be over so soon. My attachment to him will be more durable. I shall think with tenderness and delight on his beautiful and smiling countenance and interesting manners till a few years have turned him into an ungovernable, ungracious fellow.[28]

Moreover, the sequence of thought, moving from the paragraph immediately preceding that on Mrs Hall, is further confirmation that Jane Austen did indeed associate books and birth:

[26] 'Jane Austen and Romantic Imprisonment', *Romantic Imprisonment*, p. 11.
[27] To Cassandra Austen, 20 November 1800; *Letters*, p. 91.
[28] *Letters*, pp. 24–5.

Your letter was chaperoned here by one from Mrs. Cooke, in which she says that 'Battleridge' is not to come out before January, and she is so little satisfied with Cawthorn's dilatoriness that she never means to employ him again.

Mrs. Hall, of Sherborne, was brought to bed yesterday . . .

Professor Auerbach is right to exhibit prominently Jane Austen's remarks about her niece Anna's frequent babies, but she coerces the quotation in her commentary:

> Later in her life, she enthusiastically supported her niece Anna's attempt to write a novel, reading her manuscript with gusto and criticizing it with professional scrupulousness; but she lost all interest in Anna when she married and had a child. In her passage from writer to mother, Anna sinks into a lower order of being, forfeiting her humanity, her youth, and perhaps life itself: 'Poor Animal, she will be worn out before she is thirty.—I am very sorry for her' (23 March 1817). Austen's dismissal suggests an unpassable abyss between writer and mother, human and animal, the dancing creativity of the mind and the monotonous attrition of the womb. In mother-hood, Anna has relinquished life rather than created it.

Well, women were cruelly worn out by child-bearing, and obstetric science was not what it should have been, and William Empson set down with level horror the thought of John Donne 'gradually killing his wife by giving her a child every year'. But it would have been a forfeiting of Jane Austen's own humanity for her to judge that Anna had forfeited hers. What makes the sentence—in context— so different in tone and in temper from Auerbach's 'dismissal' is the position, poignant and rueful (hard on the heels not only of the Donkey but of 'Anna') of 'Poor Animal':

Anna has not a chance of escape; her husband called here the other day, & said she was *pretty* well but not *equal* to so long a walk; she *must come* in her *Donkey Carriage.*—Poor Animal, she will be worn out before she is thirty.—I am very sorry for her.—Mrs Clement too is in that way again. I am quite tired of so many Children.[29]

Very sorry for her, yes, because sorry for any woman who has *so many children*, not for her having a child at all. The stress in that last sentence—'I am quite tired of so many Children'—is, I take it, upon *I*: even I, who am not bearing them, am tired. Very sorry for

[29] To Fanny Knight, 23 March 1817; *Letters*, p. 488.

her, and this because the equation of writer = human, mother = animal, is *not* crassly asserted.

This flattening or oppression visited upon Jane Austen's tone is clearest when Nina Auerbach engages head-on with what she believes to be Jane Austen's collusion with the baby/book metaphor. Nina Auerbach does not deny that Jane Austen uses it—famously, of *Pride and Prejudice* ('I want to tell you that I have got my own darling child from London')[30] and of *Sense and Sensibility*. But the feminist critic needs to show that Jane Austen was in bad faith in using it, and chooses the worst possible ground on which to contest the matter.

When *Sense and Sensibility*, her first published novel, was in proof, she wrote exultantly to Cassandra: 'No indeed, I am never too busy to think of S & S. I can no more forget it, than a mother can forget her sucking child' (25 April 1811).[31] This triumphant letter contains one of the very few conventionally maternal images in all of Jane Austen's writings, and it is also one of her sparse employments of formal figurative language. The unaccountable conventionality of this metaphor, compared to the indelible portrait of Mrs. Hall of Sherbourne, is underlined by its appropriation from Isaiah 49: 15: 'Can a woman forget her sucking child, That she should not have compassion on the son of her womb?' In casting about for a form for the unprecedented elation of success, Jane Austen seems to have turned to the Bible rather than life. Perhaps she might later have dismissed this sentence, along with its self-consciously biblical simile, as 'thorough novel slang.' Though a Freudian might suggest that her unconscious broke through her defenses just this once, the second-hand language and metaphor make their emotional validity dubious: in Austen's letters as in her novels, true feeling cannot express itself in clichés. Though the tangible accomplishment of her first set of proofs made art and motherhood leap together in her language, the borrowed equation seems less a vehicle of spontaneous joy than an index of the paucity of language defining women's achievements.

What are we to make of the antithesis in 'Jane Austen seems to have turned to the Bible rather than life'? For Jane Austen, the Bible was central to life, and to turn to the Bible was to turn to a way of having life more abundantly. Similarly, the easy assimilation by the critic of a biblical allusion (beautifully bantering in Jane Austen, and with that comedy of seriousness that only a believer could muster) to a *cliché* is as blank as the assimilation of the biblical turn in 'forget her sucking child' to 'thorough novel slang'. The

---

[30] To Cassandra Austen, 29 January 1813; *Letters*, p. 297.
[31] *Letters*, p. 272.

'thorough novel slang' of 'a vortex of Dissipation' (Jane Austen's instance) could scarcely be more different, and when in that other letter Jane Austen went on to imagine that the slang was as old as Adam, she was not imagining it in the Bible: 'it is such thorough novel slang—and so old, that I dare say Adam met with it in the first novel he opened.'[32]

The nephew who said that she 'took a kind of parental interest in the beings whom she had created' seems to me better attuned to Jane Austen, in sensing a benign metaphor not a sexist oppression such as bred bad faith, than is her modern appropriator. For Nina Auerbach is more in favour of childlessness than Jane Austen was:

> During her last illness she wrote wearily, 'I am quite tired of so many Children' (23 March 1817), as if they were a symptom of the illness that was wearing down her life. The tone of this letter is echoed in her last and most romantic novel: in *Persuasion*, Captain Wentworth signals his continuing love for Anne Elliot by removing a burdensome child from her back; most nineteenth-century heroes would deposit the child in the heroine's arms. Adult love becomes the ally of art in redeeming the dutifully maternal woman by an alternative world.

But this is a very perverse reading of that great love-scene in *Persuasion*, which gets much of its force from the fact that 'by removing a burdensome child from her back', Captain Wentworth would be making possible Anne's maternal attention to the other child, the sick child—while at the same time Captain Wentworth shows himself likely to make an excellent father, firmly active. 'She could not even thank him. She could only hang over little Charles, with most disordered feelings' (ch. ix). *Children* are not being removed from Anne; Wentworth loves Anne in part for her loving young Charles, and for being sure to have proved at least a better mother to the boisterous 2-year-old Walter than Walter's own mother was.

For Nina Auerbach, 'Jane Austen's fiction subtly reinforces her allegiance to childless adulthood. . . . Like Jane Austen, Emma preserves the fine distinction between the artist as aunt and the "Poor Animal" as parent.' But there is something very unconvincing about using the word 'childless' and the word 'motherless' (Emma 'is motherless herself') in the same paragraph as if they were parallels.

[32] To Anna Austen, 28 September 1814; *Letters*, p. 404.

Emma, after all, had had a mother. William Empson has said that
'a monk oughtn't to have a baby, but somebody else has to have
babies, if only to keep up the supply of monks'.[33] A maiden aunt
oughtn't to have a baby, but somebody else has to have babies, if
only to keep up the supply of maiden aunts. Jane Austen's novels
are magnanimously aware of this. She might have liked the thought
that, though a feminist of Nina Auerbach's persuasions oughtn't to
have a baby, somebody else has to have babies, if only to keep up
the supply of feminists.

[33] (1964); *Argufying*, ed. John Haffenden (1987), p. 615.

VICTORIAN LIVES

Condescension has long been visited upon biography, especially Victorian. Virginia Woolf began her essay on 'The Art of Biography' (1939): 'The art of biography, we say—but at once go on to ask, Is biography an art? The question is foolish perhaps.' No, not perhaps. Humphry House, in 'The Present Art of Biography' (1948), added a word to Virginia Woolf's title, but not a word of dissent: 'biography should not properly be spoken of as an art. An artist creates his own limits without the violation of anything except his own larger designs.'[1]

The show of reason always proffered is that biography, unlike— they say—art (or unlike literature), is fettered to facts. But the glum power of 'fetters' would be changed if we thought rather of *bonds*, that is of relations and restraints which certainly may thwart but which may be ties that rightly bind, the conditions of responsibility, love, respect for things *other* than one's 'own larger designs', and such service as is perfect freedom.

Even when something more is graciously granted to biography these days, this is often the expected surprise. You might include biography in the current catalogue of impossibilities:

we see that the true subject of the *Life* [Boswell's *Life of Johnson*], as of all biographies, is the impossibility of the biographical enterprise, not presence but the illusion of presence ultimately revealed as an illusion, the dilemma of narrative trying and failing to reach through to a world beyond itself.[2]

Not '*a* subject', not even '*a* true subject', but 'the true subject' of all biographies 'is the impossibility of the biographical enterprise'. This, the modish old story, lacks enterprise.

Or you might reconstitute things in a new condescending order. Ira Bruce Nadel, in what is theoretically an account of biography (*Biography: Fiction, Fact and Form*), insists that 'the biographer is akin more to the creative writer than the historian'. This dissents from, or rather switches around, Leon Edel, who had announced for his part that 'the biographer, like the historian, is a slave of his

---

[1] *All in Due Time* (1955), p. 267.
[2] William C. Dowling, *Language and Logos in Boswell's Life of Johnson* (1981), p. 97; quoted by Ira Bruce Nadel, *Biography: Fiction, Fact and Form* (1984), p. 231.

documents'.[3] Either way the historian would do well to remonstrate. And so would those who are aware that Professor Edel has been insufficiently the slave of his documents, since he is often remiss in transcribing them. As with the famous letter by Henry James (5 October 1901), to Sarah Orne Jewett, 'in which', Edel says in his life of James, 'he suddenly cast aside "the mere twaddle of graciousness" and criticized her historical novel, *The Tory Lover*, as a falsified pastiche'.[4] The letter has twice been printed by Edel. Spot the wrong word. (The clue is the false ring of *and*, in 'and in its essence'):

You may multiply the little facts that can be got from pictures and documents, relics and prints, as much as you like—*the* real thing is almost impossible to do, and in its essence the whole effect is as nought:

—'and in its essence'? No: 'and in its absence the whole effect is as nought'. The word *absence* is unmistakable—well, clearly not that— in the letter itself in the Houghton Library. 'You may multiply the little facts': but first you must get them right.

For Woolf, the achievement of biography is manifestly lesser, 'a different life from the life of poetry and fiction—a life lived at a lower degree of tension'. The biographer is 'a craftsman, not an artist; and his work is not a work of art but something betwixt and between'. And this, she holds, because of subservience to fact.

But the masterpieces of Victorian literary biography bear witness to such imaginative freedom as is made possible only by a respect for facts. Since even to speak of fact these days is to risk being accused of naïvety (invaluably cheap label), we might invoke as an epigraph the words of a great Victorian biographer, James Anthony Froude. Froude wrote in 1851 in his essay on Homer:

Facts, it was once said, were stubborn things; but in our days we have changed all that; a fact, under the knife of a critic, splits in pieces, and is dissected out of belief with incredible readiness. The helpless thing lies under his hand like a foolish witness in a law court, when browbeaten by an unscrupulous advocate, and is turned about and twisted this way and that way, till in its distraction it contradicts itself, and bears witness against itself; and to escape from torture, at last flies utterly away, itself half doubting its own existence.

[3] *Literary Biography* (1957), p. 5.
[4] *Henry James: The Master* (1972), p. 263. *Selected Letters of Henry James* (1956), p. 234. *Henry James: Letters*, iv (1984), p. 208.

This anticipates, albeit with scepticism about the excesses of scepticism, the movement of deconstruction, the bearing witness against itself.

The world in the old days was not peopled only by a primitive tribe of raw empiricists. Fact. 1851, J. A. Froude. 1916, T. S. Eliot:

Facts are not merely found in the world and laid together like bricks, but every fact has in a sense its place prepared for it before it arrives, and without the implication of a system in which it belongs the fact is not a fact at all. The ideality essential to fact means a particular point of view, and means the exclusion of other aspects of the same point of attention. There is a sense, then, in which any science—natural or social—is *a priori*: in that it satisfies the needs of a particular point of view, a point of view which may be said to be more original than any of the facts that are referred to that science. The development of a science would thus be rather organic than mechanical; there is a fitness of the various facts for each other, with that instinctive selection and exclusion which is a characteristic of human personality at its highest.[5]

The biographer is someone gifted to exercise that instinctive selection upon this characteristic itself, alive to human personality at its highest.

The theorist of biography, Ira Nadel, quotes Nietzsche: 'there are no "facts-in-themselves," for a sense must always be projected into them before there can be "facts" '; this, Nadel immediately describes as 'a philosophic concept that casts suspicion on their validity'.[6] Suspicion, eh . . . Remark the prophylactic quotation-marks when it is a matter of someone else's claim to be dealing in facts (theirs are only 'facts'); but remark too that Nadel, on this same page, says unmisgivingly of Florence Nightingale that, *pace* Lytton Strachey, 'in fact, her room faced south'. And again: 'The aim of biography is not so much to convey the "facts," which it linguistically cannot do objectively, but to present an attitude, perspective or point of view regarding those "facts" '—this being on the same page on which he says, again unmisgivingly, that 'Ernest Kris in fact has argued that. . . .'[7]

Even Alan Shelston, who has given us an undeniably valuable edition of E. C. Gaskell's *Life of Charlotte Brontë*, deprecates the

---

[5] *Knowledge and Experience in the Philosophy of F. H. Bradley* (1964), pp. 60–1.

[6] *Biography: Fiction, Fact and Form*, p. 5.

[7] Ibid., p. 208. In fact the name was Ernst Kris, not—as Nadel thrice has it—Ernest.

Victorians' 'belief in the undeniable value of "fact"' [inverted commas], and then in the next sentence says: 'Add to this the fact that biography, by its very nature . . .' [no inverted commas].[8]

Undeniable? What should not be denied, although it has been, is the value of the great Victorian literary biographies, and preeminently Gaskell's Brontë, Froude's Carlyle, and Tennyson's Tennyson.

[8] *The Life of Charlotte Brontë* (1975), Introduction, p. 19. On the twisters' rhetoric of the institutionalized subversives such as Jonathan Dollimore, see a cogently hilarious essay by Richard Levin, 'Leaking Relativism', *Essays in Criticism*, xxxviii (1988), 267–77.

E. C. GASKELL'S CHARLOTTE BRONTË

Plunged into diverse controversy—including threats of a lawsuit—
by her *Life of Charlotte Brontë* in 1857, E. C. Gaskell was grateful to
an ironist:

I have had a preface to my (forthcoming) third edition sent to me, which
I dare not insert there; but it is too good to be lost, therefore I shall copy
it out for you:
'If anybody is displeased with any statement in this book, they are re-
quested to believe it withdrawn, and my deep regret expressed for its insertion,
as truth is too expensive an article to be laid before the British public.'
But for the future I intend to confine myself to lies (*i.e.* fiction). It is safer.[1]

But the *Life of Charlotte Brontë* was repeatedly truthful. Shakespeare's
Troilus speaks of 'truth tired with iteration'; Shakespeare's Pericles,
more truly, craves iteration:

> For truth can never be confirm'd enough,
> Though doubts did ever sleep.

As early as the fourth paragraph of the *Life of Charlotte Brontë*
(1857), E. C. Gaskell says 'as I have said', and two pages later, 'as
I mentioned'; and throughout the book she casts herself and her
words so. This is not a capitulation to the inattentive, but a recap-
itulation for the attentive, and its retrospection is braced against the
equally-frequent prospective glance: half-a-dozen pages into the book,
there is, 'to which I shall have occasion to allude again more particularly'—this turn, too, is active throughout, itself constituting the
promise of a hereafter ('of which I shall have more to say hereafter').
   As a chapter-opening (ch. v), 'For the reason just stated . . .' is
at once flat and extraordinary; and there is more than an alerting
tap in such a chapter-opening as this: 'The reader will remember
that Anne Brontë had been interred in the churchyard of the Old
Church in Scarborough' (ch. xxv).[2]

[1] To William Fairbairn, probably June 1857; *The Letters of Mrs. Gaskell*, ed.
J. A. V. Chapple and Arthur Pollard (1967), p. 458.
[2] *The Life of Charlotte Brontë* was published in March 1857. Quotations here are from
Gaskell's revised edition, respecting her right to change her phrasing and her judgements, and to correct matters of fact. She made many such changes, as well as additions, for the third edition, November 1857; I have given the chapter-numbering

Plainly these authorial enjoinings are conventions and conveniences, but they also form a tissue which is alive to more than the plain. They shape the story, in a biography by a novelist which asks, as many nineteenth-century novels are acknowledged to ask, to be read too as a dramatic poem.

E. C. Gaskell's repetitions incarnate a response to the desolate repetitions within Charlotte Brontë's life, the repetitions of family death, familiar death:

The little church lies, as I mentioned, above most of the houses in the village; and the graveyard rises above the church, and is terribly full of upright tombstones. (ch. i)

'Upright tombstones' is unmistakable, neither making nor asking comment. There are no meaningful glances, simply a literal record alive with unignorable meaning. In ch. iii: 'Haworth Parsonage is— as I mentioned in the first chapter—an oblong stone house . . . The graveyard lies on two sides of the house and garden'. In ch. vii:

In many, living, as it were, in a churchyard

—'as it were' faintly touches 'living' there, and not only bears upon 'in a churchyard'—

In many, living, as it were, in a churchyard, and with all the sights and sounds connected with the last offices to the dead things of every-day occurrence, the very familiarity would have bred indifference. But it was otherwise with Charlotte Brontë. One of her friends says:—'I have seen her turn pale and feel faint when, in Hartshead church, some one accidentally remarked that we were walking over graves.'

In the *Life of Charlotte Brontë*, we walk over graves, and a reminder has a grim likelihood of being a *memento mori*.

It is not images, figurative understandings, which recur, but literal sights, there on two sides, descriptions with a hold.

The *Life* begins with a vivid, and justly famous, evocation of what it is like to journey to Haworth—the temptation to say 'make a pilgrimage' is understood and is resisted. The railway is succeeded by the carriage, and the approach concentrates:

(i–xxviii) from my copy of 1866. The first edition, though, furnishes the text for the best and most accessible of current editions, that by Alan Shelston (Penguin, 1975); to calculate the chapter-references for this, note that the first edition was in two volumes, each having its chapters i–xiv, whereas the later edition, followed here, runs i–xxviii.

For a short distance the road appears to turn away from Haworth, as it winds round the base of the shoulder of a hill; but then it crosses a bridge over the 'beck,' and the ascent through the village begins. The flag-stones with which it is paved are placed end-ways, in order to give a better hold to the horses' feet; and, even with this help, they seem to be in constant danger of slipping backwards. The old stone houses are high compared to the width of the street, which makes an abrupt turn before reaching the more level ground at the head of the village, so that the steep aspect of the place, in one part, is almost like that of a wall. But this surmounted, the church lies a little off the main road on the left; a hundred yards, or so, and the driver relaxes his care, and the horse breathes more easily, as they pass into the quiet little by-street that leads to Haworth Parsonage.

This sympathetic dexterity (prose should be at least as well written as poetry) is relaxedly authoritative, like the driver; and thanks to the syntax, it is not only the horse who comes to breathe more easily.

More than four hundred pages later, the time comes to tell, not of the generalizable stranger's visit to Haworth, but personally, of the author's.

Towards the latter end of September [1853] I went to Haworth. At the risk of repeating something which I have previously said, I will copy out parts of a letter which I wrote at the time. (ch. xxvii)

It is odd, though clear, for her to say 'at the risk of repeating . . .', since there is not the risk of this happening, there is the certainty of it. The risk is other: that an impatient reader will not realize what is gained by such repeating; and when the author tells us that she 'will copy out parts of a letter', the action is both copying out and copying. What we then read both is and is not what we have read before:

Haworth is a long, straggling village: one steep narrow street—so steep that the flag-stones with which it is paved are placed end-ways, that the horses' feet may have something to cling to, and not slip down backwards . . .

The pleasure of meeting that admirable evocation again is in its giving us something to cling to, its looking backwards while not slipping down backwards; and Gaskell's letter immediately saves itself from slipping backwards by moving on to an epistolary inform-ality such as would not have suited the decorum of her opening chapter:

and not slip down backwards; which if they did, they would soon reach Keighley. But if the horses had cats' feet and claws, they would do all the better. Well, we (the man, horse, car, and I) clambered up this street . . .

It is not only that this very late stage of the story (the penultimate chapter) circles back to the starting-point, but that the energetic physical descriptions, like the flag-stones, are placed end-ways.

This is muscular writing. Elsewhere such repetitions enact movements which announce themselves less through muscles than through nerves. Take the reiterated *pacings*, themselves paced within the book. The first telling of these family footfalls takes care openly to acknowledge, in aftersight and foresight, all that they eventually gathered to themselves:

> It was the household custom among these girls to sew till nine o'clock at night. At that hour, Miss Branwell generally went to bed, and her nieces' duties for the day were accounted done. They put away their work, and began to pace the room backwards and forwards, up and down,—as often with the candles extinguished, for economy's sake, as not,—their figures glancing into the fire-light, and out into the shadow, perpetually. At this time, they talked over past cares and troubles; they planned for the future, and consulted each other as to their plans. In after years this was the time for discussing together the plots of their novels. And again, still later, this was the time for the last surviving sister to walk alone, from old accustomed habit, round and round the desolate room, thinking sadly upon the 'days that were no more.' But this Christmas of 1836 was not without its hopes and daring aspirations. (ch. viii)

Tennyson's 'the days that are no more' has become the 'days that *were* no more' (yet within quotation-marks), obdurately doubly past though not yet *written* by Tennyson at the time of which Gaskell writes, and this moment of Tennyson is then at once succeeded by a different embodiment of a still later Tennysonian elegiac memory, a once-happy Christmas of the 1830s (as in *In Memoriam*) and its holly boughs. 'Make one wreath more for Use and Wont.'

The evocation—like the allusion and the description—itself paces backwards and forwards, in sympathetic repetition, and in a way it left nothing 'for the future'—given this chapter viii, there was no *need* to mention this household custom again. But the next chapter, as if recalling 'perpetually', takes a brief glance at this continuing habit ('glancing into the fire-light, and out into the shadow, perpetually'), but this time with a different energy, with a more tingling step:

and by nine he, the aunt, and Tabby, were all in bed,—the girls free to
pace up and down (like restless wild animals) in the parlour, talking over
plans and projects, and thoughts of what was to be their future life.

The parenthesis, '(like restless wild animals)', which endearingly
follows upon the servant's tame name 'Tabby', sees the whole ritual
under a different aspect; the brackets look as if they are caging the
simile, one which is thereby held in strange play with the word
'free': 'the girls free to pace up and down (like restless wild animals)
in the parlour . . .'

In ch. xv, we hear again that 'The sisters retained the old habit,
which was begun in their aunt's lifetime, of putting away their work
at nine o'clock, and commencing their study, pacing up and down
the sitting room'. But by now, this is more than just the *sisters'* habit,
and is more than a habit, and the parenthetical words, 'which was
begun in their aunt's lifetime', compound the biographical truth
that the essential milestone was a gravestone.

By ch. xviii, there are two more gravestones.

She went on with her work steadily. But it was dreary to write without
any one to listen to the progress of her tale—to find fault or to sympathise
—while pacing the length of the parlour in the evenings, as in the days
that were no more.[3] Three sisters had done this—then two, the other sister
dropping off from the walk—and now one was left desolate, to listen for
echoing steps that never came, and to hear the wind sobbing at the win-
dows, with an almost articulate sound.

But the elegiac poetry of this vision is not the last word; one more
time, Charlotte Brontë is heard to pace, or rather now to walk, in
the faithful prose and in the down-to-earth hearing of Elizabeth
Gaskell, as she herself reports it in the *Life* in the closing words of
that letter about her visit to Haworth: 'We sit up together till ten,
or past; and after I go, I hear Miss Brontë come down and walk
up and down the room for an hour or so' (ch. xxvii).

The ending of this penultimate chapter of the *Life* (the book's
consummation—the two pages which follow are a summation) has
rightly been judged perfect in its clarity of grief, a grief felt especially
by the bereaved father and by the husband and especially for them:

Early on Saturday morning, March 31st, the solemn tolling of Haworth
church-bell spoke forth the fact of her death to the villagers who had

---

[3] No quotation marks for Tennyson now; the transplant has taken.

known her from a child, and whose hearts shivered within them as they thought of the two sitting desolate and alone in the old grey house.

Nothing could be more direct, and yet rippling too, since the tacit urging is to sympathize with those who sympathize with the bereaved, and since these succinct sentences ripple back to so much else within the book, all of it 'known' and to be 'thought of': all the occasions on which we have imagined those who sat there in that house of death. At the death of Aunt Branwell, the two sisters return:

They sailed from Antwerp; they travelled night and day, and got home on a Tuesday morning. The funeral and all was over, and Mr. Brontë and Anne were sitting together, in quiet grief for the loss of one who had done her part well in their household for nearly twenty years, and earned the regard and respect of many who never knew how much they should miss her till she was gone. (ch. xi)

At the imminent death of Emily Brontë, what she endured and what she would not endure:

She made no complaint; she would not endure questioning; she rejected sympathy and help. Many a time did Charlotte and Anne drop their sewing, or cease from their writing, to listen with wrung hearts to the failing step, the laboured breathing, the frequent pauses, with which their sister climbed the short staircase; yet they dared not notice what they observed, with pangs of suffering even deeper than hers. They dared not notice it in words, far less by the caressing assistance of a helping arm or hand. They sat, still and silent. (ch. xvi)

The profound sympathy (again including those whose suffering is sympathy) is there in the syntax of laboured breathing, of the participles, of the frequent pauses, to which we too 'listen with wrung hearts'; the stoicism is there in the Augustan dignity of differentiation: 'they dared not notice what they observed'. But Gaskell dares to notice it in words. And these, as the book brings home, are the accents and thoughts of Charlotte Brontë herself, turning and returning to the times she sat there:

'Now I sit by myself—necessarily I am silent. I cannot help thinking of their last days, remembering their sufferings, and what they said and did, and how they looked in mortal affliction.'

'To sit in a lonely room—the clock ticking loud through a still house— and have open before the mind's eye the record of the last year, with its shocks, sufferings, losses—is a trial.' (ch. xvii)

(A syntax which could so easily have been anticlimactic—'is a trial' after more than thirty words—here incarnates an endurance.)

'I sat in my chair day after day, the saddest memories my only company. It was a time I shall never forget; but God sent it, and it must have been for the best.' (ch. xxiv)

Nor does the reader ever forget. And so to the loss of her, of her company, and 'the two sitting desolate and alone in the old grey house'—a sadly lucid paradox, the two who are alone, compounded by a sense of what obtained between the Revd Patrick Brontë and his little-welcomed son-in-law the Revd Arthur Nicholls.

Shivering, too, is a form of rippling, and it may be registered (observed whether noticed or not) in the tissue of the *Life*. The page which follows 'They sat, still and silent' has a personal memory of Charlotte Brontë by Gaskell which (memory within memory, 'I remember . . . [her] recalling') we too would do well to remember when the book later comes to pause, not to rest, for the last time:

But Emily was growing rapidly worse. I remember Miss Brontë's shiver at recalling the pang she felt when, after having searched in the little hollows and sheltered crevices of the moors for a lingering spray of heather—just one spray, however withered—to take in to Emily, she saw that the flower was not recognised by the dim and indifferent eyes. (ch. xvi)

'shiver . . . heather . . . however withered': or rather,

remember . . . shiver . . . shelter[ed] . . . linger[ing] . . . however withered . . . flower . . . indifferent

—this is the writer whose ways with words have been condescended to.

But this was not the only shiver which Gaskell witnessed: at Charlotte Brontë's visit to the Gaskells in Manchester, 'I saw a little shiver run from time to time over Miss Brontë's frame' (ch. xxvi). Soon the shiver was to overrun her frame:

She did not achieve this walk of seven or eight miles, in such weather, with impunity. She began to shiver soon after her return home, in spite of every precaution, and had a bad lingering sore throat and cold, which hung about her, and made her thin and weak. (ch. xxvii)

It is only two or three pages later that, chilled, we shiver in sympathy with those neighbours who did so in sympathy for the two intimates and for the one who had shivered so:

Early on Saturday morning, March 31st, the solemn tolling of Haworth church-bell spoke forth the fact of her death to the villagers who had known her from a child, and whose hearts shivered within them as they thought of the two sitting desolate and alone in the old grey house.

We too have known her from a child, thanks to the *Life*. And this without sentimentality. Even a moment which might have been suspect, so perfect are its cadences and its conclusion, is vindicated by a simple fact, an implicit reminder, which protects it against the exquisite. I am thinking of that earlier chapter-ending, when the schoolchild is glimpsed among her fellows:

And the girls talked of the little world around them, as if it were the only world there was; and had their opinions and their parties, and their fierce discussions like their elders—possibly, their betters. And among them, beloved and respected by all, laughed at occasionally by a few, but always to her face—lived, for a year and a half, the plain, short-sighted, oddly-dressed, studious little girl they called Charlotte Brontë. (ch. vi)

What strengthens, and saves from plangency, the conclusion, '. . . they called Charlotte Brontë', is the fact that in due course the world was to pass through calling her Currer Bell, and her intimates were to delight in her being called, though for all too short a date, C. B. Nicholls. Mrs Gaskell (and this is an occasion when for once it may be right to call *her* '*Mrs* Gaskell', rather than the 'E. C. Gaskell' which she preferred even when inscribing a copy of one of her books for her husband, the 'E. C. Gaskell' whom, since we have no difficulty in saying W. H. Auden and E. Nesbit—and A. S. Byatt, we too should prefer)—Mrs Gaskell refers to her as Mrs Nicholls, and the penultimate chapter draws to its close with those two last letters signed C. B. Nicholls.

The 'studious little girl they called Charlotte Brontë' had not enjoyed a girlhood. 'Beyond her years': it is a commonplace phrase which Gaskell commonly uses, but far from commonplacely.

Maria Brontë at 6 was 'grave, thoughtful, and quiet, to a degree far beyond her years' (ch. iii); but then it was reported of all the Brontë children that 'They were grave and silent beyond their years' (*grave* again; ch. iii); and Charlotte Brontë's 'loving assumption of duties beyond her years, made her feel considerably older than she really was' (ch. v). The melancholy precocity is deepened by the consciousness, which Charlotte Brontë felt (and which therefore Gaskell does not need to assert and need not be privilegedly knowing

about), that there is a darker sense to 'beyond her years', as there
would be to 'before her time': such years, such time, were probably
never going to be granted, were doubly 'beyond'. 'She looked a
little old woman', said Mary Taylor of her first glimpse of Charlotte
Brontë trying to glimpse things, at the age of 14 at Roe Head: 'She
looked a little old woman, so short-sighted that she always seemed
to be seeking something, and moving her head from side to side
to catch a sight of it' (ch. vi). She looked a little old woman, and
was never to be so. In later life (but she did not sufficiently enjoy
a later life), she knew the pathos of this, and characteristically declined
to soften it, at the age of 27, into self-pity: 'I have an idea that I
should be of no use there [at home]—a sort of aged person upon
the parish' (ch. xii). In March 1847, when she was nearly 31:

'I'll take care not to tell you next time, when I think I am looking specially
old and ugly; as if people could not have that privilege, without being
supposed to be at the last gasp! I shall be thirty-one next birthday. My
youth is gone like a dream; and very little use have I ever made of it. What
have I done these last thirty years? Precious little.' (ch. xvi)

It was for Gaskell to take up that word 'precious', and to protect
with it the self-punitive user of it. Gaskell's tact is entire; she remarks nothing, but a few lines later, the word is used to mean
indeed *precious* ('the precious remnants of his [Mr Brontë's] sight');
and another few lines later, the progress has been to the novel of
insight and blindness: 'In the intervals of such a life as this, "Jane
Eyre" was making progress.' *Not* 'precious little', then. But Gaskell's
courteous dissent from Charlotte Brontë's self-stricture with its modest
retorting of the word *is* precious. She was not forgetting one of the
letters which Charlotte Brontë wrote to her, which is given later in
the *Life*: 'You charge me to write about myself. What can I say on
that precious topic?' (ch. xxiv)

'Looking before and after' is a capability we all have, but aftersight
and foresight constituted unusually much of Charlotte Brontë's life
and, in consequence and with consequence, much of the *Life*. This
is the plight (the predicament and the troth) of any biographer, at
once blessed and cursed with aftersight such as only tactful foresight
can protect against the easy ironies of hindsight.

Especially when near death. It was one of the most odious features of the religious, or rather religiose, prose of the Revd Mr
Carus Wilson, of Cowan Bridge School (he issued in Mr Brocklehurst

of Lowood School), that he couched Christian insistences in such
a story as that of Edward, aged 5, dead of the bite of a mad dog:
'My dear young friends, how necessary it is to be prepared to die:
when Edward rose in the morning he little thought what would
happen to him. . . .'[4]

'Little thought' is a phrase to be used only after much thought,
with much delicacy and with no relish.

Chapter ii of the *Life* makes a good end:

> Into the midst of this lawless, yet not unkindly population, Mr. Brontë
> brought his wife and six little children, in February, 1820. There are those
> yet alive who remember seven heavily-laden carts lumbering slowly up the
> long stone street, bearing the 'new parson's' household goods to his future
> abode.
>
> One wonders how the bleak aspect of her new home—the low, oblong,
> stone parsonage, high up, yet with a still higher back-ground of sweeping
> moors—struck on the gentle, delicate wife, whose health even then was
> failing.

There, nothing is lumbering except those carts; nothing insists on
fusing the words 'his wife and six little children, in February, 1820',
with the immediately following words: 'There are those yet alive
who. . . .' The future ('*his* future abode') is known to the biographer,
as it is known to us (in ch. i we have just read—have already read—
the funeral inscriptions of the wife and of the six children, including
Charlotte Brontë), but there is nothing *knowing* about the biographer's writing, which is itself as 'gentle, delicate' as the wife whose
failing health bleakens the chapter's pausing close.

'One wonders . . .': the very sound (with its compassionate impersonality) allows Gaskell to respect that which must remain unknown,
a matter for wondering, in the midst of so much whose outcome
is all too clear.

But Winifred Gérin was ill-advised to end a paragraph of her life
of Gaskell with the hindsight of a sentence of death:

> Nothing could have been further from Elizabeth's thoughts than that the
> just-engaged Charlotte, aged thirty-eight, would be dead within the year.[5]

Gaskell herself bore all such prospects and retrospects in mind:

---

[4] Winifred Gérin, *Charlotte Brontë: The Evolution of Genius* (1967), p. 12.
[5] *Elizabeth Gaskell: A Biography* (1976), p. 149.

And it must likewise be borne in mind—by those who, surviving her, look back upon her life from their mount of observation—how no distaste, no suffering ever made her shrink from any course which she believed it to be her duty to engage in. (ch. x)

For a 'mount of observation' is too easy a place from which to speculate condescendingly.

So, on such occasions (a visit to London, two years before Charlotte Brontë's death, for instance), the wording which Gaskell responsibly needs is *one cannot but . . .* , with its acknowledged reluctance, its siege of contraries, its concession that here too (for the biographer as well as the subject) it would have been unutterably better if things could have been otherwise:

But looking back, with the knowledge of what was then the future, which Time has given, one cannot but imagine that there was a toning-down in preparation for the final farewell to these kind friends, whom she saw for the last time on a Wednesday morning in February. (ch. xxvi)

The first chapter of the *Life* comes to an end with that dread sequence of funeral inscriptions which tolled the story of the Revd Patrick Brontë, his wife, and his six children—every one of whom he had now survived. Gaskell avails herself of the unique force of the simple word *is*, at the introduction to the Revd Mr Brontë in the opening words of chapter iii: 'The Rev. Patrick Brontë is a native of the County Down in Ireland. . . . Even in his old age, Mr. Brontë is a striking-looking man, above the common height, with a nobly-shaped head, and erect carriage. In his youth he must have been unusually handsome.'

The first tablet-inscription commemorates his wife Maria, dead 'in the 39th year of her age' (words to be exacted again for Charlotte Brontë), with a text from St Matthew: 'Be ye also ready: for in such an hour as ye think not the Son of Man cometh.'

For the Brontës, though, the hour in which that agent of the Son of Man, the Angel of Death, might come was seldom 'such an hour as ye think not'. 'Nothing could have been further from Elizabeth [Gaskell]'s thoughts'? But except at rare moments, nothing could have been closer to Charlotte Brontë's.

It is Charlotte Brontë's own unremitting sense of the future which grants to her biographer, in loving sisterhood, the needed protection against the perils of *knowing all along*. It is more than a motif, it is a motivating energy, in the *Life* that Charlotte Brontë can so often be heard in it speaking of what the future is likely to be. Her wisdom she herself judged to reside in her 'sad presages' (ch. xxvii) even when these happily (too seldom) proved false. As she wrote— brief biographer herself—in the biographical notice of her sisters (which Gaskell quotes), on the dying of Emily, 'Affliction came in that shape which to anticipate is dread; to look back on grief' (ch. xvi). And a letter in 1849 sees with clear eyes the likelihoods for Anne: 'The thought of what may be to come grows more familiar to my mind; but it is a sad, dreary guest' (ch. xvii). Later, she is weighed upon by 'deep, heavy mental sadness, such as some would call *presentiment*—presentiment indeed it is, but not at all supernatural' (ch. xix).

> Presentiment—is that long Shadow—on the Lawn—
> Indicative that Suns go down—
>
> The Notice to the startled Grass
> That Darkness—is about to pass—

Quite early in the book (ch. vii), Gaskell contemplated the shadowed side and the shadowed faces within a portrait. The year is 1835 (Charlotte Brontë is 19), but because the subject is Branwell Brontë's ambition as painter, Gaskell avails herself of the biographer's prerogative and recalls a later moment (though this may seem an Irish way to put it) when she was shown one of his paintings during her visit to Haworth in 1853. But it is a moment, two years before Charlotte Brontë died, when (as Gaskell now recalls two years after the death) she, Elizabeth Gaskell, in looking at a painting, was looking into the future, hoping to glimpse for Charlotte Brontë such a prospect as she, Elizabeth Gaskell, now fully knows, and even then half-feared, would not come to pass.

But they all thought there could be no doubt about Branwell's talent for drawing. I have seen an oil painting of his, done I know not when, but probably about this time. It was a group of his sisters, life-size, three-quarters' length; not much better than sign-painting, as to manipulation; but the likenesses were, I should think, admirable. I could only judge of the fidelity with which the other two were depicted, from the striking resemblance which Charlotte, upholding the great frame of canvas, and consequently standing right behind it, bore to her own representation, though it must have been ten years and more since the portraits were taken. The picture was divided, almost in the middle, by a great pillar. On the side of the column which was lighted by the sun, stood Charlotte, in the womanly dress of that day of gigot sleeves and large collars. On the deeply shadowed side, was Emily, with Anne's gentle face resting on her shoulder. Emily's countenance struck me as full of power; Charlotte's of solicitude; Anne's of tenderness. The two younger seemed hardly to have attained their full growth, though Emily was taller than Charlotte; they had cropped hair, and a more girlish dress. I remember looking on those two sad, earnest shadowed faces, and wondering whether I could trace the mysterious expression which is said to foretell an early death. I had some fond superstitious hope that the column divided their fates from hers, who stood apart in the canvas, as in life she survived. I liked to see that the bright side of the pillar was towards *her*—that the light in the picture fell on *her*: I might more truly have sought in her presentment—nay, in her living face—for the sign of death in her prime. They were good likenesses, however badly executed. (ch. vii)

The language is alive to the principled 'manipulation' of the multiple stationings in time: the Victorian reader's present (but itself aspiring to future readerships, eyes yet unborn); the distant past of the painting's creation; the more recent past of its being shown to Gaskell at Haworth—and, within that recency, the hope of a future that was subsequently denied: '. . . who stood apart in the canvas, as in life she survived'. 'Survived': there is a dignified pathos in that past tense (within the past) which had been true enough but was not enough, was no longer true at the time of writing.

'I had some fond superstitious hope . . .'—*fond*, as at once foolish and loving. The hope was not just that Charlotte Brontë would live, but that the painting, dividing as it did her in sunlight from her shadowed sisters, augured this, promised it. In the sentence that immediately follows, Gaskell uses the words 'augured truly' (of Branwell's talents). And the word 'presentment'—'I might more truly have sought in her presentment . . .'—is perfectly judged, incomparably finer than *representation* (the sufficient word used earlier in the sequence) would have been here. I am thinking in part of *presentment*'s aptness to a Parsonage (*OED* 1), and of its sense of a 'mental perception' (such as we readers are being granted—*OED* 6), but mostly of its combining portraiture with dramatic representation (*OED* 5): Gaskell is painting a *scene* here, with Charlotte Brontë holding up the painting in which she and her sisters figure, and the union of the dramatic and the portrait senses may be clear in the tacit antithesis between 'the counterfeit presentment of two brothers' in *Hamlet* and this genuine presentment of three sisters by a brother.

Added to which there is the hesitating of 'presentment' upon the brink of 'presentiment'; it is impossible to read the sequence 'shadowed . . . trace . . . mysterious . . . foretell . . . superstitious . . . fates . . . sign . . . [with its beautiful development from 'not much better than sign-painting' earlier] . . . augured', and not feel that some pressure is put upon 'presentment' within the sequence to colour it with a word so important to Charlotte Brontë herself, in her letters and in her novels, as 'presentiment'.

This is the kind of achievement which should have rendered impossible the condescension which has long been visited upon the *Life*. Henry James should have known better:

> Were we touching upon her [Gaskell's] literary character at large, we should say that in her literary career as a whole she displayed, considering her success, a minimum of head. Her career was marked by several little literary indiscretions, which show how much writing was a matter of pure feeling with her. Her 'Life of Miss Brontë,' for instance, although a very readable and delightful book, is one which a woman of strong head could not possibly have written; for, full as it is of fine qualities, of affection, of generosity, of sympathy, of imagination, it lacks the prime requisites of a good biography.[6]

Wrong. There are in a biography no requisites as prime as affection, generosity, sympathy, and imagination. This, from the author of *William Wetmore Story and His Friends*, who manages to find 'delightful' the tragic poignancy of the *Life*. And writing was not 'a matter of pure feeling with her', because this, the greatest of her books, incarnates the principle which T. S. Eliot expressed, 'a recognition of the truth that not our feelings, but the pattern which we may make of our feelings, is the centre of value'.[7]

There is more than one height from which Gaskell may be treated *de haut en bas*. There is, for instance, the height of professional priority. In a work called *Writing a Woman's Life* (1988), Carolyn Heilbrun has judged that the following two sentences constitute a sufficient account of the *Life of Charlotte Brontë*:

> Elizabeth Gaskell, until recently the most salient of female biographers, did not celebrate Charlotte Brontë's genius, but rescued her from the stigma

---

[6] *Nation*, 22 February 1866.

[7] 'A Brief Introduction to the Method of Paul Valéry', *Le Serpent* (1924).

of being a famous female writer, an eccentric. Carefully, Gaskell restored
Brontë to the safety of womanliness.[8]

As if that rare thing, a biography which is a true work of art (nobly
praised by G. H. Lewes—whom Charlotte Brontë had not spared—
for its 'artistic power'), would have ceased to be 'salient' because
of a political shift within a branch of the academic profession.

In the fourth paragraph of the *Life*, Gaskell introduces, perfectly
simply, a simple deep word of the greatest importance to Charlotte
Brontë and therefore to her biographer: *disappointment*.

> In a town one does not look for vivid colouring; what there may be of
> this is furnished by the wares in the shops, not by foliage or atmospheric
> effects; but in the country some brilliancy and vividness seems to be in-
> stinctively expected, and there is consequently a slight feeling of disap-
> pointment at the grey neutral tint of every object, near or far off, on the
> way from Keighley to Haworth.

It would be idle to list all the occasions on which the 'cruel chill
of disappointment'—with its cognates and neighbours (*hope*, for
instance)—is felt by Brontë or by Gaskell. The *Life* is steeped in
disappointment. Yet, in some ways, unexpectedly so. For, first, the
sufferings of Charlotte Brontë and of the entire family were so intense and immense as to make the thought of *disappointment*, one
would think, fall cruelly short. When, one by one, your mother,
your four sisters, and your brother die, what comes to mind, and
to heart, might not be disappointment.

Second, pressing from the opposite direction, the story of Charlotte Brontë's life as an artist, for all her personal tragedy, is one
of achievement and success, not of disappointment: her triumph in
writing great novels, in having them (against all-but-all odds) published and immediately recognized as such, and (supremely) her
effecting her greatest work in her last novel, *Villette*.

Next, the hopelessness of Charlotte Brontë might be thought to
be incompatible with disappointment; to have ceased to hope, or
(more) to be constitutionally incapable of it, might be expected to
have at least this consolatory power: 'So farewell Hope, and with
Hope farewell Fear'—including the fear of disappointment.

Disappointment asks thought. But then so does hope, which Wittgenstein pondered à propos the forming of an adult and of a life:

[8] p. 22.

Someone says: 'Man hopes.' How should this phenomenon of natural history be described?—One might observe a child and wait until one day he manifests hope; and then one could say 'Today he hoped for the first time'. But surely that sounds queer! Although it would be quite natural to say 'Today he said "I hope" for the first time'. And why queer?—One does not say that a suckling hopes that . . . , but one does say it of a grown-up.— Well, bit by bit daily life becomes such that there is a place for hope in it.[9]

Did, bit by bit, daily life become for Charlotte Brontë such that there was a place for hope in it? Rather the reverse?

Of Charlotte Brontë and her correspondence at 16, Gaskell writes:

In looking over the earlier portion of this correspondence, I am struck afresh by the absence of hope, which formed such a strong characteristic in Charlotte. At an age when girls, in general, look forward to an eternal duration of such feelings as they or their friends entertain, and can there-fore see no hindrance to the fulfilment of any engagements dependent on the future state of the affections, she is surprised that 'E.' [Ellen Nussey] keeps her promise to write. In after-life, I was painfully impressed with the fact, that Miss Brontë never dared to allow herself to look forward with hope; that she had no confidence in the future; and I thought, when I heard of the sorrowful years she had passed through, that it had been this pressure of grief which had crushed all buoyancy of expectation out of her. But it appears from the letters, that it must have been, so to speak, constitutional; or, perhaps, the deep pang of losing her two elder sisters combined with a permanent state of bodily weakness in producing her hopelessness. If her trust in God had been less strong, she would have given way to unbounded anxiety, at many a period of her life. As it was, we shall see, she made a great and successful effort to leave 'her times in His hands.' (ch. vii)

This passage is the nub of the book's understanding of Charlotte Brontë, an understanding inseparable from its imaginative intelli-gence and principled puzzlement about her searchability and un-searchability. The sense of this characterization stands in no need of comment, but some of its details ask attention.

For instance, the reference, twice, to 'looking forward to' (in a passage which ends with 'we shall see'—there is a play of aftersight and foresight in the sequence 'As it was, we shall see, . . .')—the words *look forward to* might make us think more than is our habit about this phrase and its asymmetry.

[9] *Remarks on the Philosophy of Psychology*, ed. G. H. von Wright and Heikki Nyman, trans. C. G. Luckhardt and M. A. E. Aue (1980), ii 4e–5e.

For the process by which 'look forward to' has come to describe an act of trust and hope is one which incarnates a modern trusting hopefulness about life, the sort of hopefulness which Samuel Beckett rebuked with his dark gnome that everything will be all right if nothing foreseen crops up. (As valuably styptic as the unexpected alerting in the remark that 'He was the most even-tempered man I ever knew, he was always angry'.)

George Eliot's Casaubon can write, in a letter, of 'looking forward to an unfavourable possibility' (see p. 207). But to 'look forward' has come to mean, not just to look into the future, 'to look ahead', but 'to look expectantly towards the future or to a coming event'—and even the *OED*'s word 'expectantly' underrates the hopefully trusting expression on the face of the phrase. Contrast the usage of 1816, straightforward, untilted towards hope or fear: 'Like chess-players, they seem always to look three moves forward' (where we should now say 'ahead'), with the hopeful sense of Foote in 1768: 'Banish your fears, and let us look forward, my love', and of Disraeli in 1837: 'His visit to the hall was looked forward to with interest.' Sometimes the phrase can be disconcertingly equivocal, since the plain sense of the phrase can never quite be extirpated by the hopeful one: as with Jowett in 1875: 'He looks forward to all future systems sharing the fate of the past.'

Gaskell says of the young that they 'look forward to an eternal duration of such feelings'; but she is aware that the phrase does not necessarily, upon reflection, contain its own internal prop; hence her adding two words next time: 'Miss Brontë never dared to allow herself to look forward with hope.'

The opposite of the brightened 'looking forward' is the darkened 'apprehension'. Charlotte Brontë herself brings out how 'looking forward' could not be other than dark for her:

'It is not right to anticipate evil, and to be always looking forward with an apprehensive spirit; but I think grief is a two-edged sword, it cuts both ways; the memory of one loss is the anticipation of another.' (ch. xxi)

She would wish (or, in her own robust turn, 'I could like . . .') to be able to trust the phrase, which comes often to her pen, but though she can say simply 'I look forward to spring as the period when you will fulfil your promise of coming to visit me', she must elsewhere use the words differently: 'I look forward to to-morrow with a mixture of impatience and anxiety' (ch. xxvii). So the crux for her is this discipline: 'I avoid looking forward or backward, and try to keep looking upward. This is not the time to regret, dread, or weep' (ch. xvii).

The progressivist phrase 'look forward' is not to be trusted, for the reason which is intimated by Gaskell's conclusion to her consummate paragraph: 'As it was, we shall see, she made a great and successful effort to leave "her times in His hands"'.

'If her trust in God had been less strong. . . .' Psalm 31: 'But I trusted in thee, O Lord: I said, Thou art my God. My times are in thy hand.'

Charlotte Brontë and Elizabeth Gaskell had different allegiances within their religion, but they were unremittingly at one in their trust that their times were in His hands. The *Life of Charlotte Brontë* is a masterpiece of religious literature, which is one reason for its being found insufficiently 'salient' at a time when all of life is supposed to be seen only under a political aspect. The strength of its religious convictions—shared by author and subject—is bent upon an understanding that disappointment is strengthless unless braced.

Against what can the secularist brace the word, the concept, 'disappointment'? It has no antonym. There is no word to describe the sense of hopes or expectations fulfilled which will do for us what the word 'disappointment' will do for hopes or expectations unfulfilled, balked. We can cobble something up phrasally (with the help of *gratified, pleased, satisfied, elated,* and so on), but nothing can give us the satisfying singleness of a positive which would be the antithetical counterpart to the negative 'disappointment'. Here, in 'disappointment', we have a ubiquitous state of mind and of heart, entirely caught for us within the one word, for which we cannot find a fitting counterword.

Henry James tried conscientiously hereabouts, setting forth on *A Little Tour of France* (1900):

We enjoyed that sensation with which the conscientious tourist is—or ought to be—well acquainted and for which, at any rate, he has a formula in his rough-and-ready language. We 'experienced,' as they say (most irregular of verbs), an 'agreeable disappointment.' We were surprised and delighted; we had for some reason suspected that Loches was scarce good. (ch. x)

Agreeable disappointment was seldom appointed for Charlotte Brontë. 'And as to disappointment, why, all must suffer disappointment at some period or other of their lives' (ch. x).

The *Life of Charlotte Brontë* is our literature's greatest study in disappointment because it realizes—makes real—that the concept of disappointment is feeble or null unless it is braced against *appointment*. That is, unless it accepts the faith wrung from Gaskell, and constituting her shortest and most bowed paragraph, when, immediately after withdrawing from Charlotte Brontë's married life ('And we thought, and we hoped, and we prophesied, in our great love and reverence'), the ensuing paragraph of chapter xxvii says with simple entirety:

But God's ways are not as our ways!

Gaskell may speak so because Brontë had done so:

'At first, I could not say "Thy will be done!" I felt rebellious, but I knew it was wrong to feel so. Being left a moment alone this morning, I prayed fervently to be enabled to resign myself to *every* decree of God's will, though it should be dealt forth by a far severer hand than the present disappointment.' (ch. viii)

It is God's appointing will which gives substance to the thought of disappointment.

There is an odious Victorian anthology of *Children's Sayings*, edited by William Canton (1900), among them this (p. 105):

An embryo divine, of six years, remarked, 'Father, you said in your sermon that *our* disappointments are *God's* appointments, but *I* think that *our* appointments are sometimes *God's* disappointments.'

This mawkish moment is a travesty of that upon which Charlotte Brontë and E. C. Gaskell concurred. Their authenticity necessarily mixes with concurrence a courteous dissent.

We talked about the different courses through which life ran. She said, in her own composed manner, as if she had accepted the theory as a fact, that she believed some were appointed beforehand to sorrow and much disappointment; that it did not fall to the lot of all—as Scripture told us— to have their lines fall in pleasant places; that it was well for those who had rougher paths, to perceive that such was God's will concerning them, and try to moderate their expectations, leaving hope to those of a different doom, and seeking patience and resignation as the virtues they were to cultivate. I took a different view: I thought that human lots were more equal than she imagined; that to some happiness and sorrow came in strong patches of light and shadow (so to speak), while in the lives of others they were pretty equally blended throughout. She smiled, and shook her head, and said she was trying to school herself against ever anticipating any pleasure; that it was better to be brave and submit faithfully; there was some good reason, which we should know in time, why sorrow and disappointment were to be the lot of some on earth. It was better to acknowledge this, and face out the truth in a religious faith. (ch. xxvii)

'Some were appointed beforehand to sorrow', 'sorrow and disappointment'. It is a lovely evocation of sisterhood in concern and grief, and the more so in that Gaskell says—needs to say—nothing of her own sorrows; she too had known what it was to be motherless in earliest childhood, and she had suffered as, in one respect, Charlotte Brontë, like her brother and sisters, never had to suffer: she suffered the deaths of two of her children, 'the never ending sorrow'. So this is not (as Gaskell's self-abnegating calmness might honourably suggest) a conversation between two people only one of whom has had to know the rougher places. 'We talked about the different courses through which life ran': but not *so* different, even if Gaskell would have been the first to concede that her lines had fallen in pleasanter places than had Charlotte Brontë's.

'To some happiness and sorrow came in strong patches of light and shadow (so to speak).' Gaskell had spoken so, and we remember the pictured light and shadow which she had pictured for us. 'On the side of the column which was lighted by the sun, stood Charlotte.' 'On the deeply shadowed side, was Emily.' 'I remember looking on those two sad, earnest shadowed faces, and wondering. . . .'

Chapter vii of the *Life* ends with the words of a letter (6 July 1835), and within them the lines of Scripture, quoted, in both senses, happily:

'Emily and I leave home on the 27th of this month; the idea of being together consoles us both somewhat, and, truth, since I must enter a situation, "My lines have fallen in pleasant places." I both love and respect Miss W——.'

This line of Scripture often came to Charlotte Brontë's mind and support and even rescue. Or rather, those lines, for there was asked great faith of her, and in her, to meet with courage Psalm 16, where the thought is ensconced within insistences upon 'inheritance' and 'heritage', words which could too much be alive with bitter family irony for Charlotte Brontë:

The Lord is the portion of mine inheritance and of my cup: thou maintainest my lot.

> The lines are fallen unto me in pleasant places; yea, I have
> a goodly heritage.

The phrase is a haunting one, not least in its being so clear and so not-quite-clarifiable: the *OED* glosses 'lines' (4c): 'Appointed lot in life. In echoes of Ps. xvi. 6, where the reference seems to be to the marking out of land for a dwelling place.' The pressure of 'appointed lot in life' is what shapes Charlotte Brontë's emending the phrase when (in a letter about *Villette* given later in the *Life*) she turned towards, not her powerlessness as a creature, but her power as a creator:

> 'If Lucy marries anybody, it must be the Professor—a man in whom there is much to forgive, much to "put up with." But I am not leniently disposed towards Miss *Frost* [Miss Snowe]: from the beginning, I never meant to appoint her lines in pleasant places.' (ch. xxv)

'The lines are fallen unto me in pleasant places': 'I never meant to appoint her lines in pleasant places.' The appointing partakes of God's prerogative, and it gives substance to the void of disappointment.

The contrast might be with the blandness of the biblical phrase as it is released by Leslie Stephen to close a section in *The Life of Sir James Fitzjames Stephen* (2nd edn, 1895, p. 358): 'Nobody could have been cheerier, more resolute, or more convinced that his lines had fallen in pleasant places.'

'As far as she could see, her life was ordained to be lonely, and she must subdue her nature to her life, and, if possible, bring the two into harmony' (ch. xxiv). She did it, heroically, in her life; Gaskell, subduing herself (the book has learnt much from Charlotte Brontë in self-denial), did it in her *Life*, where she gave body to the thoughts which she couched in a letter to John Greenwood (5 May 1855), two months after Charlotte Brontë died:

> I know how great a trial her loss must be to you in some measure. But remember how brave *she* was, all through her many sorrows; and to whom she always looked as the Sender both of Sunshine & of Storm. She was a wonderful creature, & her life was wonderfully appointed; full of suffering as it was.[10]

A wonderful creature is one who acknowledges the Creator and his wonders, and one for whom disappointment is swallowed up in the appointed.

[10] *The Letters of Mrs. Gaskell*, p. 343.

If 'disappointment' is the single word, the singular word, which stands at the heart of the *Life*, what surrounds it, and presses upon it from many directions, is an atmosphere of pressure. Gaskell, in that crucial paragraph on 'the absence of hope', speaks within the one sentence both of being herself 'painfully impressed' by Charlotte Brontë's hopelessness and of 'this pressure of grief which had crushed all buoyancy of expectation out of her'. Hope is a pressure.

There is hardly a page of the book which does not speak, either in Charlotte Brontë's words or in its own, of pressure of some sort: pressure, oppression, repression, suppression, expression, impression, depression. This last is ubiquitous, and now asks an effort of historical imagination since 'depressed' and 'depression' have become both trivialized and professionalized. The force of all such words is evident enough, though often, once again, they present themselves as no more than literal, as in the letters of the memorial inscription at the end of chapter i:

At the upper end of this tablet ample space is allowed between the lines of the inscription; when the first memorials were written down, the survivors, in their fond affection, thought little of the margin and verge they were leaving for those who were still living.[11] But as one dead member of the household follows another fast to the grave, the lines are pressed together, and the letters become small and cramped. After the record of Anne's death, there is room for no other.

So ends the paragraph, as if there were room for no other. 'After the first death there is no other.' Yet there was already, by the date of Gaskell's writing, and recorded here by her, another tablet, for Charlotte Brontë.

'The survivors, in their fond affection, thought little of the margin and verge . . .': the aftersight is not contaminated by 'little did they think'.

In this unpleasant place, 'the lines are pressed together'. Not 'The lines are fallen unto me in pleasant places'.

The *Life* brings home to us 'the pressure of difficulties', the 'pressure of school', 'the pressure of starvation and misery', 'the pressure of grief', 'the constant pressure of misery', 'the pressure of worldly interests', the 'constant pressure of anxiety', 'the gnawing pressure of daily-recurring cares'.

[11] How poignantly 'leaving' turns to 'living'.

'Now and then, the silence of the house, the solitude of the room, has pressed on me with a weight I found it difficult to bear, and recollection has not failed to be as alert, poignant, obtrusive, as other feelings were languid. I attribute this state of things partly to the weather.' (ch. xix)

—pure Charlotte Brontë, in the unvisionary resilience which can repel ('difficult to bear', not impossible) but cannot dispel—

'I attribute this state of things partly to the weather. Quicksilver invariably falls low in storms, and high winds, and I have ere this been warned of approaching disturbance in the atmosphere by a sense of bodily weakness, and deep, heavy mental sadness, such as some would call *presentiment*,— presentiment indeed it is, but not at all supernatural. . . .'

But against these ugly pressures, the *Life* sets and shares Charlotte Brontë's vision of all such suppressions and repressions as are noble. For this she finds herself deprecated these days by the enlightened, the heirs of those in whose writing on the emancipation of women she herself found a sad hiatus: 'What is this hiatus? I think I know; and, knowing, I will venture to say. I think the writer forgets there is such a thing as self-sacrificing love and disinterested devotion' (ch. xxiv).

The *Life of Charlotte Brontë* makes the most extraordinarily diverse and humane use of *first impressions*: Gaskell's own, and everybody else's, of Charlotte Brontë, and Charlotte Brontë's own. This, despite her not much trusting her first impressions of other people and not much liking other people's first impressions of her.

'I distinctly recollect your account of Emily's appearance & manners—but I forget what you said was the first impression made by Charlotte on any casual observer,' Gaskell wrote in a letter of enquiry.[12] Chapter i describes the first impression made by Haworth; chapter ii begins by speaking of 'her own and her sisters' first impressions of human life'; and the impress of this, throughout the book, stamps itself upon such a characteristic citation as this:

I find, in a letter to a distant friend, written about this time, a retrospect of her visit to London. It is too ample to be considered as a mere repetition of what she had said before; and, besides, it shows that her first impressions of what she saw and heard were not crude and transitory, but stood the tests of time and afterthought. (ch. xxiv)

---

[12] *The Letters of Mrs. Gaskell*, p. 406, to Laetitia Wheelwright, 22 August 1856.

Yet not everything in the first edition of the *Life* stood the tests of time and afterthought.

For there are bad and good forms of pressure and of suppression. Gaskell was herself famously required to suppress: prior to publication, any revelation of Charlotte Brontë's intensely unrequited passion for M. Heger; and following publication of the first edition, in reconsideration of the Revd William Carus Wilson and Cowan Bridge School; of Mrs Robinson (later Lady Scott) and the seduction-destruction of Branwell Brontë; and of the violent and extreme domestic ways of the Revd Patrick Brontë.

The case of Mr Carus Wilson she handled with typical firmness: where she was persuaded that she had misrepresented conditions at Cowan Bridge (had too much identified it with Lowood School, too much trusting to Charlotte Brontë's bitter memories), she mitigated her strictures. Locally revised, these chapters continue to tell the same story, and the book is the better for that. For it is not just a true story, but was told truly, with grievance subordinated to grief.

Yet, contrary to one's usual sense of these things, the book is also the better for the substantial rescindings which were pressed upon Gaskell, by the threat of litigation in the case of Mrs Robinson and by the slowly-dawning charge of injustice from the Revd Mr Brontë.

For Gaskell, as a novelist and consequently as a biographer, was prone to melodrama.

'The dramatic value of the ruin of Branwell Brontë to the story of his sister's life', Winifred Gérin has written, 'was apparent from the first to her biographer, who was, it must never be overlooked, before all else a novelist with a strong sense of drama and pathos'.[13] But the trouble with the 'ruin' of Branwell was that it had, not dramatic value, but melodramatic valuelessness. And, irrespective of the truth of the case, the false accents of melodrama proved all too audible here.

The legal and evidential objections to the presentation of the Mrs Robinson story (seducing the tutor), and of the father's eccentricities (burning boots, banning meat, shooting pistols, and shredding clothes—all these anecdotes deriving from gossip and subsequently needing to be 'remedied', in Gaskell's word), proved happily to be at one with an artistic objection—an objection which Gaskell probably never recognized intrinsically, and would not have heeded had

---

[13] *Elizabeth Gaskell*, p. 167.

her hand not been forced. Better, though, to have a forced hand than to have forced it oneself, into a forced style.

The woman—to think of her father's pious name—the blood of honourable families mixed in her veins—her early home, underneath whose rooftree sat those whose names are held saintlike for their good deeds,—she goes flaunting about to this day in respectable society; a showy woman for her age; kept afloat by her reputed wealth. I see her name in county papers, as one of those who patronize the Christmas balls; and I hear of her in London drawing-rooms. Now let us read not merely of the suffering of her guilty accomplice, but of the misery she caused to innocent victims, whose premature deaths may, in part, be laid at her door. (ch. xiii)[14]

He died! she lives still,—in May Fair. The Eumenides, I suppose, went out of existence at the time when the wail was heard, 'Great Pan is dead.' I think we could better have spared him than those awful Sisters who sting dead conscience into life.

I turn from her for ever. (ch. xvi)[15]

The artistic objection to this is not only that it is as unjust to someone travestied as a middle-aged married seductress called Mrs Robinson as was the film *The Graduate* (though it is) but that it is unjust to those mortal sisters who ask no capital letter, and particularly to Charlotte Brontë, whose tragedy stands in no need of having the Eumenides machinated in. Another way of putting the same point is that Gaskell's accents here are betrayingly at one with those of the victimized self-destructive Branwell Brontë himself.

Mary Taylor, the most humanely intransigent of Charlotte Brontë's friends, deplored Gaskell's revision: 'As to the mutilated edition that is to come, I am sorry for it. Libellous or not, the first edition was all true'—but even she was moved at once to add: 'and except the declamation [on Mrs Robinson] all, in my opinion, useful to be published.'[16] But it is not useful to a biography to publish untruths, or to publish that which, even if true, does not ring true, that which moves a biographer to be more declamatory, less *intelligent* than is her wont, in the sense which William Empson threw off, with inspired casualness, when he spoke of Aristotle and Copernicus as

---

[14] Dropped from the third edition; quoted here from Alan Shelston, the first edition, vol. i, ch. xiii.

[15] Dropped from the third edition; quoted from Alan Shelston, the first edition, vol. ii, ch. ii.

[16] Gérin, *Charlotte Brontë*, p. 575.

'more intelligent (less at the mercy of their own notions)', than had been supposed.[17]

Editorial reinstatements are now all the thing, it being tenderly supposed that any artistic decisions that were arrived at in respect of external contingencies (publishers' readers, or threats of litigation) constitute a form of censorship, a misguidance such as can belatedly be resisted and rectified. But in the case of the *Life of Charlotte Brontë*, the third edition is—*pace* the modern editor Alan Shelston—to be preferred, not only as newly including some of the most poignant reminiscences by, for one, Mary Taylor herself, but as newly *exclud*-ing all the throbbing melodrama, and thereby leaving the true drama of Charlotte Brontë and her family free to be felt.

What makes this a matter of central pertinence to the book, and not just of local loss and gain, is the susceptibility of Charlotte Brontë herself. Early in the *Life*, we hear the letter of 1833 (she was 16) in which she describes a character in Scott's *Kenilworth* as 'certainly the personification of consummate villainy'. Gaskell remarks this:

she, knowing nothing of the world, both from her youth and her isolated position, has yet been so accustomed to hearing 'human nature' discussed, as to receive the notion of intense and artful villainy without surprise. (ch. vii)

The surprise is Gaskell's. But if the young Charlotte Brontë received the notion of villainy without surprise, in her mature art she re-ceived it with two-edged vigilance, and by 1847 she took seriously the allied admonition of G. H. Lewes: 'You warn me to beware of melodrama': 'If I ever *do* write another book, I think I will have nothing of what you call "melodrama"' (ch. xvi).

In its 'nothing *of what you call . . .*', this is immitigably Charlotte Brontë, exactly that for which she is not only honoured but loved; and the more so in that the sentence continues: 'I think I will have nothing of what you call "melodrama"; I *think* so, but I am not sure.' For she is quick to see that a narrow imagination might deplore as melodrama anything beyond its passional ken. She therefore makes no promises, but what she evinces is at once a scepticism as to melodrama and a scepticism as to those who too promptly and pejoratively invoke the word.

The essential criticism, then, of the lurid pictures of parlour life

[17] (1930); *Argufying*, ed. John Haffenden (1987), pp. 531–2.

at the Parsonage and of drawing-room life in London, is not just their being untrue but their being false, audibly false. As can be heard if we juxtapose Gaskell's tones there with one of her own juxtapositions elsewhere. Gaskell on the wrongdoer:

> The story must be told. If I could, I would have avoided it; but not merely is it so well-known to many living as to be, in a manner, public property, but it is possible that, by revealing the misery, the gnawing, life-long misery, the degrading habits, the early death of her partner in guilt— the acute and long-enduring agony of his family—to the wretched woman, who not only survives, but passes about in the gay circles of London society, as a vivacious, well-dressed, flourishing widow, there may be awakened in her some feelings of repentance.[18]

Set against this, first, Charlotte Brontë at sweet-ish 17, to a friend who had tasted London society:

> 'Few girls would have done as you have done—would have beheld the glare, and glitter, and dazzling display of London with dispositions so unchanged, heart so uncontaminated. I see no affectation in your letters, no trifling, no frivolous contempt of plain, and weak admiration of showy persons and things.' (ch. vii)

And second, the great Gaskell, who is immediately to be heard, not in orotund rebuke of Mrs Robinson, but in respectful banter of Charlotte Brontë. For, commenting directly on this youthful melo-dramatization, the biographer shows a heart so uncontaminated here by melodrama:

> In these days of cheap railway trips, we may smile at the idea of a short visit to London having any great effect upon the character, whatever it may have upon the intellect. But her London—her great apocryphal city— was the 'town' of a century before, to which giddy daughters dragged unwilling papas, or went with injudicious friends, to the detriment of all their better qualities, and sometimes to the ruin of their fortunes; it was the Vanity Fair of the 'Pilgrim's Progress' to her.

This has all Gaskell's 'better qualities', ideally complementary to Charlotte Brontë's young self: humour, sympathy, shrewdness. Gaskell's next sentence distinguishes Charlotte Brontë's throbbing vibrancy from her more characteristic authenticity of judgement: 'But see the admirable sense with which she can treat a subject of

---

[18] Dropped from the third edition; quoted here from Alan Shelston, the first edition, vol. i, ch. xiii.

which she is able to overlook [survey] all the bearings.' In its own admirable sense, Gaskell's commentary constitutes the essential critique of her exorbitant dealings elsewhere with the 'apocryphal' story of the 'ruin' wrought by Lydia Robinson.

It would not make sense to say of Gaskell that she knew too much to argue or to judge. But the judgements to which the Mrs Robinson/Branwell Brontë entanglement moved her were not ones which she could *authenticate* to herself or to others.

Let her live and flourish! He died, his pockets filled with her letters, which he had carried perpetually about his person, in order that he might read them as often as he wished. He lies dead; and his doom is only known to God's mercy. When I think of him, I change my cry to heaven. Let her live and repent! That same mercy is infinite.

This is presumptuous; it affects not to know God's mercy, but it all too assuredly knows its own justice, and the book—in its third edition—is better without it. For the conviction that E. C. Gaskell's *Life of Charlotte Brontë* is one of the great biographies and for many of us the greatest life of a woman by a woman, magnificently magnanimous, is grounded elsewhere: where, for instance, an initial unclamorous act of judgement proceeds, not to a changed cry to heaven, but to changed accents to others and to oneself:

It is true that he [the Revd Patrick Brontë] had strong and vehement prejudices, and was obstinate in maintaining them, and that he was not dramatic enough in his perceptions to see how miserable others might be in a life that to him was all-sufficient. But I do not pretend to be able to harmonize points of character, and account for them, and bring them all into one consistent and intelligible whole. The family with whom I have now to do shot their roots down deeper than I can penetrate. I cannot measure them, much less is it for me to judge them. (ch. iii)

FROUDE'S CARLYLE

E. C. Gaskell's *Life of Charlotte Brontë* was originally published as one work in two volumes, and so was Hallam Tennyson's *Alfred Lord Tennyson: A Memoir*. James Anthony Froude's Carlyle, though, must stand as another story, or rather as stories told seriatim. The series comes to variegate all of which it is composed; and the opportunities and perils of aftersight and foresight are alive here, not within a single biography but within a body of biographical works, constituting —as first issued—eleven volumes in all. The Froude/Carlyle controversy has always proved addictive; additive is the nature of Froude's great editorial and biographical enterprise.

Carlyle died, at the age of 85, in February 1881.

One month later, there appeared in two volumes Carlyle's *Reminiscences*, edited by Froude, and consisting of four memorial characterizations by Carlyle: of his father, James Carlyle, written in the month of his father's death, January 1832; of the preacher Edward Irving (died 1834), written in 1866–7; of the critic and judge-advocate Francis Jeffrey (died 1850), written in 1867; and of Jane Welsh Carlyle (died 1866), written from 1866 and in 1869.

It was the death of his wife which precipitated Carlyle's reminiscences of Irving (whom she had loved and who had loved her) and of Jeffrey (whose affection was returned by her): 'It was her connection with them that chiefly impelled me.' Carlyle's direct memories of Jane Welsh Carlyle comprise almost half of the total pages, and she is recurrently the focus of the other reminiscences, including that of Carlyle's father.

Carlyle had not been clear about publication, but Froude was (fortunately, since the *Reminiscences* must be one of Carlyle's best books):

'In the ancient county town of Haddington, July 14, 1801, there was born' [etc.]

These are the words in which Mr. Carlyle commenced an intended sketch of his wife's history, three years after she had been taken from him; but finding the effort too distressing, he passed over her own letters, with notes and recollections which he had written down immediately after her death, directing me as I have already stated [in the preface to volume i] either to destroy them, or arrange and publish them, as I might think good. I told him afterwards that before I could write any biography either of Mrs. Carlyle or himself, I thought that these notes ought to be printed in the shape in which he had left them, being adjusted merely into some kind of order. He still left me to my own discretion; on myself therefore the responsibility rests entirely for their publication.[1]

Froude had begun his biography of Carlyle while his friend and master yet lived—a particular day in 1880 is specified near the end of the early life: 'at the moment when I am writing these words (June 27, 1880)'.[2] So with promptitude there could be published in March 1882 the two volumes of *Thomas Carlyle: A History of the First Forty Years of His Life 1795–1835*. But what next followed was importantly not the last two volumes of the biography, but the three volumes of the *Letters and Memorials of Jane Welsh Carlyle*, published exactly a year later in March 1883. The conclusion of the biography, *Thomas Carlyle: A History of His Life in London 1834–1881*, appeared in October 1884.

To these works in nine volumes should be added two outriders: Carlyle's *Reminiscences of My Irish Journey in 1849*, which Froude lightly edited and which was published in 1882; and *My Relations with Carlyle*, which Froude wrote in self-defence in 1887 when he was being defamed, and which was posthumously published by his vindicating children in 1903.

The main sequence, then, intercalates the writing of the Carlyles, edited by Froude, with Froude's own writing: first, Carlyle's *Reminiscences*; then *The First Forty Years of His Life*; next, Jane Welsh Carlyle's *Letters and Memorials*; then *His Life in London*. Froude had wished to complete his biographical work before his second editorial task: he said in a letter in 1881, '*Mrs Carlyle's* letters are a far more difficult problem. . . . I *ought* to write and publish *his* Life before I publish them, but this too Mary Carlyle's action has complicated' (she being Carlyle's niece and Froude's opponent).[3] But the order which was not of his making proved to be the making of his art, its ordonnance.

For Froude (and for everyone not blinded by Froudophobia), the most important experience of Carlyle's life, the one which gave tragic shape and tragic depth to his life, was the recognition, forced

---

[1] *Reminiscences by Thomas Carlyle*, ed. James Anthony Froude (1881), ii 69–70.

[2] *Thomas Carlyle: A History of the First Forty Years of His Life 1795–1835*, by James Anthony Froude (1882), ii 356.

[3] Waldo Hilary Dunn, *James Anthony Froude: A Biography* (1961–3), ii 490–1.

upon him, at the age of 70, by reading his wife's journal and letters after her death at 65, of how profoundly unhappy she had been and of how much he was to blame. Carlyle's remorse came to constitute not only his present and his future (he was to live, against his will, for another fifteen years) but the aspect under which he viewed all his past. The aftersight seared his eyeballs. But because it lacerated Carlyle to a humanity which had not hitherto been his, it opened Froude's eyes to Carlyle's central self—and to Froude's own central self. So Froude saw it, in *My Relations with Carlyle*:

He had seemed to me like a person apart from the rest of the world, with the mask of destiny upon him, to whom one could not feel exactly as towards a brother mortal. Another side of his character was now opened to me—the agony of his remorse for a long series of faults which now for the first time he saw in their true light. For the next four years I never walked with him without his recurring to a subject which was never absent from his mind. His conversation, however it opened, always drifted back into a pathetic cry of sorrow over things which were now irreparable. It was at once piteous and noble; for it was manifest that his faults, whatever they had been (and I did not then know completely what they had been), were no faults in his real nature. A repentance so deep and so passionate showed that the real nature was as beautiful as his intellect had been magnificent. He was still liable to his fits of temper. He was still scornful and overbearing and wilful; but it had become possible to love him— indeed, impossible not to love him.[4]

Of his dead father, Carlyle had written immediately: 'He "had finished the work that was given him to do" and finished it (very greatly more than the most) as became a man. He was summoned too before he had ceased to be interesting—to be loveable.'[5] Carlyle never ceased to be interesting, and he himself was not summoned before he had ceased to be *un*loveable. He had never failed to love his wife, but he had often failed in his love for her. The loss of her gained him his soul.

This well-attested story is manifest from the biography itself and from everything which Froude said about it. But remorse proved to be the aspect not only under which Carlyle viewed his life but under which Froude wrote the Life, detailed it and shaped it.

Imaginative tact was fostered in the biographer by the sequence of the volumes in the vast and patient enterprise. For before the

[4] (1903), p. 12.   [5] *Reminiscences*, i 4–5.

literary world came to read, in Froude's telling in the closing volumes, the story of Carlyle's remorse, there had already been granted
a preliminary revelation of the tragedy, first in Carlyle's words in
his *Reminiscences* of Jane Welsh Carlyle, and then in her own words—
movingly commented upon by Carlyle himself in his stricken bereavement—in her *Letters and Memorials*. The fact that such intimacies
had been touched upon or dwelt upon earlier within the sequence
or series (itself the artistic counterpart to that 'long series of faults'
which brought Carlyle home to himself): this made it possible for
Froude to handle, without any abuse of dramatic irony, his and our
own aftersight and foresight.

Take a reiterated particular in the biography, a fact simple and
suggestive. Very early in the Life (Carlyle at 19), we survey a landscape:

Broad Annandale stretches in front down to the Solway, which shines like
a long silver riband; on the right is Hoddam Hill with the Tower of Repentance on its crest, and the wooded slopes which mark the line of the river.[6]

Froude's eye will later return to the Tower of Repentance; here he
remarks nothing. But if he is not giving anything away, he is not
throwing anything away either. For in the published *Reminiscences* we
have earlier witnessed Carlyle's own alertness:

My poor little establishment at Hoddam Hill (close by the 'Tower of
Repentance,' as if symbolically!) I do not mean to speak of here; a neat
compact little farm (i 285)

—but Carlyle *had* spoken, couched within the curve of his syntac-
tical inversion, and with all the paradox of parenthesis (with its
unique feeling of being at once a crux and an aside, at once an
inescapable honourable admission and something which may then
be honourably passed over); and the fact that Carlyle had done so,
and that we have heard what he said (thanks to Froude's good
offices, since not only was Froude the editor of the *Reminiscences* but
they would not have seen the light of day if he had decided otherwise), this must validate the abstinence of Froude's landscape, moving
on at once without comment: 'on the right is Hoddam Hill with
the Tower of Repentance on its crest, and the wooded slopes which
mark the line of the river'.

[6] *The First Forty Years*, i 35–6.

By the time Carlyle was 30 (more than two hundred pages later), he was nearing marriage to Jane Welsh, and he was nearing Hoddam Hill and the Tower: in Froude's words,

Two miles from Mainhill, on the brow of a hill, on the right as you look towards the Solway, stands an old ruined building with uncertain traditions attached to it, called the Tower of Repentance. Some singular story lies hidden in the name, but authentic record there is none. The Tower only remains visible far away from the high slopes which rise above Ecclefechan.[7]

But there has already been revealed to us what—*for Carlyle*—lay crucially 'hidden in the name' (as always for Carlyle, an *open secret*), and of that there was certainly 'authentic record' as well as the beginnings of a 'tradition' within the biography itself. 'The Tower only remains visible far away . . .'

On the next page, we read Carlyle's letter to Miss Welsh, sketching this home of his at Hoddam:

The views from it are superb. There are hard smooth roads to gallop on towards any point of the compass, and ample space to dig and prune under the pure canopy of a wholesome sky. The ancient Tower of Repentance stands on a corner of the farm, a fit memorial for reflecting sinners.

And for reflecting biographers, especially those granted such 'ample space' as Froude—following Carlyle as a biographer in this—possessed. What the young Carlyle then reflected on had as yet none of the depth with which both he (in the *Reminiscences* of Irving, written immediately after Jane Welsh Carlyle died) and Froude here in the Life invested their backward glance. ('The views from it are superb'—and are a rebuke to *superbia*.) No ironies of biographical privilege are indulged, not only because Froude was not a man who gloated but because the biographer, even if he had wished to murmur 'Little did he know', had been anticipated by Carlyle himself—and had already recorded this particular anticipation, outside the biography proper but within the biographical and autobiographical sequence.

We respond the more to the unwittingness of the young Carlyle, or the half-wittingness, because no commentary is passed upon it. The Life-and-Letters (routinely deplored these days as monumentally dull or dully monumental) proves itself characteristically capacious

---

[7] *The First Forty Years*, i 297.

and flexible. So on the very next page (i 299), Carlyle writes again
to Miss Welsh:

Earth, sea, and air are open to us here as well as anywhere. The water
of Milk was flowing

—this is just the kind of enhancing suggestion which Carlyle felt
himself sent to the planet to register, Milk being, Froude notes,
'One of the small tributaries of the Annan' ('as if symbolically!', one
wants to take up from Carlyle, there in his dour land which yet
flowed with Milk if not honey)—

The water of Milk was flowing through its simple valley as early as the
brook Siloa, and poor Repentance Hill is as old as Caucasus itself. There
is a majesty and mystery in nature, take her as you will.

The tones of majesty and mystery are there, take them as you
will, and they need not—must not—be glossed by retrospection's
condescension.

Long after, volumes later, Carlyle writes to his aged mother from
Goethe-country, and brings the sights home to her: 'There is also
of course a wall all round—a donjon tower, standing like Repentance.'[8] Froude's note is topographical alone: 'The Tower of Repentance on Hoddam Hill', except that he adds: 'Carlyle illustrates
throughout from localities near Ecclefechan which his mother would
know.' And which the reader would know, further in the here and
now, and would have come to know in aptness.

The saddest occurrence of the place, in Carlyle's life and in the
Life, comes when Carlyle is 63, and is suffering a remorse about
his wife's unhappiness such as is both truly deep and grimly *less*
hideous than that which he would feel a few years later. 'What a
suffering thou hast had, and how nobly borne!'[9]

Froude draws no attention whatsoever to the old long-standing
name as it figures within the journeying, and he casts no glance
forward to the even worse remorse which was to follow, but his
lucid prose spares nothing:

All this was extremely morbid; but it was not an unnatural consequence
of habitual want of self-restraint, coupled with tenderness of conscience
when conscience was awake and could speak. It was likely enough that in
those night-watches, *when the scales fell off* [this taken up from the preceding

[8] *His Life in London*, ii 109.   [9] Ibid., ii 212.

letter to Jane Welsh Carlyle], accusing remembrances might have risen before him which were not agreeable to look into. With all his splendid gifts, moral and intellectual alike, Carlyle was like a wayward child, a child in wilfulness, a child in the intensity of remorse. His brother James provided him with a horse—

—a brisk transition, vaulted in the simple unexpected internal rhyme: 'the intensity of remorse. His brother James provided him with a horse'—

a 'dromedary,' he called it, 'loyal but extremely stupid'—to ride or drive about among the scenes of his early years. One day he went past Hoddam Hill, Repentance Tower, Ecclefechan churchyard, &c., beautiful, quiet, all of it, in the soft summer air, and yet he said, 'The valley of Jehoshaphat could not have been more stern and terribly impressive to him. He could never forget that afternoon and evening, the old churchyard tree at Ecclefechan, the white headstones of which he caught a steady look. The deepest *de Profundis* was poor to the feeling in his heart.' The thought of his wife, ill and solitary in London, tortured him.

Thirty words after the 'intensity of remorse', the riding past 'Repentance Tower': the collocation (which does not identify remorse with repentance) cries out for the complacencies of irony, and Froude declines to furnish them. He is assisted in this by the fact that Carlyle was quite sufficiently sensitive to such ironies. Froude's editor and commentator, John Clubbe, has written of 'the omnipresent irony'[10] in Froude; but Froude does not enjoy making ironies, and though he often finds them, he abstains from announcing his findings. He was also against the omnipresent, and would have appreciated the adjuration of John Crowe Ransom: 'we should be so much in favour of tragedy and irony as not to think it good policy to require them in all our poems, for fear we might bring them into bad fame.' What Froude explicitly found both chilling and admirable in history, as written and lived, was the passivity of its irony: 'In all or any of these views, history will stand your friend. History, in its passive irony, will make no objection. Like Jarno, in Goethe's novel, it will not condescend to argue with you, and will provide you with abundant illustrations of any thing which you may wish to believe.'[11] But in Carlyle's hands, tragedy and irony were ever-active: 'The picture was set out with the irony of which Carlyle was so unrivalled

---

[10] *Froude's Life of Carlyle*, abridged and edited by John Clubbe (1979), p. 46.
[11] 'The Science of History' (1864); *Short Studies on Great Subjects*.

a master, with the indignation of which irony is the *art*.'[12] As John Holloway has shown, irony for Carlyle the historian gravitates to dramatic irony:

when King Louis is brought in procession from Versailles to Paris (6th October 1789) he writes, 'Poor Louis has Two other Paris Processions to make: one ludicrous-ignominious like this; the other not ludicrous nor ignominious, but . . . sublime.'[13]

This, because it glimpses the sublime (which is incompatible with any easy irony), is dramatic irony as the chastened clairvoyance of the retrospectator, not as the self-hugging of a gloater spectator flattered by the parties' deafness, to a pun, say:

> Goe, bid thy Master rise, and come to me,
> And we will both together to the Tower,
> Where he shall see the Boar will use us kindly.
>
> (*Richard III*, III ii)

Carlyle's sombre fortitude of dramatic irony may sometimes be felt to harden from aftersight into the harsher thing hindsight. This can then elicit from him only that obdurate compassion which makes him so often intone 'Poor' So-and-So, as in that 'Poor Louis'. But what saves even this perilous propensity from becoming crass is its laying claim less to any unique prophetic powers than to the generally-available purchase given by hindsight, and therefore its being self-attentive too: 'My poor little establishment at Hoddam Hill', looked back upon but not down upon.

Henry James, Sr. was acutely comic about Carlyle's brand of pity:

His own intellectual life consisted so much in bemoaning the vices of his race, or drew such inspiration from despair, that he could not help regarding a man with contempt the instant he found him reconciled to the course of history. Pity is the highest style of intercourse he allowed himself with his kind. He compassionated all his friends in the measure of his affection for them. 'Poor John Sterling,' he used always to say; 'poor John Mill, poor Frederic Maurice, poor Neuberg, poor Arthur Helps, poor little Browning, poor little Lewes,' and so on; as if the temple of his friendship were a hospital, and all its inmates scrofulous or paralytic.[14]

---

[12] *His Life in London*, i 287.   [13] *The Victorian Sage* (1953), p. 63.
[14] *The Literary Remains of the Late Henry James*, ed. William James (1885), p. 424.

It is a measure of Froude's justified confidence that he can compassionately retort this turn upon Carlyle himself, as when—after
quoting Jane Welsh Carlyle's serious comic masterpiece, her detailed 'budget' (12 February 1855), eleven pages in folio, about
domestic economies at Cheyne Row, addressed to her husband—
Froude turns to being exact with his own balance-sheet, and lightly
fingers 'Poor Carlyle!' with the money-matters of the poor:

> No man ever behaved better under such a chastisement. Not a trace is
> visible of resentment or impatience, though also less regret than a perfect
> husband ought to have felt that he had to a certain extent deserved it.
> Unfortunately, knowing that he had meant no harm and had done all that
> he was asked to do the instant that the facts were before him, he never
> could take a lesson of this kind properly to heart, and could be just as
> inconsiderate and just as provoking on the next occasion that arose. Poor
> Carlyle! Well he might complain of his loneliness! though he was himself
> in part the cause of it. Both he and she were noble and generous, but his
> was the soft heart, and hers the stern one.[15]

With what admirable justice the alternative to the soft heart turns
out not to be the hard one but the stern one.

This is the place to speak of a well-intentioned but misguided
service rendered to Froude's Life of Carlyle, when John Clubbe in
1979 published a one-volume abridgement, 'pruned' to 'about three-
eighths of its original length'. Because the cuts are seldom of Froude's
own words, Clubbe is confident that his abridgement is pure gain
and will do right by those 'who have not the stoicism to plow through
the full text'. Not without hubris, he claims that 'This abridgment,
shorn of great chunks of heaped-up documentation, does have a
coherence that the original volumes lacked'.[16] A Life-and-Letters is
thereby reduced to a one-voiced biography; Carlyle's letters and
journal go, and so, among much else, do Jane Welsh Carlyle's. This
dissolution, which is described as 'presenting the work basically on
its own terms', abolishes much of the disposition, distinction, and
tissue of Froude's masterpiece.

What this tissue is may be seen in the difference which it makes,
here in the matter of the domestic economies at Cheyne Row, to
read the original as against the book-Clubbe version. Clubbe does
not include, even in part, Jane Welsh Carlyle's dramatized cogent
memorandum, hilariously shrewd, which Carlyle delightedly endorsed

---

[15] *His Life in London*, ii 171.   [16] *Froude's Life of Carlyle*, p. 62.

'Jane's Missive on the Budget'. Not only does the absence render null what it then means to speak of Carlyle's not having felt resentment or impatience in the face of Jane's dear acerbities, but it changes the intonation of Froude's words—which are always alert to the words which he has just quoted, so that it is mistaken of Clubbe to suppose that Froude's words are left intact or untouched when others' words in their immediate vicinity are excised.

So when Froude says, 'less regret than a perfect husband ought to have felt that he had to a certain extent deserved it', his impulse can be weighed only by those who have just taken up the opportunity (which Froude gave them and Clubbe withdraws) to hear the words of the Missive itself. Jane, having put into Carlyle's mouth the words she would have liked to hear him volunteer to her—'My dear, you *must* be dreadfully hampered in your finances', etc.—goes on characteristically, generously and ruefully: 'That is the sort of thing you would have said had you been a perfect man; so I suppose you are not a perfect man.'[7] Froude's words a little later—'less regret than a perfect husband ought to have felt'—get their force, their nuance, and their absence of presumption, from their play with the wife's strict loving joke (partly self-directed), of which they acknowledge in every way the priority. Perfectly judged. And perfectly judging. And so distorted by Clubbe's false economies, which assume that Froude's words are not only distinguishable from the Carlyles' but are entirely distinct.

This is a matter of the tissue of the prose, and of how Froude understands the craft of the Life-and-Letters and its intergraftings. The larger dispositions suffer a similar loss under Clubbe. Take the Greek chorus.

Clubbe makes a great deal of Froude's few mentions of the Greek chorus, partly because Clubbe's reading of the biography as a whole is to see it through the lens of the (one) allusion to Iphigenia and her sacrifice, and through Oedipus (to whom there is no allusion in the Life, though there is in Froude's posthumous *My Relations with Carlyle*).

Both Froude's point here and his tone must be acknowledged as typical of the biography's strength, respect, and ironic independence, evident in the conviction that Froude's Carlyle had to be Jane Welsh Carlyle as well as Thomas Carlyle:

[7] *His Life in London*, ii 163.

The functions of a biographer are, like the functions of a Greek chorus, occasionally at the important moments to throw in some moral remarks which seem to fit the situation. The chorus after such a letter [from Carlyle the suitor to Jane Welsh, 20 January 1825] would remark, perhaps, on the subtle forms of self-deception to which the human heart is liable, of the momentous nature of marriage, and how men and women plunge heedlessly into the net, thinking only of the satisfaction of their own immediate wishes. . . . [Froude's ellipsis] Self-sacrifice it might say was a noble thing. But a sacrifice which one person might properly make, the other might have no reasonable right to ask or to allow. It would conclude, however, that the issues of human acts are in the hands of the gods, and would hope for the best in fear and trembling. Carlyle spoke of self-denial. The self-denial which he was prepared to make was the devotion of his whole life to the pursuit and setting forth of spiritual truth; throwing aside every meaner ambition. But apostles in St. Paul's opinion were better unwedded. The cause to which they give themselves leaves them little leisure to care for the things of their wives.[18]

Froude's words have not only comic but tragic irony, for the Greek chorus takes on a darker hue when it involves itself, and not heedlessly, in 'the net' which trapped both the wife who spread it and the doomed husband who was tangled in it. Clubbe does not remark on this; more crucially, by omitting entirely Carlyle's four-page letter of love, Clubbe makes it impossible to gauge the justice and the penetration of Froude's analysis and adducing. And yet the very difference between the abridged and the thorough work can prove an illumination of just those qualities of Froude's.

But there is another omission (in consequence of another act of abridgement such as underrates the virtues of the Life-and-Letters) which substantially changes the effect of this appeal to the Greek chorus. Clubbe says that Froude 'introduced the device of the Greek chorus to allow him to comment obliquely', and again that 'the device of the Greek chorus came conveniently to mind'.[19] But it was importantly not Froude who *introduced* it, and Froude's was not the mind to whom it first conveniently came: it had earlier come to the mind of the Carlyles' friend Edward Irving, who was putting it into Carlyle's mind (and thereby, thanks to Froude, into ours). Although no reader of Clubbe could register as much, since he cuts out Irving's letter, it makes a great difference that Froude is, yet once more, imaginatively availing himself of something which he has shown,

---

[18] *The First Forty Years,* i 284-5.   [19] *Froude's Life of Carlyle,* pp. 9-10.

earlier in the biography, to have been not of his making, not of his introduction, though newly turned by him.

Irving, whose own life was to prove a tragedy (as a reader of Froude's Life already knew from Froude's edition of Carlyle's *Reminiscences*), had written to Carlyle (4 June 1819) about an incident fit for 'a modern tragedy', and had added:

occasionally I confess to have the privilege of the ancient chorus, of moralising a little, or rather not a little, upon the passing events; and occasionally to reach an admonition or a consolation to the suffering hero or heroine of the piece.[20]

So that when Froude turned to the Greek chorus, then, and to throwing in 'some moral remarks', he was returning to Irving and to the ironies of the triangular relationship of Irving and the Carlyles. (Carlyle, it may be recalled, became the husband of Jane Welsh only because Irving—who loved her and whom she loved—was unable to break off his engagement to another.) What in Irving's letter to Carlyle had been the faintly ironical and formulaic 'suffering hero or heroine of the piece' was to become strongly ironical, and, within the sacrifices inflicted by Carlyle's self-dedication, was to become true suffering for a hero and a heroine.

To forgo Irving's letter, and the one by Carlyle which prompted Froude's remarks about the Greek chorus, is not to lose, as Clubbe self-servingly supposes, 'great chunks of heaped-up documentation', but great elements of what Froude in his genius saw and showed.

Irony is not 'omnipresent' in Froude's Life; remorse and repentance all but are. There is an irony in Froude's description of Carlyle's sufferings when, in the wake of his wife's death, he looked through her papers, her notebooks and journals: 'His faults rose up in remorseless judgment.'[21]

It would not be true to say that Froude spares no opportunity to expose Carlyle's remorse; rather, he denies Carlyle no opportunity to expose it. What saves this from being cruel or inordinate is, first, that from the beginning Carlyle is shown to have no monopoly of remorse; second, that remorse towards Jane Welsh Carlyle is shown to have no monopoly within Carlyle; and third, that no finger points towards the pattern which forms.

Five pages into the Life (fifteen-hundred pages in all), we meet

---

[20] *The First Forty Years*, i 70.   [21] *His Life in London*, ii 323.

a drunken schoolmaster, 'shattered and remorseful'.[22] Two pages later, there is Carlyle's memory of a justified act of physical violence when a loutish adversary was humbled by his father: 'He would say of such things, "I am wae to think of it"—wae from repentance. Happy he who has nothing worse to repent of!' End of paragraph. The closing thought is both generalizable good-sense and Carlyle's individual self-rebuke. There is no word from Froude. But again two pages later, there is a sequence—engaging Carlyle's earliest childhood recollection—which cannot but carry, though it refrains from enforcing, a sense of that ultimate nexus of loss, remorse, and death which made all of Carlyle's life fall into shape, a shape at which he winced but from which he did not flinch:

Like the Carlyles generally he had a violent temper. John, the son of the first marriage, lived usually with his grandfather, but came occasionally to visit his parents. Carlyle's earliest recollection is of throwing his little brown stool at his brother in a mad passion of rage, when he was scarcely more than two years old, breaking a leg of it, and 'feeling for the first time the united pangs of loss and remorse.' The next impression which most affected him was the small round heap under the sheet upon a bed where his little sister lay dead.[23]

Carlyle's words, 'feeling for the first time the united pangs of loss and remorse': but not for the last time.

One might think that Froude, in denying himself any glance towards the reader, may be achieving an honourable continence but is forfeiting the possibility of any such intimation as I sense here. But this would be to forget that it is not only (valuable though this would be) *in retrospect*, in the retrospect of the Life as a whole, that this knowledge is available; for the story of Carlyle's feeling, at the death of his wife, the united pangs of loss and remorse had already been told in the *Reminiscences*, where moreover there had also figured this earliest childhood recollection of loss, remorse, and sequent death. The sequence of volumes made possible for Froude both the maximum abstention from hints at foreknowledge and the maximum availing himself of Carlyle's own already-encountered retrospect.

Much else in the *Reminiscences* had turned upon repentance (and so duly *informs* in both senses the Life). Edward Irving had somewhat condescended to Carlyle but had been his staunch friend too (and would have had Jane Welsh's hand had it not been that he was affianced to another who would not release him). Irving was destroyed by a 'pulpit-popularity' which came and went and left him exposed to the fanatical religiosity of 'the Tongues'. His early death moved Carlyle to a sense of how like and how unlike he and Irving had been. There had even been a schoolfellow named Irving Carlyle; the name and the character are mentioned but the coincidence is left unremarked although it is remarkable.[24]

When Carlyle says, 'It must be said that Irving nobly expiates whatever errors he has fallen into',[25] he is trusting that the same may come to be said of him; when he says of a wrong done by Irving, 'Perfect absolution there had long been without enquiring after penitence',[26] he knows that the same could never be said of him, since there was no absolution for him other than through overt penitence and remorse.

But turn to the crucial remorse, crucial because it recurs within the volumes' sequence and then gathers immensely much to itself; crucial too because it is a remorse not towards but *of* Jane Welsh Carlyle. Never was Carlyle more moved to a sense of his own wrongdoing than when he learnt, immediately after her death, of his wife's remorse at her wrongdoing.

Upon the death of her mother, Jane Welsh Carlyle, away at the time from Carlyle, was racked with remorse, as we hear at that moment in the Life:

Extreme, intense in everything, she could only think of her own shortcomings, of how her mother was gone now, and could never forgive her. The strongest natures suffer worst from remorse. Only a strong nature, perhaps, can know what remorse means. Mrs. Carlyle had surrendered her fortune to her mother, but the recollection of this could be no comfort; she would have hated herself if such a thought had occurred to her. Carlyle knew what she would be suffering.[27]

But what Carlyle could not know, did not know until immediately upon *her* death, though we already know it from earlier within the sequence (not from earlier in the Life and indeed not from later in the Life, by an extraordinary abstention), was her proleptic act of expiation. 'The strongest natures suffer worst from remorse': this speaks of Jane Welsh Carlyle, but it speaks to Carlyle's case (and

---

[24] *Reminiscences*, i 99.   [25] Ibid., i 335.   [26] Ibid., i 193.
[27] *His Life in London*, i 234–5.

to Froude's), as to ours. 'Carlyle knew what she would be suffering'; and he was to know her suffering.

Carlyle was to arrive at a time when he likewise could only think of his own shortcomings, of how she was gone now, and could never forgive him. This future was ushered in (*before* he came to read his dead wife's journal, with its entries revealing how profoundly he had hurt her with his platonic subservience to Lady Baring, Lady Ashburton), by what he learnt immediately upon her death.

Carlyle in the *Reminiscences* had glanced at Jane Welsh Carlyle's posthumous expiation of her unkindness to her mother, jaggedly at first in describing a visit by her mother:

> She came perhaps three times; on one of the later times was that of the 'one soirée,' with the wax-candles on mother's part—and subsequent remorse on daughter's! 'Burn these last two on the night when I lie dead!' Like a stroke of lightning this has gone through my heart, cutting and yet healing.[28]

The lighting and the lightning are one, and they are themselves finally illuminated at the close of the *Reminiscences*, in a report by Geraldine Jewsbury with a comment by Carlyle. Froude subsequently quoted this same incident as part of 'a fit close' to the *Letters and Memorials of Jane Welsh Carlyle*, with a well-grounded and unstated sense of how much the incident meant.

This goes unstated within the Life itself—and here it has an odd affinity with another burning abstention by Froude. For chapter i of *His Years in London*, on the appalling accidental burning, in the John Stuart Mill household, of the manuscript of *The French Revolution*, volume i, does not exactly report that the manuscript was burned. This calamity is visible in the harrowing chapter, but only in the chapter-summary and page-heading, 'The Burnt Manuscript', nowhere in the text itself. But retrospectively and prospectively, the next chapter begins: 'To resolve to rewrite the burnt volume was easier than to do it.'[29] And previously the burning had been described in the *Reminiscences* (ii 177–9); had been alluded to in *His Early Years* (ii 477: 'the first volume, for the cause mentioned in the "Reminiscences," had to be written a second time'); and had been explicitly recalled in the *Letters and Memorials*.

Relatedly, Jane Welsh Carlyle's posthumous expiation lives tacitly in the Life but had been twice *told* earlier in the sequence of

[28] *Reminiscences*, ii 188.   [29] Chapter ii, *His Life in London*, i 33.

volumes. As in the *Recollections* (ii 302–4), with Geraldine Jewsbury recalling the day of Jane's death, and Carlyle commenting:

On that miserable night, when we were preparing to receive her, Mrs. Warren[30] came to me and said, that one time when she was very ill, she said to her, that when the last had come, she was to go upstairs into the closet of the spare room and there she would find two wax candles wrapt in paper, and that those were to be lighted, and burned. She said that after she came to live in London, she wanted to give a party. Her mother wished everything to be very nice, and went out and bought candles and confectionary: and set out a table, and lighted up the room quite splendidly, and called her to come and see it, when all was prepared. She was angry; she said people would say she was extravagant, and would ruin her husband. She took away two of the candles and some of the cakes. Her mother was hurt and began to weep [I remember the 'soirée' well; heard nothing of this!—T.C.]. She was pained at once at what she had done; she tried to comfort her, and was dreadfully sorry. She took the candles and wrapped them up, and put them where they could be easily found. We found them and lighted them, and did as she had desired.

G. E. J.

What a strange, beautiful, sublime and almost terrible little action; silently resolved on, and kept silent from all the earth, for perhaps twenty-four years! I never heard a whisper of it, and yet see it to be true. The visit must have been about 1837; I remember the 'soirée' right well; the resolution, bright as with heavenly tears and lightning, was probably formed on her mother's death, February 1842. My radiant one! Must question Warren the first time I have heart (May 29, 1866).

I have had from Mrs. Warren a clear narrative (shortly after the above date). Geraldine's report is perfectly true; fact with Mrs. Warren occurred in February or March 1866, 'perhaps a month before you went to Edinburgh, sir.' I was in the house, it seems, probably asleep upstairs, or gone out for my walk, evening about eight o'clock. My poor darling was taken with some bad fit ('nausea,' and stomach misery perhaps), and had rung for Mrs. Warren, by whom, with some sip of warm liquid, and gentle words, she was soon gradually relieved. Being very grateful and still very miserable and low, she addressed Mrs. Warren as above, 'When the last has come, Mrs. Warren;' and gave her, with brevity, a statement of the case, and exacted her promise; which the other, with cheering counter-words ('Oh, madam, what is all this! you will see me die first!') hypothetically gave. All this was wiped clean away before I got in; I seem to myself to half recollect one evening, when she did complain of 'nausea so habitual

---

[30] The housekeeper in Cheyne Row. [Froude's note]

now,' and looked extremely miserable, while I sat at tea (pour it out she always would herself drinking only hot water, oh heavens!) The candles burnt for two whole nights, says Mrs. W. (July 24, 1866).

The action of Jane Welsh Carlyle speaks louder than words. But notice its anticipation of Carlyle's own posthumous expiation. For like his wife he felt remorse as soon as the loved one was dead, and like her he left the expiation until after he was gone, asking Froude (his Mrs Warren) to enact for him an elaborated counterpart to the simple ritual of the candles. Counterpart, and burning pain of re-enactment, since the expiation is, among so much else, the telling of this very story of Jane's expiation. Froude too burns the candles, of praise and penitence.

There is only one illustration set within the text of the four volumes of the Life, and it is the emblem of a candle:

Here, on the same page [of his journal], Carlyle sketched the emblem of the wasting candle, with the motto written on it, 'Terar dum prosim.' 'May I be wasted, so that I be of use.' He goes on:—
    'But what if I do not prosum? Why then terar still, so I cannot help it.'[31]

By a terrible irony, the image of self-sacrifice was to become the emblem of the self-punishment exacted upon (and then visited by) Jane Welsh Carlyle, when—by coincidence of social fact and domestic fret—she found herself forced to expiate her unkindness to her mother in the matter of mere candles. And later duly racked her remorseful husband the more.

Coincidence, but one which could take its place within a double prospect, since—as Froude makes clear without in any way drawing out any of these implications—the emblem of the candle had formed part of this nexus of feelings, long before the expiation of Jane's unkindness to her mother and therefore long before Carlyle's taking this to himself, in his posthumous expiation, as at once grief and balm.

The context of this other intersection in the biography is Mrs Welsh's disapproval of the prospective marriage of her daughter to Carlyle. Mrs Welsh and Carlyle had not hit it off. (Not unrelatedly, Froude's Life of Carlyle is wiser and fairer about in-laws than any other book I know.)

[31] The First Forty Years, i 197.

She [Mrs Welsh] had obstinate humours, and Carlyle, who never checked his own irritabilities, was impatient and sarcastic when others ventured to be unreasonable. She had observed and justly dreaded the violence of his temper, which when he was provoked or thwarted would boil like a geyser. He might repent afterwards of these ebullitions; he usually did repent. But repentance could not take away the sting of the passionate expressions, which fastened in the memory by the metaphors with which they were barbed, especially as there was no amendment, and the offence was repeated on the next temptation. It will easily be conceived, therefore, that the meeting between mother and daughter after the Hoddam visit, and Miss Welsh's announcement of her final resolution, was extremely painful. Miss Welsh wrote to Carlyle an account of what had passed. His letter in reply bears the same emblem of the burning candle, with the motto, '*Terar dum prosim,*' which he had before sketched in his journal. He was fond of a design which represented life to him under its sternest aspect.[32]

Yet the sternest aspect of the candle in its relation to Jane Welsh Carlyle, to Mrs Welsh, and to remorse, was not to be visible to him for many years.

'Why', Carlyle asked in *The Life of John Sterling* (Part I, ch. xiv), 'Why, like a fated Orestes, is man so whipt by the Furies, and driven madly hither and thither, if it is not even that he may seek some shrine, and there make expiation and find deliverance?'

Expiation haunts the life of Carlyle. The revelation which struck when he read his wife's journal following her death in 1866 was the more powerful as revelation because it was also a confirmation of everything he had always believed. He had always identified repentance and remorse as the mark or brand of spiritual election. His review in 1832 of the Croker edition of Boswell's *Life of Johnson* had already seized Johnson's expiation of his 'breach of filial piety' in the rain at Uttoxeter market as the tragical height of Johnson's life. Carlyle's breach of marital piety came home to him:

His faults rose up in remorseless judgment, and as he had thought too little of them before, so now he exaggerated them to himself in his helpless repentance. For such faults an atonement was due, and to her no atonement could now be made. He remembered, however, Johnson's penance at Uttoxeter; not once, but many times, he told me that something like that was required from him, if he could see his way to it.

At any rate it was round this hope and round his own recollections and remorse that our conversations chiefly turned when we took up our walks

[32] *The First Forty Years,* i 314–15.

again; the walks themselves tending usually to the spot where Mrs. Carlyle was last seen alive; where, in rain or sunshine, he reverently bared his head.[33]

'The Hero as Prophet' in 1841 located heroism here:

What are faults, what are the outward details of a life; if the inner secret of it, the remorse, temptations, true, often-baffled, never-ended struggle of it, be forgotten? 'It is not in man that walketh to direct his steps.' Of all acts, is not, for a man, *repentance* the most divine?[34]

Or there is Carlyle's most staunchly humane book, *The Life of John Sterling*. 'What', someone asked Jane Welsh Carlyle, 'What has Sterling done that he should have a Life?' And she: 'Induced Carlyle somehow to write him one!'[35] But what induced *The Life of John Sterling* in 1851 was Carlyle's intense comprehension that nothing mattered more to Sterling than his remorse at the deaths of Boyd and the others in the political folly of the Torrijos adventure in Spain:

and repentances enough over many things were not wanting. But here on a sudden had all repentances, as it were, dashed themselves together into one grand whirlwind of repentance; and his past life was fallen wholly as into a state of reprobation. A great remorseful misery had come upon him. Suddenly, as with a lightning-stroke, it had kindled into conflagration all the ruined structure of his past life. (Part i, ch. xiv)

But in Carlyle's case, the sudden lightning-stroke kindled into conflagration but did not ruin the structure of his own life, and it kindled a structure for his wife's past life: the *Letters and Memorials of Jane Welsh Carlyle*.

We owe them to Froude, in that they would not have been published then (probably ever) if he had ruled otherwise. To Jane Welsh Carlyle, we owe the indefatigable wit, acumen, and tragic resilience of the letters and journals themselves. And to Carlyle, the pathos, dignity, and self-knowledge with which he commented upon them, kindly explaining their coterie-speech and their family-jokes, and acknowledging his own unkindness, insensitivity, and hurtfulness. This took courage, and love. The three volumes constitute a unique creation and a unique experience; nowhere else is such a

---

[33] *His Life in London*, ii 323–4.
[34] *On Heroes, Hero-Worship and the Heroic in History*, Lecture II.
[35] *Reminiscences*, ii 230.

process of married text and commentary—felicitous and desolating text and commentary—so burnt through. In the distant past (we know from Froude), the Carlyles had proposed to write books in concert. And so in the end, and with great pain, they did, uniquely. Carlyle's contribution, both in the form of his own words and in his allowing, half-urging, Froude to publish the *Letters and Memorials of Jane Welsh Carlyle*, did much to redeem the condescension which he had once bent upon her: 'so we will be content with Goody whether she ever comes to a book or not'.[36]

Carlyle's remorse came not to dominate but to dispose the entire biographical and autobiographical sequence of Froude's enterprise. For remorse was the shaping spirit of Froude's imagination here too.

In one crucial respect, Froude was free of remorse, and thereby enabled to deal freely with Carlyle's. Here, Froude could afford to suffer with those whom he saw suffer. He had twice been left a widower, once before the death of Jane Welsh Carlyle, and once between her death and Carlyle's death. (His first wife, dying, had hoped that Froude would marry the intimate friend of hers whom he did indeed marry.) It is clear that twice he suffered great grief but felt no remorse or self-reproach, and there is every reason to believe that he had no occasion to feel either. He was therefore in a position both to feel greatly for Carlyle in his bereaved grief *and* to maintain an independence of Carlyle's remorse.

The relation of remorse to Froude's achievement is rather this: that it was only the example of Carlyle's courage in remorse which saved Froude from a capitulation which would have ended in re-morse. For Froude was very tempted to evade the charge which Carlyle had laid upon him. Here he was not (as in the matter of his dead wives) free of remorse, but freed from the very real threat of incurring remorse.

The revelation of the true unhappiness of the Carlyles' marriage, for all the marital triumphs which were not a matter of happiness: had this revelation been a command to Froude, a clear insistence, there would have been no temptation. Froude would certainly have obeyed it, and he would have been able to cite explicit warrant for his conduct. But Carlyle laid a much harder duty upon Froude. Carlyle havered. He did and did not want these materials published,

---

[36] *His Life in London*, i 355.

whether the *Reminiscences* or the *Letters and Memorials of Jane Welsh Carlyle*; and he did and did not want his biography to be written. The only thing which stood steady throughout all his vacillations— and is evinced by all of them—was his not wishing to take final responsibility.

But Carlyle had staked everything upon the fearless pursuit of the truth, and—in words which Froude was to quote at length in the preface to the first volume of the Life—he detested above all other things those mealy-mouthed biographies which revered not truth but the British goddess Respectability.

Froude's duty, as is now well-known, was at once perfectly clear and imperfectly clarified. So more than once he prayed that this cup might be taken from him. Nevertheless . . .

The guilt which he most feared, and which would have caused him immitigable remorse, was cowardice. When Carlyle first came to know Froude, he thought less well of Froude than of Clough as, in essence, less brave. It took courage, though, for Froude to tell us of this. Nor did he exempt himself from the charge that he had been insufficiently brave in the face of Carlyle; he is among those of whom he speaks when he regrets that, in London, 'From first to last he was surrounded by people who allowed him his own way'.[37]

Cowardice is the censure which Froude passes on himself in the second volume of *His Life in London*, in the matter of not supporting Governor Eyre's brutally punitive measures in the West Indies; after quoting a fiery letter by Carlyle, Froude says:

> I was myself one of the cowards. I pleaded that I did not understand the matter, that I was editor of 'Fraser,' and should disturb the proprietors; mere paltry excuses to escape doing what I knew to be right. Ruskin was braver far, and spoke out like a man. (ii 329–30)

But by this date, concluding the four volumes of the Life, Froude had shown in the biographical enterprise such courage as allowed him to acknowledge a cowardice.

There had been poignant moments in the first two volumes when it was clear, with aftersight or with foresight, that Froude was thinking of the duty which had been laid upon him and was still not sure whether he would carry it through. For *The First Forty Years* could be seen as still a holding operation. Froude could say to himself that

---

[37] *His Life in London*, ii 233.

he had sufficiently discharged his obligations to truth and to Carlyle by publishing the *Reminiscences*. Or, after *The First Forty Years*, by publishing (it might be) the *Letters and Memorials of Jane Welsh Carlyle*, the issuing of which quite sufficiently involved Froude in controversy and censure.

When the young Carlyle let his name go forward for the professorship of Astronomy, the words of Froude are none of them inattentive to Carlyle but they tell another story too:

It was a last effort to lay down the burden which had been laid upon him, yet not a cowardly effort—rather a wise and laudable one—undertaken as it was in submission to the Higher Will.[38]

For Froude nearly reneged. 'Had I considered my own comfort or my own interest, I should have sifted out or passed lightly over the delicate features in the story.'

He continued, in the pages introductory to *His Life in London*:

Had I taken the course which the 'natural man' would have recommended, I should have given no faithful account of Carlyle. I should have created a 'delusion and a hallucination' of the precise kind which he who was the truest of men most deprecated and dreaded; and I should have done it not innocently and in ignorance, but with deliberate insincerity, after my attention had been specially directed by his own generous openness to the points which I should have left unnoticed.

These are the accents of a man who, by this stage, had conquered the temptation to betray his master.

But earlier 'I had drifted towards a cowardly conclusion that I would suppress Mrs. Carlyle's letters after all.'[39] And if those, then a suppression of so much else.

Froude spoke openly of this towards the end of *His Years in London*, in closing chapter xxxii, when again he feels obliged to use the word 'cowardly' but rightly declines to be abject about it. In 1873, 'without note or warning he sent me his own and his wife's private papers, journals, correspondence, "reminiscences," and other fragments':

The new task which had been laid upon me complicated the problem of the 'Letters and Memorials.' My first hope was, that, in the absence of further definite instructions from himself, I might interweave parts of Mrs. Carlyle's letters with his own correspondence in an ordinary narrative,

---

[38] *The First Forty Years*, ii 390.
[39] *My Relations with Carlyle*, pp. 30–1.

passing lightly over the rest, and touching the dangerous places only so far as was unavoidable. In this view I wrote at leisure the greatest part of 'the first forty years' of his life. The evasion of the difficulty was perhaps cowardly, but it was not unnatural. I was forced back, however, into the straighter and better course.[40]

It is characteristic of Froude's central dignity that he should make no claim to a sudden rush of courage. 'I was forced back, however, into the straighter and better course.'

His first biographer, Herbert Paul, put it well: 'He conceived himself to be under a pledge. He had given his word to a dead man, who could not release him.'[41] Moreover, the dead man in question had given the words of a dead woman, who could not release *him*. But Froude, even when insisting that he had done the right thing, was careful always to qualify his description of Carlyle's legacy of duty. As Froude said in a letter,

Only remember this: that it was Carlyle's own determination (or at least desire) to do justice to his wife, and to do public penance himself—a desire which I think so noble as to obliterate in my own mind the occasion there was for it.[42]

Froude was to protest at Tennyson's having said he 'had sold [his] Master for thirty pieces of silver'. Hallam Tennyson placated him, denying the rumour since Tennyson had said no more than that 'it would have been better if you had omitted 3 or 4 pages'.[43] And this, before the much more revelatory final volumes were out. Froude would have ruefully relished the sentiments of Sir John Skelton: 'he may have been sometimes tempted to wish that the prophet (whose love of silence was, as his wife said, purely Platonic) had done his penance in person, and not by proxy.'[44]

Finally, there is another nexus by which remorse shaped the Life, and made for an animating conjunction of the men and the moment: the conjunction of saints' lives, repentance, and the ethics of biography.

The first volume of *His Life in London* ends with Froude's first meeting with Carlyle, who was then 54, Froude 31:

---

[40] *His Life in London*, ii 414–15.   [41] *The Life of Froude* (1905), p. 305.

[42] Dunn, *James Anthony Froude*, ii 497.

[43] See the notes to Tennyson's 'The Dead Prophet' (1885), in *The Poems of Tennyson*, ed. Christopher Ricks (1987), iii 111.

[44] Dunn, *James Anthony Froude*, ii 500.

Of me, with good reason, he was inclined to think far less favourably [than of Clough]. I had written something, not wisely, in which heterodoxy was flavoured with the sentimentalism which he so intensely detested. He had said of me that I ought to burn my own smoke, and not trouble other people's nostrils with it. Nevertheless, he was willing to see what I was like. James Spedding took me down to Cheyne Row one evening in the middle of June [1849]. We found him sitting after dinner, with his pipe,

—this is the sort of move which Froude likes to effect drily and slily, 'burn my own smoke . . . with his pipe'—

We found him sitting after dinner, with his pipe, in the small flagged court between the house and the garden. He was studying without much satisfaction the Life of St. Patrick by Jocelyn of Ferns in the 'Acta Sanctorum.' He was trying to form a notion of what Ireland had been like before Danes or Saxons had meddled with it, when it was said to have been the chosen home of learning and piety, and had sent out missionaries to convert Northern Europe. His author was not assisting him. The life of St. Patrick as given by Jocelyn is as much a biography of a real man as the story of Jack the Giant-killer. When we arrived Carlyle had just been reading how an Irish marauder had stolen a goat and eaten it, and the Saint had convicted him by making the goat bleat in his stomach. He spoke of it with rough disgust; and then we talked of Ireland generally, of which I had some local knowledge.[45]

A happy fecund coinciding, that the first meeting of Carlyle and his great biographer should have entailed their talking about superstition, sanctity, and the biography of a real man. Froude never forgot the saints' lives. 'Of all the collections of ecclesiastical biographies the most interesting by far which I have ever met with is Colgan's *Lives of the Irish Saints*.'[46] Froude could neither accede to nor disown the traditional claims for such lives. It was repentance which aptly fretted him.

'This Patrick,' they said, 'teaches repentance, and the doctrine of repentance is such that, if a man believes, he may commit a crime and repent, and then it will be well with him; he will go away and do as he lists.' The Druids' objection has still some sense in it.

Yet only some sense, so Froude objected to the objection too:

[45] *His Life in London*, i 458–9.   [46] Dunn, *James Anthony Froude*, i 77.

The old pagan Irish were afraid of Christianity, because it preached the acceptance of repentance. They said if repentance is accepted men will sin freely and will say, I will repent and all will be well. They were wrong.[47]

Froude understood his era as confused not only about the choice of life but the choice of Lives. In 1850 he wrote:

If we wanted proof of the utter spiritual disintegration into which we have fallen, it would be enough that we have no biographies. We do not mean that we have no written lives of our fellow creatures; there are enough and to spare. But not any one is there in which the ideal tendencies of this age can be discerned in their true form; not one, or hardly any one, which we could place in a young man's hands, with such warm confidence as would let us say of it,—'Read that; there is a man—such a man as you ought to be; read it, meditate on it; see what he was, and how he made himself what he was, and try and be yourself like him.'

But how were 'the ideal tendencies' of the age to be protected against the falsities of idealizing?

The age of the saints has passed; they are no longer any service to us; we must walk in their spirit, but not along their road; and in this sense we say, that we have no pattern great men, no biographies, no history, which are of real service to us.[48]

How to combine the exemplary virtues of a saint's life with a Carlylean distrust of saintliness? (Froude: 'The modern Englishmen have been offered the saints' biographies, and have with sufficient clearness expressed their opinion of them.') By bringing home that the modern saint is someone who inspires us by recognizing the error of his or her ways, by embracing repentance with pain and without shrugging, and by acceding to tragedy.

The shape of Carlyle's life, revealed by remorse, was such as to make clear what the acceptance of repentance must mean in the nineteenth century. 'Such a man as you ought to be': this must mean, not the idealized or the idolized, but a nature open to remorse, in acknowledgement and confession.

Enter 'the ethics of biography'. Such was the title of Margaret Oliphant's essay, published in reproof of Froude in 1883, the year between *The First Forty Years* and *His Life in London*. She claimed to know how 'a high-minded man' would have behaved: 'rather than

---

[47] Letter to Kingsley; Dunn, *James Anthony Froude*, i 191.
[48] 'Representative Men'; *Short Studies on Great Subjects*.

be the instrument of ruining a virtuous reputation, and betraying the secret weakness of a man whom the world held in honour, he would retire from the field altogether'. 'It is impossible that a man could be compelled to criminate his friend, or to soil an established reputation entrusted to his care.'[49] But Froude's sense of his duty was exactly that his friend had craved his assistance in revealing, and therefore not *betraying*, his secret. The reputation that is here unjustly soiled, the friend unjustly criminated, is not Carlyle but Froude, who respected what Carlyle himself would have judged to be in truth high-minded.

Samuel Johnson, a great biographer and the greatest of biographical opportunities, knew the wisdom of acknowledging the weaknesses of great men.

If nothing but the bright side of characters could be shown, we would sit down in despondency, and think it utterly impossible to imitate them in *any thing*. The sacred writers related the vicious as well as the virtuous actions of men; which had this moral effect, that it kept mankind from *despair*, into which otherwise they would naturally fall, were they not supported by the recollection that others had offended like themselves, and by penitence and amendment of life had been restored to the favour of Heaven.[50]

The manifestations of remorse in Jane Welsh Carlyle and in Thomas Carlyle, and—prompted by them—the averting of remorse by Froude: but these leave another visitation of remorse, upon Froude's readers. Some of his first readers persisted, remorselessly, in their persecution of him for his acts of brave and candid love. Others, over the years, gradually relented and even repented. But remorse may still sharpen its tooth for all those, then and since, who—while granting abstractly that Froude's Carlyle may well be a masterpiece—have casually failed to live in its company.

[49] *Contemporary Review* (July 1883); reprinted in James Clifford, *Biography as an Art: Selected Criticism 1560–1960* (1962), pp. 101–2.
[50] Recorded by Malone; Boswell, *Life of Johnson*, ed. Hill and Powell, iv 53.

TENNYSON'S TENNYSON

'The worth of a biography depends on whether it is done by one who wholly loves the man whose life he writes, yet loves him with a discriminating love.'[1]

The words are Alfred Tennyson's, within the *Memoir* by his son Hallam Tennyson.

To Virginia Woolf, the *Memoir* was 'an amorphous mass'. To Humphry House, it was 'an obvious example' of how right Lytton Strachey was to decant Victorian biography.[2] But these were unimaginative engagements with a book too prejudicially judged to be unimaginative, a book sadly underrated in itself and in its kind, the Life-and-Letters.

Its title-page has to be the place to start. Its title:

ALFRED LORD TENNYSON

Straightforward, but with its own *furthermore*, for it is the title which was Alfred Tennyson's for the final tenth of his long life. He had been ennobled *for* as well as *by* his art, a bequeathable tribute such as no English poet before or since has secured.

A reader, at the very beginning, is stationed at the end of the poet's life, for the poet was not Alfred Lord Tennyson until 1884, for the last eight of his eighty years. The portrait—by Samuel Laurence—which faces the first volume's title-page is a portrait not of Alfred Lord Tennyson, but of Alfred Tennyson, 30, dashing, and beardless. But then the frontispiece to the second volume, which faces the all-but-identical title-page (differentiated only by VOLUME II), is not a portrait of Alfred Lord Tennyson either, since its photograph, by John Mayall, was taken in 1864, twenty years before the peerage. It shows a much later man than does Volume I, but an earlier man than Alfred Lord Tennyson, not identical though having the same identity.

In 1897, when the *Memoir* appeared, the identity of Lord Tennyson had changed. Hallam Tennyson well knew himself to have inherited the peerage but not the poetic powers which had gained the

---

[1] *Alfred Lord Tennyson: A Memoir* (1897), ii 165.
[2] 'The New Biography' (1927). (1948), *All in Due Time* (1955), p. 258.

peerage, those powers which had long ago imagined a succession. 'Ulysses' was written when Tennyson was in his early twenties:

> This is my son, mine own Telemachus,
> To whom I leave the sceptre and the isle—
> Well-loved of me, discerning to fulfil
> This labour, by slow prudence to make mild
> A rugged people, and through soft degrees
> Subdue them to the useful and the good.
> Most blameless is he, centred in the sphere
> Of common duties, decent not to fail
> In offices of tenderness, and pay
> Meet adoration to my household gods,
> When I am gone. He works his work, I mine.

Since a peer has the privilege of signing himself simply, say, 'Tennyson', the given name will on a formal occasion fall away, and the son's distinguished continuity with the father (when he is gone) be manifest. Continuity, but not indistinguishability; Tennyson's Tennyson is a son's life of his father, and it embodies (not, in my judgement, 'enshrines') Tennyson's own sense of self, but it does not assimilate father to son, and though it may be thought of as a peer's life of a peer, this is not because the son ever thinks himself his father's peer.

Hallam Tennyson, as is well known, deliberated the book's title. The offices of tenderness which he had contemplated while his father still lived, he did not complete until five years after his father's death. The biographer had revised variously, repeatedly, needing to reduce drastically the vast materials which came to him (some 40,000 letters for a start); these protracted feats of cutting and of concatenation may fortify the conviction that the final shaping of the *Memoir* did not lightly befall.

An earlier title, as all this accrued, had been *Materials for a Life of A.T. Collected for My Children*. Another title, to which he returned some years later for a supplementary volume in 1911, had been *Tennyson and His Friends*.

The matter of titles surfaced, as something of a pun, in a letter by Gladstone given in the *Memoir* itself, where early in the story of the poet's life Hallam Tennyson reports having enquired of Gladstone immediately upon Tennyson's death in 1892. The reader comes upon this reply unexpectedly (flexing the years), ensconced within

1837–8, with Gladstone recalling the year when Tennyson first called upon him, impelled by Gladstone's having been the schoolfriend of the dear dead Arthur Hallam. Now, more than half a century later, Tennyson too is dead. More than half a century later than the young years which it shadowily summons, there comes an imperfect remembering, emanating from the station of the highest office:

10 DOWNING STREET, WHITEHALL, *October*, 1892

—the month of Tennyson's death. Gladstone's letter ripely, prime-ministerially, regrets his not being at leisure to furnish the information which Hallam Tennyson sought, but the Grand Old Man's unmassive missive earned its place in the *Memoir* (rather than in the *Journal of Negative Results*) by virtue of its ending:

I am greatly pleased to hear that you have undertaken the 'Life,'—doubtless an arduous task, but one to which your titles are multiple as well as clear. (i 164–5)

The son is entitled to undertake it, as is manifest—among other things—from his title's now being Lord Tennyson.

After the poet's death and the title's passing to Hallam Tennyson, Emily Lady Tennyson 'asked not to be addressed as the Dowager Lady Tennyson but as Emily Lady Tennyson: "A small matter but there seems to be in it a feeling that one is still his wife as one feels that one is." '[3] An exquisitely English triple 'one'—there was, after all, only one person who was or had been his wife. For the devout widow, he was still alive. 'Peace, let it be! for I loved him, and love him for ever: the dead are not dead but alive': one of Tennyson's greatest endings in its confidence of unending personal survival, the true 'Vastness'. For Emily Tennyson to call herself in her widowhood Emily Lady Tennyson was to keep him alive as the Dowager Lady Tennyson would not.

And then below the book's title there comes the subtitle.

ALFRED LORD TENNYSON
A MEMOIR

This will prove felicitously to combine memoir and memoirs. Memoirs are 'a person's written account of incidents in his own life, of the

---

[3] Robert Bernard Martin, *Tennyson: The Unquiet Heart* (1980), p. 583.

persons whom he has known, and the transactions or movements in which he has been concerned; an autobiographical record' (*OED*). *A Memoir* is to some degree Hallam Tennyson's memoirs; he had lived forty years in the company of his father. Hallam Tennyson lived half of his all-but-eighty years so, as his father lived half of his eighty years in the company of his son. The death of Tennyson folds the two lives.

A memoir is defined as 'a biography or biographical notice' (*OED* 4, from 1826); but this ignores the fact that a memoir carries some implication of personal knowledge, and that like memoirs it engages with persons whom you have known.

ALFRED LORD TENNYSON
A MEMOIR

A dignified dubbing, this rings more true than the poetical wrestings which have lately become the academic thing. Robert Bernard Martin's intelligently sceptical biography of Tennyson, substantial and almost entirely substantiated, invaluable for its stringency and astringency, does permit itself a prompt throb: *Tennyson: The Unquiet Heart*. Yet there the epigraph points to something askew, and not just because it disregards Tennyson's indentation:

> . . . for the unquiet heart and brain,
> A use in measured language lies;
> The sad mechanic exercise,
> Like dull narcotics, numbing pain.
>
> *In Memoriam*, V.

Lopping off Tennyson's words 'and brain', reducing 'the unquiet heart and brain' to *Tennyson: The Unquiet Heart*—is Martin entitled, qualified, to practise lobotomy? Tennyson's brain is not much in evidence in the modern biography, and is believed by Martin not to have been much in evidence all along. True, Tennyson was not an intellectual (is he the only one of our great poets of the last 150 years not to have been?), but it is a brainlessness of intellectuals to suppose that they have a monopoly of brains. In 1918, T. S. Eliot, himself an intellectual, praised Tennyson with discriminating reluctance, allowing him a brain of a kind:

I cannot see the resemblance to Tennyson which people often remark in Georgian poetry. I do not care to pose as a champion of Tennyson, and

Mr. Chesterton's approval makes one uneasy about him. But Tennyson was careful in his syntax; and, moreover, his adjectives usually have a definite meaning; perhaps often an uninteresting meaning; still, each word is treated with proper respect. And Tennyson had a brain (a large dull brain like a farmhouse clock) which saved him from triviality.[4]

Since Tennyson is the poet of Mariana and of 'the slow clock ticking', Eliot's wit is not merely disparaging—any more than it was when he wrote (notoriously) of Henry James that 'He had a mind so fine that no idea could violate it'.[5]

ALFRED LORD TENNYSON
A MEMOIR
BY HIS SON

No name. The reader can guess at the author's name, because in being the son of the (late) Alfred Lord Tennyson he has a sporting chance that his name is Lord Tennyson too. But it never says the name Hallam Tennyson on the title-page, or indeed anywhere else within the book. The author's name is to be found with but not within the book (*il y a de hors-texte?*), on the spine of the English edition. Not, though, in or on the American edition.

The English edition has at its spine: TENNYSON / A / MEMOIR / HALLAM / LORD TENNYSON. The spine of the American edition pre-empts the words of the title-page. So that if at the end of last century you had bought the American edition, you could have read the entire book and never found it explicitly stated that its author is Hallam Tennyson.

Hallam Tennyson had originally intended to refer to the poet throughout the *Memoir* as A.T. It was Emily Tennyson who secured his doing otherwise, by saying, with all her indeflectible mildness, 'I had rather myself that you said my father'.[6] BY HIS SON: Tennyson had three sons. The eldest son—that is, the one who would have been Lord Tennyson—was still-born in 1851, the year after the wedding of his parents. He was to his father the 'dear little nameless one' (i 330), and immediately after the birth of his third son in 1854, in a letter to Julia Margaret Cameron, Tennyson

---

[4] *The Egoist*, March 1918.
[5] *Little Review*, v (1918), 46; previously in *The Egoist*, January 1918.
[6] *Materials*, iv 6; quoted by Philip L. Elliott, *The Making of the Memoir* (1978), p. 16.

remembered in sorrow this first nameless one: 'The first we had was born dead (a great grief to us), really the finest boy of the three; and I nearly broke my heart with going to look at him' (i 375).

Hallam Tennyson, who was to make known those words, was the second son, born in 1852; on this title-page he too is a nameless one, since it simply says—sadly need say no more than—BY HIS SON.

For finally there was Lionel Tennyson, born in 1854 but dead before his father. So that of the three Tennyson sons, the eldest was dead at birth, and the youngest dead in his early thirties, in 1886, six years before his father's death. By the time of Tennyson's aged death, there was only the one son left. BY HIS SON has a particular pathos in that this son was not an only child though in adulthood he had become such.

The same tragic story was to be visited upon Hallam Tennyson himself, who came to survive two of the three children, the three sons, with whom he was blessed at the time of the *Memoir*. And visited, again, upon the poet's grandson, Sir Charles Tennyson, and his three sons.

Emily Lady Tennyson set down 'Recollections of my early Life', and when her son came to print these, it was with the inscription 'Written for her son in 1896'.[7] The poignancy is not only in this then being the year of her death (the year before the *Memoir* was published), but in the further recollection that when long ago she originally recorded these memories they had been 'Written For My Sons'. There were then two, or rather only two of the three; by the time she died in 1896 there was only the one son left. He, blessedly, was decent not to fail in offices of tenderness.

It is much to the credit of the *Memoir* itself that Hallam Tennyson thinks of himself so little, although he rightly did not think little of himself. In the year 1852, at the top of the page (i 357), are the words BIRTH OF A SON. What is set down is simply the journal-entry ('Hallam born on the 11th of August'), plus the grave mirthful letters which the father penned:

Everything, I believe, is going on well, tho' the mother suffers from an almost total want of sleep, and the little monster does anything but what Hamlet says Osric did in his nursery-days.[8] I found him lying alone on

---

[7] *Tennyson and His Friends* (1911), p. 3.
[8] 'He did Complie with his Dugge before hee suck't it'; *Hamlet*, v ii.

the third day of his life, and, while I was looking at him, I saw him looking at me with such apparently earnest, wide-open eyes, I felt as awe-struck as if I had seen a spirit.

A spirit: it was in 1852, this year of Hallam Tennyson's birth, that the poet began his sombre and majestic poem on gestation, 'De Profundis', a poem the gestation of which itself lasted twenty-eight years:

> Out of the deep, my child, out of the deep,
> From that great deep, before our world begins,
> Whereon the Spirit of God moves as he will—
> Out of the deep, my child, out of the deep,
> From that true world within the world we see,
> Whereof our world is but the bounding shore—
> Out of the deep, Spirit, out of the deep,
> With this ninth moon, that sends the hidden sun
> Down yon dark sea, thou comest, darling boy.

Positioned at the line-ending as weighed there with 'darling boy', 'hidden sun' hides and yet reveals, as ripe pregnancy does, its sometime-hidden homophone, *son*. BY HIS SON. Here, *for* his son.

And then, on the title-page of the *Memoir*, below the words BY HIS SON, there is the epigraph:

> I have lived my life, and that which I have done
> May He within Himself make pure!

This, without attribution or identification. Not to recognize the lines of the poem, it is intimated, might verge on a disqualification for entering upon a memoir of the poet. Any reader of a poet's life who did not already know the poems themselves (and *a fortiori* the famous enduring ones) would probably be the trifling truffle-snuffler whom Tennyson—we learn from the *Memoir* itself—most detested:

What business has the public to want to know all about Byron's wildnesses? He has given them fine work, and they ought to be satisfied. It is all for the sake of babble. As for the excuse, 'Tôt ou tard tout se sait,' nothing can be falser as far as this world is concerned. The surface of the *tout* may be, but the *tout* never is, correctly known. (ii 165)

For Tennyson's biographer to have attributed or identified the lines of the epigraph would have been an insult. And any reader who stood in need of such attribution or identification would probably not be 'pure' but profane.

The epigraph functions, as epigraphs always do, as a threshold, and this one speaks of being made pure. As does George Herbert:

> *Superliminare*:
> Avoid, Profaneness; come not here:
> Nothing but holy, pure, and cleare,
> Or that which groneth to be so,
> May at his perill further go.

> I have lived my life, and that which I have done
> May He within Himself make pure!

Who speaks? The dying King Arthur. And yet not dying, since 'King Arthur is not dead', Arthur the special case of what is for the Christian always the case, since 'the dead are not dead but alive'. Arthur speaking in words with which he was endowed by Tennyson, words which are now ('From the great deep to the great deep') returned in a reciprocity of application to the poet himself, whose own life has now at last been fully lived.

But following as it does the words BY HIS SON, the epigraph is alive to enhancing suggestions. For each of the three sons has too a claim upon the father's words 'I have lived my life'. Our eldest-born, speak first—yet never really born, back in 1851, the eldest son, *of*—and *to*—whom ('him' turning at once to 'thou') Tennyson wrote in 1851 (it is quoted in the *Memoir*):

Dead as he was I felt proud of him. To-day when I write this down, the remembrance of it rather overcomes me; but I am glad that I have seen him, dear little nameless one that hast lived tho' thou hast never breathed, I, thy father, love thee and weep over thee, tho' thou hast no place in the Universe. Who knows? It may be that thou hast. (i 340)

A supreme mystery, in life and death, rested for Tennyson in the compacting of life and death in this being 'that hast lived tho' thou hast never breathed'. In the midst of death, we are in life.

'The remembrance of it rather overcomes me.' The remembrance of the three sons comes over the entire *Memoir*, shaping and shading it. Tennyson is our greatest poet of intimate bereavement (or, granting Hardy his greatness, we may say, of certain bereavements), and it is Hallam Tennyson's apprehension of this which grants him the insight that in this life of the poet, as in the life's work of the poet, the shaping aftersight and foresight are those which are intimate with bereavement. Which is why the three sons, of whom one lives to tell the tale, constitute not just a subject but an element by which the *Memoir* lives and breathes.

To this his first son, Tennyson wrote of his bereavement, addressing him (again 'He' becoming 'thou') as 'blind and mute' but not as inaccessibly deaf. The poem was not made public either by the poet-father or by the biographer-brother:

> Little bosom not yet cold,
> Noble forehead made for thought,
> Little hands of mighty mould
> Clenched as in the fight which they had fought.
> He had done battle to be born,
> But some brute force of Nature had prevailed
> And the little warrior failed.
> Whate'er thou wert, whate'er thou art,
> Whose life was ended ere thy breath begun,
> Thou nine-months neighbour of my dear one's heart,
> And howsoe'er thou liest blind and mute,
> Thou lookest bold and resolute,
> God bless thee dearest son.

In some ways, for ever and not invidiously, for reasons which every parent can understand, this first son could not but remain the 'dearest son'.

But then all three of the sons, and again not invidiously, were in different ways the dearest son. The younger, who would have been the youngest, Lionel (born 1854), had—as is clear from the family correspondence and memories—this prerogative of the youngest, a claim (at once traditional and individual) brought hideously home by his death in early manhood. Lionel manifestly was not the self-sacrificing type, except in the largest sense. Robert Bernard Martin has remarked that

The speed with which Lionel became engaged at the age of twenty-one was a gesture of independence making it clear that he was going to lead his own life and that he had no intention of remaining unmarried to take care of his parents, as Hallam seemed set to do.[9]

But Lionel's proved to be a life the leading of which was not in his hands, a life tragically done before his father's:

> I have lived my life, and that which I have done
> May He within Himself make pure!

[9] *Tennyson: The Unquiet Heart*, p. 515.

When Lionel died in 1886, his grieving father at once set within his new poem 'Locksley Hall Sixty Years After' a tribute to his dead son, in lines which find a place in the *Memoir* and which, Hallam Tennyson records, 'were written immediately after the death of my brother, and decribed his chief characteristics': 'The Good, the True, the Pure, the Just!'

There is, then, a poet's suggestiveness in the decision to follow the title-page authorship BY HIS SON with an epigraph which, though plainly its central impulse is to pay tribute in his own words to the poet-father, yet speaks diversely to and of each of the three sons.

But before turning to the surviving 'dearest son', one might first contrast Hallam Tennyson's title-page with the differently valuable determination of two other such title-pages. There is the life of the poet in 1949 by his grandson, Charles Tennyson, the biography which first revealed so many truths about Tennyson and particularly about his life as a son, a biography which long held the field and will never, so evocative is it of a Victorian family-life which Sir Charles could recall, be dispensable. (Sir Charles, as many will remember, did not quite make one hundred; we were all set to celebrate him even more than usual, when, bright as a berry, in 1977 he died in his 98th year—died, in the dear word of his son, 'unexpectedly'.) The title-page:

ALFRED
TENNYSON

by his grandson
Charles Tennyson

This makes the family continuity clear and paramount; it effects nothing less; it seeks to effect nothing more; and it is unequivocal, since it gives both the relationship (*by his grandson*) and the name (*Charles Tennyson*—there had been more than one grandson of the poet, which is why the man who became Sir Charles Tennyson was not Lord Tennyson).

Something of the same happy unmistakability can be seen in the title-page of one of the earliest such biographies of an English poet, a life especially notable for the tender grace of its record of a death, the life of George Crabbe by his son. There are two title-pages in 1834. The first: THE / POETICAL WORKS / OF THE / REV.

GEORGE CRABBE: / WITH / HIS LETTERS AND HIS
JOURNALS, / AND HIS LIFE, / BY HIS SON. / IN EIGHT
VOLUMES. No name yet; instead the filial dignity only. And then,
as the following leaf: LIFE / OF THE / REV. GEORGE CRABBE,
LL.B. / BY HIS SON, / THE REV. GEORGE CRABBE, A.M.
   Not, any longer, just BY HIS SON, though this likewise has a
line to itself, but BY HIS SON, / THE REV. GEORGE CRABBE,
A.M. The assured differentiation between father and son is that of
their university degrees. A second differentiation: the father's name
is in larger print than the son's, as it should be.
   Hallam Tennyson, like the younger George Crabbe unrepiningly
no poet, was nevertheless quite sufficiently sensitive and imaginative
to be aware of what he might elicit when he succeeded the statement of authorship, BY HIS SON, with his, the father's, lines as
epigraph, epigraph as epitaph:

> I have lived my life, and that which I have done
> May He within Himself make pure!

For these words, and in particular the opening ones, constitute a
courteous tacit repudiation of what was everywhere said by those
who presumed to judge the life-choices of Hallam Tennyson. The
thing that was said of this son who was 40 when his father died,
and 45 when he completed this further task of dedication to his
dead father's life-work, was that he had not had a life, had not *lived
his life* but had given it up totally to his father and mother.

Someone once said of his ministrations to them—that he was son and
daughter combined—and he really seemed to be living their lives rather
than his own.[10]

Living their lives: Emily Tennyson too might say, from beyond the
grave by 1897, 'I have lived my life.'
   So when Hallam Tennyson followed his words BY HIS SON
with his, simultaneously his father's, words, 'I have lived my life . . .',
he was not only speaking as King Arthur (whose both having and
not having a father was indispensable to his mythic standing) but
speaking about his own relations to his father. He has something
to say in his unobtrusive person, and the better because not in his
own words but in his father's: contrary to what people will tell you,

---

[10] Elliott, *The Making of the Memoir*, p. 4, quoting a typescript of Elspeth Grahame,
in the Tennyson Research Centre, Lincoln.

given that self-sacrifice, far from being a way of losing one's life, is the only true way to gain it, *I have lived my life.*

There is a touching turn in the *Memoir* when Hallam Tennyson is brought back from Cambridge in 1875–6, breaking—for good and all—his undergraduate education at Trinity College. This calling-home was, for all its love, the rending re-enactment of the summons which had once been visited upon the young Alfred Tennyson, likewise called home in a family emergency and never returning to complete his degree at Trinity.

Hallam Tennyson reports this choice of life with economical equanimity, levelly framing it within, first, 'our daily life', and then 'Our life':

> In April 1874 the regular journal, giving the bare facts of our daily life, which my father had wished my mother to keep for his private use, comes to an end, so that I have no longer this on which to depend for the exact date as to days.
>
> Owing to my mother's illness I did not return to Cambridge after the Christmas of 1875, but remained at home as my father's secretary, a capacity in which there was much to be done.
>
> Yet he would willingly have set me free for a more definite career; and at one time he consulted Mr Gladstone as to my taking up a political life. Gladstone wrote in answer that my father must recollect that a political life was 'surrounded by an adamantine wall,' that a man in politics was apt to 'lose the finer moral sense,' and that the political outlook ahead was full of 'storms.'
>
> Our life did not undergo much change. (ii 208–9)

The touching life of this is all in the transitions, with their dignified subordination. Hallam Tennyson's own life has become enfolded within 'our daily life'; what 'comes to an end' is not just the family journal of their lives but his irrecoverable life as an undergraduate at Cambridge; the exoneration of his father ('Yet he would willingly have set me free') is proffered with what is itself evidence in Hallam Tennyson of just that 'finer moral sense' which political calculation may contaminate (Gladstone's warning); and when the last paragraph there begins anew with 'Our life did not undergo much change' (not 'Our lives'), any uncynical reader will be moved by Hallam Tennyson's fretless simplicity, alive with such an irony—like all worthwhile ironies—as is true to some degree in both senses, since though from one point of view Hallam Tennyson's abrupted life at Cambridge could hardly have undergone a greater change, from

another it is plain that this change was no more than the consummation of his earlier self-surrender, a homecoming to as well as by
his central self.

'We are grieved that our absolute need of Hallam at home has
prevented him from accomplishing his university career', wrote
Tennyson to the Master of Trinity.[11] Both parents were duly, rightly,
uneasy. The day before Tennyson died, Jowett wrote to Hallam
Tennyson: 'There was nothing that he would have desired more
than that you should make a name and career for yourself in your
own way, worthy of that which he bequeaths to you: he regretted
that he had been a drag upon you.'[12] With such potentialities for
parental guilt in the air ('Yet he would willingly have set me free'),
it is not surprising that Emily Tennyson should have said of the
peerage: 'That Hallam should inherit the duties belonging to this
distinction is cause of deep thankfulness to me'; she was thankful
'that he should have an honourable career marked out for him
when his work for his father has ceased'.[13] Hallam Tennyson's work
for his father ('He works his work, I mine') was not to cease until
his father ceased, or rather not even then, since prior to any
honourable career there was his honourable obligation to the task
of the *Memoir*. In due course a political career was to be his, but
only after he had done his best by his father's life. The peerage
brought its inherited duties, as his mother had hoped. It would be
to underrate him to say that he owed his becoming Governor-General
of Australia only to his peerage, but presumably being Lord Tennyson
was no hindrance.

Every page of the book carries, necessarily, Hallam Tennyson's
impress, but he did not impose himself upon it. When (this is given
in the *Memoir*) Bishop Brooks recorded his visit in 1883 to the
Tennysons' home and his meeting Mary Boyle and her niece Audrey,
Hallam Tennyson saw no occasion even to hint to the reader that
Miss B. with the loveliest smile is the woman whom he was soon
to marry, an incipient and further Mrs Tennyson. The Bishop's
sequence makes its own way:

[11] 29 March 1876; *The Letters of Alfred Lord Tennyson*, ed. Cecil Y. Lang and
Edgar F. Shannon, Jr., iii (1990), 126.
[12] Evelyn Abbott and Lewis Campbell, *The Life and Letters of Benjamin Jowett* (1897),
ii 458.
[13] To Gladstone, 27 September 1883; *Letters*, iii 264. Charles Tennyson, *Alfred
Tennyson* (1949), p. 472.

Dinner was very lively. Mrs Tennyson is a dear old lady, a great invalid, as sweet and pathetic as a picture. Then there are staying here Mr Lushington, a great Greek scholar, a Miss B., who knows everybody and tells funny stories, and another Miss B., her pretty niece, with the loveliest smile. After dinner, Tennyson and I went up to the study again, and I had him to myself for two or three hours. We smoked, and he talked of metaphysics, and poetry, and religion, his own life, and Hallam, and all the poems. (ii 295–6)

His own life, and Hallam: which Hallam? Probably Arthur Hallam, who even or especially in death had given such life to Tennyson, but we have the anecdote thanks to Hallam Tennyson, who lived his own life in living for his father.

> I have lived my life, and that which I have done
> May He within Himself make pure!

The *first* person who is the first-person 'I' there is, as it should be, Tennyson, who has lived his life, which is why there can now be a completed memoir of him. 'I', next: the speaker within the poem, King Arthur, in the poem 'Morte d'Arthur'—or rather in either that poem or in 'The Passing of Arthur' or in both; for these lines, it should be emphasized, carry an unusual emphasis in that they are among the few which Tennyson elected should be heard twice within his collected poems. Since the whole of 'Morte d'Arthur' is taken up, with additions, within 'The Passing of Arthur', these are lines which Tennyson twice asks us to attend to, lines which have a context diversely germane:

> The old order changeth, yielding place to new,

Not only in the body of the poems (as against within each of the poems), 'Morte d'Arthur' changed, yielding place to 'The Passing of Arthur', but also in the setting of the *Memoir*, where 'Not Amurath an Amurath succeeds', but Tennyson Tennyson:

> 'The old order changeth, yielding place to new,
> And God fulfils Himself in many ways,
> Lest one good custom should corrupt the world.
> Comfort thyself: what comfort is in me?
> I have lived my life, and that which I have done
> May He within Himself make pure! but thou,
> If thou shouldst never see my face again,
> Pray for my soul.'

The central two lines derive from Tennyson's love of his dead Arthur, Arthur Hallam without whose early death ('I have lived my life') we should not have either Tennyson's 'Morte d'Arthur' or the name of Hallam Tennyson, here an unnamed author. (Alan Sinfield's 1986 book on Tennyson created a poem for our time with its inadvertent index-entry 'Morte d'Authur'.)

The second line of the epigraph is there left incomplete: 'May He within Himself make pure!' It waits for ever for the words which both complete the line and begin the succeeding thought: 'but thou,'. What was asked of Sir Bedivere was such love as is asked of Hallam Tennyson.

The two lines are benignly retorted upon Tennyson himself, who did not believe himself pure but did believe that he was such as Christ could within Himself make pure. 'Pray for my soul': the *Memoir* might itself be construed as a prayer for the soul of Alfred Tennyson. We are not prevented from praying for his repose.

There is, it has to be acknowledged, some invitation to take the He ('May He within Himself') as Tennyson. We may receive this with reluctance; such a capital H when the He is Human does grate upon modern sensibilities; but in her journal Emily Tennyson did not shrink from rendering her Husband a capital H as He. She was not alone in this; the creepy schoolmaster Henry Graham Dakyns, tutor to the Tennyson boys Hallam and Lionel, later laid this unction to them:

To avoid repetition and for reverence' sake, I shall speak of Lord and Lady Tennyson as Him and Her, and of yourselves, my two pupils, by your names. If I have occasion to mention myself (your old tutor) I will use the symbol Δ, the first letter of Δακυντδιον, which, being interpreted, is 'Little Dakyns,' by which name your father spoke of me, at least on one occasion.[14]

Hallam Tennyson, serving but unservile, shared something of this feeling that his father was He. And if we judge that this makes Tennyson disconcertingly like God, I think that the *Memoir* would be prepared to meet that, not least because such a belief would not have discomposed the poet. The Mediator makes use of other mediators, beyond the grave, there where Arthur Hallam may help to make pure that which we have done which we ought not to have done.

[14] *Tennyson and His Friends*, p. 188.

> Be near us when we climb or fall:
> Ye watch, like God, the rolling hours
> With larger other eyes than ours,
> To make allowance for us all.
>
> (*In Memoriam*, li)

'Like God': Hallam Tennyson's last quotation in the *Memoir* is from the 'Ode on the Death of the Duke of Wellington', imaginatively refocused on the death of Tennyson and his funeral. The passage (the last sixteen lines of the poem) ends: 'God accept him, Christ receive him.' It begins: 'On God and Godlike men we build our trust'.

To move from the title-page to the dedication is to see not only Hallam Tennyson's privilege as the son of the poet but his necessary independence of his father, because the first thing that he did, having quoted on the title-page from his father's published work, was to quote something unpublished, indeed a rejected version of a published poem.

Tennyson did not wish 'the chips of the workshop' to be made public, and it was for this reason that Hallam Tennyson, when he made his magnificent munificent gift of Tennyson manuscripts to Trinity College in 1924, did so on the condition that though they be exhibited, they not be copied or quoted *in perpetuity*. This interdiction the College (wisely choosing one form of piety over another) decided to annul in 1969, at the urging of the fourth Lord Tennyson and of Sir Charles Tennyson—honour, honour, honour to them, and to the then College Librarian, Philip Gaskell.[15]

---

[15] Engaged in 1966 in editing the poems of Tennyson (published 1969), and working under the interdiction, I deprecated the fact 'that there can be no authoritative correction of the many errors in transcription which Hallam Tennyson himself made in publishing poems from these manuscripts. In 1913 he published a fragment about Semele, which begins:

> I wish'd to see Him. Who may feel
> His light and love? He comes.

"Love" is an error; the manuscript clearly reads: "Who may feel / His light and . . ."—but the correct reading may not be quoted. Since apparently no other manuscript of "Semele" survives, an editor has either to perpetuate the error "love", or to amend it without being able to cite his authority. In the circumstances, one is tempted to go in for crossword-clues: this is an evil setback' ('Tennyson's Methods of Composition', *Proceedings of the British Academy*, lii, 210). I fear that few of my listeners or readers understood that the evil setback is *live*.

In honouring his father, Hallam Tennyson is moved to override the poet's wishes while showing himself sensitive to what is at issue.

THESE VOLUMES ARE DEDICATED

BY PERMISSION

TO THE QUEEN.

Whereupon Hallam Tennyson preserves an essential continuity by putting forward as his dedication a poem which Tennyson himself had proffered as a dedication, and yet uniquely does so in that the world had never seen this version of this poem.

An Unpublished Version of 'To the Queen,' 1851.

THE NOBLEST MEN METHINKS ARE BRED
OF OURS THE SAXO-NORMAN RACE;
AND IN THE WORLD THE NOBLEST PLACE,
MADAM, IS YOURS, OUR QUEEN AND HEAD.

YOUR NAME IS BLOWN ON EVERY WIND,
YOUR FLAG THRO' AUSTRAL ICE IS BORNE,
AND GLIMMERS TO THE NORTHERN MORN,
AND FLOATS IN EITHER GOLDEN IND.

I GIVE THIS FAULTY BOOK TO YOU,
FOR, THO' THE FAULTS BE THICK AS DUST
IN VACANT CHAMBERS, I CAN TRUST
YOUR WOMAN'S NATURE KIND AND TRUE.

And just as the epigraph on the title-page acknowledged its selector's implication in that which more importantly had independent point, so the dedication of the *Memoir* is in its quiet way self-referential: in speaking of the faults of a book, it at once concurs with the poet (he had been right to publish, at the head of the edition of his poems which followed his just having become Poet Laureate, not this but the reconsidered version of the poem) and acknowledges the *Memoir*'s own limitations and shortcomings.

Setting aside Tennyson's too-easy faith in the British Empire, and our too-easy want of faith in it, I note in passing what it meant to Hallam Tennyson to summon this sometime pride in the two Indias, 'either golden Ind'. Between Tennyson's writing of this version of the 1851 dedication, and Hallam Tennyson's use of it as the dedication in 1897, there had supervened the tragedy which left grimly unambiguous the authorship BY HIS SON. Lionel Tennyson's Ind had not proved golden; he gave his life for the India Office, having gone to India and contracted the fever which killed him as he was returning. The whole of the *Memoir* is shadowed by the fraternal aftersight of this family filial tragedy, this maternal and paternal heartbreak.

'I give this faulty book to you': Hallam Tennyson is not only speaking through lines which his father had indeed found faulty (An Unpublished Version) but speaking of the inescapable faults of the biography itself. But there was no fault in the dedicatory choice of this poem, perfect as to stanza form, where there coincided the elegiac stanza of *In Memoriam* and the patriotic stanza which Tennyson had developed in poems of the 1830s. 'To the Queen', the first poem which Tennyson published as Poet Laureate, his first Laureate act (and it was *In Memoriam* which had won him the Laureateship in 1850), is a patriotic poem which is here turned to elegiac purposes, an *In Memoriam* not only for Tennyson but for Lionel Tennyson.

It is often said or implied that Hallam Tennyson was a dullard and couldn't possibly have shaped a book well or written it well. But his evocation of Queen Victoria, when he was a child, might begin a questioning of this condescension. In May 1863, at the age of 10, he manifested an economical acumen:

> The Queen wears a locket round her neck with thin black velvet. The Queen is not stout. Her Majesty has a large mind and a small body to contain it therein.
>
> *Observations:*—You must always say 'Mam' when in her Majesty's presence. You must stand until the Queen asks you to sit down. Her Majesty does not *often* tell you to sit down.
>
> Finis[16]

Ask you to sit down / tell you to sit down: to be asked by the Queen is to be told.

Hallam Tennyson lived for forty years in the immediate loving presence of a man intensely sensitive to words; the supposition that none of this came home to him is implausible.

The shape of the *Memoir* is this: it begins with the dedication to the Queen, and it draws to an end, after the body of the book, after Tennyson's death, after his funeral service and the plaque which

---

[16] Hope Dyson and Charles Tennyson, *Dear and Honoured Lady* (1969), p. 78.

honours him, with a complete page in square brackets [square brackets having as usual the function of containedly deepening and recessing, the editor's prerogative], this page not being part of the book proper but a grave coda to it:

[It has taken me four years to complete this Memoir of my father. Throughout, my mother's assistance has been invaluable. She passed away peacefully at Aldworth, August 10th, 1896 (having entered her eighty-fourth year, the age at which my father died), and we laid her to rest in the quiet churchyard at Freshwater. A few days before her death she expressed her satisfaction that she had lived long enough to help me to correct the proofs for the press. . . .] (ii 432)

This last page is dedicated to his mother, *his* Queen. It has at its head:

MY MOTHER'S DEATH   [1896

and it concludes with the church inscription 'to the memory of my father and mother'. Contained within its square brackets, it affords Emily Lady Tennyson a finely judged tribute, distinguishing her as she would have wished. She was not a poet; she was not wronged, unappreciated, or a 'marginalized' genius; there would have been no *Memoir* of her, though her son's book is, among much else, a memoir of her.

Whereupon you turn the page, and enter the correspondence with Queen Victoria.

Framing this intensely patriarchal book, then, are acts of tribute by men of power to women of power, overt and covert: first, Tennyson's, and Hallam Tennyson's, dedication to the Queen; then, in the penultimate moment of the book, the tribute to Emily Lady Tennyson; and finally the return to the Queen in her relations to the poet.

After the dedication, the preface too opens with unpublished verses (again an act of privilege and of independence):

Unpublished Sonnet
(*Written originally as a preface to 'Becket'*).

Just as for his dedication Hallam Tennyson had chosen something written by the poet as a dedication but not used by him, so for the preface he resurrects a preface that had been willingly let die.

Old ghosts whose day was done ere mine began,
If earth be seen from your conjectured heaven,
Ye know that History is half-dream—ay even
The man's life in the letters of the man.
There lies the letter, but it is not he
As he retires into himself and is:
Sender and sent-to go to make up this,
Their offspring of this union. And on me
Frown not, old ghosts, if I be one of those
Who make you utter things you did not say,
And mould you all awry and mar your worth;
For whatsoever knows us truly, knows
That none can truly write his single day,
And none can write it for him upon earth.

It proves to be the Victorian writers (the poet and his biographer), not the modern ones, who have the surer sense of the ultimate unknowability even of the best-attended-to biographical subject. The line these days is that all we do is impose ourselves, as upon everything else; all biographies are fictions, since everything is a fiction; and all biographies are autobiographies.

This half of the truth, pressed in our day to the point of half-truth or heresy (in T. S. Eliot's understanding of the term), is more inwardly understood by Hallam Tennyson than by his modern academic counterparts. For one thing, Hallam Tennyson understands that it is half of the truth, and he braces it against the daunting possibility of substantial understanding. For another, he writes, *pace* all those who unstrenuously deplore his piety, without complacency.

Professor Martin, in his comparable preface, insists on candour—rightly, but rightly because of what Hallam Tennyson had effected and had left still to be done. Martin insists upon much more candour than any Victorian biography would have felt wise: 'To ignore the imperfections of a man is to patronize him, as if the whole truth of his character were not to be faced.' But the whole truth of a man's character is not to be found. Which is why Hallam Tennyson opens his preface with this curiously haunting admission of inevitable failure which yet—since he is concurring with his father's poem—is witness to an act of understanding.

For whatsoever knows us truly, knows
That none can truly write his single day,
And none can write it for him upon earth.

Perhaps in the great book of heaven it will be written, but here upon earth it cannot be written.

An offspring of Tennyson cites a poem about further forms of 'offspring': lives and letters. The poem unostentatiously realizes the half of the truth of which our time believes itself fully in possession (too fully, I believe): 'Sender and sent-to go to make up this'. What saves the poem, as it saved both Tennyson and his son, from being paralysed by such concession, is faith in a cognate religious mystery: the humanly-unknowable man, 'As he retires into himself and is', partakes in this of the divine: 'Though I uncircumscrib'd my self retire'. No man, not only no God, can be circumscribed (with 'Word' reaching to 'uncircumscrib'd'):

> And thou my Word, begotten Son, by thee
> This I perform, speak thou, and be it don:
> .   .   .   .
>
> Boundless the Deep, because I am who fill
> Infinitude, nor vacuous the space.
> Though I uncircumscrib'd my self retire,
>
> *(Paradise Lost*, vii 163–4, 168–70)

Without impiety (though risking blasphemy, as any serious religious utterance must), Tennyson's begotten son mediates the word. Rather, the words—those of Milton that had been taken up within Tennyson's poem.

The preface, then, at once constitutes the acknowledgements, the immediate acknowledgement: you are not going to know my father; you would not *know* him even if you had lived with him as I did; and you must not suppose that the promise made (a preface is a promise) is that you will *know* him. An 'innermost sanctuary' is sacred, and we may seek it only on the strict condition that we know we will not find it, as Hallam Tennyson promptly moves to remind us:

> 'History is half-dream—ay even
> The man's life in the letters of the man';

but besides the letters of my father and of his friends there are his poems, and in these we must look for the innermost sanctuary of his being. For my own part, I feel strongly that no biographer could so truly give him as he gives himself in his own works;

—a lovely turn upon what it is to *give yourself*, in that self-giving which is self-portrayal and self-surrender, in art, love, and worship—

as he gives himself in his own works; but this may be because, having lived my life with him,

—'I have lived my life . . .'—

having lived my life with him, I see him in every word which he has written; and it is difficult for me so far to detach myself from the home circle as to pourtray him for others. (i xi–xii)

'The innermost sanctuary of his being': Hallam Tennyson's mother had written to him, when he was 20, 'Be very careful about thy language, old darling—no slipshod above all things. Go as far as possible into the innermost depths of thy being. What comes there expresses itself naturally in clear forceful language.'[17]

Clear forceful language animates the preface, as when he speaks of 'the journal of our home life': 'This last is a simple record of daily something-nothings' (i xvi). An excellent phrase, 'a simple record of daily something-nothings'. When I first met it, I thought to myself, This is a real writer; and then, upon reflection, not less of a writer in making something anew of others' words. Not stealing them. The phrase is a benign reimagining of the malign energy of Iago ('Who steales my purse, steales trash: 'Tis something, nothing'); but the phrase had already been graced with such benignity by Tennyson himself. Hallam Tennyson's crisp simplicity, 'a simple record of daily something-nothings', is achieved by courtesy of his father, who had created for *Becket* the exchange: 'What did you ask her?' 'Some daily something nothing' (III i).

It is on the second page of the first chapter of the *Memoir* that Alfred Tennyson enters the world. The paragraph begins:

Here, on the 6th of August, 1809, was born, in his father's rectory, Alfred Tennyson.

The next paragraph begins: 'In 1892'. 1892 was the year of Tennyson's death, and the consecutive openings ('1809, was born' / 'In 1892') cannot but suggest that the poet's death is already colouring, shadowing, the page on which he is born. Both of the paragraphs, though, modify a reader's propensities, in their tissue of life and death.

[17] 12 May 1873; *The Letters of Emily Lady Tennyson*, ed. James O. Hoge (1974), p. 301.

Here, on the 6th of August, 1809, was born, in his father's rectory, Alfred Tennyson. He was the fourth of twelve children, eight sons and four daughters, most of them more or less true poets, and of whom all except two have lived to 70 and upward. Dr Tennyson baptized the boy two days after he was born, following the Prayer-book instruction that people 'defer not the Baptism of their children longer than the first or second Sunday next after their birth.'

> 'Here's a leg for a babe of a week!' says doctor; and
>   he would be bound,
> There was not his like that year in twenty parishes round,

was said of him; nevertheless during his infancy three times after convulsions he was thought to be dead.
    In 1892 I visited the old home,

—at which point, my first thought as a reader is that Tennyson is being remembered as having died. This, not only because the two lines from 'The Grandmother' (Hallam Tennyson identified them in a footnote) are from a poem on her first, still-born, child *and* on the recent death (at nearly 70—'lived to 70 and upward') of her eldest son. There are other intimations of mortality. The previous paragraph had ended, of the infant Tennyson, 'three times after convulsions he was thought to be dead', and the next paragraph at once opens with the year of Tennyson's death: 'In 1892 I visited the old home'. But, happily as life and as biographical art, the memory is other:

> In 1892 I visited the old home, and when I returned, told my father that the trees had grown up obscuring the view from the Rectory, and that the house itself looked very desolate. All he answered was, 'Poor little place!'

'The house itself looked very desolate': 'Your house is left unto you desolate.' The author of *Aylmer's Field* was still alive, at this recorded moment in 1892, but standing on the very verge of his confine.
    This unsentimental tremulousness shines through all the opening pages, as when two pages later there is a return to this return by Hallam Tennyson in 1892:

> When there I looked in vain for the words 'Byron is dead,' which he had carved on a rock when he was fourteen, on hearing of Byron's death (April 19th, 1824), 'a day when the whole world seemed to be darkened for me.'

As the whole world was to be darkened for Hallam Tennyson and Emily Tennyson many years later than 1824 but only a few months later in 1892.

Or again there is the unforgettable description ('I shall never forget . . .') of his father's last reading of *Maud*, which is placed, by another of Hallam Tennyson's perfectly simple but inspired temporalities, not at the time when it occurred, two months before Tennyson died in 1892, but within the year in which *Maud* appeared, 1855: 'I shall never forget his last reading of *Maud*, on August 24th, 1892. He was sitting in his high-backed chair, fronting a southern window which looks over the groves and yellow cornfields of Sussex' (i 395).

Joy culminates in 'Come into the garden, Maud,' and my father's eyes, which were through the other love-passages veiled by his drooping lids, would suddenly flash as he looked up and spoke these words, the passion in his voice deepening in the last words of the stanza:

> She is coming, my own, my sweet;
>   Were it ever so airy a tread,
> My heart would hear her and beat,
>   Were it earth in an earthy bed;
> My dust would hear her and beat,
>   Had I lain for a century dead;
> Would start and tremble under her feet,
>   And blossom in purple and red.

(i 397)

By the time Hallam Tennyson tells us this, his father is earth in an earthy bed, but his father's heart still lives and beats in these lines themselves. (He has now lain for a century dead; his lines, if we allow ourselves truly to hear them, still start and tremble and blossom.) Remembering this moment—within two months of it, Tennyson lay dead, and in the year of the *Memoir*'s publication, he had lain for a lustrum dead—Hallam Tennyson was himself moved to create a love-passage. Perhaps some part was played by the coincidence that, as Hallam Tennyson knew, this stanza, recorded thanks to an emissary of Edison's at the end of the poet's life, would allow the hearts of subsequent generations to hear the poet read the poem. 'My heart would hear her and beat.' This is the stanza of life beyond the grave, and it should not be only Tennyson's eyes that flash.

It is because of such passages, such passings, as these that I am vexed by those who, without ever showing so or even feeling obliged to argue the matter sustainedly, assert that Hallam Tennyson was not up to it; that it is not he who is exercising imagination but I who, in being stirred by his words and his transitions, am imagining things.

So he was not a poet, but that would not have to mean that he could not write at least as well as a professor. 'A simple absence of curiosity'?

But we are dealing here, of course, with a rather unimaginative writer, who would probably never have written a biography if he had not been the son of a great and much-revered father.[18]

A. O. J. Cockshut is likely to be right in thinking that this was the only biography which Hallam Tennyson would ever have been moved to write, but this has no bearing on whether, when so moved, Hallam Tennyson was capable of imagination. 'But we are dealing here, of course, with a rather unimaginative writer.' Of course.

If I had to select a tissue of particular moments of transparent success, it would be constituted of chronographia, a figure—a picture of the passing of time—particularly valuable in elegiac biography, and more than usually so in the life of a poet as diversely sensitive to time as Tennyson was. In picturing in his memory's eye, and hearing in his memory's ear, that last reading of *Maud*, Hallam Tennyson was drawn naturally to a parenthetical glimpse of his father's high-domed head 'outlined against the sunset-clouds seen through the western window'. And there is a finely-etched and finely-judged chapter-ending for 1880, perfect in its chronographia of twilight and eyesight, when Hallam Tennyson quotes 'Frater Ave atque Vale' in its entirety, doubly an elegy, Catullus's and Tennyson's for *his* brother, and now triply an elegy, since for Tennyson too. And then the chapter immediately concludes with these observant paragraphs:

Miss Ritchie was staying at Farringford when we came back from our foreign travels. To her he dwelt with more pleasure on the row to Desenzano than on almost anything else, and on the associations of Sirmione with Catullus. The long July twilight had at last died away whilst he talked of all he had been seeing, and lights were brought, and I fetched him a volume of Catullus.

He made Miss Ritchie, who was no Latin scholar, follow the words as he read through some of his favourite poems. His finger moved from word to word, and he dwelt with intense satisfaction on the adequacy of the

---

[18] *Truth to Life* (1974), p. 39.

expression and of the sounds, on the mastery of the proper handling of quantity, and on the perfection of the art. (ii 248)

Such a chapter-ending is itself an intense satisfaction, a proper handling, the perfection of an art. Once again, Hallam Tennyson shows his mastery of others' words, for here he adapted Emily Ritchie's own account, paraphrasing and reordering, and by turning it into the third person, endowing it with a dignity even greater than she had elicited.[19]

Chapter xxiii of volume ii is called THE LAST CHAPTER. It is the last chapter of the *Memoir*, and the last chapter of Tennyson's life; that Tennyson never wrote in chapters permits the book to maintain its due distance from the art which it honours.

My sense of the *Memoir*'s prospects and architectonics asks that attention be paid to chapter xvii of volume ii:

DEATH OF LIONEL. 'LOCKSLEY HALL SIXTY YEARS AFTER.' 1886.

The chapter begins by quoting four and a half lines from Tennyson's great poem 'To the Marquis of Dufferin and Ava', without naming it, and then moves directly to the tragic context:

> Not there to bid my boy farewell,
> When That within the coffin fell,
> Fell and flash'd into the Red Sea,
> Beneath a hard Arabian moon
> And alien stars.

We had always been so united a family that my brother Lionel's death, in April 1886, as he was returning from India, was an overwhelming grief to us, 'a grief as deep as life or thought.'

---

[19] Tennyson, *Letters*, iii 197 n, quotes Emily Ritchie, from *Materials*: 'He made me who am no Latin scholar follow the words as he read through some of his favourite poems. Never was so inspiring an initiation into classic beauty. His finger moved, from word to word, dwelling with the most intense satisfaction on the perfection of the art, on the adequacy of the expression and of the sounds, and the mastery of the proper handling of quantity.' Hallam Tennyson forewent the fervour of 'Never was so inspiring an initiation into classical beauty', which is too rich for the twilit colouring and for the tender grace of the occasion; he moved 'the perfection of the art' so that it came at the conclusion, instead of the lesser thing, 'the proper handling of quantity'; and he stationed the whole touching reminiscence as an elegiac ending to a chapter.

And then after thirty lines devoted to the thirty years of Lionel's brief life:

He started for home from Calcutta at the beginning of April. Then came the last days on the Red Sea. He spoke little and did not suffer much pain. He passed away peacefully at three in the afternoon of April 20th. The burial service was at nine that same evening, under a great silver moon. The ship stopped: and the coffin was lowered into a phosphorescent sea. (ii 322–3)

Whereupon the page is ruled by a line, dividing with decorum this mortal rite of passage from all which follows. Then the rule is followed:

In June Dr Oliver Wendell Holmes and his daughter visited us at Farringford. My father told him that he admired his 'Chambered Nautilus.' When they parted, Wendell Holmes said to him, 'We have points of contact, have we not?' Which was true enough, especially in their humour.

It is a charming and consolatory evocation of life's proper resumption, social life at Farringford, with humour too, after a lonely death beneath alien stars. But in the transition (passage again), Hallam Tennyson's unassuming sequence is much more than a reassuming. 'We have points of contact, have we not?'

Holmes and his daughter met Tennyson and his son, now his only surviving son. 'My father told him that he admired his "Chambered Nautilus".' These transitions and juxtapositions are those of recorded life itself, and Hallam Tennyson is reporting no more than what happened; and yet, given the multifarious materials at hand, he chose a sequence, one which then invokes at exactly the right moment—following 'and the coffin was lowered into a phosphorescent sea'—Tennyson's appreciation of 'The Chambered Nautilus', a poem devoted to the death of the body, the soul's immortality, and 'life's unresting sea'.

> Build thee more stately mansions, O my soul,
>   As the swift seasons roll!
>   Leave thy low-vaulted past!
> Let each new temple, nobler than the last,
> Shut thee from heaven with a dome more vast,
>   Till thou at length art free,
> Leaving thine outgrown shell by life's unresting sea!

Yet 'The Chambered Nautilus' has none of the immitigable ache at the heart, despairing of theodicy though not of God's love, of Tennyson's elegy at 80 for Lionel at 32, 'To the Marquis of Dufferin and Ava':

X

And sacred is the latest word;
  And now the Was, the Might-have-been,
  And those lone rites I have not seen,
And one drear sound I have not heard,

XI

Are dreams that scarce will let me be,
  Not there to bid my boy farewell,
  When That within the coffin fell,
Fell—and flashed into the Red Sea,

XII

Beneath a hard Arabian moon
  And alien stars. To question, why
  The sons before the fathers die,
Not mine! and I may meet him soon;

XIII

But while my life's late eve endures,
  Nor settles into hueless gray,
  My memories of his briefer day
Will mix with love for you and yours.

The poem is bowed with grief; there at the end it bows, in loving courtesy, to those—the Viceroy of India and his family—who had been good to the member of Tennyson's family. How firmly and how delicately the inversion ('To question, why / The sons before the fathers die, / Not mine!') manages to combine—as the ordinary order would not—an insistence that such a question inevitably cries out, with the insistence that it can be truly curbed by Christian resignation. And how little the plural ('The sons'), because it is paired with 'the fathers',[20] insists on an individual life-story (more than one son dead) rather than the story of life, while at the same time, 'The sons', being so true to Tennyson's own pangs.

[20] Robert Bernard Martin gives the lines as 'To question, why / The sons before the father die'; remarkable what a difference the singular 'father' makes to the poem's solicitous range (*Tennyson: The Unquiet Heart*, p. 558).

An anguished pathos ('That a sorrow's crown of sorrow is re-membering happier things') has come to fall, by the time of the *Memoir*, upon the level anecdotes of Lionel as a child:

My father was always interested in the imaginative views which we chil-dren took of our surroundings. Of these I may give one instance: how Lionel had been brought from his bed at night, wrapt in a blanket, to see the great comet, and suddenly awaking and looking out at the starry night, asked, 'Am I dead?' (i 370)

The starry night of the English skies, as against 'a hard Arabian moon / And alien stars'. Am I dead? Is he dead?

'Sometimes', Hallam Tennyson writes of his bereaved father, 'when he was with us alone he would say, "The thought of Lionel's death tears me to pieces, he was so full of promise and so young"' (ii 324).

But far from tearing the *Memoir* to pieces, Lionel's death does much to compose it as an imaginative work. Again and again there are intimations of mortality which are yet entirely free from any abuse of either aftersight or foresight, as in that story 'Am I dead?', set down without fudging or nudging, and followed immediately (the next words, beginning the next paragraph) by: 'The chief anxiety of my parents, I remember . . .' It is not Hallam Tennyson's place to comment on these shadowings, but his placing them within the book, and his placing them where he does, must often give them a sombre weight. I think for instance of two long letters from Benjamin Jowett back in 1858, suggesting possible subjects for poems. To Professor Martin, Jowett is fatuous here:

Truly, as Jowett said, 'Subjects like blackberries seem to me capable of being gathered off every hedge'. And those he suggested were often worth about as much as blackberries.[21]

But Hallam Tennyson judged Jowett's long letters worth including, and it is worth bringing ourselves to ask why. The answer is not that Jowett was an eminent Victorian, a handsome ornament to this monument, but that among Jowett's urgings, twenty-eight years before India killed Lionel Tennyson ('India was his fate') and before Tennyson in his grief turned yet once more to the *In Memoriam* stanza, there had been this adjuration of Jowett's:

---

[21]   *Tennyson: The Unquiet Heart*, p. 424. *Memoir*, i 433.

I want to suggest something that would 'express the thoughts of many hearts,' which I must always think to be the highest excellence of poetry, and afford a solace where it is much needed. The subject I mean is 'In Memoriam' for the dead in India. It might be done so as to include some scenes of Cawnpore and Lucknow; or quite simply and slightly, 'Relatives in India,' the schemings and hopings and imaginings about them, and the fatal missive suddenly announcing their death. They leave us in the fairness and innocence of youth, with nothing but the vision of their childhood and boyhood to look back upon, and return no more.

Perhaps you know what sets my thoughts upon this, the death of my dear brother, the second who has died in India. It matters nothing to the world, for they had never the opportunity of distinguishing themselves, but it matters a great deal to me. They were dear good disinterested fellows, most unselfish in their ways, and as grateful to me for what I did for them when they were boys, as if it had been yesterday. I like to think of them in the days of their youth busying themselves with engineering which was their great amusement. They were wonderfully attached to each other. The younger one especially, who died first about five years ago, was one of the sweetest dispositions I ever knew.

If I did not venture to look upon you and Mr Tennyson as something like friends, I should not venture to trouble you with this sorrow about persons whom you have never seen or heard of. (i 435)

In the *Memoir*, Jowett's letter is respected in itself, as it should be; the letter is not inserted to serve the biographer's turn, though— under the pressure of prospect and retrospect ('the Was, the Might-have-been')—it does take on the dark colouring of the family tragedy. This letter of Jowett's in December 1858 had expressed its gratitude for 'the two sweet letters of the children': 'Lionel's epistle especially is just a picture of a child's mind' (i 434).

Such an effect is possible only within a Life and Letters, a genre within biography that is now thoughtlessly underrated and misrepresented, uniquely imaginative in its variety of textures and of metabolism.

Let me take a sequence of a letter within journal entries, again with the thought of Lionel's death in our minds though it could not at the time, 1871, have been in Tennyson's, except in so far as any parent who joins in mourning must spare a thought for his own children, and especially any parent who has already lost a child. The letter, naturally enough but at a price that we should recognize, can find no place within a persistingly single biographical format, tone and procedure, like Professor Martin's, a format which now has the monopoly.

The following letter was written by A. to Mrs Elmhirst (née Rawnsley) on the death of her son:

HASLEMERE, June, 1871.

MY DEAR SOPHY,

I ought to have written to you before to express my sympathy with you on the loss of your son, and I thought of writing at the moment when I first heard of your great affliction, but somehow I myself have always felt that letters of condolence, when the grief is yet raw and painful, are like vain voices in the ears of the deaf, not heard or only half heard. 'The heart knoweth its own bitterness,' and a stranger intermeddleth not therewith, though I am not a stranger indeed, but your old friend from your childhood. However, when Drummond and Catherine were here the other day, he said he thought you would be soothed by hearing from me; so I write, though I doubt whether I can bring you any solace, except indeed by stating my own belief that the son, whom you so loved, is not really what we call dead, but more actually living than when alive here.

You cannot catch the voice, or feel the hands, or kiss the cheek, that is all; a separation for an hour, not an eternal farewell. If it were not so, that which made us would seem too cruel a Power to be worshipped, and could not be loved, but I trust that you believe all this, and by this time have attained to some degree of tranquillity: and your husband also.

I hear that *he* was very amiable and full of promise, and the manner of his death, and its taking place far away from you, and its suddenness, must have so added sorrow to sorrow, that I almost fear you will think I write coldly, but I do not feel coldly. Kindest remembrances to Elmhirst, and also to the Hallidays, and

Believe me affectionately yours,

A. TENNYSON.

June 22nd. A. and Hallam went to town for the Royal Academy.

June. Aldworth. Tourgueneff the Russian novelist (whose *Lisa* and *Pères et Enfants* A. liked much) and Mr Ralston arrived. Tourgueneff (a tall, large, white-haired man with a strong face) was most interesting, and told us stories of Russian life with a great graphic power and vivacity. (ii 105–6)

The letter of condolence is loving; the immediate journal-juxtaposition ('A. and Hallam', *Fathers and Sons*) invites an affectionate thinking about such feelings; and the two combine with the past loss of one of Tennyson's sons and the future loss of another ('its taking place far away from you, and its suddenness': this would prove tragically apt), to create a weight achievable only when working with materials of such a differing weave as these, and not in the smoother fashioning of what has become in biography the usual wear.

Later, far later, in 1891, the year before Tennyson died, there is this succession, entirely straightforward and profoundly suggestive (and again not such as would figure within our current biographical conventions):

> My father wrote in July to Gladstone about the death of his eldest son:
>
> MY DEAR FRIEND,
>
> Only one word from myself and my wife to say how fully we sympathize with you. More than this one word at the present moment would be intrusive.
>
> He spent his birthday, Aug. 6th, quietly, talking over old days with Aubrey de Vere. (ii 389)

The death of an old friend's son, the birthday of an old man: thou met'st with things dying, I with things far from new born. But Tennyson's, though not Gladstone's, eldest son is alive to set this down; and yet not the eld*est*, and for this reason all too aware of what was passing through his father's mind when he sent these condolences to a friend. 'The sons before the fathers die.' And for Hallam Tennyson too, recording this letter of condolence, to say even 'one word at the present moment would be intrusive'.

The *Memoir* has its coda; an account of the *Memoir* may have one: this, on a lack in Lives.

Philip Larkin tilted at Tennyson in the second of two (unpublished) poems celebrating 'The Literary World':

> Mrs Alfred Tennyson
> Answered
>   begging letters
>   admiring letters
>   insulting letters
>   enquiring letters

> business letters
> and publishers' letters.
> She also
> looked after his clothes
> saw to his food and drink
> entertained visitors
> protected him from gossip and criticism
> And finally
> (apart from running the household)
> Brought up and educated the children.
>
> While all this was going on
> Mister Alfred Tennyson sat like a baby
> Doing his poetic business.

By the poet who gave us (with irony, but) 'Books are a load of crap'. Larkin did well not to print 'The Literary World'. Just a smack at Tennyson, since it too much smacks of the infantile itself. But something catches the mind in that glimpse of Tennyson ruling the house less as patriarch than as baby.

The greatest biography in the language, and perhaps in any language, is of a man who had no child: Samuel Johnson.

Charlotte Brontë did not live to have a child. The Carlyles, though they lived long, had no child. (Jane Austen, George Eliot, Henry James, T. S. Eliot, D. H. Lawrence, Samuel Beckett: childless.) The life of Tennyson offers an unusual opportunity and challenge; it might evince a half of the truth not addressed by Hallam Tennyson and not entertained by Professor Martin since biographers do not seriously entertain it: the understanding that, not only are children formed by their parents, but parents are formed by their children. In life, though not in Lives, children are formers as well as formees. This reciprocity, not (it must be granted) equipollence, goes neglected.

We have a deep reluctance to admit about family life what we casually grant elsewhere: that, say, teachers are changed by their students, as well as students by their teachers. Lionel Trilling, him-self a fine contributor to Victorian Lives, took comfort from his confidence in Freud's conviction of 'a hard, irreducible, stubborn core of biological urgency, and biological necessity, and biological *reason*, that culture cannot reach'.[22] Trilling went on to a reminder:

---

[22] (1955), *Beyond Culture* (1966), p. 115.

We must not permit ourselves to be at the mercy of the terrible pendulum of thought and begin now to discredit all that we have learned about cultural influence or conclude that parents have been suddenly relieved of all responsibility for their children's psychic destinies.

I should wish to offer a plea: that children not be relieved of all responsibility for their parents' psychic destinies. It is both a glory and a peril of the English language that someone who is no longer a child remains your child.

An even more true biography of Tennyson than Hallam Tennyson's would have to be imaginatively interested in the ways in which the son came to shape the life and not just the Life of his father.

The usual half of the truth is more socially serviceable. But your children do change you, inexorably. Larkin, childless on principle ('And don't have any kids yourself'), caught this in his evocation of young mothers at the playground, 'Afternoons':

> Their beauty has thickened.
> Something is pushing them
> To the side of their own lives.

This something is their own new young lives, pushing them to the side of their own lives. And this is quite as true of modern lives as of Victorian lives.

GEORGE ELIOT:
'SHE WAS STILL YOUNG'

She died, in December 1880, seven months after she married young John Cross, more than twenty years younger than she. Her great successor Henry James wrote home in a letter:[1]

This event is really very sad: she, poor woman, had begun a new (personal) life: a more healthy, objective one than she had ever known before. I doubt whether she would have written, but she would have lived—and after all, at sixty, and with a great desire to live, she was still young.

She was not 60 when she died, but 61; not that this would matter if it were not that she had apparently permitted herself the smallest possible form of a traditional vanity, by sometimes making out that she was one year younger than she really was. Her coffin carried the untrue touching date of birth, '1820'.[2]

When you speak of someone else as still young, you are not thinking only of that someone else's age: Henry James was 37, and he was writing to his mother who was 70. 'At sixty, and with a great desire to live, she was still young': more than twenty years earlier, back in her first work of fiction, *Scenes of Clerical Life*, George Eliot had imagined an elderly man hoping for an heir, a grand-nephew, 'whom he might even yet live to see a fine young fellow with at least the down on his chin. Why not? one is still young at sixty.'[3] But it is characteristic of George Eliot that she was alive not only to the hope but to the despair which could be still young; the words 'she was still young' occur not only in Henry James's letter but in one of George Eliot's novels which James had reviewed, *Felix Holt*, and there—in imagining the remorseful peril of Mrs Transome in her mid-fifties—the words dip sickeningly: 'She was still young and ardent in her terrors; the passions of the past were living in her dread' (ch. xxxiv). And in one of George Eliot's most distinctive achievements, the letter in *Middlemarch* sent by the dry, sad scholar Edward

---

[1] To Mrs Henry James, Sr., 10 January 1881; *Letters*, ed. Leon Edel, ii (1975), 332.

[2] *The George Eliot Letters*, ed. Gordon S. Haight (1954–78), ii 79 n.

[3] 'Mr. Gilfil's Love-Story', ch. v.

Casaubon—nearing 50—as a proposal of marriage, the words 'I am still young' are desolating:

> I await the expression of your sentiments with an anxiety which it would be the part of wisdom (were it possible) to divert by a more arduous labour than usual. But in this order of experience I am still young, and in looking forward to an unfavourable possibility I cannot but feel that resignation to solitude will be more difficult after the temporary illumination of hope. (ch. v)

Of her earlier novel, *Romola*, she said: 'I began it a young woman, —I finished it an old woman.'[4] She did not mean that it had taken years, but that it had taken its toll. Yet had she really been a young woman when she began it at 41? When she died, was she still young? Or was she as young as she had ever been? That is, not exactly young at all.

She was sceptical of mystery, but Henry James was right to use that word when he reviewed Cross's *Life* of this woman who had died as Mrs Cross, had lived as Mrs Lewes (married, perhaps, in the eyes of a God in whom she perhaps did not believe), and had originally been Miss Evans:

> There are critics who refuse to [her] the title of a genius; who say that she had only a great talent overloaded with a great store of knowledge. The label, the epithet, matters little, but it is certain that George Eliot had this characteristic of the mind *possessed*: that the creations which brought her renown were of the incalculable kind, shaped themselves in mystery, in some intellectual back-shop or secret crucible, and were as little as possible implied in the aspect of her life. There is nothing more singular or striking in Mr. Cross's volumes than the absence of any indication, up to the time the *Scenes from Clerical Life* were published, that Miss Evans was a likely person to have written them; unless it be the absence of any indication, after they were published, that the deeply-studious, concentrated, home-keeping Mrs. Lewes was a likely person to have produced their successors.[5]

What she had once most wished to escape was the oppressive consciousness of having done so little with her years. In 1857, the year in which her first volume of fiction appeared, she forbore to remind Lewes of her birthday: 'Anniversaries are sad things—to

---

[4] J. W. Cross, *George Eliot's Life as Related in Her Letters and Journals* (1885), ii 352.
[5] (1885), *Partial Portraits* (1888). *Essays on Literature: American Writers, English Writers*, ed. Leon Edel and Mark Wilson (1984), p. 995.

one who has lived long and done little.'[6] Not that we should simply expect to be happier if we were to live long and do much, as is clear from her poem *The Legend of Jubal*, coolly summarized by Henry James:

Jubal invents the lyre and teaches his companions and his tribe how to use it, and then goes forth to wander in quest of new musical inspiration. In this pursuit he grows patriarchally old, and at last makes his way back to his own people. He finds them, greatly advanced in civilization, celebrating what we should call nowadays his centennial, and making his name the refrain of their songs. He goes in among them and declares himself, but they receive him as a lunatic, and buffet him, and thrust him out into the wilderness again, where he succumbs to their unconscious ingratitude.[7]

If you are still alive, do not turn up incognito—or cognito—for the centenary of your birth, or it may turn out be exactly a century prior to the centenary of your death.

'She did not look young when I first saw her, and I have no recollection of her ever looking much older': the words are those of a friend who got to know her in her early thirties.[8] In what was, apart from a poem, her first published original writing, 'Poetry and Prose, from the Notebook of an Eccentric', when she was 27, there is a poignant tale, protected by its title, 'A Little Fable with a Great Moral'. It tells of two wood-nymphs, one of whom 'grew old without finding it out, for she never looked for herself in the lake'; who lived for centuries, and who was spared the knowledge of age: 'And while she was dreaming this, men came and cut down her tree, and Hieria died without knowing that she had become old.'[9]

Hieria's creator lived knowing that she had early become old, the sap in her tree at risk.

Perhaps you would find some symptoms of age creeping over me if you were with me now, and you would accuse me of being too old for five-and-twenty, which is a sufficiently venerable sum of years in the calendar

---

[6] To Sara Hennell, 23 November 1857; *Letters*, ii 404–5. Compare, also to Sara Hennell, 23 November 1842; *Letters*, i 152: 'My birthday (the 23d) I celebrated yesterday, much, I fancy, as the oysters on the rock celebrate theirs.'

[7] *North American Review*, October 1874; *Essays on Literature: American Writers, English Writers*, p. 970.

[8] Bessie R. Belloc; Gordon Haight, *George Eliot: A Biography* (1968), pp. 102–3.

[9] *Essays of George Eliot*, ed. Thomas Pinney (1963), p. 22.

of young ladies generally. But I can laugh and love and fall into a fit of enthusiasm still, so there is some of the youthful sap left.[10]

But what most moved her and her art was not the promise of the sap but the threat of being sapped. The Epilogue to 'Mr. Gilfil's Love-Story', in her first book *Scenes of Clerical Life*, says: 'But it is with men as with trees: if you lop off their finest branches, into which they were pouring their young life-juice, the wounds will be healed over with some rough boss, some odd excrescence.' And in an essay on 'The Too Ready Writer' in her last book, *Impressions of Theophrastus Such*, she pities these losses: these things 'which were once but the joyous mounting of young sap, are already taking shape as unalterable woody fibre'.

Even Maggie Tulliver, in *The Mill on the Floss*, who is one of George Eliot's freshest creations, was—like her creator—'strangely old for her years';[11] and there is a dark tragic counterpart to such childhood pathos in the paralysis and imbecility, the second childhood, of Mr Transome in *Felix Holt* (ch. i): 'But he's not much over sixty-five, is he?' 'Sixty-seven, counting by birthdays; but your father was born old, I think.' George Eliot was moved to pity by a proper self-attention here (not self-pity), for perhaps she too had been born old. In *Theophrastus Such*, the essay 'So Young!', which she wrote when she was old, imagines a writer who continues to be famous for being young, and who complains about it to the narrator.

'Well,' said I, 'youth seems the only drawback that is sure to diminish. You and I have seven years less of it than when we last met.'

'Ah?' returned Ganymede, as lightly as possible, at the same time casting an observant glance over me, as if he were marking the effect of seven years on a person who had probably begun life with an old look, and even as an infant had given his countenance to that significant doctrine, the transmigration of ancient souls into modern bodies.

George Eliot told Dr Thomas Allbutt, 'It is in vain to get one's back and knees in the right attitude if one's mind is superannuated.'[12] But her mind had long been annuated—and her body too. She was particularly vexed that this did not even bring such advantages as might have been expected; she was still under 30 when she wrote in a letter from Switzerland: 'I confess I am more sensitive than I

---

[10] To Martha Jackson, 21 April 1845; *Letters*, i 189.
[11] Book IV, ch. ii.   [12] 1 November 1873; *Letters*, v 451.

thought I should be to the idea that my being alone is odd. I thought
my old appearance would have been a sufficient sanction and that
the very idea of impropriety was ridiculous.'[13]

What was felt to be the impropriety of her marriage to—or rather
her living with—G. H. Lewes was then compounded by her marriage, so soon after Lewes's death, to John Cross. Cross himself said
that after their marriage, and as a result of travelling, 'She began
at once to look many years younger.'[14] But not enough years younger,
even for her ('The only point to be regretted in our marriage is that
I am much older than he'[15]), and certainly not for those who maliciously condescended to her, such as Mrs Jebb, who does not waste
a word:

George Eliot, old as she is, and ugly, really looked very sweet and winning
in spite of both. She was dressed in a short dark soft satin walking dress
with a lace wrap half shading the body, a costume most artistically designed to show her slenderness, yet hiding the squareness of age. . . . In the
evening she made me feel sad for her. There was not a person in the
drawing-room, Mr. Cross included, whose mother she might not have been,
and I thought she herself felt depressed at the knowledge that nothing
could make her young again; to her we were all young of a later generation. She adores her husband, and it seemed to me it hurt her a little to
have him talk so much to me. It made her, in her pain, slightly irritated
and snappish, which I did not mind, feeling that what troubled her was
beyond remedy. He may forget the twenty years difference between them,
but she never can.[16]

T. S. Eliot once remarked that the test of a true poet is that he
writes about experiences before they have happened to him.[17] George
Eliot's second marriage may have taken her back to *Middlemarch*,
three paragraphs from its end:

Sir James never ceased to regard Dorothea's second marriage as a mistake;
and indeed this remained the tradition concerning it in Middlemarch, where

[13] To Mr and Mrs Charles Bray, 28 August 1849; *Letters*, i 301.

[14] *George Eliot's Life*, iii 417.

[15] To Isaac Evans, 26 May 1880; *Letters*, vii 287.

[16] Haight, *George Eliot*, p. 545, quoting the deliciously titled book, *With Dearest
Love to All*.

[17] William Empson: 'As a young man I snatched at any chance to hear wisdom
drop from Mr T. S. Eliot, and he once remarked that the test of a true poet is
that he writes about experiences before they have happened to him; I felt I had
once passed this test, though I forget now in which poem' (*Essays on Renaissance
Literature*, i. *Donne and the New Philosophy*, ed. John Haffenden (1993), p. 127).

she was spoken of to a younger generation as a fine girl who married a sickly clergyman, old enough to be her father, and in little more than a year after his death gave up her estate to marry his cousin—young enough to have been his son, with no property, and not well-born.

No, not young enough to have been *Dorothea's* son. But Mrs Jebb's beady eye had seen no one there in the drawing-room 'whose mother she might not have been'.

She had no children, and she had little or no childhood, being known as Little Mamma and 'finding it impossible to care for childish games and occupations'.[18] There is a memory of her, which has become famous,

at a children's party at her [Miss Shaw's] mother's—about 9 or 10 years old, she thinks. Mary Anne sat apart from the rest, and Mrs. Shaw went to her and said, 'My dear, you do not seem happy; are you enjoying yourself?' 'No, I am not', said Mary Anne. 'I don't like to play with children; I like to talk to grown-up people'.[19]

The anecdote calls up Virginia Woolf's praise of 'the mature *Middlemarch*, the magnificent book which with all its imperfections is one of the few English novels written for grown-up people'.[20] But the affinity is not simply a happy one, since there are particular pains and dangers in writing for grown-up people when even as a child they were all you liked to talk to.

'You talk as if you had never known any youth. It is monstrous— as if you had had a vision of Hades in your childhood, like the boy in the legend': the expostulation is Will Ladislaw's, in *Middlemarch* (ch. xxii). A feat of detection by Gillian Beer tracked down the boy in the legend: Anskar, a ninth-century missionary to Scandinavia.[21] When he was 5, 'having given himself to boyish levity', he saw his dead mother; to come to her, he had to 'flee every kind of vanity, and put away childish jests and have regard to the seriousness of life. . . . Immediately after this vision he began to be serious and to avoid childish associations, and to devote himself more constantly to reading and meditation.' Gillian Beer brings out the 'beautiful appropriateness to Dorothea's problems and fate' of Anskar's story,

---

[18] Edith Simcox, quoting Maria Lewis; Ruby V. Redinger, *George Eliot: The Emergent Self* (1975), p. 77.

[19] Miss Hennell, reporting Miss Shaw; *Letters*, i 41 n.

[20] *Times Literary Supplement*, 20 November 1919.

[21] *Darwin's Plots* (1983), p. 175.

and of his martyrdom being that he will not find martyrdom. (John Donne knew that 'to some / Not to be martyrs, is a martyrdom'.) What might be stressed as well is the appropriateness of the legend not only to Dorothea but to Dorothea's creator. At the age of 5, to 'put away childish jests':

> When I was a child, I spake as a child, I understood as a child, I thought as a child: but when I became a man, I put away childish things.

Would George Eliot have been able to say quite this?

Mature is Virginia Woolf's word for *Middlemarch*, as it was the word of innumerable reviewers of George Eliot, and repeatedly a word of the novels themselves. But there was never an easy commerce between what was mature in George Eliot and what was not or what had not been; her greatest achievements come when such commerce is less her assurance than her hope, and when she conveys a chastened sense of how difficult is the enterprise which W. H. Auden later set down so equably:

> To grow up does not mean to outgrow either childhood or adolescence but to make use of them in an adult way. But for the child in us, we should be incapable of intellectual curiosity; but for the adolescent, of serious feeling for other individuals. . . . All that a mature man can give his child and adolescent in return for what they keep giving him are humility, humour, charity and hope.[22]

George Eliot came late—or at least believed that she came late—to the writing of fiction. By September 1856, when she began her first story, she was a woman of nearly 37, and she had behind her a substantial body of writing: translations, essays, and other editorial contributions. She had long wanted to write fiction, but something—or some things—had stopped her, or so it seemed to her. Yet apart from Dickens, none of her contemporaries had made *so* early a start as a novelist as to cause her any sensible shame, and some had been even later developers.

Then again there are good reasons for not writing novels at all. No novel is ever published without hurting the feelings of someone, and as well as the possibilities of pain and the violations of privacy, there are other kinds of possible damage. At the age of 19, George Eliot—or rather, Marian Evans—had been insistent about the perils

[22] *New Statesman*, 18 May 1957.

of novels and romances; we may find her tone inordinately right-
eous, but we should not find her position foolish, when she ventures

to believe that the same causes which exist in my own breast to render
novels and romances pernicious have their counterpart in that of every
fellow-creature.

I am I confess not an impartial member of a jury in this case for I owe
the culprits a grudge for injuries inflicted on myself. I shall carry to my
grave the mental diseases with which they have contaminated me. When
I was quite a little child I could not be satisfied with the things around
me; I was constantly living in a world of my own creation, and was quite
contented to have no companions that I might be left to my own musings
and imagine scenes in which I was chief actress. Conceive what a character
novels would give to these Utopias. I was early supplied with them by those
who kindly sought to gratify my appetite for reading and of course I made
use of the materials they supplied for building my castles in the air. But
it may be said, 'No one ever dreamed of recommending children to read
them; all this does not apply to persons come to years of discretion, whose
judgments are in some degree matured.' I answer that men and women
are but children of a larger growth; they are still imitative beings.[23]

Yet even in the repudiation there is a life in the language which
is halfway to the vitality of great fiction. For behind her references
to 'my appetite for reading' and to men and women as 'but children
of a larger growth', there is a play of mind in the allusion to Dryden's
lines from *All for Love* (Act IV), where Dolabella says:

> Men are but Children of a larger growth,
> Our appetites as apt to change as theirs.

Dryden had said 'Men'; Lord Chesterfield had turned it to 'Women,
then, are only children of a larger growth'; and young Marian Evans,
with characteristic resistance and impartiality, averred: 'Men and
women are but children of a larger growth'—following this at once
with 'they are still imitative beings', she herself having just imitated
Dryden. We are in the presence of a writer.

When she died, *The Times* spoke of her 'years of painful, yet ardent
growth' (24 December 1880). Lewes had described her—or 'him',
'George Eliot'—to her first publisher Blackwood as someone who
'has passed the middle of life without writing at all, and will easily
be made to give it up'.[24] 'Unlike most writers', George Eliot 'is

---

[23] To Maria Lewis, 16 March 1839; *Letters*, i 22–3.
[24] Lewes to Blackwood, 12 July 1857; *Letters*, ii 364.

more anxious about *excellence* than about appearing in print—as his waiting so long before taking the venture proves'.[25] From the beginning of her career as a novelist, Lewes protected her from reviews, aware of 'that excessive diffidence which prevented her writing at all for so many years, and would prevent her now, if I were not beside her to encourage her'.[26] She herself hoped to 'sprinkle some precious grain as the result of the long years in which I have been inert and suffering'[27]—suffering under what seemed to her to be inertia. 'It is necessary to me, not simply to *be* but to *utter*.'[28]

Journalism and editorship, however high-minded, were not full utterance. As early as 1846, when she was 26, her friends had known of her creative ambition: 'Mary Ann looks very brilliant just now—we fancy she must be writing her novel.'[29] *Brilliant* there has a physical immediacy, a glow as of a woman who has happily conceived. But it was not until ten years later, in April 1856, that there came what Cross—specifying these weeks as perhaps 'the most important and interesting of all in George Eliot's development'— was to call 'unmistakable signs of the rising of the sap of creative production'.[30] In July 1856 she wrote:

> I am anxious to begin my fiction-writing, and so am not inclined to undertake an article that will give me much trouble, but, at all events, I will finish my article on Young.[31]

This article on the eighteenth-century poet Edward Young clarified her mind, with its sense of the poet's tardiness; she expanded Pope's remark about Young into 'a foolish youth and *middle age*', with this being tacitly played against the fact that he was called Young. Then there followed another article, 'Silly Novels by Lady Novelists', which still further clarified her thoughts and feelings: eleven days after sending it off, she began her first fiction, a woman novelist whose novels are far from silly. 'How I Came to Write Fiction': on 6 December 1857 she was to set down her record of September 1856:

> September 1856 made a new era in my life, for it was then I began to write Fiction. It had always been a vague dream of mine that some time

[25] Lewes to John Blackwood, 22 November 1856; *Letters*, ii 276.
[26] Lewes to Sara Hennell, 12 September 1862; *Letters*, iv 58.
[27] Journal, 2 January 1858; *Letters*, ii 416.
[28] To John Sibree, 8 March 1848; *Letters*, i 255.
[29] Sara Hennell; Haight, *George Eliot*, p. 61.
[30] *George Eliot's Life*, i 285.   [31] Cross, *George Eliot's Life*, i 296.

or other I might write a novel, and my shadowy conception of what the novel was to be, varied, of course, from one epoch of my life to another. But I never went farther towards the actual writing of the novel than an introductory chapter describing a Staffordshire village and the life of the neighbouring farm houses, and as the years passed on I lost any hope that I should ever be able to write a novel, just as I desponded about everything else in my future life. . . . Still, he [Lewes] began to think that I might as well try, some time, what I could do in fiction, and by and bye when we came back to England and I had greater success than he had ever expected in other kinds of writing, his impression that it was worth while to see how far my mental power would go towards the production of a novel, was strengthened. He began to say very positively, 'You must try and write a story,' and when we were at Tenby he urged me to begin at once. I deferred it, however, after my usual fashion, with work that does not present itself as an absolute duty. But one morning as I was lying in bed, thinking what should be the subject of my first story, my thoughts merged themselves into a dreamy doze, and I imagined myself writing a story of which the title was—'The Sad Fortunes of the Reverend Amos Barton.' I was soon wide awake again, and told G. He said, 'O what a capital title!' and from that time I had settled in my mind that this should be my first story.[32]

'A new era in my life, for it was then I began to write Fiction': and the fiction itself uses those *opening* words. 'I am thinking', says Lydgate in *Middlemarch*, 'of a great fellow, who was about as old as I am three hundred years ago, and had already begun a new era in anatomy' (ch. xlv). And there is Harold Transome in *Felix Holt* (ch. xliii): 'Though I am close on thirty-five, I never met with a woman at all like you before. There are new eras in one's life that are equivalent to youth—are something better than youth.'

On 18 October 1859, George Eliot wrote to her friend François d'Albert-Durade in Switzerland:

But in these last three years a great change has come over my life—a change in which I cannot help believing that both you and Madame d'Albert will rejoice. Under the influence of the intense happiness I have enjoyed in my married life from thorough moral and intellectual sympathy, I have at last found out my true vocation, after which my nature had always been feeling and striving uneasily without finding it. What do you think that vocation is? I pause for you to guess.

I have turned out to be an artist—not, as you are, with the pencil and the pallet, but with words. I have written a novel [*Adam Bede*] which people

[32] George Eliot's Journal; *Letters*, ii 406–7.

say has stirred them very deeply—and *not* a *few* people, but almost all reading England.

I think you will believe that I do not write you word of this out of any small vanity:— my books are deeply serious things to me, and come out of all the painful discipline, all the most hardly-learnt lessons of my past life. I write you word of it, because I believe that both your kind heart and Madame d'Albert's too, will be touched with real joy, that one whom you knew when she was not very happy and when her life seemed to serve no purpose of much worth, has been at last blessed with the sense that she has done something worth living and suffering for.[33]

The depth of feeling is there in the transition from 'an artist [. . .] with words' to 'write you word of this'; and the feeling spends itself in the sigh 'at last': 'has been at last blessed'. Why had it to be 'at last'? We may look ahead to her message of advice to a young hopeful: 'in my opinion, at the age of twenty only a rare genius could produce anything really valuable in the form of fiction.'[34] Or we may adduce her natural and principled reluctance to hasten: her distrust of 'The Too Ready Writer'; her sense of a proper 'retar-dation' (she uses the word beautifully,[35] and Henry James praised her for a 'retarding persuasiveness which allows her conjured im-ages to sink slowly into your very brain'[36]); and her grounded fear of precipitancy. When, at 25, she broke off an incipient love-affair with someone who (a friend reveals) 'from youth—or something or other, did not seem to her half so interesting as before', she insisted that she had 'dismissed it from my mind, and only keep it recorded in my book of reference, article *"Precipitancy, ill effects of"* '.[37] So we may concur with Leslie Stephen:

I do not think that any one who has had a little experience in such matters would regard it as otherwise than dangerous for a powerful mind to be precipitated into public utterance. The Pythagorean probation of silence may be protracted too long; but it may afford a most useful discipline: and I think that there is nothing preposterous in the supposition that George

---

[33] *Letters*, iii 186–7.   [34] To Charles Lewes, 2 July 1879; *Letters*, vii 178.

[35] For instance, *Felix Holt*, ch. xxxviii: 'the inestimable interest of retardation'; *Daniel Deronda*, ch. xv: 'notwithstanding the fashionable retardation of most things from dinners to marriages'.

[36] *Nation*, 16 August 1866; *Essays on Literature: American Writers, European Writers*, p. 910.

[37] Mrs Charles Bray to Sara Hennell, 30 March 1845; *Letters*, i 183–4. George Eliot to Sara Hennell, 6 April 1845; *Letters*, i 186.

Eliot's work was all the more powerful because it came from a novelist who had lain fallow through a longer period than ordinary.[38]

'Nothing preposterous' is good, since preposterous means before-after. Yet George Eliot's pain at her own delay was genuine, and it is not possible to be fascinated by her genius and not want to hazard some guess as to what it was in 1856 which—in the words of her strange story 'The Lifted Veil'—'carried off some dull obstruction'.

It was, I believe, the decision not to have children that brought to birth George Eliot's novels. Or that lent a soft obstetric hand. It is apparently the case that in July 1856 Lewes and George Eliot, who had set up home the previous year, came to practise birth control, intending to have no children.[39] This year saw the combination of this decision with her becoming stepmother to Lewes's three sons. Her maternal feelings will have been at once intensified and dissolved. Lewes was to speak of her to his sons, stepping into a foreign language for this stepmother, as 'the Mutter'.[40] When she became 'the Mutter', it was accepted that she was never to be a mother; but no longer as a writer did she have to mutter ('It is necessary to me, not simply to *be* but to *utter*'). She was nearly 37,

[38] *Cornhill*, February 1881; *George Eliot: The Critical Heritage*, ed. David Carroll (1971), pp. 466–7.

[39] Haight, *George Eliot*, p. 205.

[40] Nina Auerbach, who rejects on political grounds George Eliot's acceptance of the familiar metaphor which relates the conceiving of books to the conceiving of children, disparages George Eliot's 'Mrs Lewes': 'As with "little Mamma," the title was more suggestive of role-playing than of reality. Eliot's testy response to a feminist who addressed her as "Miss Evans" shows her clinging to the name as an index of social acceptance: "when I tell you that we have a great boy of eighteen at home who calls me 'mother,' as well as two other boys, almost as tall, who write to me under the same name, you will understand that the point is not one of mere egoism or personal dignity, when I request that any one who has a regard for me will cease to speak of me by my maiden name" (1 April 1861)'. George Eliot's tone there does not seem to me testy, unlike her disparager's word 'testy'; relatedly, I see nothing in her dignified sentences that would justify the description of her as 'clinging to the name as an index of social acceptance'. George Eliot, in her life with Lewes, manifested incomparably more courage in confronting slanderous social and sexual spite than is asked of any late-twentieth-century feminist professor, and she was not one to 'cling' to things for the sake of 'social acceptance', even though she desisted from such empty provocations as would damage the lives of those whom she loved, including those three boys. (Auerbach, 'Artists and Mothers: A False Alliance', 1978; *Romantic Imprisonment*, 1985, p. 180.) On the stultifying self-contradiction in Auerbach's position, see p. 107 above.

and the decision now not to have children was a decision not to have children.

I never saw such a woman. There is nothing a bit masculine about her; she is thoroughly feminine and looks and acts as if she were made for nothing but to mother babies. But she has a power of *stating* an argument equal to any man; equal to any man do I say? I have never seen any man, except Herbert Spencer, who could state a case equal to her.[41]

This was John Fiske, in 1873. Her most substantiated biographer, Gordon Haight, wrote that the fallibility of phrenology as a guide to character is manifest in George Combe's report that George Eliot's bump of philoprogenitiveness was rather small.[42] But was Combe altogether right to equate philoprogenitiveness with 'love of children'? She loved children, but she did not bear them. When Lewes's son—whom she called 'Our poor boy'—was gravely ill in 1869, she wrote to Mrs Mark Pattison, a propos of having shown too much effusiveness, '(of that dumb sort which is the more apt to come when one has not full opportunity of speech)':

But in proportion as I profoundly rejoice that I never brought a child into the world, I am conscious of having an unused stock of motherly tenderness, which sometimes overflows, but not without discrimination.[43]

Her own fullest opportunity of speech was a use of that unused stock of motherly tenderness, and it came as soon as she had decided never to bring a child into the world. The intimate conjunction is clear in a letter to Harriet Beecher Stowe, where George Eliot, speaking of the possibility that letters may be misconstrued, goes on:

But I have little anxiety of that kind in writing to you, dear friend and fellow-labourer—for you have had longer experience than I as a writer, and fuller experience as a woman, since you have borne children and known the mother's history from the beginning.[44]

A fellow-labourer as to the pains of a novelist, but not as to labour-pains.

George Eliot was stepmother to and sometimes a mother to the Lewes boys, but she was not their mother.

It was her books to which she gave birth. Cross introduced her account of September 1856, the new era, with the words: 'We have

[41] Haight, *George Eliot*, p. 468.   [42] *George Eliot*, p. 101.
[43] 10 August 1869; *Letters*, v 52.   [44] 8 May 1869; *Letters*, v 31.

now arrived at the period of the new birth.' A misogynistic reviewer of Cross's *Life* repudiated the metaphor:

The pangs of childbirth are usually considered the most dreadful physical torments entailed on women for the sin or indiscretion of Eve. In reading this biography we are made to believe that they are slight in comparison with the pangs of bookbirth.[45]

'But she is gestating, and gestation with her is always perturbing. I wish the book were done with all my heart.' So wrote Lewes about her writing.[46] Many a true word spoken in gestation, especially about her true words. 'Certainly', said her publisher, 'she does seem to feel that in producing her books she is producing a living thing, and no doubt her books will live longer than is given to children of the flesh.'[47] Sometimes the metaphor is muffled: 'I am finishing a book, which has been growing slowly like a sickly child, because of my own ailments; but now I am in the later acts of it. I can't move till it is done.'[48] Muffled, and yet the phrases 'because of my own ailments' and 'I can't move' do suggest a sickly *unborn* child. Often the metaphor (which is more than analogy, is impulse and deepest creative hope) is not muffled in the slightest:

Exultation is a dream before achievement, and rarely comes after. What comes after, is rather the sense that the work has been produced within one, like offspring, developing and growing by some force of which one's own life has only served as a vehicle, and that what is left of oneself is only a poor husk.[49]

This letter to Mrs Peirce in 1866 is among the most deeply informed and informative that George Eliot ever wrote, and it moves naturally from its insistence that her novels are like offspring to a consolatory admonition about age:

I want to tell you not to fancy yourself old because you are thirty, or to regret that you have not yet written anything. It is a misfortune to many that they begin to write when they are young and give out all that is genuine and peculiar in them when it can be no better than trashy, unripe fruit. There is nothing more dreary than the life of a writer who has early exhausted himself.

[45] Quoted by Redinger, *George Eliot: The Emergent Self*, pp. 20–1.
[46] To T. A. Trollope, 8? February 1866; *Letters*, viii 361.
[47] John Blackwood to William Blackwood, 22 April 1875; *Letters*, ix 149.
[48] To Barbara Bodichon, 10 April 1866; *Letters*, iv 236.
[49] To Harriet Peirce, 14 September 1866; *Letters*, viii 383.

Unless it be the life of a writer who has early exhausted herself. And from there, again with untroubled continuity, to her own arrival at her creativity:

Before that, I was too proud and ambitious to write: I did not believe that I could do anything fine, and I did not choose to do anything of that mediocre sort which I despised when it was done by others. I began, however, by a sort of writing which had no great glory belonging to it, but which I felt certain I could do faithfully and well. This resolve to work at what did not gratify my ambition, and to care only that I worked faithfully, was equivalent to the old phrase—'using the means of grace.' Not long after that, I wrote fiction which has been thought a great deal of—but the satisfaction I have got out of it has not been exactly that of ambition. When we are young we say, 'I should be proud if I could do that.' Having done it, one finds oneself the reverse of proud.

The novels themselves, and not only their creator's sense of self, take seriously and imaginatively the metaphor which relates childbirth to bookbirth. Among the reasons why Casaubon, in *Middlemarch*, is supremely touching is the depth of George Eliot's commiseration with his inability to write his grand or grandiose book, a commiseration the humour of which does nothing to lessen the sadness of *any* authorship as a posterity to take the place of children. Casaubon contemplates marriage:

On such a young lady he would make handsome settlements, and he would neglect no arrangement for her happiness: in return, he should receive family pleasures and leave behind him that copy of himself which seemed so urgently required of a man—to the sonneteers of the sixteenth century. Times had altered since then, and no sonneteer had insisted on Mr. Casaubon's leaving a copy of himself; moreover he had not yet succeeded in issuing copies of his mythological key; but he had always intended to acquit himself by marriage, and the sense that he was fast leaving the years behind him, that the world was getting dimmer and that he felt lonely, was a reason to him for losing no more time in overtaking domestic delights before they too were left behind by the years. (ch. xxix)

For Casaubon, like George Eliot, had been an old head on young shoulders. 'Oh, he dreams footnotes, and they run away with all his brains. They say, when he was a little boy, he made an abstract of "Hop o' my Thumb", and he has been making abstracts ever since' (ch. viii). This is spirited, the way 'footnotes' runs into 'run' and then 'Hop', and acutely unlike the stiff gait of Casaubon. His theory of the mythologies, Dorothea had come to admit to herself, was 'already withered in the birth like an elfin child' (ch. xlviii).

Manifestly there is a political dimension to this, and Dale Spender, in her book *Man Made Language* (1980), does well to remind us how many of the great or notable women writers have been childless. Nina Auerbach is no less insistent, as is indicated by her title 'Artists and Mothers: A False Alliance', that the metaphor is an oppression by males, and that George Eliot, like Jane Austen, was confused and gulled when she voiced it. But the political considerations, which have their interest, should not thrust aside the consideration of childlessness within the novels themselves.

George Eliot, the stepmother, is especially attentive in the novels to foster-parenthood. Mostly she displaces herself so that the foster-parent (a benign step-parent in some ways) is a father and not a mother. And these deep circumstances are at once a mythic or fairy-tale heart to the novels and the prompter of the active head, the brain power, which substantiates them.

Tito in *Romola* has a foster-father. Daniel Deronda grew up with his uncle, who is suspected of being his father. Harold Transome, in *Felix Holt*, grew up with his 'father', who is suspected of not being his father. And so, in a very different way, did Esther Lyon, as unaware of her true father as Eppie is in *Silas Marner*.

It is perhaps *Silas Marner* that best conveys the dignity of foster-parenthood and the indignity of a childlessness perversely self-inflicted, since Godfrey Cass was not man enough to claim his baby by his shameful dead wife, and so must live as at once childless and a bereaved father. 'Meanwhile, why could he not make up his mind to the absence of children from the hearth brightened by such a wife?' (ch. xvii) Because *the absence of children* is a finely judged and judging way of putting it. There is a child, and she is absent, and this is something other—even more painful than—the usual 'child-less hearth'.

'But one morning as I was lying in bed, thinking what should be the subject of my first story, my thoughts merged themselves into a dreamy doze, and I imagined myself writing a story of which the title was—"The Sad Fortunes of the Reverend Amos Barton"'. And what were his sad fortunes? They were not his fortune or lack of it, his financial embarrassments and plights; real though these are, they pale beside his saddest of fortunes: the death of his wife Milly after childbirth. 'Lying in bed': Cross cut out those words when he

printed the journal-entry, as too domestic or intimate. But if we ask
what bed it is which looms in 'The Sad Fortunes of the Reverend
Amos Barton', and constitutes 'the subject of my first story'—the
bed of sleep, of sickness, of love, of childbirth, of death—the answer
is the conjunction of the last two: childbed and deathbed. George
Eliot's journal does justice to the story as well as to its genesis when
she records that 'There still remained the question whether I could
command any pathos, and that was to be decided by the mode in
which I treated Milly's death'. She tells too of a letter from someone
'saying he had never read anything that affected him more than
Milly's death'.

'The birth came prematurely', and so then did the death of 'the
beloved wife of Amos Barton, who died in the thirty-fifth year of her
age' (ch. vii, ch. x). Years later, when Amos Barton visits the grave
with his daughter: 'She was about thirty, but there were some premature lines round her mouth and eyes, which told of early anxiety'
(Conclusion). Yet George Eliot had not herself been premature in
telling of these anxieties and these sad fortunes. From this first story
on, the word 'premature' was always to figure importantly for her.

Naturally she did not get everything right in this first book, *Scenes
of Clerical Life*, though it is an excellent book, compact and comical
and poignant. Critics have remarked that mother-love is always a
fatal subject for George Eliot in the *Scenes of Clerical Life*; perhaps
one should say rather than when the love does not prove fatal to
the mother it may prove fatal to the novelist. For George Eliot isn't
really thinking when she mourns Janet Dempster's childlessness, in
the story 'Janet's Repentance'. Since both Janet and her husband
are alcoholics, and he is brutal and violent, we cannot simply or
easily share the sadness of childlessness as the author wishes us to
do. Yet it was child-bearing and childlessness which moved her
imagination—set it in motion—in this first book as in many subsequent ones. 'Lisbeth Bede loves her son with the love of a woman
to whom her first-born has come late in life' (ch. iv): these are the
words of a novelist to whom this first-born novel, *Adam Bede*, had
come late in life, and the words love the mother-love which they
contemplate, without envy and yet with a warm exasperation at
Lisbeth Bede's ways. But then Adam Bede's mother is set against
the girl whom he loves, Hetty Sorrel, and Hetty's desolating inflic-
tion of childlessness upon herself by infanticide. Hear the evidence
of the labourer, John Olding, at her trial:

'And just as I was stooping and laying down the stakes, I saw something odd and round and whitish lying on the ground under a nut-bush by the side of me. And I stooped down on hands and knees to pick it up. And I saw it was a little baby's hand.' (ch. xliii)

In its naturalness and oddity, this is great art, truly realistic and yet raised to the heights of imaginative discretion by the life with which it moves: from 'down on hands and knees' to 'pick it up' to 'baby's hand': 'And I stooped down ... to pick it up. And I saw it was a little baby's hand'. I cannot respect the flippancy with which Nina Auerbach, determined to disparage any alliance between artists and mothers (especially in those such as Jane Austen and George Eliot, who explicitly embraced the metaphor), speaks of such a tragic moment: 'Though in her ambiguous role as "Mrs. Lewes", George Eliot took the name of "mother" solemnly, her novels do not. Infanticide is a persistent, and sometimes tempting, activity.' Auerbach condescends to George Eliot for her 'insufferably cute toddlers' and for 'these genuflections to motherhood'.[50] Against the professorial sarcasm of 'genuflections' I should set that moment when someone genuinely kneels: 'And I stooped down on hands and knees to pick it up. And I saw it was a little baby's hand.' Infanticide as, drawledly, a 'sometimes tempting activity'? As often, the new politics is the flip side of the old, at one for instance with the pseudo-fastidious grimace of a Victorian reviewer at Hetty Sorrel's misery:

Hetty's feelings and changes are indicated with a punctual sequence that makes the account of her misfortunes read like the rough notes of a man-midwife's conversations with a bride. This is intolerable. Let us copy the old masters of the art, who, if they gave us a baby, gave it us all at once. A decent author and a decent public may surely take the premonitory symptoms for granted.[51]

And the postmonitory symptoms? There is a hateful grating of the haughty thought, 'who, if they gave us a baby, gave it us all at once', against the mutilating thought, 'And I saw it was a little baby's hand'. George Eliot may have become an author because she did not take the premonitory symptoms for granted.

When in *Scenes of Clerical Life* she spoke of the old maids, the Miss Linnets, as having 'seven or eight lustrums',[52] she did not conceal

[50] *Romantic Imprisonment*, pp. 182, 178.
[51] *Saturday Review*, 26 February 1859; *George Eliot: The Critical Heritage*, p. 76.
[52] 'Janet's Repentance', ch. iii.

from herself with this old-world phrasing that her age was theirs, between 35 and 40. (And a lustrum was originally a purificatory sacrifice, a washing.) Getting on for 40: this is an age with which she was properly preoccupied in her novels. She had no sympathy with affectations of youthfulness in the middle-aged (these were the subject of her earliest surviving manuscript, written at school), but she had much sympathy with those who, like Madame de Sablé in 1635—she had been born in 1599—'had nearly crossed that table-land of maturity which precedes a woman's descent towards old age'.[53] This is from an essay which precedes the fiction which she began at exactly that age; in her last novel, *Daniel Deronda*, she could be more playful with the same metaphor, playing it not upon 'Woman in France' but upon man in Britain: Mr Bult in *Daniel Deronda* 'had the general solidity and suffusive pinkness of a healthy Briton on the central table-land of life' (ch. xxii).

Her unsentimentality about children was hard-won. In her first published prose-work, 'From the Notebook of an Eccentric', her thoughts on 'The Wisdom of the Child' were wishful and wistful:

It may not be an original idea, but never mind, if it be a true one, that the proper result of intellectual cultivation is to restore the mind to that state of wonder and interest with which it looks on everything in childhood.[54]

But is it a true one?

Self-renunciation, submission to law, trust, benignity, ingenuousness, rectitude,—these are the qualities we delight most to witness in the child, and these are the qualities which most dignify the man.

But what the novelist in George Eliot rightly delighted most to witness in children was very different: their self-assertion, their tousled refusal to submit, their aggrievedness and cunning—all of these capable of unexpected sweetness, and all of them looking like an exhilarating travesty of adult ways.

'Now, which'll you have, Maggie—right hand or left?'
'I'll have that with the jam run out,' said Maggie, keeping her eyes shut to please Tom.
'Why, you don't like that, you silly. You may have it if it comes to you fair, but I shan't give it you without. Right or left—you choose, now. Ha-

---

[53] *Westminster Review*, October 1854; *Essays*, p. 62.   [54] *Essays*, pp. 19–20.

a-a!' said Tom, in a tone of exasperation, as Maggie peeped. 'You keep your eyes shut, now, else you shan't have any.'

Maggie's power of sacrifice did not extend so far; indeed, I fear that she cared less that Tom should enjoy the utmost possible amount of puff, than that he should be pleased with her for giving him the best bit. So she shut her eyes quite close, till Tom told her to 'say which,' and then she said, 'Left-hand.'

'You've got it,' said Tom, in rather a bitter tone.

'What! the bit with the jam run out?'

'No; here, take it,' said Tom, firmly, handing decidedly the best piece to Maggie.

'O, please, Tom, have it: I don't mind—I like the other: please take this.'

'No, I shan't,' said Tom, almost crossly, beginning on his own inferior piece.

Maggie, thinking it was no use to contend further, began too, and ate up her half puff with considerable relish as well as rapidity. But Tom had finished first, and had to look on while Maggie ate her last morsel or two, feeling in himself a capacity for more. Maggie didn't know Tom was looking at her: she was seesawing on the elder bough, lost to almost everything but a vague sense of jam and idleness.

'O, you greedy thing!' said Tom, when she had swallowed the last morsel. He was conscious of having acted very fairly, and thought she ought to have considered this, and made up to him for it. He would have refused a bit of hers beforehand, but one is naturally at a different point of view before and after one's own share of puff is swallowed. (Book I, ch. vi)

Self-renunciation, submission to law, rectitude? Children are but men and women of a smaller growth.

George Eliot was precocious as a child, but gravely not glitteringly so. As an adult novelist, her sense of adults was wisely alert to their childishness and was unwisely credulous about their childlikeness. Whenever she speaks of someone (it is usually a woman) as 'childlike', we are in the vicinity of gullibility and implausibility, and George Eliot's vigilance—which did not have to narrow its eyes—has slackened into the wide-eyed. Dorothea in *Middlemarch* is repeatedly childlike: 'Dorothea's voice, as she made this childlike picture of what she would do, might have been almost taken as a proof that she could do it effectively' (ch. lxxvi). But what we ask for is not proof that Dorothea could do it effectively, but evidence that George Eliot can do it effectively—can attribute the childlike to this grave heroine.

The childlike grave-eyed earnestness with which Dorothea said all this was irresistible—blent into an adorable whole with her ready understanding of high experience. (Of lower experience such as plays a great part in the world, poor Mrs. Casaubon had a very blurred shortsighted knowledge, little helped by her imagination.) (ch. lxxvi)

Irresistible should incite us to resist, since the author calls upon it to cow us; and the parenthesis about 'lower experience' is a low piece of rhetoric, designed to avert our attention from the implausibility, the insubstantiality, of Dorothea's childlikeness. 'While she said in a sobbing childlike way, "We could live quite well on my own fortune"' (ch. lxxxiii). I cannot imagine, let alone hear, the words 'We could live quite well on my own fortune', as utterable in a childlike way. The true art is to be found elsewhere, for instance in the meeting of a middle-aged childishness with a middle-aged callousness, as when in *Daniel Deronda* the discarded wife Mrs Glasher ('hardly less than seven-and-thirty') unexpectedly resists her obdurate husband Grandcourt:

She kept hold of her purpose as a child might tighten its hand over a small stolen thing, crying and denying all the while. Even Grandcourt was wrought upon by surprise: this capricious wish, this childish violence, was as unlike Lydia's bearing as it was incongruous with her person.[55]

The difference between the false throb and the true pulse can be heard in the famous or notorious evocation of Saint Theresa at the beginning and end of *Middlemarch*. 'Many Theresas have been born who found for themselves no epic life.' 'Here and there is born a Saint Theresa, foundress of nothing.' Could there be a Saint Theresa in a town like Middlemarch? Some such question waited for more than a century for an unsoft answer.

One day God summoned Saint Theresa and sent her to earth for three days to walk among mortals. The first day, Saint Theresa called God in utter despair. 'God,' she said 'I'm in New York and there is no beauty, no love, no religion, no kindred spirit. It's an awful world, God, I want to come home.' No, God said to Saint Theresa, continue your sojourn on earth. On the second day, Saint Theresa called God. 'God,' said Saint Theresa, 'I'm in Chicago and it's worse than New York. There is no humanity and there is so much suffering of the human soul. I must come back to heaven immediately'. No, God said to Theresa, continue your

---

[55] *Daniel Deronda*, ch. xxx.

sojourn on earth. On the third day, Saint Theresa called again. 'God, darling, it's Terry. I'm in L.A.'[56]

Yet there was another side to George Eliot's preoccupation with Saint Theresa, something very different from the high orotundity which invites the low joke. For the first sentences of the Prelude to *Middlemarch* had presented us with a different Theresa, evoked in different accents, in childhood with her brother:

> Who that cares much to know the history of man, and how the mysterious mixture behaves under the varying experiments of Time, has not dwelt, at least briefly, on the life of Saint Theresa, has not smiled with some gentleness at the thought of the little girl walking forth one morning hand-in-hand with her still smaller brother, to go and seek martyrdom in the country of the Moors? Out they toddled from rugged Avila, wide-eyed and helpless-looking as two fawns, but with human hearts, already beating to a national idea; until domestic reality met them in the shape of uncles, and turned them back from their great resolve.

'In the shape of *uncles*': this has prophetic soul, the shape and the substantiality of art.

In *Romola* (ch. xxxiv), Tito placates Tessa by giving a butterfly-kiss to the baby:

> He satisfied her by giving the small mummy a butterfly kiss, and then putting his hand on her shoulder and turning her face towards him, said, 'You like looking at the baby better than looking at your husband, you false one!'

This moment of Tito's, false, is necessarily less poignant in its airy lightness than the butterfly-kiss which George Eliot imagines for the saddening irresponsible lovers in *Adam Bede*. Barbara Hardy, one of the best critics of George Eliot, settled upon this lovers' butterfly-kiss as having a particular pathos and irony. And if we ask what makes it so real for us, what fends off sentimentality, one answer is the play of the fantastical butterfly-kiss against the simple making of butter. For Arthur had seen Hetty's beauty and felt her attraction as he watched her making butter. Later:

> It was a pity they were not in that golden age of childhood when they would have stood face to face, eyeing each other with timid liking, then given each other a little butterfly kiss, and toddled off to play together.

[56] This fable, from David Mamet, reported in *Rolling Stone*.

He actually dared not look at this little buttermaker for the first minute
or two. (ch. xii, in two consecutive paragraphs)

It is *golden*—'that golden age'—which helps to effect the move from
the 'little butterfly kiss' to the 'little buttermaker'. That golden age,
soon to be leaden. We are to think back to that earlier meeting,
and to recall the discreet and warm art by which butterflies were
succeeded by butter, and impalpable arms by busy hands (ch. ix):

Young souls, in such pleasant delirium as hers, are as unsympathetic as
butterflies sipping nectar; they are isolated from all appeals by a barrier
of dreams—by invisible looks and impalpable arms.
   While Hetty's hands were busy packing up the butter, and her head
filled with these pictures of the morrow, Arthur Donnithorne, riding

—and we are back riding with the narrative. George Eliot does not
break the butterfly in valuing the butter. She herself once pointed
out that one hand of hers was broader across than the other, because,
she thought, of making so much butter and cheese.[57] But whatever
the discrepancy between her hands, her art was even-handed.
   The life of her writing is often a matter of these small movements, a maturing of one word into another. When she writes of
'a vague caution', her art is cautious but not vague in its movement:
'like that of an insect whose little fragment of earth has given way,
and made it pause in a palsy of distrust'.[58] The movement from
pause to *palsy* is itself a trembling and an inertia. Or there is the
movement of a sad crystallizing, as when Lydgate, pressed by debts
and needing to take back the extravagant 'bridal present' of am-
ethysts which he had given Rosamond, is glintingly glimpsed as
'intensely miserable, this strong man of nine-and-twenty and of many
gifts' (ch. lviii). When the infant Eppie reaches out to Silas Marner's
face—'the small hand began to pull Marner's withered cheek with
loving disfiguration' (ch. xiii)—the words are themselves a loving
disfiguration of the way in which you might have expected such a
thing to be put.
   George Eliot knows perfectly well that age may be neither here
nor there. 'What's age got to do with it, I wonder?', asks Adam
Bede (ch. i), and later his youth is not held against him when it
comes to the right job: 'And as for age, what that's worth depends
on the quality o' the liquor' (ch. xxi). Still, the general impulse of

   [57] Haight, *George Eliot*, p. 28.   [58] *Romola*, ch. xxx.

her work is of a considerable and carefully considered sympathy with both childhood and middle-age, held in tension with an alertness about the particular delusions to which youth is liable.

Somehow we got to talk of the Mill on the Floss. She said her sole purpose in writing it was to show the conflict which is going on everywhere when the younger generation with its higher culture comes into collision with the older. . . . She spoke of having come into collision with her father and being on the brink of being turned out of his house. And she dwelt a little on how much fault there is on the side of the young in such cases, of their ignorance of life, and the narrowness of their intellectual superiority.[59]

This has something of her own *transitional* life, in the movement here: 'on the brink of being turned out of his house. And she dwelt . . .'

She reserved her sharpest contempt for those who made excuses for the young, those who do not forgive them but exculpate them. As in the chapter of *The Mill on the Floss*, 'St. Ogg's Passes Judgment' (Book VII, ch. ii): 'Mr. Stephen Guest had certainly not behaved well; but then, young men were liable to those sudden infatuated attachments', and 'still she was very young'—so different, and not only in timbre, from 'she was still young'. Of all her central characters, the one from whom she most shrank in revulsion was Tito in *Romola*. The gems he sold were not his but his foster-father's, 'in the narrow sense by which the right of possession is determined in ordinary affairs; but in that large and more radically natural view by which the world belongs to youth and strength, they were rather his who could extract the most pleasure out of them' (ch. xi). W. B. Yeats said that great literature is

the Forgiveness of Sin, and when we find it becoming the Accusation of Sin, as in George Eliot, who plucks her Tito in pieces with as much assurance as if he had been clockwork, literature has begun to change into something else. George Eliot had a fierceness hardly to be found but in a woman turned argumentative, but the habit of mind her fierceness gave its life to was characteristic of her century[60]

—a deft and odious snitching of one of her favourite words, argumentative. Yet one of her strengths is her fierce refusal to accede to youth's self-estimate.

---

[59] Emily Davies to Jane Crow, 21 August 1869; *Letters*, viii 465–6.
[60] 'At Stratford-on-Avon' (1901); *Selected Criticism*, ed. A. Norman Jeffares (1964), pp. 97–8.

Not that he was in a sentimental stage; but he was in another sort of contemplative mood perhaps more common in the young men of our day—that of questioning whether it were worth while to take part in the battle of the world: I mean, of course, the young men in whom the unproductive labour of questioning is sustained by three or five per cent on capital which somebody else has battled for. (*Daniel Deronda*, ch. xvii)

Justice in these matters will depend upon the utmost exactitude. 'The difficult task of knowing another soul is not for young gentlemen whose consciousness is chiefly made up of their own wishes' (*Middlemarch*, ch. xii). A comma after 'gentlemen' would have made it inordinate and unjust, as if the consciousness of all young gentlemen were chiefly made up of their own wishes; as it stands, poised, it looks as if is it set to indict all young gentlemen, and then limits the charge, chasteningly.

But George Eliot's weakness or limitation is, on the one hand, that she does sometimes prosecute those, say, in their twenties to the point of persecution; and on the other hand, that she is reduced to guessing and gesturing when she tries to imagine them, not in unhappy collusion (like Lydgate and Rosamond—this, she is laceratingly happy at), but in happy community, like Felix Holt and Esther Lyon. 'They laughed merrily, each holding the other's arms, like girl and boy. There was the ineffable sense of youth in common' (ch. li). *Ineffable* comes too conveniently. George Eliot had not found ineffable the sense of childhood in common, or the sense of *lack* of youth in common.

She finds it all but impossible to create young people (not children) whom she greatly likes or greatly respects, leave alone both. Her good young people make for bad art. Yet her art is to be respected for its resistance to the cult of youth.

In 1919, which was as it happens the centenary of George Eliot's birth, T. S. Eliot deplored the cult of youth as manifested in an over-valuation of the poetry of those who had died in the Great War:

Important truth comes to the young only in rare flashes of genius. There are no flashes; some of the men had a nice honesty in detail, in accounting for their lives in France—but not that great honesty of the general scheme, that superhuman honesty which is realized only by years of observation and thought and which constitutes the genius of middle age.

We are a little wearied, in fact, by the solemnity with which Mr. Osborn accepts the youthful mind and the youthful point of view. 'Youth knows more about the young,' he says, 'than old age or middle age.' If this were so, civilization would be impossible, experience worthless. *Hommes de la trentaine, de la quarantaine*, assert yourselves. Sympathy with youth is life; but acceptance of youth at its own valuation is sentiment; it is indifference to serious living.[61]

George Eliot, that *femme de la trentaine, de la quarantaine*, had behind her art—and within it—the honesty which is realized only by years of observation and thought and which constitutes the genius of middle age.

Casaubon was middle-aged and prematurely old, and his proposal of marriage could not itself have the bloom of youth:

I have discerned in you an elevation of thought and a capability of devotedness, which I had hitherto not conceived to be compatible either with the early bloom of youth or with those graces of sex (ch. v)

—bloom of youth? Samuel Beckett, that genius of ageing, wrote in *Company*: 'Bloom of adulthood. Imagine a whiff of that.' (There in a story which speaks too of the 'bump of philogénitiveness'.) George Eliot did imagine a whiff of that, sometimes with a genial robustness, as when in her first story Mr Fellowes says, 'It isn't all of us that can make conquests when our ugliness is past its bloom.'[62]

She had not enjoyed youth. 'Few women, I fear, have had such reason as I to think the long sad years of youth were worth living for the sake of middle age.'[63] But then perhaps few women had found their years of youth so long and sad. When George Eliot pretended that things had been otherwise, her metaphors twisted in her hands, as in the weirdest fiction she ever wrote, 'The Lifted Veil', the story of someone who can read other people's thoughts, except those of the woman whom he desires and fears. When she again possessed his senses and imagination,

It was a moment as delicious to me as the waking up to a consciousness of youth after a dream of middle age.

But this is itself a deadly and delusive dream. For George Eliot, whose long sad years of youth had been worth living only for the sake of middle age, the true happy waking up would have had to be the other way round: the waking up to a consciousness of middle

[61] *Athenaeum*, 4 April 1919.   [62] 'Amos Barton', ch. vi.
[63] Redinger, *George Eliot: The Emergent Self*, p. 50.

age after a dream of youth. In *Adam Bede*, 'Hetty did not understand how anybody could be very fond of middle-aged people' (ch. xv). George Eliot is not fond of her for this, but she does not deduce from it that nobody could be very fond of young people. She retained a comfort which she had gained in her twenties:

> Then the sorrows of older persons which children see but cannot understand are worse than all. All this dear Sara, to prove that we are happier than when we were seven years old, and that we shall be happier when we are forty than we are now, which I call a comfortable doctrine and one worth trying to believe.[64]

She didn't really have to try. Not that she was sentimental about old age. Featherstone in *Middlemarch* would be enough to prove that, and so would her quoting this proverb: 'One is never too old to learn, said an old woman; so she learned to be a witch.'[65]

A learned man may be too old to learn that all his labours have been an arid futility. Yet Casaubon is not too old to learn this, and George Eliot pities him, not for his unresponsive hardness to Dorothea, but for his being responsive as to need to harden himself against her and against the recognition which now comes with her:

> His glance in reply to hers was so chill that she felt her timidity increased; yet she turned and passed her hand through his arm.
> Mr. Casaubon kept his hands behind him and allowed her pliant arm to cling with difficulty against his rigid arm. (ch. xlii)

Cling, not *to*, but *against*.

For Leslie Stephen, Casaubon was merely 'a consummate pedant, who is pitilessly ridiculed for his petty and hidebound intellect'.[66] *Pedant . . . pitilessly . . . petty*: this has something of Milton's satirical wit. But Casaubon is pitied. I for one would rather be married to Casaubon than to anyone else in the book, and George Eliot was not being concessively personal when she drily wrote to Harriet Beecher Stowe, 'I fear that the Casaubon-tints are not quite foreign to my own mental complexion. At any rate I am very sorry for him.'[67] In answer (this has become famous) to the question, 'But from whom, then, did you draw Casaubon?', she pointed, 'with a

---

[64] To Sara Hennell, 3 March 1844; *Letters*, i 173.
[65] *Westminster Review*, July 1856; *Essays*, p. 277.
[66] *George Eliot: The Critical Heritage*, p. 480.
[67] October? 1872; *Letters*, v 322.

humorous solemnity', to her own heart:[68] she herself had conceived him, and he was herself. No fool, she looked in her heart and wrote.

For Leslie Stephen, 'Casaubon is a wretched being because he has neither heart nor brains.' But it is not a man without heart whom we hear—very soon after his unresponsive hardness to Dorothea—on the occasion when she waits up for him:

'Dorothea!' he said, with a gentle surprise in his tone. 'Were you waiting for me?'
'Yes, I did not like to disturb you'.
'Come, my dear, come. You are young, and need not to extend your life by watching'. (ch. xlii)

'With a gentle surprise in his tone': this comes as a gentle surprise not only to Dorothea but to us—and perhaps even to the creator of Casaubon, since the greatest effects in art are felicities, not determinations. The old need to extend their life by watching, they need all the hours they can get. George Eliot extends her own imaginative life, and ours, by comprehending, with gentle surprise, a Casaubon who would be moved to say such a thing.

'You are young.' Casaubon's creator was not young, and she knew what it meant to him, 'the autumnal unripeness of his author-ship' (wherewith the unseasonable months endowed him), his hope that 'there might still be twenty years of achievement before him, which would justify the thirty years of preparation' (ch. xlii). Of Daniel Deronda's mother, George Eliot wrote: 'You might have imagined her a sorceress who would stretch forth her wonderful hand and arm to mix youth-potions for others, but scorned to mix them for herself, having had enough of youth' (ch. liii). But George Eliot, having had enough of youth, did not mix youth-potions for others, or when she did, they did not work. What she was potent at was middle-age potions.

Circle back to Henry James, and to his first description of her, when she was 49. When he met her in 1869, he was touched to humorous puzzled rapture and self-protection:

I was immensely impressed, interested and pleased. To begin with she is magnificently ugly—deliciously hideous. She has a low forehead, a dull grey eye, a vast pendulous nose, a huge mouth, full of uneven teeth and a chin and jaw-bone *qui n'en finissent pas.*

[68] Haight, *George Eliot*, p. 450, from F. W. H. Myers.

Now in this vast ugliness resides a most powerful beauty which, in a very few minutes steals forth and charms the mind, so that you end as I ended, in falling in love with her. Yes behold me literally in love with this great horse-faced blue-stocking.[69]

It was left to Robert Lowell to see the powerful beauty in this perturbing exasperating record by Henry James (a record as much of his delicious hideousness as of hers), and to compact its uneasy truths, and other truths, into a rhymeless sonnet in her honour, about her honour:

> A lady in bonnet, brow clearer than the Virgin,
> the profile of a white rhinoceros—
> like Emerson, she hated gardens, thinking
> a garden is a grave, and drains the inkwell;
> she never wished to have a second youth—
> as for living, she didn't leave it to her servants,
> her union, Victorian England's one true marriage,
> one Victorian England pronounced *Mormonage*—
> two virgins; they published and were childless. Our writers often
> marry writers, are true, bright, clashing, though lacking
> this woman's dull gray eyes, vast pendulous nose,
> her huge mouth, and jawbone which forbore to finish:
> George Eliot with Tolstoy's once inalienable eye,
> George Eliot, a Countess Tolstoy . . . without Tolstoy.

[69] *Letters*, ed. Leon Edel, i (1974), 116.

A NOTE ON
HARDY'S 'A SPELLBOUND PALACE'

A SPELLBOUND PALACE
(Hampton Court)

On this kindly yellow day of mild low-travelling winter sun
　　The stirless depths of the yews
　　Are vague with misty blues:
Across the spacious pathways stretching spires of shadow run,
And the wind-gnawed walls of ancient brick are fired vermilion.

　　Two or three early sanguine finches tune
Some tentative strains, to be enlarged by May or June:
　　From a thrush or blackbird
　　Comes now and then a word,
While an enfeebled fountain somewhere within is heard.

　　Our footsteps wait awhile,
　　Then draw beneath the pile,
　　When an inner court outspreads
　　As 'twere History's own asile,
Where the now-visioned fountain its attenuate crystal sheds
In passive lapse that seems to ignore the yon world's clamorous clutch,
And lays an insistent numbness on the place, like a cold hand's touch.

And there swaggers the Shade of a straddling King, plumed, sworded,
　　with sensual face,
And lo, too, that of his Minister, at a bold self-centred pace:
　　Sheer in the sun they pass; and thereupon all is still,
Save the mindless fountain tinkling on with thin enfeebled will.

A haunted haunting poem, like so many of Hardy's.

Seldom can tourists, let alone visionary sightseers, have been less spellbound, if within that word there lurks some hope of fairy-tale fancies. The palace, spellbound, casts a spell all right, but a grim one; its spires of shadow cast a shade, which then in the end lengthens and erects itself, capitally, as a Shade, and then as two such. Hampton Court darkly feels not far enough from the Tower (as a favoured Minister of Henry VIII would do well to bear in mind), and Tower-tourism would have its sombre side.

The day is kindly (something other than kind, but not nothing), yet it is yellow too. Not mellow, exactly; the misty blues in the winter sun are other than the mists of mellow fruitfulness and of the autumn sun. Birds that manage to sing are held sanguine — there is a dry repressing of *sang* in the movement 'Two or three early sanguine finches tune / Some tentative strains', and those strains are audibly under strain. The fountain, its lassitude caught inattentively from, oh, somewhere within, sounds enfeebled, to put it mildly; next the sight of it duly proves numbing; and the fountain at the end, unextinguished though, is uncompromisingly mindless and enfeebled to the last. But, for there is always a But, the exquisitely enervated assonances within 'tinkling on with thin enfeebled will' find themselves braced disconcertingly by the unremittingness of the will. There is something the opposite of *enfeebled* about the word itself once it recurs, as if there need be no end of enfeeblement.

The first stanza sets a scene, not itself stirless for all its mildness; presentiment and premonition are felt to be playing their vague and spacious part, and unexpected energies ignite as the first stanza completes its architectonics. All bricks are fired, their making merely, but these walls of ancient brick are fired vermilion. How irresistibly *vermilion* sweeps in, gathering all attention to itself, a veritable cynosure, not only as putting in their place those everyday yellows and blues, and as royally imperious, but as being, of the stanza's rhyme-words, the first not to be a humbly ministering monosyllable. It is conclusive, the fourfold or quadrangular 'vermilion'. Meanwhile the compounded attrition of 'wind-gnawed walls' bides its time. What king's name is not Ozymandias?

The first stanza's opening sights and colours and darkenings (those 'spires of shadow' are secular as well as saecular, for Hampton Court, though Cardinal-built, is no cathedral), are succeeded by the desultory and ineffectual sound-effects of a bird-song so half-hearted as for once to make Keats's 'And no birds sing' sound as if it might be a relief. The birds' strains will, it is trusted, be 'enlarged by May or June' (*by* as agency as well as date), but this is a thin-lipped prophecy even if 'enlarged' does intimate not only a musically courting expansiveness but also freedom from captivity — the birds caught there in the grandiose cage that is Hampton Court. And who wants from a bird 'a word' exactly?

Meanwhile (each of the four stanzas draws to a Meanwhile) there is the background unmusic of the fountain. 'While an enfeebled fountain somewhere within is heard.' The syntax of the line is a masterpiece of flat fatigue: *is heard*, my word. The numbing flatness,

the razing of a fountain, is characteristic of Hardy's aptitude for the
apt however uningratiating. Too self-respecting a Creative Writing
Programme would counsel a budding poet against such enacted
entropy. What sort of gratitude can be breathed as thanks for five
lines, about sounds, which travel with lethal indeflectibility to '. . . is
heard'?

The third stanza immediately stations the poem's spectators within
a present-tense reminiscence, while necessarily beckoning the poem's
readers with the other hand of 'Our': 'Our footsteps wait awhile'.
Deep, and rather chastening, the way our footsteps—not even our
feet—are differentiated from us (they are ours, though they are not
we); they wait, as if they have a life of their own. Very true this
is too, partly as the unforthcoming visitors' being possessed by the
place, and partly as a matter of your usual sightseeing sleepwalking.
The feet walk on as and when it pleases them.

This stanza insists upon weight; the word *wait* hardens, is aggravated, before our very ears as it draws 'beneath the pile':

> Our footsteps wait awhile,
> Then draw beneath the pile,

—where *beneath* refuses to rest simply in the less-pressed preposi-
tional sense of 'close in against', but accrues an obdurate gravity
of oppression, weighted upon by so noble a pile. ('Lie heavy on him,
Earth! for he / Laid many heavy loads on thee!'—but then Hampton Court does not have Vanbrugh's unmisgiving tonnage.)

Hampton Court feels like what it often was, a madhouse:

> Where an inner court outspreads
> As 'twere History's own asile,

—the expansiveness of 'outspreads' (opening out at the unpunctuated
line-ending too) is at once dementedly contracted to 'asile', an asylum
in both senses of the word, and with the archaic form of the word
enforcing with all the more weight the conviction that asylums never
can be obsolete. The line combines a burly brutality (unmistakable
in its thrust and timbre) with a riddling quality, for does 'History's
own asile' see History as the warder or the lunatic, the refuge or
the refuge-seeker? Whereupon the weighty bricks give way to the
scarcely less weighty water. Water congeals, its 'passive lapse'
stalagtitic, with geology as the thinking man's history. The fountain
sheds crystal, attenuate crystal but obdurate (a dark chandelier now?),

so that it crystallizes into a solidity which may seem to ignore the world's clamorous clutch but not because of any watery levity with gravity, only because it is busy pressing its own unclamorous clutch of a claim, and laying 'an insistent numbness on the place'. The rhyme of *clutch* and *touch* has a simple grip, an unignorable directness—try arguing with that.

And then, then and there ('And there swaggers . . .'), there erupts the Shade of a straddling King. What, are *you* here, King Henry? It is as if 'on the place, like a cold hand's touch' had promptly precipitated—had conjured up within the circle of these courts— these immitigable apparitions. This, with 'on the place' releasing the ensuing rhyme, *face/pace*, and with *clutch/touch* feeling for our most tactile of monarchs.

'And there swaggers' is at once (as immediately and as both) the two different kinds of *there*, the stressed deictic one which points, and the unstressed one which (in the endearing terms of the dictionary) is 'used without any meaning of its own to allow the subject to follow the predicate'. (And here, the subject to follow the king.) 'And there swaggers . . .' perfectly combines the drama which points and the neutrality which records. Shades they may be, these two men, but how massively unmistakably corporeal they are, bodily enough to cast shadows themselves, and still alive to all their different physical being, their two bodies, their body politic. And altogether male. This place is still the stamping ground of the one, and the pacing ground of the other, and it always will be. Nothing will ever enfeeble them, Sheer in the sun.

And if King Henry VIII is 'plumed, sworded', we should cock an ear ('somewhere within is heard') for the other side of his swaggering grandeur: *sordid*. A homonym which Geoffrey Madan stigmatized as absurd ('Julian Grenfell's "Orion's sworded hip" was often quoted with appreciation')[1] is here a triumph of the studied *sotto voce*. The king, even at this distance of date, is still felt as dangerous; preserve, then, the civilities; admire his being 'plumed, sworded', while—within your own asile of an aside not even needing to be separately uttered—preserving your self-respect by knowing to yourself in the same breath that he is sordid. Watch your tongue (and keep your ears). The syllables can be sounded both ways: Hardy's 'sworded', in a poem which rhymes 'a word'

---

[1] *Geoffrey Madan's Notebooks*, ed. J. A. Gere and John Sparrow (1981), p. 68.

with 'heard', is keeping close to its chest such cards as Byron threw down:

> Oh, Wellington! (or 'Vilainton'—for Fame
> Sounds the heroic syllables both ways).
>
> (*Don Juan*, IX 1–2)

'A Spellbound Palace' is a poem of magnificence, with something of the superficially-obsolete inconvenient grandeur of a great pile, and with an entirely living sense of that which can never be exorcised, as well as of the fact that even if such shades could be exorcised, this would not be the death of them, merely their eviction. In the poem, reluctant admiration practises its awkward honourable straddling, in the company of bold and rightly self-centred art. For Hampton Court endures as beauty, whatever tyrannies and corruptions went to its making, and Henry's face may have been sensual but was not mindless, any more than were his Ministers, those Ministers who are at once servants and anything but. It was handsome of Wolsey, and prudent withal, to present Hampton Court to Henry VIII, as a gift and not just as a sight. Hardy here has not only Henry and Wolsey in his sightseeing, but Holbein.

A friend of mine, when I recently presented him with 'A Spellbound Palace', said, with simple truth, 'There's *always* another Hardy poem.' But then a Hardy poem itself feels the touch of other poems, of others' poems. Hardy might, for instance, have grimly enjoyed the prospect of Gray, who opens his 'Ode on a Distant Prospect of Eton College' royally:

> Ye distant spires, ye antique towers,
> That crown the watery glade,
> Where grateful Science still adores
> Her HENRY's holy Shade.

More than roman numbering separates Henry VI from Henry VIII; the founder of Eton College from the bounder of Hampton Court; 'Henry's holy Shade' from 'And there swaggers the Shade of a straddling King'.

Again, Hardy's 'numbness' here may invite us to hear ('somewhere within' again) a poem which offers an enlarged birdsong:

> My heart aches, and a drowsy numbness pains
> My sense . . .

Hardy has, likewise in two successive lines (but unlikewise, with a stanza-fissure between them), 'numbness' and, not 'sense', but 'sensual', a fine coarsening. Again, when we learn—from Samuel Hynes's excellent edition of Hardy's poems—that in manuscript the title of 'A Spellbound Palace' had been 'A Sleeping Palace', we may register the poem as another of Hardy's inspired dispiriting renderings-down of Tennyson, for whom 'The Sleeping Palace' had figured within a sequence which arrives at the fairy-tale ending proper to the next poem in sequence, 'The Sleeping Beauty'. Tennyson had bent less attention upon a king than upon a fairy prince: 'A fairy prince, with joyful eyes' (not a solid king with piggy ones), 'and lighter-footed than the fox'. Tennyson's sequence is 'The Day-Dream', Hardy's poem is by way of being a real-life nightmare.

And there enters a modern-day real-life nightmare.

SWEENEY ERECT

> *And the trees about me*
> *Let them be dry and leafless; let the rocks*
> *Groan with continual surges; and behind me*
> *Make all a desolation. Look, look, wenches!*

Paint me a cavernous waste shore
  Cast in the unstilled Cyclades,
Paint me the bold anfractuous rocks
  Faced by the snarled and yelping seas.

Display me Aeolus above
  Reviewing the insurgent gales
Which tangle Ariadne's hair
  And swell with haste the perjured sails.

Morning stirs the feet and hands
  (Nausicaa and Polypheme).
Gesture of orang-outang
  Rises from the sheets in steam.

This withered root of knots of hair
  Slitted below and gashed with eyes,
This oval O cropped out with teeth:
  The sickle motion from the thighs

Jackknifes upward at the knees
  Then straightens out from heel to hip
Pushing the framework of the bed
  And clawing at the pillow slip.

    Sweeney addressed full length to shave
        Broadbottomed, pink from nape to base,
    Knows the female temperament
        And wipes the suds around his face.

    (The lengthened shadow of a man
        Is history, said Emerson
    Who had not seen the silhouette
        Of Sweeney straddled in the sun.)

    Tests the razor on his leg
        Waiting until the shriek subsides.
    The epileptic on the bed
        Curves backward, clutching at her sides.

    The ladies of the corridor
        Find themselves involved, disgraced,
    Call witness to their principles
        And deprecate the lack of taste

    Observing that hysteria
        Might easily be misunderstood;
    Mrs. Turner intimates
        It does the house no sort of good.

    But Doris, towelled from the bath,
        Enters padding on broad feet,
    Bringing sal volatile
        And a glass of brandy neat.

Whether the relation between Hardy's poem and Eliot's be that of
analogue or source (or a will o' the wisp), here are, at the least,
coincidences enough. Eliot:

    (The lengthened shadow of a man
        Is history, said Emerson
    Who had not seen the silhouette
        Of Sweeney straddled in the sun.)

Hardy: 'shadow', 'History', 'straddling' ('the Shade of a straddling'),
'in the sun'—and these occurring in the same order as in Eliot.
    The run of overlappings or adjacencies is this (I set aside words
like 'this' but include Eliot's epigraph):

Hardy	*Eliot*
stirless	leafless / stirs
shadow	shadow
footsteps	feet / feet

wait	waiting
History	history
clutch	clutching
hand's	hands
Shade	[shadow]
straddling	straddled
face	Faced / face
bold	bold
in the sun	in the sun
still	unstilled
mindless	[leafless]

Added to which, there are overlappings both large and small. Small, for instance, in the way in which Hardy's 'low' and 'lo' might be heard in Eliot's 'below . . . oval O'. Large, in the way in which both poems begin with wind and water, among the trees too (and with rocks or bricks); or the parallel between Eliot's sardonic Marvellian adaptation of the old patriotic genre 'Instructions to a Painter' ('Paint me . . .') and Hardy's sense of historic Instructions to an Architect (and to a Minister).

What might be made of any consanguinity of the Eliot and the Hardy poems, if still believed?

The first thing of which to take the force is that, if acquisition there be, Eliot is not the borrower but the lender. 'Sweeney Erect' was published in 1920; 'A Spellbound Palace' in 1925, in *Human Shows, Far Phantasies*.

We know from Lennart Björk's edition of Hardy's *Literary Notebooks* (I learn from Michael Millgate and from Dennis Taylor, whom I thank) that Hardy transcribed 23 lines from 'The Love-Song of J. Alfred Prufrock', subscribing them:

T. S. Eliot—a poet of the vers-libre school—quoted in 'From Shakespeare to O. Henry' by S. P. B. Mais—Grant Richards 1917

Professor Millgate has further informed me that Hardy cut out of *The Daily News* for 11 August, and inserted loose in his notebook, a review of J. C. Squire which quoted Eliot's 'Miss Helen Slingsby'.

As to 'A Spellbound Palace', Professor Millgate tells me that he would 'hazard a guess (no more)' that there may be an autobiographical source in the visit paid by Hardy and Emma Hardy to Hampton Court in 1874–5. There is no reason to suppose, though, that 'A Spellbound Palace' was written much earlier than its publication in 1925 (Hynes cites nothing). If then, as is likely, Eliot's poem has the priority, then Hardy's initial readings, in manuscript or in proofs, may be called in evidence when weighing the likelihood that the coincidings are not coincidences. Hardy's 'numbness' had been 'stillness' (Eliot's epigraph has 'unstilled', and Hardy 'still'); more interestingly, there is 'wind-gnawn', which had once been 'bare-gnawed', and where Hardy at one stage 'cancelled -*gnawed*, and wrote in the margin *wiped* and *whetted*' (Hynes). Sweeney, bare, 'wipes the suds around his face', and he 'Tests the razor', lest it need whetting.

There would be something pleasing, and salutary, about any such reversal of our expectation, in this small jolt to literary history or rather of it (especially given two poems about history), and with Eliot ministering to Hardy (whose poems Eliot saddeningly condescended to). I don't suppose that Hardy's poem alludes to Eliot's, but I think it more than likely that Hardy's would not have taken quite the form, and quite the wording, it has, were it not for Eliot's. Hampton Court—in a complication of historical similitude and dissimilitude such as Eliot subtly relished, particularly in *The Waste Land* (1922)—bore more than a little resemblance to a brothel. 'Look, look, wenches!' (Listen, listen, finches!)

If the lengthened shadow of a man is history, there must be no Emersonian sentimentality, no flinching from some unlovely lengthenings. Few men have cast a longer shadow than Henry VIII, over history, over church and state, and marriage, and the relations of men to women and of beauty to power. He 'knows the female temperament', does Henry Erect. Perhaps Hardy, who had an ear for such things, was grimly tickled by the rub of the very names here, names so potent as not even needing to be named (there's glory for you): Henry, Wolsey, Sweeney—and, attending, Hardy.

But if you prefer something more burly, to the point of genial brutality, there is always as, well, a *coda*, Gavin Ewart (*TLS*, 18 September 1992):

DISCOVER THE TRUE STORIES OF A ROYAL HOME
(ADVERTISEMENT ON THE LONDON UNDERGROUND)

> At Hampton Court, fat Henry's Royal Palace,
> Discover the True Stories of a Royal Home!
> He was no niggard with his active phallus
> At Hampton Court, fat Henry's Royal Palace—

Not different much from oil-rich lust in Dallas
Or what the Popes were into, in old sexy Rome!
At Hampton Court, fat Henry's Royal Palace,
Discover the True Stories of a Royal Home!

RACINE'S *PHÈDRE*, LOWELL'S *PHAEDRA*

No translator has had the gifts or the luck to bring Racine into our culture. It's a pity that Pope and Dryden overlooked Racine's great body of works, close to them, in favor of the inaccessible Homer and Virgil.

(Robert Lowell, 'On Translating *Phèdre*,' *Phaedra*, 1961)

Lowell set himself to translate Racine in the knowledge that this was a field which had never been won. Extremity was forced upon Lowell. After such knowledge, what forgiveness? Lowell's critics have proved duly unforgiving: they have refused to admit that here the history of unsuccess had been such as to call for extreme measures.

Here is the emergency.

First, Racine has always frustrated English hopes, being one of the great writers (European, too) never brought home in English translation. There is no Racine alive in the language as Dryden's Juvenal is, or even Florio's Montaigne. More: no translation of Racine into English has ever made anybody's modest enduring reputation; there is no equivalent of Cary's staunch dominie Dante.

Second, nothing of any central lasting importance has ever been said, even as a succinct tip, about Racine in English (the contrast might be with Baudelaire or Proust), and no great writer in English has been profoundly fecundated by Racine or by translations of Racine.

Third, there is something resolutely equivocating about English relations to the French neoclassical ideal and therefore to Racine. Even T. S. Eliot, the most imaginative proponent of classicism in a romantic age, did not make good his account of the matter:

My own opinion is, that we have no classic age, and no classic poet, in English; that when we see why this is so, we have not the slightest reason for regret; but that, nevertheless, we must maintain the classic ideal before our eyes. Because we must maintain it, and because the English genius of language has had other things to do than to realize it, we cannot afford either to reject or to overrate the age of Pope.[1]

Eliot never explains why there is not the *slightest* reason for regret, and so this assurance comes out as too simply reassuring. Since a

[1] 'What is a Classic?' (1944); *On Poetry and Poets* (1957), pp. 59, 63, 66–7.

classic age and a classic poet must presumably be able to effect *some* achievements not otherwise possible, it feels like a mere rallying by Eliot, this telling the English that they have forgone nothing; and if they have forgone anything at all, there must be some reason for regret even if none for repining. A stricter acknowledgement is made by Eliot in this address when, thinking still of the classic poet, he speaks of Racine:

> In modern European literature, the closest approximations to the ideal of a common style, are probably to be found in Dante and Racine; the nearest we have to it in English poetry is Pope, and Pope's is a common style which, in comparison, is of a very narrow range.

Yet the very narrow range of Pope's common style must bear some relation to his not being a classic poet, and must constitute some reason for regret.

It is not that there is a knock-out competition, Shakespeare vs. Racine. Nevertheless, one aspect of the matter, both cause and consequence of what has been Racine's untranslatability for us, is the English tradition of being negatively willing not to reject Racine but positively eager not to overrate him. Eliot himself, who insisted that Pope's style is of a very narrow range in comparison with Racine, was moved to insist too that Racine's language is of a very narrow range in comparison with Rabelais and Villon:

> The French language has seemed to be much more clearly tethered to a normal style; yet, even in French, though the language appeared to have established itself, once for all, in the seventeenth century, there is an *esprit gaulois*, an element of richness present in Rabelais and in Villon, the awareness of which may qualify our judgment of the *wholeness* of Racine or Molière, for we may feel that it is not only unrepresented but unreconciled.

Behind Eliot's admonitory reservation, there was Arnold, who told the English that they could not afford to overrate the age of Pope but who turned even this to a national pride:

> We English had Shakspeare waiting to open our eyes, whensoever a favourable moment came, to the insufficiencies of Pope. But the French had no Shakspeare to open their eyes to the insufficiencies of Corneille and Racine.[2]

---

[2] 'The French Play in London' (1879); *English Literature and Irish Politics*, ed. R. H. Super (1973), p. 75.

Such is Arnold's cool composure; earlier in this history of resistance, there had been Coleridge's torrid discomposure, conceding that the excesses of the drama of his day extorted some admission of Racine's merits and yet eager, even so, not to overrate the Frenchman:

for such is the *kind* of Drama, which is now substituted every where for Shakespeare and Racine. You well know, that I offer violence to my own feelings in joining these names; but however meanly I may think of the French serious Drama, even in its most perfect specimens; and with whatever right I may complain of its perpetual falsification of the language, and of the connections and transitions of thought, which Nature has appropriated to states of passion: still, however, the French Tragedies are consistent works of art, and the Offspring of great intellectual power. Preserving a fitness in the parts, and a harmony in the whole, they form a nature of their own, though a false nature.[3]

In the doubting dubious light of such a tradition, it is as if not only the art but the very name of Racine cannot be brought over into English. Beckett when young had yearned in English for French virtues, Belacqua/Beckett being 'the man with a style' emulous of 'the writing of, say, Racine or Malherbe':

They have no style, they write without style, do they not, they give you the phrase, the sparkle, the precious margaret. Perhaps only the French can do it. Perhaps only the French language can give you the thing you want.
    Don't be too hard on him, he was studying to be a professor.[4]

Beckett later found himself unable or unwilling to give the English something he was not sure that they wanted anyway, the name and example of Racine: one difference between *Premier amour* (1945) and Beckett's translation of it as *First Love* (1973) is that the following flight was omitted in the English, perhaps because Racine could neither be carried over nor be replaced by an English counterpart:

Donnez un vase de nuit, dis-je. J'ai beaucoup aimé, enfin assez aimé, pendant assez longtemps, les mots vase de nuit, ils me faisaient penser à Racine, ou à Baudelaire, je ne sais plus lequel, les deux peut-être, oui.[5]

Pope is perhaps (as Eliot suggested) our nearest counterpart to Racine, but there would be no felicitous incongruity between Pope and the

---

[3] *The Friend*, 7 December 1809.
[4] *Dream of Fair to Middling Women* (1992), p. 48.
[5] *Premier amour* (1970), p. 44.

English for 'vase de nuit', Pope being in *The Dunciad* the poet of the chamber-pot.

'To bring Racine into our culture': for Lowell, *our* has to be partly English, partly American, and altogether historically subsequent. The principle of Johnson's admonition, in attending to Pope's *Iliad*, has endured through such a passing of years as it invoked:

In estimating this translation, consideration must be had of the nature of our language, the form of our metre, and above all of the changes which two thousand years have made in the modes of life and the habits of thought.[6]

Lowell translated *Phèdre* as he did because of an unignorable historical change in the modes of life and the habits of thought. His apprehending this change should at least have protected him against the charge of perversity.

This crucial and undisputed change is our unremitting consciousness of and self-consciousness about sexuality. 'Such sly audacity!' (*Phaedra*, IV i): Lowell's slyly audacious translation is for our time and our world the only imaginable one, or at any rate the only consistently imagined one—imagined so as to be neither prurient nor vacant. The vacant translations have no difficulty in not being prurient, and no achievement either. Lowell sacrifices much of Racine's banked richness, but the loss is a calculated and calculable one, and *Phèdre* is itself a play sensitive (as was its author) to the inescapability of sacrifice, just as Lowell is a translator sensitive to sacrifice as any translator's servitude and grandeur.

Prurience is the nub, not because Racine is prurient but because things which were not so within his culture present a sacrificial emergency when they are to be brought over into ours. Prurience's snigger or snicker is not just incompatible with such tragedy but fatal to it.

The word *prurient* apparently entered the English language in the year of Racine's birth, 1639 (apparently, in that the *Oxford English Dictionary* records the fact, on the authority of Todd in 1818, but lacks the citation). *Pruriency* arrived in 1669 and *prurience* in 1688; *Phèdre* was of 1677. But the three English words had as their energy in the seventeenth century the literal root-meaning: 'that itches physically', 'the quality of itching', 'the physical fact or sensation of

---

[6] *Life of Pope.*

itching'. The movement into what is now the sense was effected via an intermediate one: '*fig.* having an itching desire or curiosity, or an uneasy or morbid craving' (from 1653), '*fig.* the quality or condition of mental itching' (from 1711).

'Your hands are moist and itching for my bed' (IV ii): Lowell lunges at prurience in this line's travesty-marriage of callous cliché and intense physicality, where Racine's cooler horror could be carried by the movement from 'le transport' to 'porté':

> Après que le transport d'un amour plein d'horreur
> Jusqu'au lit de ton père a porté sa fureur

Yet when even so accomplished a translator as Richard Wilbur seeks to translate faithfully this horrifying infidelity, his coolness feels relaxed, not taut:

> Now that your vile, unnatural love has led
> You even to attempt your father's bed[7]

The *OED* relaxes its attention when it comes to define *prurient* in the sense now dominant (recording the adjective since 1746 and the nouns since 1781 and 1795). For the dictionary is insufficiently alert to the intermediate sense and does not exactly catch the intimated relation to sexuality:

prurient Given to the indulgence of lewd ideas; impure-minded; characterized by lasciviousness of thought or mind.

prurience, pruriency Liking for or tendency towards impure or lascivious thought.

But someone's mind could be impure or lascivious without being prurient exactly: the dictionary's word *indulgence* is what has to be pondered. The concept of prurience implies an attitude toward one's own impure, lewd, or lascivious imaginings, an impurity not of the imaginings but of the attitude toward them, an attitude of cherishing, fondling, slyly watching, or preferring (preferring imagining to acting). Art is obliged to be especially interested in prurience, since prurience is a disease of the imagination; prurience is not unimaginativeness, a failure of imagination, but a corrupt success of it. *Fondling* is a member of the family of disconcerting words here, not because fondling is in itself contaminated but because it is not an action healthily appropriate to one's imaginings, especially of other people's

---

[7] *Phaedra* (1987).

—and, above all, one's father's and mother's—physical acts of love. Racine's style of steel is supple but unfondling when it contemplates, imagines somebody imagining, these acts of love. Théramène's first speech, the second speech of the play, is in reply to Hippolyte.

> Qui sait même, qui sait si le Roi votre père
> Veut que de son absence on sache le mystère?
> Et si, lorsque avec vous nous tremblons pour ses jours,
> Tranquille, et nous cachant de nouvelles amours,
> Ce héros n'attend point qu'une amante abusée ...

Wilbur's translation, with its powerful 'fondling', hovers equivocally between the chaste coldness of Racine and a fully candid admission of the sexual energies:

> Who knows, indeed, if he wants the truth about
> His long, mysterious absence to come out,
> And whether, while we tremble for him, he's
> Not fondling some new conquest at his ease
> And planning to deceive her like the rest?

Theseus's long mysterious something comes out suggestive, and *tremble*, though a direct translation of Racine's *tremblons*, is disconcertingly activated into displaced sexuality by Wilbur's *fondling*, which is absent from Racine. It is not that Wilbur's translation here lacks energy, but that the hiding places of its power feel intimate with prurience's pleasures as Racine's lines do not.

Lowell, sensing that the effect least faithful to Racine is any that might incite prurience, drives not for an intermediate effect but for an extreme explicit one, making the truth indeed come out:

> One even doubts
> if noble Theseus wants his whereabouts
> discovered. Does he need helpers to share
> the plunder of his latest love affair;
> a shipload of spectators and his son
> to watch him ruin his last Amazon—

(I i)

Lowell gets out into the open not only the active sexual energies of Theseus but the more insinuating ones which threaten any such vivid imagining of his (another's, especially your father's) acts. The prurience of voyeurism or scopophilia does not know where to look when it meets the bold stare of

> a shipload of spectators and his son
> to watch him ruin his last Amazon

Neither tragedy nor comedy is as confident how to deal with prurience as farce is. Fire drives out fire; the itch to laugh derisively and decisively drives out the other itch. Lowell seeks a modern counterpart to what Eliot in 1919 seized in Marlowe, 'the farce of the old English humour, the terribly serious, even savage comic humour'.[8] Like Marlowe, Lowell aims at a paradox which is caught in Eliot's unremarked divergency of praise: on the one hand, Marlowe's is an art of 'prodigious caricature'; on the other, his is a 'style which secures its emphasis by always hesitating on the edge of caricature at the right moment'. The closest thing in English literature to Lowell's creation, in *Phaedra* and elsewhere, of something which both is and is not caricature (both being it and hesitating on the edge of it), is the Marlovian extreme, the ball of wild-fire, which Eliot exultantly swung:

> And after him, his band of Myrmidons,
> With balls of wild-fire in their murdering paws...
>
> At last, the soldiers pull'd her by the heels,
> And swung her howling in the empty air...
>
> We saw Cassandra sprawling in the streets...

Prurience is a contaminated propriety. As such, it may collude with the imbalance or dislocation which has overtaken Artemis/Diana. In Euripides' world of the story, there are *two* divine forces, terrible, awe-inspiring, equipollent; but the transition into Racine's world constitutes a shift, an acknowledgement (in Hippolyte's love for Aricie) that there is now only one, Venus; and the movement from Racine to our world has to acknowledge the furthering of this imbalance. Venus remains immitigably herself, the heyday in the blood and more; but what is now felt as the *force* of Diana? She would seem to have dwindled to cold baths, Olympic Games, and *pudeur*.

Lowell, then, understands prurience as the greatest threat to an honourable translating of Racine. There are three pertinent pruriences, of sexuality, of violence, and of irony. All are opposed by Lowell's ways in translation. Sexuality and violence are protected against prurience by a candour such as necessarily courts indignity

---

[8] 'Christopher Marlowe' (1919); *Selected Essays* (1932), 1951 edn, pp. 123–4.

in its overtness; and irony, particularly the pruriently knowing (to which dramatic irony is so tempted), is persistently extirpated by Lowell.

The critic J. F. Crick has complained that Lowell's *Phaedra* is 'post-Freudian, post-Kinsey'.[9] But what exactly would it be for a translation effected after Freud and after Kinsey *not* to be post-them? 'It is Freud crossed with Cotton Mather, Jonathan Edwards and Hawthorne, and with a dash of Emily Dickinson.' But Emily Dickinson is exactly the instance to challenge any such unmisgiving confidence that nothing particularly has *happened*, that a translator may proceed as if pre-Freudian achievements could in our day effectively be translated within good old pre-Freudian terms. Much of Dickinson's best poetry could not now be written as she wrote it, for its unmisgiving tacit eroticism (something quite other than the 'naive') could scarcely affect not to notice that the erotically tacit has yielded since Dickinson's day to the knowing, something everywhere in the air, an air at once 'frank' and 'suggestive'. Her accents are quite other.

> In Winter in my Room
> I came upon a Worm—
> Pink, lank and warm—
> But as he was a worm
> And worms presume
> Not quite with him at home—
> Secured him by a string
> To something neighboring
> And went along.
>
> A Trifle afterward
> A thing occurred
> I'd not believe it if I heard
> But state with creeping blood—
> A snake with mottles rare
> Surveyed my chamber floor
> In feature as the worm before
> But ringed with power—
> The very string with which
> I tied him—too
> When he was mean and new
> That string was there—

---

[9] *Robert Lowell* (1974), p. 72.

> I shrank—'How fair you are'!
> Propitiation's claw—
> 'Afraid,' he hissed
> 'Of me'?
> 'No cordiality'—
> He fathomed me—
> Then to a Rhythm *Slim*
> Secreted in his Form
> As Patterns swim
> Projected him.
>
> That time I flew
> Both eyes his way
> Lest he pursue
> Nor ever ceased to run
> Till in a distant Town
> Towns on from mine
> I set me down
> This was a dream.

Here is no explicit consciousness of the unconscious, and this coolth issues in one of the greatest erotic poems in the language, a poem fascinating in being exactly, in the old way, fascinated as the victim is by the snake. It is more than hard to imagine Dickinson's poem as existing in another language and therefore as needing to be translated into the English language of our day, but it is no less hard to conceive of how it *could* be translated for our day without radically re-effecting a relation of the conscious to the unconscious in matters of sexuality. In other words, how one would carry this poem into a post-Freudian world without stationing the poem so differently as to bring about a quite different equation of gain and loss when it comes to the co-operative unconscious both in artist and in audience.

What does this suggest as to the possibility of translating the secreted sexuality of Racine?

John Bayley saw what Lowell was doing but did not really ask why Lowell was doing it.

I take it that the triumph of Racine is somehow to have admitted the predestinate obsessions of lust, and the misery of monstrous longings, within the strict limits of a classic poetry; and that the miracle of the thing is its exhibited control. Venus is suggested in all the grossness of her power, but she is never allowed to disturb the Apollonian clarity of speech. In destroying this balance Lowell destroys dignity. 'Frothing with desire', his Phèdre is almost as energetically ludicrous a figure as the poisoned Nourmahal in Dryden's *Aurengzebe*. She calls on Hippolytus—in a phrase which mocks the simmering coolness of the Racinian confrontation,—for his 'sword's spasmodic final inch'.[10]

'The triumph of Racine is somehow to . . .': but the translator is someone who, even more than the critic, cannot afford to rest content with a *somehow*. *How?* And is any such *how* available now? The critic can, though he or she had better not make a habit of it, speak of a miracle ('the miracle of the thing'); the blessed translator has a task in hand. 'Venus is suggested in all the grossness of her power': but there may no longer be any prophylaxis such as can protect what was once suggested against what is now suggestive. The fate of the word *suggestive* might suggest this. From 1631, it had a broad sense, and did not have to suggest certain sorts of thing; and then from 1889 it narrowed and provoked: '*euphem.* Apt to suggest something indecent. Gunter, *That Frenchman*: Her incomparable drolleries and naughtinesses, in some suggestive opera bouffe, some musical debauch.'

No one is going to doubt or underrate the steely dignity of Racine's *Phèdre* or of Racine's art at that climactic moment:

> Au defaut de ton bras prête-moi ton epée.
> Donne.

Lowell will have known what he was forgoing when he rendered this thus:

> Look, this monster, ravenous
> for her execution, will not flinch.
> I want your sword's spasmodic final inch.

(II v)

The dilation of *flinch* so that it becomes '*f*ina*l inch*' is appalling: 'spasmodic' is a hideous compacting of love and death: 'I want' is lack and desire: 'final' is a sword's tip, and a sword to the hilt, and a life's end. The intense physicality lacks dignity, but it has corporeality, and it transmits more of the energy of Racine, albeit in a harshened form, than does, say, Wilbur's inoffensive moment, which may hew close to Racine's words but has no power to *hew*:

---

[10] *London Magazine*, June 1966; collected in *Robert Lowell: A Portrait of the Artist in His Time*, ed. Michael London and Robert Boyers (1970), p. 197.

> If you'll not stain your hand with my abhorred
> And tainted blood, lend me at least your sword.
> Give it to me!

And Wilbur's earlier lines in the speech—

> In haste to expiate its wicked lust,
> My heart already leaps to meet your thrust—

seem to me to have just the suggestiveness which Lowell is at such audacious pains to eschew.

Louis Simpson, in deploring Lowell's line 'I want your sword's spasmodic final inch', makes what purports to be a historical point as if all that were really involved were the simple avoidance of anachronism. The line

is not Racine—it is pure Lowell, and a distortion. Racine's Phèdre is not self-consciously making an up-to-date sexual metaphor; to her, a sword is a sword. 'A primrose by the river's brim / A simple primrose was to him.'[11]

But one need not suppose that Phèdre was being self-consciously sexual, or that her creator Racine was being so, to resist Simpson's assumption that, in the absence of anything you could call a self-consciously up-to-date sexual metaphor, there can be no erotic suggestion or implication in Racine's lines. Phallic symbols were in some ways enfranchised by Freud, but he did not own the franchise of them. The uneasiness of Simpson's insistence (as if in those days such a thought could never have entered anyone's head) is manifest in the invoking of Peter Bell, whose Wordsworthian lineaments ('a solemn and unsexual man') are even more distant from those of Racine's Phèdre than are those of Lowell's Phaedra.

While some critics were deploring Lowell for making erotic what had not been so, others were granting that such a moment was erotic but rejecting Lowell's dealings with this. Michael Black, who would presumably have to answer to Louis Simpson, says of Phèdre's speech here, 'at the end of all this the gasped-out *Donne* is a plea for a sexual release'; so Lowell is to be differently deprecated now:

It [the climactic-erotic] emerges almost grotesquely in Robert Lowell's translation of the passage. Indeed I would say he makes it over-explicit and disconcertingly jaunty.[12]

[11] *Hudson Review*, xiv (1961–2); collected in *Robert Lowell: A Portrait of the Artist in His Time*, ed. London and Boyers, p. 111.

[12] *Poetic Drama as Mirror of the Will* (1977), pp. 184–5.

I hear nothing jaunty in the clenched-teeth rhythm of 'I want your sword's spasmodic final inch.' But then I hear something evasive in '*almost* grotesquely' (where the critic's responsibility is rather to say in just what ways *grotesque* is and is not the right word here). Black sees that the 'over-explicit' is a nub, but he then has no interest in what might move Lowell to such a calculation or miscalculation. The alternative to the over-explicit might, after all, be something implicatedly implicit, smutched with the prurient. Black himself often sounds jaunty, edgy, nervous, and *under*-explicit. (There is something of a tradition, revealingly, of this in Racine studies, where even someone as stalwart as Martin Turnell will permit himself the ill-judged prurient word *sexiness* for Phèdre's imagining Hippolyte with Aricie.) 'I seem to hear,' says Black, dangerously playing safe as prurience does, 'I seem to hear a certain salivation in *lâchement enchantée*.' 'Her speech reaches what I can only call a climax (meaning just that).' 'Aricie's salivating ch's and g's and j's (if I can put it that way).' Her C's, her U's, and her T's. Not since the days when I used to register the pleasure H. A. Mason took in referring to Juliet 'in her nightie' have I so heard the accents of prurience. Black's nervous eagerness of imagining, in its relation to prurience, is what Lowell, or any unflinching translator of Racine, is up against.

'The gasped-out *Donne*': so take the word *gasp*.

> Hélas! du crime affreux dont la honte me suit
> Jamais mon triste coeur n'a recueilli le fruit.
> Jusqu'au dernier soupir, de malheurs poursuivie,
> Je rends dans les tourments une pénible vie.

'Au dernier soupir' goes easily into English, but (sigh) all too easily since it arrives at a cliché: 'last gasp'. Kenneth Muir avails himself of this but fails to breathe any new life into a phrase which is itself at its last gasp:

> Dogged by miseries
> To the last gasp, in torture, I render up
> A life I long to lose.[13]

But Lowell gasps out, grasps at, clasps, a rhyme, having stationed 'last gasp' as the last word of its line, and he gives the phrase something desperately climactic, swathed in a heady dying alliterative lure:

[13] *Five Plays of Jean Racine* (1960).

> I killed myself—and what is worse I wasted
> my life for pleasures I have never tasted.
> My lover flees me still, and my last gasp
> is for the fleeting flesh I failed to clasp.
>
> (IV vi)

Nothing ventured, nothing gained, whether as tragic heroine or as tragic translator. Set such a gasp against the ones heard by Louis Simpson, telling how he was unable to get someone to disapprove of the movement of Lowell's translation.

When I complained about it to a man of the theater, he said that, to the contrary, Lowell's run-on couplets are very pleasing. You hear the rhyme as an echo, a pleasant assonance—not falling with the regularity of a bellclapper, as in the original. I sighed and withdrew my objection. To me, one of the sweetest sounds in the world is Racine's end-stopped couplets being inhaled by an audience of schoolgirls at the Comédie Française, and their punctual little gasps.

I sighed and withdrew. But not before wondering what region of the imagination those schoolgirls had punctually surfaced from, with their 'punctual little gasps'.

It stands to reason that Simpson is right to see that Lowell pays a price. But it is never established that the price paid by Lowell amounts to bankruptcy, or that the other, less bold, ways of translating Racine do not pay a crippling price.

To translate Phèdre's description of Theseus:

> Volage adorateur de mille objets divers

into this:

> lascivious eulogist of any belle
>
> (Act 2, sc. v)

is a gross lapse of diction. The word *belle* conjures up Gibson Girls, *The Belle of New York*, etc. In such cases, a neutral word would be better.[14]

A neutral word such as what? The translators converge gleefully upon *fickle* as their adjectival salvation, but it doesn't help them to render the tauntingly cool *objets divers*.

---

[14] *Robert Lowell: A Portrait of the Artist in His Time*, p. 110.

> The fickle admirer of countless nameless women
> (Black)
> The fickle worshipper at countless shrines
> (John Cairncross)[15]
> The fickle worshiper of a thousand maids
> (Wilbur)
> a fickle lover, bent
> To stain great Pluto's bed
> (Muir)

Muir musters an interesting and faintly disgusting corporeality in 'bent / To stain great Pluto's bed', but neither he nor the others could come up with a 'neutral' word for the women. The effect is not neutral but neutered. At which point one wonders whether there is not something to be said for the vulgar vibrancy of 'lascivious eulogist of any belle'.

Prurience is the charge which Theseus makes against Hippolytus. Here is how Edmund Smith rendered the speech, in his translation or imitation of Racine, *Phaedra and Hippolitus* (1707), at a time when the modern sense of prurience was establishing itself, and when Pope—who was indebted to this translation for two lines in *Eloisa to Abelard*—was often to be accused of prurience.

> What, no remorse! No qualms! No pricking pangs!
> No feeble struggle of rebelling honour!
> O 'twas thy joy! thy secret hoard of bliss,
> To dream, to ponder, act it o'er in thought;
> To doat, to dwell on; as rejoicing misers
> Brood o'er their precious stores of secret gold.
>
> (Act IV)

'What is sometimes called "vulgarity" is therefore one thing that has not been vulgarized.'[16] But Eliot would have acknowledged that this truth too is subject to history. Lowell's sense of the sacrifices which history demands of us, and which a translator must not try to elude, prompted him to challenge the three pruriences. First, that of violence, by—for instance—not veiling the brute brutality of Hippolyte's death: 'his body was a piece of bloody meat.' If this leaves less to the imagination than Racine did, that is partly because

---

[15] *Phaedra & Other Plays* (1963).　　[16] T. S. Eliot, *Tyro* i (1921).

the imagination is not these days to be trusted to have as much left to it. In Edmund Smith's words: 'To dream, to ponder, act it o'er in thought.' In the same spirit, Lowell reduces, either in frequency of occurrence or in force, the dramatic ironies which can laxly prompt a corrupted imagining, a secret doting and hoarding. Most crucially, in the very tissue of the verse, he leaves no room for the suggestive. In so doing, he necessarily sacrifices many enhancing and chastening suggestions but he creates a translation of Racine such as succeeds in precluding the snicker, the snigger and the knowing finger laid against the nose, and precludes all these by something other than lifelessness.

Lowell knew himself to be, as translator, the heir of Pound, not of Gilbert Murray. 'We need a careful study of Renaissance Humanists and Translators, such as Mr. Pound has begun,' Eliot wrote in 1920, and at once continued:

We need an eye which can see the past in its place with its definite differences from the present, and yet so lively that it shall be as present to us as the present. This is the creative eye; and it is because Professor Murray has no creative instinct that he leaves Euripides quite dead.[17]

Lowell, it is true, judged that he had no choice but to amputate, but at least he preserved Racine's life.

[17] 'Euripides and Professor Murray' (1920); *Selected Essays*, p. 64.

AUSTIN'S SWINK

'How shal the world be served?
Lat Austyn have his swynk to hym reserved!'

The author of *How to do things with Words*[1] knew how to do things with such wording as constitutes allusion—as is clear from J. L. Austin's having given the world *Sense and Sensibilia.*

The famous joke, which is not without pride and prejudice, is more than a quip because the displaced word *sensibility* so much enters, not into the equation, but into the opposite of equation. For a start, the register of 'sensibilia' is deliciously registered as cold-shouldering the warm thought of 'sensibility'.

sensibile. *Philos.* Usu. in pl. **sensibilia**. A term popularized by Bertrand Russell to denote the kind of thing which, if sensed, is a sense-datum.

The *Oxford English Dictionary*'s final citation (1962) is the witticism to which Austin was onomastically entitled; its first is knotty Hinton in 1856 on 'the "properties" or "sensibilia"'.

The gap between the obdurately professional term 'sensibilia' and the flexibly personal word 'sensibility' (cognate, to boot) is wide enough to challenge any spark. But Austin's leap is sure-footed just because his own sensibility is such an important part of his being, both personal and professional. Of the twentieth-century English philosophers he is the one who is most to be relished for his sensibility and for what he makes of it in his word-work. And his witticism is not cheaply at the expense of Jane Austen, being itself a tribute to the wit that she was and that she mustered. *Sensibilia* emends *Sensibility* as little, and yet as much, as Austin emends Austen.

Yet there is something askew here. For Austin's condescension towards literature has been persuasively specified and cogently indicted by Geoffrey Hill in his profound essay 'Our Word Is Our Bond' (1983). Not that Hill lacks pleasure in Austin's world:

The system within which Austin exercises his discriminations is not quite a comedy of manners and not quite a line of wit. When a man named

---

[1] I preserve the running title of the 1962 edition (Clarendon Press, and Harvard University Press), capitalized so; the title page had the title in capitals throughout.

Austin entitles his lectures 'Sense and Sensibilia' he is simultaneously being precise and asserting something: he is accepting the gift, the aptness of the thing given, and he is displaying his own 'gift,' his aptitude for making the most of the *donnée*, in a pleasing way, to himself and to us, though the pleasure is of a minor kind.[2]

Not as minor as all that, one might mildly remonstrate, while finding Hill's pages on Austin a uniquely formidable encounter of a poet's exactions with a philosopher's slighting of the poet's enterprise.

Granted, Austin was right to distinguish art-speech from direct utterance; was right to judge that a 'performative utterance' ('I name this ship . . .') cannot be thought exactly to perform itself when it figures within the different kind of occasion which is a poem. But Austin was wrong—and Hill's stringency is the more telling because there can be no doubt of his brooding respect for so much in Austin— to speak as if the difference in question came down to a matter of the serious or (Austin's prophylactic quotation marks) of the 'serious'.

Hill's epigraph for his great enquiry (it is nothing less than a Defence of Poetry for our age) is Austin's unruffled lapse:

And I might mention that, quite differently again, we could be issuing any of these utterances, as we can issue an utterance of any kind whatsoever, in the course, for example, of acting a play or making a joke or writing a poem—in which case of course it would not be seriously meant and we shall not be able to say that we seriously performed the act concerned.[3]

There is a true gist here, and we should not suppose that Austin, of all people, is being merely dismissive of 'making a joke' and consequently of 'writing a poem'. But *seriously* is an evasion of the work which needed to be done. What Austin did was resort to the word. He used it not twice but thrice in the paragraph just quoted, which continued: 'If the poet says "Go and catch a falling star" or whatever it may be, he doesn't seriously issue an order.' There is something in this, but *seriously* is busy ducking and weaving, and the effect of Austin's following Donne's words with 'or whatever it may be' is to intimate, wearily, that not only does the poet not seriously issue an order, the poet does not seriously issue anything. Elsewhere Austin reached for quotation marks ('it may figure in a context not

[2] *The Lords of Limit* (1984), p. 146.
[3] 'Performative Utterances' (1956); *Philosophical Papers* (1961), 1979 edn, pp. 240-1.

wholly "serious," in a play, perhaps, or in a poem'),[4] but such inverted commas suggest both an averting and something of an aversion.

We, in our turn, may feel an aversion for Austin's underdescribed and prejudicial dependence on the word 'parasitic':

> For example, if I say 'Go and catch a falling star,' it may be quite clear what both the meaning and the force of my utterance is, but still wholly unresolved which of these other kinds of things I may be doing. There are parasitic uses of language, which are 'not serious,' not the 'full normal use.' The normal conditions of reference may be suspended, or no attempt made at a standard perlocutionary act, no attempt to make you do anything, as Walt Whitman does not seriously incite the eagle of liberty to soar.[5]

The move, from the quasi-qualification (left uninvestigated) of 'which are "not serious"' to the unaccommodated 'does not seriously incite', is at one with the coercively pejorative word *parasitic*. It is far from 'quite clear what both the meaning and the force of' Donne's line could be for Austin, or what serious inciting Whitman might be engaged in, given that it isn't any literal one. And it ill becomes Austin at this point to invoke the 'parasitic'. For Whitman came here to Austin's mocking mind via Max Beerbohm's mocking mind, the conjunction in Beerbohm's caricature of a gay bard flinging his arms and a sullen bird clenching its wings: 'Walt Whitman, inciting the Bird of Freedom to Soar.' 'Walt Whitman does not seriously incite the eagle of liberty to soar.' Austin had himself been incited. Perhaps he was being more than parasitic, perhaps he was alluding to Beerbohm's own allusive play.[6]

---

[4] 'Performatif-Constatif' (1958); translated from the French by G. J. Warnock, in *Philosophy and Ordinary Language*, ed. C. E. Caton (1963), as 'Performative/Constative' (p. 24); the quotation marks round the translated 'serious' are presumably Austin's own.

[5] *How to do things with Words*, p. 104.

[6] The word *incite* is not to be found in the poem Beerbohm presumably had in his sights (a poem, it seems, of Horace Traubel's making, for Whitman had left it as prose):

TO SOAR IN FREEDOM AND IN FULLNESS OF POWER

I have not so much emulated the birds that musically sing,
I have abandon'd myself to flights, broad circles.
The hawk, the seagull, have far more possess'd me than the canary or
    mocking-bird,
I have not felt to warble or trill, however sweetly,
I have felt to soar in freedom and in the fullness of power, joy, volition.

Alluding to a Beerbohm caricature, that allusive thing, is a meta-
matter, and sometimes Austin not only invokes such a regress, he
does so by courtesy of the progressing regression which is allusion.
'Of course comments on comments, criticisms of criticisms, are subject
to the law of diminishing fleas . . .' How dextrously this second
sentence of 'Unfair to Facts'[7] allusively does what it speaks of, and
returns not only to the law of diminishing returns but to Swift's
fleas, which themselves return elsewhere in Austin on Excuses: 'Here
is matter both contentious and practically important for everybody,
so that ordinary language is on its toes: yet also, on its back it has
long had a bigger flea to bite it, in the shape of the Law, and both
again have lately attracted the attentions of yet another, and at least
a healthily growing, flea, in the shape of psychology.'[8] And so *ad
infinitum*. But the especial Austin touch is the flea-leap, very light on
its feet, from 'on its toes' to 'on its back'.

The same meta-matter arises whenever there is allusion to a parody,
since parody is itself allusive; this colours Austin's pleasure in playing with Lewis Carroll, which thereby becomes something more
than the usual Oxford philosopher's child's-play.[9]

> Oxbridge philosophers, to be cursory,
> Are products of a middle-class nursery:
> Their arguments are anent
> What Nanny really meant.
>
> (W. H. Auden, 'Academic Graffiti')

Austin on one occasion did let slip a reference to 'nannies' in 'Ifs
and Cans', 'as perhaps our nannies once told us to' (he is like Empson
in being class-bonded without being class-bound); elsewhere he made
more of a nursery-memory.

But the belief [Ayer's] that really there *are* only sense-data emerges again,
more clearly and much more frequently, in the final chapter, significantly
entitled 'The Constitution of Material Things.' ('What are material things
made of?')[10]

---

[7] (1954); *Philosophical Papers*, p. 154.
[8] 'A Plea for Excuses' (1956–7); *Philosophical Papers*, p. 185.
[9] There are the dealings with Father William in 'The Meaning of a Word'
(1940); *Philosophical Papers*, p. 59; the dark footnote in 'Other Minds' (1946): 'The
awkwardness about some snarks being boojums', *Philosophical Papers*, p. 89; and the
appearance of 'the slithy toves' in *How to do things with Words*, p. 96.
[10] *Sense and Sensibilia* (1962), p. 106.

Answer to the questioner who sits so sly: frogs and snails and puppy-dogs' tails, as well as sugar and spice and all things nice.

The paradox, or at least the contradiction between what Austin explicitly maintains and what he implicitly practises, is manifest when we notice how it is that Austin leads into such a thought as this, with its belittling use of 'not seriously' and 'parasitic' and 'etiolations':

Language in such circumstances is in special ways—intelligibly—used not seriously, but in ways *parasitic* upon its normal use—ways which fall under the doctrine of the *etiolations* of language.[11]

For the odd thing is that Austin is able to arrive at this only with the aid of the poetry of Shakespeare, the previous sentences constituting this sequence:

a performative utterance will, for example, be *in a peculiar way* hollow or void if said by an actor on the stage, or if introduced in a poem, or spoken in soliloquy. This applies in a similar manner to any and every utterance—a sea-change in special circumstances. Language in such circumstances is in special ways—intelligibly—used not seriously . . .

Now it is true that *The Tempest*'s 'sea-change' has itself suffered a sea-change, and even something of an etiolation; but it is far from hollow and void to Austin, who has recourse to those words with as grateful a frequency as did T. S. Eliot.[12]

Austin's inspired ubiquitous play with literary allusions confirms that his pseudo-professional—unthinking or thoughtless—denigration of literature was not altogether true to himself. But in commenting now on some of his allusive feats, I am concerned not just to secure attention for the particularities of his wit, or to praise his sensibility (which he sold short in this insufficiently serious talk of the *serious*), but to suggest that literary allusion has its bearing on Austin's duly extraordinary relation to 'ordinary language'.

Our common stock of words embodies all the distinctions men have found worth drawing, and the connexions they have found worth marking, in the lifetimes of many generations: these surely are likely to be more numerous, more sound, since they stood up to the long test of the survival of the fittest, and more subtle, at least in all ordinary and reasonably practical

---

[11] *How to do things with Words*, p. 22. Austin has (on p. 92) a brief footnote on etiolation 'as it occurs when we use speech in acting, fiction and poetry, quotation and recitation'.

[12] For instance, *How to do things with Words*, p. 149; 'How to Talk' (1953); *Philosophical Papers*, p. 145.

matters, than any that you or I are likely to think up in our arm-chairs of an afternoon—the most favoured alternative method.[13]

He did not invoke 'ordinary language' as an authority, let alone as the judge, but as an indispensable witness. Yet he needed somehow to reconcile his conviction that the daily language was magnificently revelatory, an unignorable body of long-standing understandings, with his equally strong conviction that ordinary people, the ordinary language users, are often wrong-headed, pigheaded, and big-headed about genuine philosophical problems.

Such a reconciliation could on occasion be effected, with something of the momentous momentaneousness of poetic insight, by combining literary allusion and ordinary language—by combining, that is, the supremely uncommon language-wielders and the common tonguesters. Austin was too dandiacal to be a populist, and too grateful for commonalty to be an idiosyncrat. On the one hand, he might (it seems from Geoffrey Warnock)[14] have concurred with H. P. Grice, 'How *clever* language is!'—though probably Austin would have been more sensitive to the tonal condescension skulking there. On the other hand, he did not sentimentalize ordinary language:

Again, thinking of 'ordinary language' as he did—as an instrument unselfconsciously evolved by speakers confronted with an immense and ever-changing variety of practical contingencies—he naturally recognized that it might in certain ways be confused or incoherent and even, for certain purposes, totally inadequate.[15]

What allusion supplied was an arching of the ordinary (with its staunchness, the common genius of the language) against the extraordinary (with its individual genius, without which the common tongue would falter or palter). That which was 'an instrument unselfconsciously evolved' might here meet that which was consciously developed, and developed not as philosophical expertise but as new language wisdom.

Although it will not do to force actual language to accord with some preconceived model: it *equally* will not do, having discovered the facts about 'ordinary usage' *to rest content* with that, as though there were nothing more

---

[13] 'A Plea for Excuses'; *Philosophical Papers*, p. 182.

[14] 'Saturday Mornings', *Essays on J. L. Austin*, by Isaiah Berlin and others (1973), p. 39.

[15] G. J. Warnock, 'John Langshaw Austin', *Proceedings of the British Academy*, xlix (1963), 359.

to be discussed and discovered. There may be plenty that might happen and does happen which would need new and better language to describe it in. Very often philosophers are only engaged on this task, when they seem to be perversely using words in a way which makes no sense according to 'ordinary usage.' There may be extraordinary facts, even about our everyday experience, which plain men and plain language overlook.[16]

But what this professional formulation (a Defence of Philosophy) leaves out is something which Austin's best practice, his very wording, often incarnates: that when we 'need new and better language' it may be to those who made it new, the great writers, that we turn, and that, given that there are indeed 'extraordinary facts, even about our everyday experience, which plain men and plain language overlook,' we should do well to turn to the better-than-plain language of the better-than-plain men, and women, the language of the great writers, which overlooks little or nothing.

Six lines after this asseveration, Austin speaks of 'the philoprogenitive'; this is not the plain language of plain men, but nor is it simply a philosopher's professional willingness to risk a hard word. For one thing, Austin has arrived at the word via *given birth to*:

far more *detailed* attention ought to be given to that celebrated question, the posing of which has given birth to, and still keeps alive, so many erroneous theories, namely: why do we call different things by the same name? In reply to this, the philoprogenitive invent theories of 'universals' and what not.

For another, this feels like Mr Eliot's Sunday Morning Service, or rather Mr Austin's Saturday Mornings:[17]

> Polyphiloprogenitive
> The sapient sutlers of the Lord
> Drift across the window-panes.
> In the beginning was the Word.

Austin, a master, was well aware that 'The masters of the subtle schools / Are controversial, polymath.'

It is, I believe, some such conjunction of the ordinary and the extraordinary which precipitates so often in Austin those allusions which are at once literary *and* commonplace—Pope being a natural resource here, and *Hamlet*, and the Bible, all simultaneously the

[16] 'The Meaning of a Word'; *Philosophical Papers*, p. 69.
[17] 'Saturday Mornings': the title of Warnock's memoir, recalling Austin's regular meetings, in *Essays on J. L. Austin*.

highest reaches and the widest reaches of the language, to the point at which the allusion has a proverbial power, with *Hamlet*, say, as made up of proverbial quotations.[18]

But first some words about Austin's love of splicing. A characteristic stylistic trick of his (sometimes a stylistic tic) is to splice a couple of proverbs, idioms, or catch-phrases. 'Lastly we may ask— and here I must let some of my cats on the table—does the notion of infelicity apply to utterances *which are statements*?'[19] The cards are on the table, and the cat is let out of the bag. And the cats are on the table instead of on the mat.[20] A clever cat's-cradle, though for my money there aren't enough interesting filaments from cats to cards to make this particular splicing worth the candle.

More consequential is a splicing like this one: 'In so far as I am merely flogging the converted, I apologize to them.'[21] There is pleasure in the phantom other-centaur (like 'Camford' instead of 'Oxbridge'), in the thought of preaching to a dead horse; and conversion and flagellation do have their joint roots. Or again: 'The average excuse, in a poor situation, gets us only out of the fire into

---

[18] Such glances as these: on misapplications within a performative utterance, ' "I give", said when it is not mine to give or when it is a pound of my living and non-detached flesh' (*How to do things with Words*, p. 34); 'liable to be *hidden*, whether it be in the future, in the past, under the skin, or in some other more or less notorious casket' ('Other Minds'; *Philosophical Papers*, p. 106); the footnote, ' "You cannot fool all of the people all of the time" is "analytic" ' ('Other Minds'; *Philosophical Papers*, p. 113; similarly *Sense and Sensibilia*, p. 11); the bringing in of Malvolio, 'To feel the firm ground of prejudice slipping away is exhilarating, but brings its revenges' (*How to do things with Words*, p. 61); a glimpse of Johnson Redivivus, 'the question always arises whether the praise, blame, or congratulation was merited or unmerited: it is not enough to say that you have blamed him and there's an end on't' (*How to do things with Words*, p. 140).

[19] *How to do things with Words*, p. 20.

[20] ' "What is the meaning of (the word) 'cat'?", "What is the meaning of (the word) 'mat'?", and so on': 'But of course "the cat is on the mat" does *not* imply "Austin believes the cat is on the mat": nor even "the speaker believes the cat is on the mat"—for the speaker may be lying' ('The Meaning of a Word'; *Philosophical Papers*, pp. 57, 64). 'Again we say (or are said to say) "It is true that the cat is on the mat" ' ('Truth' (1950); *Philosophical Papers*, p. 117). 'It may be the case at once that the cat is on the mat but I do not believe that it is' (*How to do things with Words*, p. 49). Austin is fond of the poor cats in the adages. 'There are more ways of killing a cat than drowning it in butter' (*How to do things with Words*, p. 48, and a footnote in 'Performative/Constative': 'English proverb. I am told that this rather refined way of disposing of cats is not found in France,' *Philosophy and Ordinary Language*, p. 27).

[21] 'The Meaning of a Word'; *Philosophical Papers*, p. 56.

the frying pan—but still, of course, any frying pan in a fire.'[22] What makes this so much more than silly-clever is not just the unexpected reversal visited by Austin upon 'Out of the frying pan into the fire', but the sudden arrival of that dousing: 'Any port in a storm.' Austin is in his elements.

Or instead of splicing there may be splitting, which on occasion comes to the same thing. The first paragraph of 'Other Minds' ends: 'And Mr. Wisdom himself may perhaps be sympathetic to-wards a policy of splitting hairs to save starting them.'[23] This pun plays on the page because it knows that it doesn't exactly work on the page: 'Other Minds' was given as a talk, when *hairs* would be indistinguishable from *hares*; with affectionate absurdity it briefly invites us to imagine starting hairs; and it not only splits the aural from the orthographic in general but the particular homophone hairs/hares—splits these so as to splice them.

Such unillusioned exuberance is at play in a sly grandeur like '*sub specie humanitatis*'; in the weirdness of a mere plural ('we shall simply make hashes of things'); in a rolling of the eyes and of a vowel ('that I had given a pretty myth-eaten description'); in a sentence with a sudden turn of speed, 'So much for the cackle.' (where Austin cuts the 'cut the'); or in a concluding admonition: 'On these matters, dogmatists require prodding: although history indeed suggests that it may sometimes be better to let sleeping dogmatists lie.'[24] But it is in splicing that Austin finds his most honest duplicity. In, for instance, the closing words of 'Other Minds':

to suppose that the question 'How do I know that Tom is angry?' is meant to mean 'How do I introspect Tom's feelings?' (because, as we know, that's the sort of thing that knowing is or ought to be) is simply barking our way up the wrong gum tree.[25]

How grimly farcical, this glueing together of 'barking up the wrong tree' and being 'stuck up a gum tree' (meanwhile *working* 'our way up'), and how endearingly false the word 'simply' is to this double or triple jeopardy.

But then Austin was happy to carry on splicing even when the jeopardy was more than intellectual, was military. Accumulating life-or-death information for D-Day, Austin compiled a 'kind of

[22] 'A Plea for Excuses'; *Philosophical Papers*, p. 177.
[23] *Philosophical Papers*, p. 76.
[24] Respectively: *Philosophical Papers*, pp. 88, 74, 154, 189, 75.
[25] *Philosophical Papers*, p. 116.

guidebook' 'for the use of the invading troops.' He gave to this more-than-vade-mecum the title *Invade Mecum*.[26] This has a touch of class, in both senses, and in its Latinity it takes long views. Moreover, it knew that this was no time for not joking.

Such a joke splices, and allusions are splicings; some of Austin's best allusions doubly so, in further enacting within themselves what they also constitute in relating 'Other Minds' to Austin's knowing his own. In allusion, the metaphysical problem of the One and the Many can seize the field-day. When Austin does as he likes with *As You Like It*—'There will not be books in the running brooks until the dawn of hydro-semantics'—it is so as to rebuke Berkeley, censured in the previous sentence: 'Berkeley confuses these two.'[27] But allusion fuses these two. Or splices them or grafts them, there being many versions of allusion, some of them pastoral. Of John Wisdom's views on 'the peculiarity of a man's knowledge of his own sensations,' Austin says:

This seems to me mistaken, though it is a view that, in more or less subtle forms, has been the basis of a very great deal of philosophy. It is perhaps the original sin (Berkeley's apple, the tree in the quad) by which the philosopher casts himself out from the garden of the world we live in.[28]

Berkeley's apple is Adam and Eve's but does take a sidelong glance at the apple of a peer of Berkeley's, acknowledging Newton's gravitational pull. And how cunningly the tree of the knowledge of good and evil is plaited with the groves of academe and with Ronald Knox's teasing of Berkeley.

> There was once a man who said 'God
> Must think it exceedingly odd
> If he finds that this tree
> Continues to be
> When there's no one about in the Quad.'[29]

---

[26] Warnock, *Proceedings of the British Academy*, xlix (1963), 350.

[27] 'Truth'; *Philosophical Papers*, p. 126. Austin's joke is a different story from Aldous Huxley's reverting Shakespeare's lines to 'sermons in books, stones in the running brooks'.

[28] 'Other Minds'; *Philosophical Papers*, p. 90.

[29] Divine intervention saves Berkeley's bacon:

> Dear Sir, Your astonishment's odd:
> *I* am always about in the Quad.
> And that's why the tree
> Will continue to be,
> Since observed by Yours faithfully, God.

The characteristic richness of Austin's prose, for all its being so drily done, is a matter of readiness for argument unpursued (to adopt Empson's characterization of richness). Sometimes the readiness is all a matter of intricate allusion. Take the opening paragraph of 'Truth':

'What is truth?' said jesting Pilate, and would not stay for an answer. Pilate was in advance of his time. For 'truth' itself is an abstract noun, a camel, that is, of a logical construction, which cannot get past the eye even of a grammarian. We approach it cap and categories in hand: we ask ourselves whether Truth is a substance (the Truth, the Body of Knowledge), or a quality (something like the colour red, inhering in truths), or a relation ('correspondence'). But philosophers should take something more nearly their own size to strain at. What needs discussing rather is the use, or certain uses, of the word 'true.' *In vino*, possibly, '*veritas*,' but in a sober symposium '*verum*.'[30]

This last remark is one of several of Austin's which grace John Gross's *Oxford Book of Aphorisms* (1983). How well-judged is Austin's modesty, professional and personal for all, the well-earned confidence of his manner: truth is too much to hope for, a philosophical symposium should be sober not intoxicated, and so let us settle for something less than truth, something true.

Or there is the play of 'We approach it cap and categories in hand,' where the interruption of the deferential sequence 'cap in hand' by those intrusive *categories* not only doffs a cap to those philosophically self-important things but creates the momentary sequence 'cap and . . . ,' for all the world as if we were on the brink of '. . . bells'. Now *that* would be foolish of philosophers.

And again there is the allusion not just to Pilate but to Bacon (a good old opening for an essay on Truth, gratefully raised now to a meta-opening), and then to the diverse operations performed by the summoned camel. Matthew 19: 24: 'It is easier for a camel to go through the eye of a needle, than for a rich man to enter into the kingdom of God.' (Bacon, you're a rich man, impeachably so.) At first the camel is admitted so that it may be needlingly unable to 'get past the eye even of a grammarian' (not A Grammarian's Funeral but a camel's), but then this biblical idiom finds itself stitched to another when we reach 'to strain at': 'Blind guides, which strain at a gnat, and swallow a camel' (Matthew 23: 24).[31] But even here,

---

[30] *Philosophical Papers*, p. 117.

[31] Samuel Butler, master-splicer, had remarked: 'One man's gnat is another man's camel.'

Austin is not yet done, for he has arrived at this 'strain at' via an odd inversion of the playground cry against the bully, *why don't you pick on someone your own size?* Trust Austin, though, to mean not bigger but smaller (given any realistic estimate of the size of philosophers): 'But philosophers should take something more nearly their own size to strain at.' Added to all of which, the camel has long knelt in the service of philosophical discourse, a joke about foreign (Germanic?) lucubration lurking within Tennyson's comment on the women in his early poems: 'All these ladies were evolved, like the camel, from my own consciousness.'

Isaiah Berlin famously wrote of Austin that he 'detested vagueness, obscurity, abstraction, evasion of issues by escape into metaphor or rhetoric or jargon or metaphysical fantasy'.[32] Perhaps *escape into* metaphor was not Austin's thing (though he was often a consummately evasive rhetorician—just look at the unpaid work he regularly extorts from the word 'surely,' four times for instance in his review of Ryle), but there was for Austin no escape *from* metaphor, first because there cannot be for anybody (language being what it is); second, because 'not all metaphors should be assumed to be misleading';[33] and third because Austin, like Aristotle, well knew that the greatest thing by far is to be a master of metaphor. As when, far from eliminating metaphor,[34] he cogently elaborates it: repudiating Strawson's claim that 'Fact is wedded to that-clauses' ('the fact that . . .'), Austin fosters the metaphor so that it burgeons:

If it is indeed so wedded, it leads, I fear, a double life. It was not born in wedlock, its marriage was a marriage of convenience and it continues to lead a flourishing bachelor existence.[35]

[32] *Essays on J. L. Austin*, pp. 1–2.

[33] Review of Ryle, *TLS*, 7 April 1950. But elsewhere Austin is more hostile: 'Now first, though the expression "deceived by our senses" is a common metaphor, it *is* a metaphor; and this is worth noting, for in what follows the same metaphor is frequently taken up by the expression "veridical" and taken very seriously. In fact, of course, our senses are dumb' (*Sense and Sensibilia*, p. 11). As elsewhere in Austin, 'seriously' gives the game away; he is not taking metaphor very seriously. Never trust anyone who follows 'In fact' with 'of course', or who, belittling metaphor, averts his mind from the fact that to say 'our senses are *dumb*' is to hire metaphor.

[34] On Descartes's division of ideas: 'if we attempt to eliminate the metaphor from the ways of acquiring property . . .' ('Are There *A Priori* Concepts?' (1939); *Philosophical Papers*, p. 47).

[35] 'Unfair to Facts'; *Philosophical Papers*, p. 163.

Allusion leads a double life, and is itself a form of metaphor, alive to similitude in dissimilitude. Just how felicitously endemic allusion is to Austin may be seen from a couple of occasions when, translating in 1950 Frege's *The Foundations of Arithmetic*, Austin finds for his own way of putting it a foundation in words which are not his own, in allusion on the verge of cliché, from Milton:

However, if confusion is not to become worse confounded, it is advisable to observe a strict distinction between unit and one.[36]

—but not too strict a distinction between Frege's German and the English rendering. Or there is Frege translated with the aid of Pope:

We might say, indeed, almost in the well-known words: the reason's proper study is itself.[37]

We might say it indeed, in what are well-known words but not the words of the original which Austin is translating:

> Know then thyself, presume not God to scan;
> The proper study of Mankind is Man.
>
>   (*An Essay on Man*, ii 1–2)

Austin's felicitous foisting-in is itself a presumption, not entirely proper, and yet the fruit of proper study. 'Presume not God to scan': but Austin has ensured that we hear 'the well-known words' (English ones, rather than German) in how we are obliged to scan his line, its cadence of Pope: 'The reason's proper study is itself.' As often in Austin, the allusive play toys with insolence. Austin has so good an ear as to encourage us, for instance, to tax him with alluding, in his new insistence '*No modification without aberration*,'[38] to the old resistance 'No taxation without representation.'

Most allusions of subtlety and efficacy are likely to be related in some important way to inheritance.[39] Austin's sense of inheritance

---

[36] Page 48 (#38), translating 'Um nicht Verwirrung einreissen zu lassen, wird es jedoch gut sein'.

[37] Page 115 (#105), translating 'Man könnte wohl mit Abänderung eines bekannten Satzes sagen: der eigentliche Gegenstand der Vernunft ist die Vernunft'. Professor Burton Dreben has kindly pointed out to me that Frege is presumably alluding to Goethe, *Elective Affinities*, part 2, ch. 7, and that Goethe had his predecessors such as Pierre Charron.

[38] 'A Plea for Excuses'; *Philosophical Papers*, p. 189.

[39] The present writer has discussed this in two essays: one on Dryden and Pope, 'Allusion: The Poet as Heir' (*Studies in the Eighteenth Century*, iii, ed. R. F. Brissenden,

has something in common with Tennyson's (the inheritance of black blood and yet of brotherhood), since what is inherited is both poison and antidote, both sickness and health—as we might expect in a philosopher drawn often to speak of the 'infected'. Sometimes we inherit something we would be better without; worse, we do not just inherit it, it has been bequeathed to us.

The pursuit of the incorrigible is one of the most venerable bugbears in the history of philosophy. It is rampant all over ancient philosophy, most conspicuously in Plato, was powerfully re-animated by Descartes, and bequeathed by him to a long line of successors.[40]

And 'I bequeath' is a performative utterance . . .[41]

Braced, though, against the bad news is the good news: that there is another inheritance: 'ordinary language . . . embodies, indeed, something better than the metaphysics of the Stone Age, namely, as was said, the inherited experience and acumen of many generations of men.'[42] The men and women have been both ordinary and extraordinary, and sometimes the extraordinary ones, the geniuses, have given word to what oft was thought but ne'er so well expressed.

The poet who gave us that uniquely indispensable formulation of commonalty is alluded to by Austin, for another proverbial accomplishment, in the second sentence of 'Other Minds': 'I feel ruefully sure, also, that one must be at least one sort of fool to rush in over ground so well trodden by the angels.'[43] What rescues this from the banal, what gives it point, is not only the turn given to the line of Pope ('well trodden' taking over territory from 'fear to tread,' while Pope's 'where angels . . .' becomes 'trodden by the angels,' *the* angels invoking theological evolutionary debate and being on the side of the angels), but the substance which is given to Austin's word 'ruefully' by the extremely soft-spoken joke lurking in 'one must be at least one sort of fool . . .' What one sort of fool? A bloody fool, *sotto voce*, Austin being too polite to say so.

The great phrases from the past can become rubbed too smooth; one of Austin's pleasures is to restore something of their original frictive force. Hamlet's 'Ay, there's the rub' has worn away its turfy

1976); the other on Tennyson, 'Tennyson Inheriting the Earth' (*Studies in Tennyson*, ed. Hallam Tennyson, 1981).

[40] *Sense and Sensibilia*, p. 104.   [41] *How to do things with Words*, p. 32.

[42] 'A Plea for Excuses'; *Philosophical Papers*, p. 185.

[43] *Philosophical Papers*, p. 76.

texture, the obstacle or impediment in bowls which hinders or diverts the bowl from its proper course. When Austin sighs (in another of those fleet of foot notes which do work of Gibbonian character), 'There is the rub,' it is within a consideration, in morbid detail, of 'the case where I miss a very short putt'.[44] The rub of the green has its memory kept green.

When Austin proffers, with what in someone else might have been inertia, 'out of joint,' he not only has his comedy with 'the three words' (which are *purpose, intention,* and *deliberation,* not the three words 'out of joint'), but he tames Hamlet's 'cursed spite' down to 'in spite of':

there are overriding considerations, which may be operative in any situation in which I act, which may put all three words out of joint, in spite of the other standard conditions for their use being satisfied.[45]

When Austin expatiates on *infelicity,* on that which renders a performative utterance ('I promise . . .') not true or false—which it cannot be—but null, he turns to *Hamlet,* or rather to *Hamlet* as it has entered into this common stock of sayings, into what if you deprecate it you will call a cliché and if you value it a great commonplace:

. . . infelicity is an ill to which *all* acts are heir which have the general character of ritual or ceremonial, all *conventional* acts.

. . . as *utterances* our performatives are *also* heir to certain other kinds of ill which infect *all* utterances.

Acts of all our three kinds necessitate, since they are the performing of actions, allowance being made for the ills that all action is heir to.[46]

But Shakespeare didn't write 'ills', he wrote 'shocks':

> The Heart-ake, and the thousand Naturall shockes
> That Flesh is heyre to.
>
> (III i)

Or rather he did write 'ills', but elsewhere in the soliloquy, just as he wrote 'action' (Austin's 'the ills that all action is heir to') elsewhere in the soliloquy. Austin splices and re-splices:

---

[44] 'Ifs and Cans' (1956); *Philosophical Papers,* p. 218.
[45] 'Three Ways of Spilling Ink' (1958); *Philosophical Papers,* p. 286.
[46] *How to do things with Words,* pp. 18–19, 21, 105.

The Heart-ake, and the thousand Naturall shockes
That Flesh is heyre to.
                    Puzels the will
And makes us rather beare those illes we have,
Than flye to others that we know not of.

And loose the name of Action.

The depths of *Hamlet* amenably allow Austin to say more than you might think. 'There is nothing either good or bad, but thinking makes it so.' Hamlet's thought underlies Austin's account of a particular philosophical relation as 'a *purely conventional* relation (one which "thinking makes so"),'[47] and he gives a twist to the thought in the title of a section of *How to do things with Words*, 'CAN SAYING MAKE IT SO?'[48]

And there is the matter of meaning. 'There are many sorts of sentence in which the words "the meaning of the word so-and-so" are found, e.g. "He does not know, or understand, the meaning of the word *hand-saw*." '[49] Austin has the eye of a hawk. The climactic destination of that *tour de force* of his which begins 'Suppose I have said 'There's a bittern at the bottom of the garden," and you ask "How do you know?" ' is not in the text proper but in the conclusive footnote at its end:

'I know, I *know*, I've seen it a hundred times, don't keep on telling me' complains of a superabundance of opportunity: 'knowing a hawk from a handsaw' lays down a minimum of acumen in recognition or classification.[50]

Note that the minimum of acumen in recognition is not just ornithological, but literary, knowing where knowing a hawk from a handsaw flies in from. 'I know a hawk from a handsaw.'

But perhaps the greatest of Austin's allusive flights arises when he imps the wing of *Hamlet* with feathers from *Macbeth*, in the footnote to the final paragraph of 'Pretending', a footnote which thereby becomes in one way though not in another the essay's closing words:

What, finally, is the importance of all this about pretending? I will answer this shortly, although I am not sure importance is important*: truth is. In the first place . . .[51]

* I dreamt a line that would make a motto for a sober philosophy: *Neither a be-all nor an end-all be.*

[47] 'Truth'; *Philosophical Papers*, p. 128.   [48] *How to do things with Words*, p. 7.
[49] 'The Meaning of a Word'; *Philosophical Papers*, p. 57.
[50] 'Other Minds'; *Philosophical Papers*, p. 80.   [51] *Philosophical Papers*, p. 271.

This, as with any living allusion, establishes Austin as both a borrower and a lender, in defiance of Polonius: 'Neither a borrower
nor a lender be.' But it does so by invoking and resisting Macbeth's
ambitions: 'that but this blow / Might be the be all, and the end
all.' A sober philosophy is without these usurpatious ambitions, and
the modesty of 'I dreamt a line . . .' is at once rueful and respectful,
both *Hamlet* and *Macbeth* being so alive to dreams ('perchance to
dream', 'what dreams may come'; 'wicked dreams', 'these terrible
dreams').[52] Austin's spliced play seems to me an even better thing
than the old devilish citing of *Hamlet* for a philosopher's purposes:
the determination that there should not be in your philosophy more
things than are dreamt of in heaven and earth.

True, the literary critic fascinated by allusion is always in danger
of imagining a play of mind where there was simply a workaday
mind. One last testing-ground might be the review of Gilbert Ryle's
The Concept of Mind which Austin published in 1950. Anonymous
though it was, the review was Austin all over, ending with some of
his best jokes, including a joke about jokes:

All, too, save those who have never learned to suspect solemnity, will join
in his enjoyment of his numerous jokes, for the most part shrewd and
spontaneous, only occasionally straying over the borderline into facetiousness. The jokes . . .[53]

---

[52] Two pertinent musings from Wittgenstein:

Shakespeare and dreams. A dream is all wrong, absurd, composite, and yet at
the same time it is completely right: put together in *this* strange way it makes
an impression. Why? I don't know. And if Shakespeare is great, as he is said
to be, then it must be possible to say of him: it's all wrong, things *aren't like that*—
and yet at the same time it's quite right according to a law of its own.

It could be put like this too: if Shakespeare is great, his greatness is displayed
only in the whole *corpus* of his plays, which create their *own* language and world.
In other words he is completely unrealistic. (Like a dream.) [1949]

During a dream and even *long* after we have woken up, words occurring in the
dream can strike us as having the greatest significance. Can't we be subject to
the same illusion when awake? I have the impression that *I* am sometimes liable
to this nowadays. The insane often seem to be like this. [1948] (*Culture and Value*,
ed. G. H. von Wright, trans. Peter Winch (1980), pp. 83, 65.)

[53] *Times Literary Supplement*, 7 April 1950. The review is neither included nor
listed in *Philosophical Papers*, so I am all the more grateful to Sir Geoffrey Warnock
for answering my enquiry about Austin's reviewing.

—where affection for Ryle is saved from leniency by the unexpected turn by which we are assured, not that we will enjoy Ryle's
jokes, but that we 'will join in his enjoyment of his numerous jokes';
and yet this without sarcasm, since Austin no less suspects the canting
solemnity which purses its lips at a man who enjoys his own jokes.
And the comic timing is so good: 'will join in his enjoyment of his
numerous jokes, for the most part . . . ,' pausing only for a comma's
worth of enjoyment by Austin of this *his* own joke.

. . . only occasionally straying over the borderline into facetiousness. The
jokes of a clown, says the professor, *are* the workings of his mind; and
certainly his own wisecracks and epigrams (though far from clowning) go
to bear out his theory in his own case. *Le style, c'est Ryle.*

It is a wonderful crowning clowning allusion; not just any man,
l'homme, but Ryle, with the extravagant absurdity which rhymes
Le style with *Ryle.* A real joke; the mind reels.

Such is the inspired ending of the review; it had begun with
something not at all a matter of Buffon-buffoonery, something more
chaste, Wordsworthian indeed. The review opens:

Even to the undergraduate, plain thinking and plain living as the work of
the past 50 years has made him, Professor Ryle's first book, long awaited,
will seem one that he cannot afford not to possess and that he can afford
to possess.

'Plain living and high thinking are no more'?[54] Well, Ryle and Austin
are concerned to bring high thinking down to earth, and to reduce
it to plain thinking, plain as unostentatious and as lucid. But then
Wordsworth animates the whole of the review.

Imagination is commonly supposed to be or to include the 'seeing' of 'mental
pictures.' Professor Ryle argues that there is no such thing; he explains
imagining as being, roughly, like pretending. Yet though, no doubt, the
extent to which people do genuinely 'see images' is often grossly exaggerated, surely they do sometimes see images. To take an obvious example,
they do see after-images. The author seems to argue that because a man
seeing Helvellyn in his mind's eye does not see Helvellyn but only 'sees'
it, therefore he 'sees' nothing; but he may 'see' something. To 'see' may
be a metaphor; but not all metaphors should be assumed to be misleading.

---

[54] Wordsworth, 'Written in London: September 1802': 'O Friend! I know not
which way I must look.'

If we ask, not 'Wherefore to Dover' but 'Wherefore to Helvellyn?,' the answer must be Wordsworth's there being a presence not to be put by.[55] And 'a man seeing Helvellyn in his mind's eye' will be grateful not only to Wordsworth for *his* mind's eye, but to the mind of the author of *Hamlet* for having seen that there is such a thing as the mind's eye.

It matters that Wordsworth looms benignly in the review of Ryle because this gives depth to what would otherwise be just a wisecrack, the moment when Austin says of Ryle 'But he is by nature a *philosophe terrible*, and has chosen therefore . . .' The splicing of *enfant terrible* with the traditions of *les philosophes* has its manifest comedy, but what gives weight to its wit is the memory of that sublime moment when the infant is seen under the aspect of the philosopher, or rather of the 'best Philosopher':

> Thou best Philosopher, who yet dost keep
> Thy heritage, thou Eye among the blind!

And this in a poem which invokes infancy. That Wordsworth's Immortality Ode weighed with Austin is clear from his turning to, and turning, the thought of 'trailing clouds of glory,' which for him becomes the subheading '*Trailing clouds of etymology*',[56] and on another occasion this: 'we might consider the trailing etymologies of

---

[55] On Wordsworth and Helvellyn, see *The Prose Works of William Wordsworth*, ed. W. J. B. Owen and Jane Worthington Smyser (1974), ii 243–4, 387, for *A Guide through the District of the Lakes* and for Helvellyn in the poems. Austin brings Wordsworth adroitly into play in remonstrating with H. A. Prichard about Aristotle and 'happiness':

It seems to me very rash to assume that in common English 'happiness' obviously means feeling pleased: probably it has several more or less vague meanings. Take the lines:

> This is the happy warrior, this is He
> That every Man at arms should wish to be.

I do not think Wordsworth meant by that: 'This is the warrior who feels *pleased*'. (*Philosophical Papers*, pp. 19–20)

[56] 'A Plea for Excuses'; *Philosophical Papers*, p. 201. 'A word never—well, hardly ever—shakes off its etymology and its formation.' Never—well, hardly ever: shades of W. S. Gilbert, not to be shaken off. Austin varies his etymology-allusion by calling upon Milton too. 'But come thou goddess fair and free, / In heaven yclept Euphrosyne' ('L'Allegro'). 'And first for that goddess fair and free (fairly fair, fraily free), divinest Etymology' ('Pretending' (1958); *Philosophical Papers*, p. 260).

the three words [intention, purpose, and deliberation]: for no word
ever achieves entire forgetfulness of its origins.'[57]

> Not in entire forgetfulness,
> And not in utter nakedness,
> But trailing clouds of glory do we come
> From God, who is our home:
> Heaven lies about us in our infancy!

Austin's trailing words do not seek forgetfulness of Wordsworth's.

It is these felicities which make *philosophe terrible* so happy a joke,
this and the yawning difference between the French and any
Englishing of it as 'a terrible philosopher'; and it is Austin's ways
with the heritage which is allusion which should move us to hail
him likewise:

> Thou best Philosopher, who yet dost keep
> Thy heritage, thou Eye among the blind!

[57] 'Three Ways of Spilling Ink'; *Philosophical Papers*, p. 283.

LITERATURE AND THE MATTER OF FACT

I

An ageing scholar takes his young bride, for their honeymoon, to Rome, a far cry from the English provincial town which gives its staunch name to George Eliot's supreme novel: *Middlemarch*. For Dorothea Brooke, now inescapably Dorothea Casaubon, the disillusionment has already begun. Rome oppresses her, though not Rome alone.

> Forms both pale and glowing took possession of her young sense, and fixed themselves in her memory even when she was not thinking of them, preparing strange associations which remained through her after-years. Our moods are apt to bring with them images which succeed each other like the magic-lantern pictures of a doze; and in certain states of dull forlornness Dorothea all her life continued to see the vastness of St. Peter's, the huge bronze canopy, the excited intention in the attitudes and garments of the prophets and evangelists in the mosaics above, and the red drapery which was being hung for Christmas spreading itself everywhere like a disease of the retina.
>
> (*Middlemarch*, ch. xx)

It is an artistic realization deservedly famous, and characteristic of George Eliot: the combination of historical weight ('the vastness of St. Peter's') with generous speculative commonalty ('Our moods'), which then culminates in a crystalline scientific particular: 'and the red drapery which was being hung for Christmas spreading itself everywhere like a disease of the retina'. It is the word 'retina' which does it. (End of sentence, and end of paragraph.) A disease of the eye might leave some hope of a second opinion; a disease of the retina, never.

Now hear the voice of the biographer. Gordon Haight is moved to adduce *Middlemarch* at the moment, ten years earlier, when George Eliot and her all-but-husband G. H. Lewes are visiting Rome (no honeymoon for them):

> The Casaubons' Roman honeymoon occurred in December. George Eliot did not realize that the liturgical colour for Christmas is white.[1]

---

[1] *George Eliot: A Biography* (1968), p. 324.

No problem? *For* 'red drapery' *read* 'white drapery'? But this would be worse than anaemic. Dorothea was not dreaming of a white Christmas.

Does it matter if George Eliot got it wrong? The answer that you give will prove central to what you imagine imagination to be, and to judging what, in works of art, distinguishes from license the responsible liberty of imagination. My position is that we must not simply relax into letting the matter pass. If George Eliot is in error here, this is not only infelicitous but damaging. For her paragraph is itself about error and imposition, about the perilous power of 'our moods' and of our propensity to impress upon external circumstance what is rather an emanation of our natures; and it therefore becomes more than usually important that the artist be vigilant and not succumb to the very pressures which she so compassionately deprecates.

In 1980, I gave a BBC talk for the centenary of George Eliot's death; on that red-carpet occasion, I did not mention red drapery since it would have been a red herring. I was pleased, though, to hear from Professor Haight, whom I had never met; he sent me an article of his, which happened to elaborate on his point of correction:

The liturgical color for Christmas, of course, is white. George Eliot had been in Rome in 1860 during Holy Week, and may have assumed that the red draperies symbolizing the Passion would also be used at Christmas. But such a mistake is unusual in her books.[2]

But now Professor Haight had jotted overleaf: 'The mistake is mine. I find that the red is a papal color, used at St. Peter's at all seasons.'

Was I right to feel so relieved that George Eliot had, after all, been in the right? Clearly it is regrettable that Haight's error, believing her in error, is still there in the paperback edition of the 'standard' biography, but does it much matter? Not but what it is a pleasant spectacle to see someone hoist with his own petard; and vistas are intriguing (one of Lichtenberg's aphorisms reads simply: 'A list of printing errors in the list of printing errors'); and then again, in an age when literary critics have been getting above themselves (and above the artists upon whom they live), it is gratifying, and may be salutary, to find that the artist knew not only better but best.

---

[2] 'Poor Mr. Casaubon', *Nineteenth Century Literary Perspectives*, ed. Clyde de L. Ryals (1974), pp. 259–60.

The point is not that a writer is always right—some of what I shall instance suggests otherwise. But we should prefer writers to be right, and we should particularly do so when their own standards would have been stringent precisely here. As so often, the alternative to respectfully holding people to high standards is the disrespect of condescension, and it would be condescending to murmur that, come now, such an error would not matter to us, as enlightened readers, even though it would assuredly have mattered to the author herself. Haight shows as much, upon the publication of *Middlemarch*. 'There were the usual pedants pointing out little errors.' (An inadvertent irony from Haight's pen. The sequence is the time-honoured one: I am scrupulous; you are fussy; he is a white-coated pedant.)

There were the usual pedants pointing out little errors. A barrister in the Temple wrote anonymously to George Eliot to say that by destroying his will, as he tried to do in Chapter 33, Featherstone could not have revived the earlier one. In the next book (Chapter 52) George Eliot let Mr. Farebrother explain that fact to Mary Garth. Paget had expressed his great delight in George Eliot's 'wonderful accuracy in medical matters.' A few days later she was distressed to receive a letter from a London surgeon declaring it wrong in Chapters 63 and 66 to describe Lydgate 'with bright, dilated eyes' from taking opium, which contracts the pupils. When she asked Paget whether she should change the passages, he replied that it was accurate enough: the eyelids can be wide with excitement even though the pupils are contracted. Nevertheless, in revising the text for the one-volume edition, she changed the passages to read 'with a strange light in his eyes' and 'the peculiar light in the eyes.'[3]

All honour to George Eliot for declining to be soothed; for refusing to be any less strict with herself than she would have been with others; and for seeing that, in such art as hers, accuracy in legal or in medical matters, though it may indeed be distinguishable from literary power, is not distinct from it. But even here one must not be sentimental, must not avert one's eyes whether dilated or not. It is not a compliment to a writer to take her will for the deed. More's the pity, then, that in relinquishing the inauthentic vividness of those dilated eyes, she was not able to achieve an authentic wording. Her 'strange light' and 'peculiar light' are no more than gestures towards a realizing, no more than the wrong kind of cry for help to the reader. (Here, you imagine it, would you?) She is merely

---

[3] *George Eliot: A Biography*, pp. 446–7.

telling us that the eyes were strange and peculiar, not seeing it and showing it.

II

The question, then, of literature and the matter of fact (in both senses) is a simple though not an easy one, an ancient though not an outdatable one: Are works of literature affected if the facts they proffer as facts are not facts, and demonstrably so?

Let me, though, make some preliminary differentiations. I set to one side the cognate questions of *belief* (what difference does it make to a reader of *Paradise Lost* that he or she is, or is not, a Christian?) and of *probability* (what is it to accept in *King Lear* the likelihood of Edgar's not revealing himself to his blinded father?).

The point is *not* that literary works which are in error become no good, since they—like people—can be very good and yet have something very wrong with them. (Randall Jarrell once defined a novel as a prose fiction of a certain length with something wrong with it.) Fidelity to fact, or accuracy, I should propose, is always a virtue, but it is not necessarily the ground of all virtues; elegance and energy are virtues too. So I am not proposing accuracy as a necessary, let alone a sufficient, condition of literary worth. Nor am I maintaining that a deft inaccuracy may not manage to bring about other valuable effects, to some degree compensatory. But I judge that it will always be critically relevant to consider accuracy and inaccuracy, and that if you decide in advance that inaccuracy is inherently irrelevant or immaterial or trivial, you strike at the roots not only of interpretation but of imaginative creation.

I shall rehearse (for they could not be new and yet must ask perennial renovation) some of the reasons behind T. S. Eliot's insistence that what distinguishes both the poet and the critic is 'the sense of fact'. My enterprise is partly an argument, partly a plea. I need to add that I don't consider this matter, in my handling of it, to be one of theory but rather of principle and tact, though I should myself be grateful for a disinterested theoretical—better still, philosophical—exploration of the whole business. I don't know of one. Aristotle's distinction between two kinds of error in poetry, essential and accidental, is little more than a searching glance.

For E. M. Forster as a critic (the novelist knew better), there was no problem, abstractly considered. 'Information is true if it is

accurate. A poem is true if it hangs together. Information points to
something else. A poem points to nothing but itself. Information is
relative. A poem is absolute.'[4]

This belle-lettristic gnome of 1925 strikingly anticipates our recent flurry of structuralist hanging-together—strikingly, were it not
that structuralism was itself a diverse energy of the 1920s, and that
anyway such a bizarre political axis is commonplace. The aesthetic
dedication from the old days would find itself at one with the
academicized ideology of our day exactly in this: in craving, albeit
for opposite reasons, to remove literature from any obligations to
referential fidelity or correspondence. For has not *language* itself (the
medium of literature) been proved, by Saussure and his set, to be
entirely without referential fidelity or correspondence? Well, No,
or even Nope, but such just now is the orthodoxy of intellectual
complaisance.

This, as against such judgements of literature as relate it directly
to 'the transactions of the world'—the great phrase (à propos of
Shakespeare) is Dr Johnson's, and it asks to be supplemented by
Wittgenstein's understanding that 'the world is everything that is
the case'. Such wider judgements are disobligingly messier, and they
permit fewer airs, than those which conveniently limit themselves
to the ways in which works of art hang together and are absolute.

The impulse to release literature from the responsibilities of fidelity
derives, within Forster's world, from a desperate wish to keep separate and uncontaminated the anti-professional realm of individual
sensibility and of feeling. The same impulse, within the world of
recent pedagogical criticism, derives from the opposite extremity:
the wish to keep separate (and uncontaminated by individual sensibility and feeling) the professional realm of politicized intellectuality.
And, from either end, to reduce literary response and judgement
to the *manageable*. Granted, the life of the critic would be much
easier if all she or he had to do was consider internal coherence,
and never, complementarily, any external correspondence. But then
our daily social life would likewise be much easier if all that needed
to be considered in a friend, a loved one, a colleague, or a politician
was internal coherence and never any fidelity to what is externally
the case.

[4] 'Anonymity: An Inquiry' (1925); *Two Cheers for Democracy* (1951), 1965 edn,
pp. 89–90.

Forster's asseveration that the truth of a poem consists solely in its hanging together, and has absolutely nothing to do with accuracy, is a recipe for an impoverished poetry and a wizened criticism. But it does wonderfully simplify the life of the mind. And this is why a good many people acquiesce promptly in the notion that literature doesn't employ facts as *facts*, but rather (with the usual prophylaxis of inverted commas) as 'facts', so that factual accuracy is irrelevant. The next step, back, under pressure (of which there is not enough around), is to grant that accuracy may sometimes be relevant but is intrinsically unimportant, a trivial consideration. We need to notice the ambiguity in the question 'Does it matter?', which sometimes means 'Is it germane?' and on other occasions 'Though admittedly germane, is it of much importance?'

Does it matter that a poem by Elizabeth Bishop apparently supposes that there is ordinarily such a thing as an eighty-watt bulb about the house?[5] Was she making a point or making a mistake, and would we ever be able to do justice to the former possibility (a hallucination dramatized, for instance) if we were to insist that a mistake was not to be thought of and that it was our duty to disattend to any such nigglings?

> Meanwhile the eighty-watt bulb
> betrays us all,
>
> discovering the concern
> within our stupefaction.
>
> ('Faustina, or Rock Roses')

Does it matter that Keats notoriously stationed 'Silent, upon a peak in Darien', a man called Cortez, or should we just make a silent unrhythmical correction in our heads (you *know*, Balboa) and agree hereafter to disattend to the error of fact?

The editors of the *Norton Anthology of English Poetry* say that the mistake 'matters to history but not to poetry'; but this convenient severance of poetry from history is not truly in the interests of either poetry or history. When a poet invokes the historical facts of the New World (reaching beyond the traversed Atlantic to the amazing Pacific), historical facts which he is contrasting both with a new world of astronomical fact ('a new planet swims into his ken') and

---

[5] I owe this instance to a review of Bishop's *Geography III*, by Anthony Hecht in the *TLS*, 26 August 1977: 'there are no eighty-watt bulbs'.

with the Old World of European imagination centred in the Mediterranean (Chapman's Homer and 'the realms of gold'), it is unwise to hire a bodyguard for the poet. There are occasions when the cost of protecting a particular poem is too high because it amounts to the selling short of poetry. Donald Davie has made clear that he differs from the Norton editors, but only in his reasons not in his ruling:

The error about Cortez doesn't matter, not for the reason the Norton editors give or imply, but because it is an error in the history of European discovery and colonising of the New World—and that is not, except incidentally, the history that Keats's poem is concerned with.[6]

There is the usual doubt as to just what is meant by 'doesn't matter'; more substantively, I should altogether dissent from this as an understanding of the poem. Far from the New World's being there only 'incidentally', I find that the awe-inspiring amplitude of the poem, its sheer reach, is dependent upon its holding so assuredly in relation the great spaces of three human endeavours: the imaginative exploration through the arts (the Old World created anew in translation), the geographical exploration (the Old World discovering the New World), and the astronomical exploration (the oldest of worlds now newly registered by man). It is exactly the imaginative concurrence of these *three* histories that, *pace* Donald Davie, 'Keats's poem is concerned with.'

I maintain, then, that the accuracy of something offered as a fact in a work of literature can never be irrelevant or immaterial, and need not be unimportant though it may be so—there is no way of knowing in advance, rather as there is no way of answering in advance A. E. Housman's question parodying the witless textual critic, 'Which weighs most, a tall man or a fat man?'

The crucial question is that of the terms on which a work of literature offers itself. I am aware that in putting it like this I am advocating a return to a contractual model in literary understanding, but I have never seen a cogent refutation, as against a scorning, of the contractual model, valuably one among several.

By proffering factuality, a work is released from certain obligations—for example, our tests of plausibility rightly become different and may even lapse. But (nothing coming easier in art which is true

---

[6] Reviewing three books on Pound, *London Review of Books*, 23 May 1985.

both to itself and to all which is not art) by the same token, a work which proffers factuality will enter into other obligations. The difference between *Crime and Punishment* and Truman Capote's *In Cold Blood* is not that the latter is based upon a murder which happened but that it proffers itself as a record of a murder which happened. The Clutter family was murdered, and by these men. It would be idle, even frivolous, to say, of these unlikely killings (the grim fruit of rumour and frustration), that you find them artistically implausible. They don't have to be plausible, since they are a matter of record. None of Capote's energies go into making a reader believe that such murders would have taken place; and released from this obligation, Capote necessarily enters into others. And if Capote had subsequently gone on television, and had roguishly revealed that he had made up the whole thing, and that the book's photographs of the murderers were in fact of some amiable clerical cousins of his, the book itself—and not just Capote's personal reputation, such as it was—would have changed. Certain questions about it which were not pertinent would have become pressing, and others would have receded.

But what critics keep doing is changing the terms so as to exculpate. When a work is acutely consonant with the facts which it adduces, it is praised for fidelity; when it lapses from its claims, the idea of *in*fidelity is held to be farcically solemn and inadmissible. This is not criticism but public relations.

One way of getting at what is at stake is to consider two corollaries of maintaining the irrelevance, the immateriality, of the matter of fact, the inherent inapplicability to literature of any such consideration as whether the facts are or are not so.

First, a writer could not ever be praised for *using* fact, for inner resourcefulness in imaginative relation to external resources. Our delight for instance in a *trouvaille* depends upon its having indeed been *found*, out there, existing prior to and independent of the artist's will; and the comedy of the *trouvaille*, like its penetration, is a consequence of the acknowledged gap between what was assuredly found and what is then visited upon it by the differentiating imagination.

Take the humble anagram. When the Prime Minister Harold Wilson was about to crown a lifetime's efforts on behalf of socialism by taking a peerage, there was much speculation as to the title he would adopt. The black art of the anagrammatist peered into the entrails of *Harold Wilson* and saw there the impending protean rearrangement: *Lord Loinwash*. And the inspired anagram would not have worked if Wilson had in fact regularly chosen to be known as Harry Wilson (compare a putative President of the United States called James Carter), any more than a David Levine caricature of Richard Nixon is allowed to give him a nose which has *no* fidelity to that especial proboscis.

We now prefer the satirical anagram to the celebratory one; but even if we are no longer moved by the Victorian allegorizing of Florence Nightingale ('Flit on, cheering angel'—did she flit? rather a heavier tread, I should have thought), we should remember the amazing grace which can be visited upon the lowly anagram. 'What is truth? said jesting Pilate; and would not stay for an answer.' *Quid est veritas?* And yet the answer was tacitly there, if Pilate had had eyes to see and ears to hear: *Est vir qui adest*: it is the man who is in your presence. Christ did not need to speak, needed *not* to speak; but Pilate (the divine anagram intimates) needed to stay for the grace of an answer which was there within his disgracefully cynical question.

Alexander Pope is our greatest poet of the *trouvaille*. We should delight in what he made from what was not of his making, for instance the facts about Lord Hervey, gifted creep to Queen Caroline.

> Let *Sporus* tremble—'What? that Thing of silk,
> *Sporus*, that mere white Curd of Ass's milk?'
>
> (*An Epistle to Dr. Arbuthnot*, 305–6)

What raises this from the irresponsibility of lampoon to the responsibility of satire, and therefore to high art, is its play with a matter of fact. For it is on record, from within the family, that Lord Hervey did indeed take asses' milk as a tonic. The sickly and sexually suggestive dismissal, 'that mere white Curd of Ass's milk', derives not from fancy but from fact; it has been found, and thereby it is founded.

Pope is a rhetorician of genius, but rhetoric can be emptily effective. What is it that informs these lines about Sporus, who is Lord Hervey raised to the corruptest power?

> Whose Buzz the Witty and the Fair annoys,
> Yet Wit ne'er tastes, and Beauty ne'er enjoys,
> So well-bred Spaniels civilly delight
> In mumbling of the Game they dare not bite.

> Eternal Smiles his Emptiness betray,
> As shallow streams run dimpling all the way. . . .
>
> (311–16)

'Eternal Smiles his Emptiness betray': what makes this so much more than emptily sententious (along the easier lines of Goldsmith, 'the loud laugh that spoke the vacant mind') is its availing itself of a fact which horribly gives body to the moral observation. 'A painted face and not a tooth in his head': such at the time was the report of the Duchess of Marlborough. In due course, Hervey graced himself with 'the finest set of Egyptian pebble teeth' ever seen.

'Eternal Smiles his Emptiness betray.' Given his pyorrhoea, Lord Hervey would have done better to settle for 'Read my lips'. But how happily the fact co-operates with the imagination here, and what a difference this makes not just to the line itself but to those which precede it—

> So well-bred Spaniels civilly delight
> In mumbling of the Game they dare not bite

—and to those which follow, hanging with fascinated revulsion upon Hervey's lips: 'Half Froth, half Venom, spits himself abroad.' In the face of Hervey's dental and other unhygiene, Pope is, truly, *mordant*.

But if Pope is right to say of himself (as he does six lines after the Sporus passage) that

> not in Fancy's Maze he wander'd long,
> But stoop'd to Truth, and moraliz'd his song:

('stooped'—swooped down upon it like a falcon), it will not do then to change the terms on those occasions when he is charged with having falsified the facts. Lord Hervey's modern biographer and advocate, Robert Halsband, has remonstrated:

> At least one detail in the portrait, among the few concrete ones, is contradicted by what is known of Hervey: can he be a 'Child of Dirt that stinks' when he bathed daily?[7]

It is a good question, and we must not take the usual easy way out and, having previously valued Pope's art exactly for its finding so much imaginative truth in the matter of fact, now start invoking, oh, mythopoeic power, transcendings, poetic licence, and the usual

---

[7] *Lord Hervey: Eighteenth-Century Courtier* (1974), pp. 176–7.

mod. cons. 'Can he be a "Child of Dirt that stinks" when he bathed daily?' If we have to admit, Well, no, then we should not abandon the principle but should reluctantly judge this poetic moment to be artistically, and not just historically, something less than Pope at his greatest. For it was a fellow-poet, Pushkin, who declared that 'Slanders, even in poems, have always struck me as unpraiseworthy.'

But then for my part I am happy to answer Halsband's question with Yes. For what Lord Hervey, daily baths and all, stank of, will not have been body odour but perfume:

> Fop at the Toilet, Flatt'rer at the Board,
> Now trips a Lady, and now struts a Lord.

> (328–9)

Not just a 'Child of Dirt' (where Halsband cuts in) but 'this painted Child of Dirt'. Hervey was, as a matter of fact, highly cosmeticized. And Pope was very hot on the ways in which perfume is 'Dirt that stinks'. For as he was soon to write in the *Epilogue to the Satires*, with just such as Hervey in mind:

> all your Courtly Civet-Cats can vent,
> Perfume to you, to me is Excrement.

> (ii 183–4)

And this too is not a flight of fancy but doubly a stooping to truth. *Civet*: 'a yellowish or brownish unctuous substance, having a strong musky smell, obtained from sacs or glands in the anal pouch of several animals of the Civet genus. It is used in perfumery.'

It is a corollary, then, of our right to appreciate an artist's responsible relationship to fact that we have not just the right but the duty to deprecate an artist's irresponsibility. But there is a second corollary. If the-facts-being-so-or-not were intrinsically immaterial, then not only could a writer never use fact, he or she could never use *non*-fact either. If literature were a-factual (on the lines of I. A. Richards's misguided belief that statements within literature are 'pseudo-statements'), *a-factual* as against deliberatedly either factual or non-factual, then literature would never be able to achieve all those effects which are created from a conscious manifestation of *what is known not to be the case*.

Think of some of the ways in which an artist uses non-fact. Surrealism, for one. The point of Magritte's amazing painting of a man, seen from the back, looking into a mirror which reflects not the front of his face but the back of his head, would be entirely lost on anyone ignorant of the properties of a mirror—and would be entirely lost too on anyone who, in the name of sophisticated art-effort, thought that it was his bounden duty to put out of his mind the actual properties of actual mirrors. Magritte's painting shows what no mirror ever shows in such a way (and thereby, incidentally, differentiates painting from mirroring), while nevertheless oddly reminding us that it is perfectly possible for mirrors to be so placed as to show you the back of your head. And even while showing us a man who is *not* what you would ordinarily call *reflected* in the mirror (though assuredly reproduced in it), the painting also shows us an unobtrusive book which *is* reflected in the mirror. It lies on the mirror's ledge, and it and the mirror have agreed to do the right thing. How come the book is reflected and the man not? Ah, but then books can't look in mirrors; and even less can they imagine looking in mirrors and for a heady moment defying mirrordom.

Surrealism, in literature as in the visual arts, more than thrives upon, it depends upon, not just realism but the immitigably real. Even relativists watch their step and furtively take heed of the law of gravity, a law openly dear to surrealists.

In the bad old days, when plays in England needed to be licensed by the Lord Chamberlain, a play by Edward Bond fell foul of the censor, and was absurdly treated. *Early Morning*, an absurdist sur-realist play about Queen Victoria, was punished for lèse-majesté. This was an act of folly, but it has to be said that the arguments that were mustered against the Lord Chamberlain's judgement were themselves foolish. A drama critic, Ronald Bryden in the *Observer*, took quite the wrong tack:

Bond says it never crossed his mind that the Lord Chamberlain would object to the play when it was submitted to him in his last months of power over the theatre, and it's hard to see what connection with reality was found to justify the subsequent ban. *Early Morning* has nothing to do with historical events. It's a wild, macabre dream set somewhere between sleep and waking (hence the title?) in which myths from our school history merge and dissolve into images from *Alice in Wonderland*. . . .

But the judgement (a true one) that the play is a 'wild, macabre dream' requires that the play possess exactly that 'connection with reality' which the critic misguidedly abrogates. If Queen Victoria had in fact been having a riotous lesbian affair with Florence Nightingale, as the play pretends to posit, the play would not be *inconceivably* funny and it would not be a wild macabre dream. Far from having 'nothing to do with historical events', *Early Morning* has everything to do with them, the everything then including the turning of them topsy-turvy and arsy-versy. Such satirical surrealism as Edward Bond's requires an unremitting connection with reality, and anyone who was oblivious of Victorian history would be in for a more than usually pointless and incomprehensible evening in the theatre.

Then again there are all the other effects which depend upon an awareness of non-fact, a dependence which is itself dependent upon the unremitting relevance of fact. When for instance a writer (poet, novelist, dramatist . . .) dramatizes a consciousness which is gullible, self-deceived, ignorant, demented, or sheerly wrong, the dramatization can be apprehended as such only by our relating what is mistakenly imagined to be the case to what we know to be the case.

It is one of the most endearing things about Robert Browning as a poet that he was able to re-create, as the persuasive dramatizing of hallucination, what had originally been no more than a slip (but Freudian perhaps?) of his own. In Browning's poem 'Prince Hohenstiel-Schwangau' there had originally been the mistaken yoking of a particular wayside-temple with a tradition of sacrifice which was really based elsewhere. Browning was vexed at having made the mistake, and he asked his friend Mrs Orr to give notice of it in her *Handbook* to his poetry, first published in 1885. But then by 1888 he thought better of it, in the best way, and converted his mortification into something newly alive: an explanation by the Prince, within the poem, of the erroneous confusion as itself dream-induced and revelatory exactly in being so. As we now have it, the passage runs with this very current:

> somehow words deflect
> As the best cannon ever rifled will.

> 'Deflect' indeed! nor merely words from thoughts
> But names from facts: 'Clitumnus' did I say?
> As if it had been his ox-whitening wave
> Whereby folk practised that grim cult of old—
> The murder of their temple's priest by who
> Would qualify for his succession. Sure—
> Nemi was the true lake's style. Dream had need

> Of the ox-whitening piece of prettiness
> And so confused names, well known once awake.
>
> (2133-43)

'Well known once awake'? We may want to retort to the emending poet, Come off it, but the poem itself came to do something with error and thereby is not in error. It dramatizes.

Again: how can hyperbole be recognized for what it is (a pleasing revelatory distortion) if its *being* a distortion is excluded from response and from consideration?

And how do we ever make, or take, an irony except by relishing the marksmanship with which it aims off?

I have seen a textbook praised for its efforts to make students 'inept'—was this perhaps an adept irony? I have heard the faculty at a university praised because the help they had given to the administration 'could not be underestimated'—should I be careful not to underestimate the irony of the praiser?

If I vow that my love for you will be constant even as the leaves of the mighty English oak keep their green stations throughout the twelve turning months of the year (you know the line of talk, in poetry and out of it), a great deal will turn on what you make of my having gone straightfacedly from the sublime to the deciduous. If you were to quiz me, would I impatiently reply, 'You know what I mean—very well then, For *oak* read, oh, *yew*'? But then perhaps I was not pledging but hedging. My love for you will be constant even as the leaves of the mighty English oak. . . .

No such effects, of ironies and jokes and hyperboles, of surrealism and dramatization, can ever be either effected or effective except by courtesy of those facts that find themselves pointedly snubbed. The great modern genre for this is the photo-bubble cartoon, the witty force of which is entirely dependent on a probity and a severance. The photo must be genuine, not a political fake, and there must be a complete severance between the factuality of the photo and the factitiousness of the bubble. Preferably a starkly black and white photo, a starkly white balloon. A clear line, which is a line of responsibility too.

I think of the *Private Eye* cover of the welcoming of Castro by Khrushchev at Moscow Airport, the greyness, the bleakness, the comradely bear hug, and from those powerful lips: 'Later, you fool.' Now the joke is funny (while also being in earnest) only because

Castro had not in fact flown across the world for an assignation and an ungovernable passion.

And something similar goes for the tragi-comedy of the photo-bubble which recorded and transmogrified the police brutality at the Olympic Games in Mexico, brutality which moved Octavio Paz to resign his ambassadorship. Within the writhing mêlée of clubbed students and clotted policemen, there issues from a desperate mouth, just below what is both unmistakably and yet mistakably a truncheon, 'Pass the baton'. And for an excruciating moment, the Olympic Games are on again, and the comic incompetence of what would have been the worst relay-team ever is there to hold its own against what was in fact so violently other.

These two *Private Eye* covers are for me classics of the genre. And how is it that the effect would be sure to evaporate if, instead of a photo, there were a shrewd pencil-sketch of such scenes, complete with caption? Because of the signal responsibilities of photography to fact—signal, but not unique; different in degree, not in kind; so that what goes for photography goes, *mutatis mutandis*, for literature.

We all now know, all too well, that of course the photographer too must inevitably select, and thereby invent and distort, and thereby etc. etc. (to the glee of those who have invested their all in the fictivity of everything). Nevertheless, there are limits, and there is a contract, sometimes even a covenant, in operation when a photograph is put before us. The photographer, let us say the war photographer to make the clearest case, does not claim, proffering a work of his or her art, that such a thing might happen, or that such things happen, but that this thing happened.

Take Robert Capa's haunting photograph, after the Liberation of France, showing the huddled women with shaven heads, women who had 'fraternized' and more with the occupying Germans. It is not just that our response would not be the same if we were to find out that the women were in fact film-extras hired for the day, but that the *photograph* would not be the same. (Film, fiction-film, has different responsibilities and opportunities.) For a photograph is not the physical print-object alone (any more than a poem is the inking on a page), but is constituted of the relation between the physical print and a claim which it honourably makes and makes good. At which point even so great a photographer as Capa, or rather especially so great a photographer, can be bad news.

For it is not just that this compelling photographer was personally a compulsive liar. The disconcerting thing is the doubt as to how far Capa's personal untruthfulness seeped into his artistic conscience. For it would be weak-minded to claim that his photographs would be the same, would be as moving or moving in the same way, if we were to learn that they were in fact film-stills, and that those people were not prisoners of war at all, or corpses, but film-extras and set-up sets.

Photography, and especially such war photography as Capa's, has a contract with its contemplators. Once all the deductions have been made that acknowledge the photographer's inescapable selection, placing, timing, and so on, the war photograph says not that this is how it might have looked, but this is how it was. Which is why I find it appalling that Capa's biographer, Richard Whelan, can in the end brush aside the question of whether Capa's most famous photograph, the falling soldier in the Spanish civil war, was faked, staged, or not.

There have long been known to be problems about the place, the time, the shadows, the sequence, all calling in question Capa's trustworthiness, and elsewhere Capa was not above issuing the false caption. 'The fact is that we shall probably never know exactly what happened on that hillside,' says Whelan with shabby relief.

To insist upon knowing whether the photograph actually shows a man at the moment he has been hit by a bullet is both morbid and trivializing, for the picture's greatness ultimately lies in its symbolic implications, not in its literal accuracy as a report on the death of a particular man.[8]

Distrust immediately anyone who invokes 'ultimately'. Any such escapology as Whelan's is itself trivializing. Would the photograph really have effectively, affectively, the same 'symbolic implications' if Capa had gone even beyond staging a soldier but had hired an actor for his shot? (An easy business, symbolism, it seems.)

Such a photograph can move us in the particular way that it does because it stands not as a feature film's fiction but as a war's fact. We take the force of it because we also take the photographer's word for it. In Vietnam, the child running in flames. The gun to the man's head. At Kent State, a woman crouched in anguish above a body. Our understanding of suffering realized in photography is based on an understanding, and faith misplaced would be art

[8] *Robert Capa: A Biography* (1985), pp. 97–100.

evacuated. It is terrible to think that Capa may have been corrupted by the devilish imposture advocated by Henry Luce as 'fakery
in allegiance to the truth'.

There is a poem by James Wright which derives from a news-
photo. Wright does something better than write a political poem,
he writes a poem politically.

EISENHOWER'S VISIT TO FRANCO, 1959

'. . . we die of cold, and not of darkness.'

—Unamuno

The American hero must triumph over
The forces of darkness.
He has flown through the very light of heaven
And come down in the slow dusk
Of Spain.

Franco stands in a shining circle of police.
His arms open in welcome.
He promises all dark things
Will be hunted down.

State police yawn in the prisons.
Antonio Machado follows the moon
Down a road of white dust,
To a cave of silent children
Under the Pyrenees.
Wine darkens in stone jars in villages.
Wine sleeps in the mouths of old men, it is a dark red color.

Smiles glitter in Madrid.
Eisenhower has touched hands with Franco, embracing
In a glare of photographers.
Clean new bombers from America muffle their engines
And glide down now.

Their wings shine in the searchlights
Of bare fields,
In Spain.

Curbing its indignation, and leveling its dismay, the poem contemplates what was truly a key moment in post-war history, the moment when, in the interests of NATO, the American victor of the
war against Fascism comes to shake hands with the Fascist dictator.
Those 'Clean new bombers' contain the undertaking that the bases
would harbour 'clean' bombs; that 'glare of photographers' is flattering

but baleful; and Wright searchlights the dark disingenuousness of
Fascism:

> He promises all dark things
> Will be hunted down.

The Fascist leader proceeds with a travesty of ordered enlightened
equability; he promises all dark things will be hunted down. No, he
really promises what was fleetingly intimated, a discreet amputation
of that, an apocalyptic line-ending:

> He promises all dark things

This is a superb poem capturing the tragic compromises with tyr-
anny which democracy may be moved to make. Realpolitik. But
then its power as a poem must derive from, though it is not
conterminous with, the real. It is not a poem which says, Let us
imagine that the leader of a country, fifteen years after the end of
a war, etc. etc.; it does not say that, it says, You know what has
happened—have you taken the force of it? The poem does not
make up a meeting, it makes something of a meeting, or rather it
deduces and educes a great deal from a meeting. And is then itself
a meeting.

In this, it resembles the greatest such poem in the language.
Marvell's 'Horatian Ode upon Cromwell's Return from Ireland'
does not ask you to imagine a political tragedy, it asks you to exercise
your imagination upon a political tragedy. The execution of King
Charles is not flinched from in any way, the poet giving credit
where credit is due and yet not denying that in the hideous equation of revolutionary emergency the King is tragically in debit too.

> He nothing common did or mean
> Upon that memorable scene;
>   But with his keener eye
>   The ax's edge did try;
> Nor called the gods with vulgar spite
> To vindicate his helpless right,
>   But bowed his comely head,
>   Down as upon a bed.

These lines earn Marvell a supreme tribute: there is no finer tribute
in English poetry to a man's dignified courage *in extremis*, and this
man was a political adversary. Yet the greatness of the poem is not

a matter of the words alone, but of the relation of the words to everything which is not a matter of words. Convictions—and facts. To put it simply: would the poem be the same if historians were now to prove that the King had in fact been dragged kicking and screaming, blubbering and pleading, to the scaffold? Does not the poem make a claim to historical justice, and to the facts of power, which goes well beyond, though it never leaves behind, the power of words? Marvell's 'Horatian Ode', though as a poem it is more than a document, is the kind of poem which is never less than a document.

Frederick Wiseman, who is something more than the *doyen* of documentary film-makers in that he continues to be also the best of them, was trained as a lawyer, and he reinstates the contractual model of art in its relations to audiences. He gives undertakings, not just to the institutions (a school, an asylum, a monastery, an intensive-care unit), but to us, and he honours all concerned. A Wiseman film operates within strict contractual constraints. These people are not actors. These pains are not imaginary even though to realize these pains will ask imagination of you. This is what happened. There is such a place.

I realize that there are those, especially in universities and especially in English departments, for whom the distinction between fact and fiction was long ago exploded. It seems that any such distinction was only ever an abuse of power anyway, and there are no such things as facts, only those inverted-comma ectoplasms 'facts'. (Such literary relativists, though, can always themselves be caught slipping into saying that *in fact*. . . .) But in our time, fiction and fictivity have aggrandized themselves not only in art but in discourse generally. It heralded a great shift, in the first decade of this century, when there entered, with coercive convenience, the terms 'non-fiction' and 'non-fictional'. Fiction was thereby granted a remarkable imperialistic status, not only as hereafter differentiating all we read or write, but as getting to define the alternative to itself so much in its own terms, so entirely as not being itself. There is fiction, and there is non-fiction.

But imagine going to the library and being asked whether a particular book was theology or non-theology, poetry or non-poetry, science or non-science.

A writer's responsibility might be put like this: you can't both lean upon historical or other fact (this being not only permissible but indispensable to many kinds of literary achievement) and at the same time kick it away from under you. You can't get mileage from the matter of fact and then refuse to pay the fare.

And where does this leave the rightly valued thing imagination? As valuable exactly insofar as we continue to distinguish it from what is not imagined, and furthermore distinguish the imaginary from such other acts of imagination as memory and sympathy. Leigh Hunt praised a particular moment in Keats's poetry as 'a fancy founded, as all beautiful fancies are, on a strong sense of what really exists or occurs'.[9]

If literature does indeed transcend historical contingency and fact, it must not be by failing to respect their dignity and their claims. A false transcendence is the subject of a true poem by D. J. Enright, called 'Streets'.[10] The principle is obdurate, though the application of it will always ask tact and a recognition of how complicated and elusive a literary understanding can be.

III

Let me call up some occasions when works of literature have been impugned for error. And let me recommence with another Victorian honeymoon, and with such social detail as might seem beneath our notice but which can carry immense weight.

On 7 March 1874, the day when the happy couple landed, Tennyson published as Poet Laureate a greeting to the Russian Grand Duchess who was entering the British Royal Family:

> Alexandrovna.
> And welcome, Russian flower, a people's pride,
>   To Britain, when her flowers begin to blow!
>   From love to love, from home to home you go,
> From mother unto mother, stately bride,
>   Marie Alexandrovna!

But before long, Tennyson was kicking himself. 'People say that the accent is on the antepenultimate, Alexándrovna. If so, it rather spoils my chorus.' Rather. For an essential element in a genuine welcome might be getting the pronunciation of someone's name right. The

---

[9] *Examiner*, June–July 1817; *Keats: The Critical Heritage*, ed. G. M. Matthews (1971), p. 59.

[10] See p. 326.

corrected 'Marie Alexándrovna' would be unspeakable as a chorus, guttering and spluttering. And it will not do to hail, as Tennyson does, the reconciliation of two nations which had recently been at war, in an English poem which proceeds to ride roughshod over a Russian claim. A trivial point? But poetry is itself a form of pronouncement to which pronunciation is crucial; words in poetry are made good through the co-operation of their sense and their sound. So that a poem of welcome which repeatedly mispronounces its honorand might start to feel like a sardonic thrust—here is how much we English have forgiven the Crimean War and how much we welcome you. . . .

The point may seem a small one; and the poem is a small one in the scale of Tennyson's accomplishment; but the objection, as Tennyson himself lugubriously acknowledged, is radical, in that the whole poem would have had to be rewritten if the error were to have been rectified. For the mis-said name 'Alexandróvna' furnishes the chorus, first the centre and then the climax of all five stanzas. The name carries great weight in the poem, and in this it differs from a less pressing, though still pertinent, point which was made about a recent Laureate effort in the face of a royal marriage. When Prince Charles made an honest Princess of Diana, there was a wedding ode from the Poet Laureate, John Betjeman. His song, he felt sure, was seconded by bird-song:

> Blackbirds in City churchyards hail the dawn,
> Charles and Diana, on your wedding morn.

A happily lugubrious letter in *The Times* said at once:

> I fear not. It is the moulting season. Patriotic blackbirds may endeavour to raise a twitter or two even if they do themselves a mischief in the attempt.
> But it has to be said—if you want blackbirds at the wedding, get married in spring.
>
> Yours faithfully . . .[11]

Faithfully is right.

Any sardonic possibility in such a mispronunciation as 'Alexandróvna' might seem not only unwanted but unwarranted. Yet one of the reasons why the British won the war against Nazi Germany (with a little help from our friends) was Churchill's refusal to pronounce the word *Nazi* as the Nazis might have wished and as weaklings and

---

[11] K. H. Oldaker, writing on 27 July 1981.

quislings did. 'Nar-zee', he growled, and crouched round the radio we felt better at once. Not only did 'Nar-zees' sound more sleazily nasty, but we took them over, we did not acquiesce, we anglicized. No pronunciation could have been less welcoming.

The minutiae of insult and of compliment are important to literature, as they are to public life. When the Warden of Wadham College, Oxford, Sir Maurice Bowra, received an honorary degree from an American university, he was goaded as well as tickled by the fact that the citation had succeeded in mispronouncing all three of his names: Cecil [See-sil] Maurice [Mo-reece] Bowra [Boe-ra] as against Cecil [Sess-il] Maurice [Morris] Bowra [Bough-ra].

A poem of compliment, such as Tennyson's 'Welcome . . .', cannot be truly a poem unless it is truly a compliment. And the same considerations apply when we turn from a real to an imagined name and its pronunciation. Take another Anglo-Russian nexus. Nabokov was once clucked at in the *Times Literary Supplement*:

The essential un-Englishness of Nabokov's English is emphasized in the lyrical passage at the beginning of *Lolita*, where he gives instructions about the pronunciation of his heroine's name ('the tip of the tongue taking a trip of three steps down the palate to tap, at three, on the teeth'). Unfortunately, however, the English 't' does not tap on the teeth at all, being— phonetically speaking—alveolar. Dental 'ts' begin, one might note, at Calais.

In an interview in the *Sunday Times*, Nabokov duly pooh-poohed the complaint:

Incidentally, speaking of my first nymphet, let me take this neat opportunity to correct a curious misconception proffered by an anonymous owl in a London weekly a couple of months ago. 'Lolita' should not be pronounced in the English or Russian fashion (as he thinks it should) but with a trilling of Latin 'l's' and a delicate toothy 't.'

Nabokov was prudent not to let the matter pass; after all, that taunting tongue-twister is quintessential Nabokov (himself a twister of tongues), and is quintessential Humbert Humbert, in its titillatory prissiness. How sexy Lolita is! Just think of what your tongue gets up to, in the mere saying of her name! 'The tip of the tongue taking a trip of three steps down the palate to tap, at three, on the teeth.' And notice that, in replying, Nabokov does not waive the principle, does not retort that he is, for Heaven's sake, a novelist, an artist, not a phonetician. He does not flash a poetic licence. Instead, he makes the surprising claim that in this novel which he wrote in English and in Russian the name ' "Lolita" should not be pronounced in the English or Russian fashion . . . but with a trilling of Latin "l's" and a delicate toothy "t".'

I used to think that this was just Nabokov as Houdini, but then a friend reminded me that Lolita isn't her real name anyway and that there are things elsewhere in the book which suggest that Humbert Humbert (and his creator) might have toyed with some such Latin trilling and thrilling. So the verdict? Not proven? But I can hear on a tape of Nabokov's reading from the book that *he* didn't pronounce the name 'with a trilling of Latin "l's and a delicate toothy "t" '.

The pronunciation of a name is a social fact which may be underwritten by a phonetician's credentials. One great poet of social fact is Pushkin, and there is a telling moment in Nabokov's idiosyncratic and fascinating edition of *Eugene Onegin*. First, Nabokov's translation from the ballroom scene:

> Up to the porch our hero now has driven;
> past the hall porter, like a dart,
> he has flown up the marble steps,
> has run his fingers through his hair,
> has entered. The ballroom is full of people;
> the music has already tired of dinning;
> the crowd is occupied with the mazurka;
> there's all around both noise and squeeze;
> there clink the cavalier guard's spurs;
> the little feet of winsome ladies flit;
> upon their captivating tracks
> flit flaming glances,
> and by the roar of violins is drowned
> the jealous whispering of fashionable women.
>
> (I xxviii)

The Commentary quotes Pushkin's manuscript note on the cavalier guard's spurs:

Inexact. Cavaliers, as well as hussars, of the guard wore court dress and low shoes for balls. A judicious remark, but the notion lends something poetical to the description. I refer to the opinion of A.I.V. [Netty Vulf].

Pushkin, then, knew—or came to know, a year after publication—what he was doing. The spurs, though, are not just 'inexact' but absurd; in so crowded a ballroom, spurs would have ripped the elaborate dresses to shreds, and this is to leave aside the fact that had the cavalier guard been so remiss as to do one of those Russian dances low to the ground, he might have done himself a serious injury. . . . Pushkin, though, wants the clink, blending in with the other sounds. Fine. But the critical question remains: is not the artistic achievement something less than the greatest when it can add 'something poetical to the description' only by overriding the matter of fact? Is it not a blemish that the description is better if you don't actually think about it, don't *realize* it? And is not Pushkin's art exactly one which elsewhere prides itself on social exactitude, on being so deliciously *au fait* with the fashionable world, not just its customs but its very costumes?

The point of such questions is to suggest not that the stanza collapses but that it is marred; Pushkin has not achieved the perfect fit of fact and suggestive enhancement which characterizes his writing at its best. He was able to introduce the cavalier guard's spurs only by being, well, cavalier. And if his friend Netty Vulf's remark was 'judicious', we may ourselves judge the matter somewhat less leniently than Pushkin.

The principle, then, may be judged to be always pertinent but not always equally pressing. We should press charges in proportion as the artist pressed claims. The traditional grounds for valuing Pushkin's art give salience to his mastery of circumstantial social detail, and it will not then do to brush aside something as mere social detail. The question of genre or kind (and of claims inherent in a genre or kind) is therefore one factor which helps assess not the pertinence but the importance of accuracy.

So critics hostile to the principle are often hostile to any generic differentiations. Instead they may differentiate the scholar from the artist along just this line, that a scholar can be in error and an artist not. There is a book by Norman Sherry which follows Conrad's footsteps; one learned review of *Conrad's Eastern World* took Professor Sherry to task, first on a point of fact and then on the point of principle. I have always liked this paragraph as a supreme instance of the academic 'of course', which means 'as I am probably the only person to have remarked but which, as a scholar and a gentleman, I shall affect to pretend we all of us know.' He quotes Sherry:

'Conrad's picture of the trading station in that part of Borneo of which he wrote was accurate.' Conrad, of course, thought that the Patusan of

Lord Jim was situated not in east Borneo but in north-west Sumatra, over a thousand miles away . . . but more disturbing is the emphasis placed on 'accurate' in the quotation. Conceivably Conrad could have been 'accurate' for all important literary purposes if he had erected Patusan on the maritime coast of Bohemia.[12]

What makes this so misguided a joke is not just the airy invoking of *The Winter's Tale*, a play which notoriously gives Bohemia a seacoast ('maritime coast' is intended as mock-pomposity), but the weirdness of the claim once you go beyond the manner to the matter. For it amounts to saying that a Conrad novel is the same kind of work, stands in the same relation to make-believe, as *The Winter's Tale*. But the Jacobean audience was not ignorant of Bohemia, and Shakespeare's reference, which was on the lines of latter-day references to the Swiss navy, was not intended to be somehow a-factual but to be an indicator that the play would be availing itself of what was known not to be fact. The art of *The Winter's Tale*, in this respect, is closer to that of Saul Steinberg than to that of Joseph Conrad.

Poets have themselves differed as to where their responsibilities lie. They have had to choose, and we as readers and critics may be obliged to choose too. Does the natural world, for instance, need to be respected in and for itself before it can be asked to furnish the energies of art? Poetry may be capable of being as culpably exploitative as anything else, and its right to be respected may be in proportion to its willingness to respect all which is not poetry or art. An early poem by Yeats, 'The Indian to His Love' (1886), has the line, 'The peahens dance on a smooth lawn.' It was objected that peahens do not dance. Yeats turned not to natural history but to literature, insisting that peahens 'dance throughout the whole of Indian poetry. . . . As to the poultry yards, with them I have no concern.'[13] But no amount of high and mighty scorn will undo the fact that a high price is paid by a poetry which invokes poultry and at the same time declares that it has no concern with the poultry yards.

The contrast would be with Tennyson, who declined to print a lovely early poem of his, 'Anacaona'. It is about Hispaniola or Hayti, where Queen Anacaona welcomed the Spanish. This poem of

[12] C. T. Watts, *Review of English Studies*, NS, xix (1968), 93.
[13] Quoted by A. Norman Jeffares, *A Commentary on the Collected Poems of W. B. Yeats* (1968), pp. 8-9.

paradise ends, in happy innocence, on the brink of slaughter. Why would Tennyson not print it, despite the urging of friends? Because, as one of them, Edward FitzGerald, said, the poet believed that the poem 'would be confuted by some Midshipman who had been in Hayti latitudes and knew better about Tropical Vegetable and Animal'.

There is perhaps no greater distinction within poets than that between those who believe that a poem can be confuted by a midshipman and those who demand a collusive jury of their peers. Tennyson's seems to me far the more honourable position—and to have made for the greater poetry.

Natural history in 'Anacaona' might have seemed a less urgent thing to Tennyson, though he invariably sought the utmost accuracy, had the poem been a poem of natural history alone; but it was a poem of imperial history, too, of exploitation and massacre. The matter of fact is intimate, in the end of the poem, with matters of life and death. And it is to those that I turn for my last instances.

On 10 March 1841, Dickens wrote to thank someone who had seen the proofs of *Barnaby Rudge*, where it was said that a man was hanged 'for passing bad one pound notes' (ch. xi). There were no one pound notes at the time of this historical novel; notes under five pounds were not issued until 1797. Dickens's letter is exemplary.

My Dear Sir
  I have looked back to the Annual Register, and find you are quite right about the one pound notes. Very many thanks to you for your kind care.

And the text as we have it now reads 'for passing bad notes'.

Exemplary, first, because it was wise to check what the man said, and to look back to the Annual Register; second, because Dickens was duly grateful; third, because he did not take the high ground and say that with the Mint and the Exchequer he had no concern.

But a corollary of giving Dickens credit here, as we should, is that we should not shrug aside, as servile lovers of Dickens do, a crux in *Great Expectations*. For Magwitch, the convict who comes back from Australia and risks his life to repay Pip, would *not* have been liable to the death penalty at that date for doing so. Yet it is essential to the novel that he should be deemed liable to the death penalty. Not only does his act thereby incarnate a supremely loving danger, but it is his being liable to the death penalty which underwrites, first, his destroying the evil Compeyson, and, second, his dying a natural death—eluding the penalty of his return—as a consequence of that violent river-struggle with his antagonist. *Great Expectations* is a great novel, but—like Magwitch himself—it pays a price for taking the law into its own hands. What might have seemed to be only a legal detail radiates into the central life of the book, and may remind us that one simple test of how important an error or a license may be to a book is how daunting an enterprise it would prove to be to put the matter of fact right.

Which brings me to a modern novel where such a crux is even more central. In William Golding's *Lord of the Flies*, Piggy's glasses are a nub.

And Piggy sat motionless behind the luminous wall of his myopia.

His specs—use them as burning glasses!

Ralph moved the lenses back and forth, this way and that, till a glossy white image of the declining sun lay on a piece of rotten wood.

Twenty-five years ago, T. Hampton saw through this, and said so in the best of fact-finding journals, *Notes and Queries* (July 1965).

This is impossible. The lenses used to correct myopia are diverging lenses and so will not bring the rays of the sun to a focus. Had Piggy been long-sighted then he would have been wearing converging lenses, which will focus light to a point. The only trouble is that then he could have survived without them, as he could have seen objects in the distance—for instance, the fatal rock.

I understand the instinct to find this criticism funny or absurd (though part of the instinct is the disreputable wish for a quiet life), but does not taking *Lord of the Flies* seriously require one to take this criticism seriously? For although the book is a Christian parable, it is also a horrifyingly realistic account of credible behaviour and of its cogent upshot. And Piggy's shortsightedness, and the glasses which counter it, are central to the architectonics of the book. Piggy cannot be longsighted; not only does he die because he is shortsighted, but the moral and spiritual impulse of the book is behind the irony that, of all the boys, he is the one who is *least* shortsighted—except physically. And then again, it is essential that it be Piggy, through those glasses, who brings fire. For if it is a Christian fable, it is also a Promethean one, and Piggy the fire-bringer is hideously sacrificed.

The point is not just a matter of glum relish, by which one might take pleasure in imagining Golding the Nobel Prize winner alone on a desert island and to his surprise deprived of the hot meal which he had supposed his glasses would muster. No, it is a critical matter of a matter of fact, and one the correction of which would entail the entire rewriting of the book. I continue to think *Lord of the Flies* an extraordinary achievement, especially for a first novel; but there was already present, if the early readers had eyes to see and were not myopic, the hubris and the overbearing which damaged his later novels, a hubris which moved Golding to say of *Pincher Martin*, 'It's going to be a blow on behalf of the ordinary universe.' For one thing, the ordinary universe really stands in no need of having blows struck on its behalf; for another, if you really want to strike a blow on behalf of the ordinary universe, one place to start would be a respect for the universe of the ordinary optician.

Meanwhile there are the literal blows which writers must not demean. Those of the Crimean War, for instance.

> Half a league, half a league,
>   Half a league onward,
> All in the valley of Death
>   Rode the six hundred.
> 'Forward, the Light Brigade!
> Charge for the guns!' he said:
> Into the valley of Death
>   Rode the six hundred.

But no sooner was the poem sent for publication than Tennyson discovered to his chagrin that the figure of six hundred might be in question. For he learnt that the leader in *The Times* on 13 November 1854 had first said 'about 700 strong' and then 'seven hundred'; it was the special correspondent's report which had given both '607 sabres' and a total of 607, and the subsequent leader of 14 November which had spoken of 600.

Tennyson and his wife fretted; the poet told the editor of the paper in which the poem was to appear that 'Six is much better than seven hundred (as I think) metrically so keep it and put the note I have made at the bottom.'[14] (The note cited the 607 sabres mentioned by the *Times* correspondent.)

Now it is easy to find Tennyson's scruples fussy or morbid; he is apparently vindicated as to the matter of fact (the modern historian

---

[14] 6 December 1854; *Letters*, ed. Cecil Y. Lang and Edgar F. Shannon, ii (1987), 101.

E. L. Woodward gives the number as 673 horsemen beginning the charge), and in any case the difference between 600 and 700 might be judged to be neither here nor there.

But what is admirable in Tennyson—and it fortifies the honour of this poem which honours the brave mis-commanded soldiers— is the awareness that the slope is slippery. For if we were to start messing with the actual figures, and to say that it really doesn't matter exactly how many soldiers there were in the Charge of the Light Brigade, where would we stop? Seven hundred is all right, say; so would it be all right if in fact the British had had 50,000 men, up against a few Russian old-age pensioners armed only with pitchforks? For at some point the realities of the engagement would simply be left behind and disgraced. And Tennyson, let us remember, did not write a poem which comes before us saying, Let us imagine an act of doomed absurd military prowess; he wrote about the meaning of such an act as had just been witnessed by the world. It would have been a derogation from the Brigade's courage to have done anything other than contemplate, with imagination, the very facts.

A paper, not Tennyson's *Examiner* but the *New York Times*, will furnish an ending. On 10 September 1990, an article on biography, novels, and biographical novels praised Julian Barnes for *Flaubert's Parrot*, 'a novel that's part biography, part literary essay, part fantasy, part homage to the Hermit of Croisset'.

I have a soft spot for *Flaubert's Parrot*, since it is the only novel which will ever have two pages about me in it. Harder is the question of what the two pages get up to.

This is how Julian Barnes opens the matter.

I'll remember instead another lecture I once attended, some years ago at the Cheltenham Literary Festival. It was given by a professor from Cambridge, Christopher Ricks, and it was a very shiny performance. His bald head was shiny; his black shoes were shiny; and his lecture was very shiny indeed. Its theme was Mistakes in Literature and Whether They Matter.

So far, so good; my head is bald and does shine on occasion; I wish that my shoes kept pace with it; and though I am not sure that I should want a lecture of mine to be remembered as shiny, this must be better than its being forgotten as dull. I respect Mr Barnes's respect for the facts and his not being afraid of the charge of baldism; after all, it would not really have been effective if he had shaped all that shiny sequence about a named individual who in fact teemed with curls.

What I am less happy about is Mr Barnes's unargued contention (complete with a swipe at 'bespectacled professors of English') that all you need do with Piggy's glasses in *Lord of the Flies* is 'detonate the error—like blowing up a small bomb with a controlled explosion. What's more, this detonation . . . doesn't set fire to other parts of the novel.' Sorry, that is just what it does do.

And then what I am least happy about is Mr Barnes's dealings with the 600 or 700 of 'The Charge of the Light Brigade': 'Tennyson wrote the poem very quickly, after reading a report in *The Times* which included the phrase "someone had blundered."' Oh no it didn't; the phrase in *The Times* was 'some hideous blunder', and Tennyson effected a profound refashioning of it:

> 'Forward, the Light Brigade!'
> Was there a man dismayed?
> Not though the soldier knew
>   Some one had blundered:
> Their's not to make reply,
> Their's not to reason why,
> Their's but to do and die:
> Into the valley of Death
>   Rode the six hundred.

In the recording of Tennyson reading the poem, made at the end of his life, his voice swoops upon 'knew' with an emphasis at once awed, exasperated, and half-incredulous at the immediately culpable folly of 'Some one'—the effect in the recording is riveting.

When I was told in *Flaubert's Parrot* that the *Times* report had included the phrase 'someone had blundered', I thought to myself that once again someone had blundered. I should like to think that it was Mr Barnes's blunder which made the judges of the Booker Prize dash the cup from his lips and not give *Flaubert's Parrot* the Prize after all.

But let me end, not with tomfoolery, but with John Ruskin's dignified and moving statement of what is at issue. In *The Seven Lamps of Architecture* (II iii), Ruskin illuminates 'The Lamp of Truth' and thereby the principled power of imagination.

For it might be at first thought that the whole kingdom of imagination was one of deception also. Not so: the action of the imagination is a voluntary summoning of the conceptions of things absent or impossible; and the pleasure and nobility of the imagination partly consist in its knowledge and contemplation of them as such, *i.e.* in the knowledge of their actual absence or impossibility at the moment of their apparent presence or reality. When the imagination deceives, it becomes madness. It is a noble faculty so long as it confesses its own ideality; when it ceases to confess this, it is insanity. All the difference lies in the fact of the confession, in there being *no* deception. It is necessary to our rank as spiritual creatures, that we should be able to invent and to behold what is not; and to our rank as moral creatures, that we should know and confess at the same time that it is not.

LITERARY PRINCIPLES AS AGAINST THEORY

Principles as against theory? What follows is an attempt to enunciate briefly some convictions and to indicate some grounds for them. This will necessarily be open to the objection which the philosopher can always make, that of being 'underdescribed' and 'underargued'. (The philosopher in turn can often be accused either of overdescription and overargument or of inhabiting a world in which the possibility of overdescription and overargument goes unimagined.)

Against the claims of theory, I set the counterclaims of principle. These may sometimes be counterclaims in the sense that they are at odds with theory's claims, and sometimes in the sense that they put in a competing bid for what will always, in teaching and out of it, be limited resources, notably those severely limited resources time and energy and attention. Very often my beliefs have been best expressed by others; this is for me not an admission but an acknowledgement, since it makes thought about literature continuous with literature, where too I repeatedly find my beliefs best expressed by others.

When Hopkins wrote of the 'teachable element' in literature, it was not of theory that he was thinking, and his words may remind us of one continuing alternative claim upon the attentions of teachers and taught, whether in school, college, or graduate school. Hopkins speaks of how poets should learn, and what he says is consonant with how we might learn about as well as from poets.

The strictly poetical insight and inspiration of our poetry seems to me to be of the very finest, finer perhaps than the Greek; but its rhetoric is inadequate—seldom firstrate, mostly only just sufficient, sometimes even below par. By rhetoric I mean all the common and teachable element in literature, what grammar is to speech, what thoroughbass is to music, what theatrical experience gives to playwrights.[1]

Hopkins enunciates a principle; because it is a principle and not a theory he is moved naturally to speak of experience, to which principle, as by definition less comprehensively ideate than theory,

[1] 7 August 1886; *The Correspondence of G. M. Hopkins and R. W. Dixon*, ed. C. C. Abbott (1935), 1955 edn, p. 141.

gives a correspondingly greater weight. Rhetoric, this teachable element in literature, is not theory, and it still has its legitimate claims and must not be ousted. Rhetoric, granted, is not literature, but that is not because this teachable element departs, rather because something else arrives, a ministering to wisdom, or to justice or to vitality or to magnanimity, such as does not rest content with persuasion. Literature is, among other things, principled rhetoric, and Hopkins's words need to be complemented by T. S. Eliot's, when, having embarked upon editorship of *The Criterion*, he spoke of principles:

A literary review should maintain the application, in literature, of principles which have their consequences also in politics and in private conduct. . . . To maintain the autonomy, and the disinterestedness, of every human activity, and to perceive it in relation to every other, require a considerable discipline. It is the function of a literary review to maintain the autonomy and disinterestedness of literature, and at the same time to exhibit the relations of literature—not to 'life,' as something contrasted to literature, but to all the other activities, which, together with literature, are the components of life.[2]

Such a sense of literature's relations is itself a statement of principle, and is incompatible with subservience. Literary study, like literature itself, has always needed to resist not only the imperialism of science, which is often frankly adversarial, but also those humanities which are literature's allies but do have their neo-imperialistic ambitions. History, with its insistence that facts are its province, and philosophy, with its confidence that truths are its province: these are often tempted to invade. One of them is always manifestly a greater threat to literature and to literary study than is the other, but therefore not for very long. It used to be history, now it is philosophy. The evidence that literary study is in danger of being philosophized out of autonomous existence is the fact that, as literary theory, it now supposes itself not just able to learn from philosophy (so it should) but able to adjudicate within the discipline of philosophy. John Searle may be wrong and Richard Rorty right, but literary study is vulnerably overextended when (as a discipline, not as individual asseveration) it presumes to rule upon the matter. The world of the philosophers is everything which is their case, and is not our oyster.

When Christopher Norris (whom I take to be one of the most

[2] *The Criterion*, i (1923), 421.

dedicated and resourceful of literary theory's advocates) applauds Rorty and deplores Searle, not for the homely reason that Rorty at present is, in Norris's judgement, of more use to literary studies, but with the interventionist claim that Rorty is philosophically in the right and Searle in the wrong, he is not so much overweening (his self-delighting word) as underwitting. For to speak of Searle's indictment of Derrida as having 'more to do with professional self-esteem than with the interests of reason and truth';[3] to say that 'Territorial imperatives were clearly at stake when John Searle . . . launch[ed] an attack on this whole new breed of overweening literary theorists'; and to sum it up as 'this aggressively self-promoting line': is all this not insouciant (naïvely so, to use their much-wielded word) about any retort of *tu quoque*? Why isn't the theorist's enterprise equally vulnerable to motive-seeking? Why aren't 'professional self-esteem' and 'territorial imperatives' and an 'aggressively self-promoting line' just as easy to retort upon the literary theorist? It is unlikely that either party has a monopoly of impure motives.

Resistance to what seem to some of us the inordinate and unspecific claims of theory will sometimes turn upon claims made *for* it and not just *by* it. Resistance will often wish to suggest the losses inseparable from a thoroughgoing dedication to theory's comprehensive articulation. So one remarkable feature of theory, its impressive intellectuality, is necessarily a limitation too, since there is a difference between intelligence and intellectuality, a difference which has often been the site of valuable disagreements between the English and the French life of the mind. T. S. Eliot wrote in his memorial of John Maynard Keynes (strangely little-known, even to economists):

What one immediately remarked, and most distinctly remembered, about Maynard Keynes, when first meeting him twenty-five or more years ago, was a very exceptional intelligence. The use of 'intelligence' here suggests the French, rather than the English associations of the word. That is already, however, making a suggestion which needs at once to be corrected. It is on a somewhat lower level, that of the most alert un-creative mind, that intelligence is a French rather than an English characteristic. When it is united to a powerful and original intellect, it is probably as rare in one race as in another. Certainly, Keynes was quite English, and, in any sense of the word, an 'intellectual'. That is to say, he was born into, and always lived in, an intellectual environment; he had intellectual tastes; and he had—what is not always denoted by 'intellectual'—an intellect. But his mind was also intelligent: it was highly sceptical, and free from the bias of enthusiasm; furthermore, it was a free mind, in that his interests were not limited by the activities in which his talents were supreme.[4]

Behind this there lie both Eliot's disagreement with and his equally substantial agreement with D. H. Lawrence about thinking and intelligence. Intelligence, as both understood and evinced by Lawrence, aspires to be continuous with that which it works upon, whereas intellectuality—with its sense of the advantages to be gained from specialization and its disjunctions—does not. The distinction is not between thinking and feeling, though it may involve very different apprehensions of the duties and priorities within thinking and feeling and the relations between them. Theory, because of its elaborated intellectuality, is not well-adapted to exactly that salience which was seized upon by Eliot (whose philosophical competence was not less than that of his recent disparagers, such as Harold Bloom and Geoffrey Hartman) in ending some reflections on contemporary poetry: 'intelligence, of which an important function is the discernment of exactly what, and how much, we feel in any given situation'.[5] This is one of the great statements of principle not only about intelligence and about literature (since Eliot, like literature itself, is so thoughtful about feeling, and so aware of the difference between the task of combining and the luxury of confusing), but also germane to that more circumscribed essential thing, the profession of teaching.

Fortunately we are not obliged to pick only one goal, but if I ever had to, as a classroom teacher, it would not be the fullest possible self-consciousness of methodology and theory, but this principle of Eliot's: 'intelligence, of which an important function is the discernment of exactly what, and how much, we feel in any given situation'. I'd select this for, above all, two reasons. First (since literary study should be instinct with social and political judgements), that the world in which we live is still one hideously imperilled by falsity of feeling, so that it is as much a responsibility of the artist and of the teacher to bring people to understand *illusions* of feeling as feelings. Eliot wrote: 'Stendhal's scenes, some of them, and some of his phrases, read like cutting one's own throat; they are a terrible humiliation to read, in the understanding of human feelings and human illusions of feeling that they force upon the reader.'[6] The sheer *understanding*

---

[4] *New English Weekly*, 16 May 1946.   [5] *The Egoist*, iv (1917), 151.
[6] *The Athenaeum*, 30 May 1919.

of this, which everywhere animates Eliot's great poems, has hardly become less needed in a society which is happy to educate us into human illusions of feeling. And my second reason for giving such priority to Eliot's insight is that the classroom teacher should maximize the advantages, and minimize the disadvantages, of one crucial respect in which she or he ordinarily differs from the author: that of being physically in the room with those whom one is to reach and teach. To teach the works of Stendhal is very different from reading them. Teaching's humanity must impinge differently—not more power-fully or more honourably but with the continual obligation to confront, even if then to affront, the feelings of those physically present, the obligation of just those living adjustments, allowances, re-adjustments, apprehensions, and concessions which it is the glory of Stendhal's art *not* to deal in. In one elementary sense, the novel says the same to its readers even though it means differently. But the classroom can never afford to be above the suspicion of condescension and of sparing or not sparing people's feelings. ('I am afraid that this is sure to hurt X's feelings,' Dr F. R. Leavis once said of a notorious disciple—'but then he has so many of them.') Intimate with feeling, the intelligence of literature, as of the classroom, is less intellectually ideate than it behooves theory, with its philosophical aspiration, to be.

The point is not any brainless accusation that theory is 'cerebral' and lacks feelings; it teems with feelings, but far from being dedic-ated to 'the discernment of exactly what, and how much, we feel in any given situation', theory's advocates often write in such a way as to preclude or occlude exactly such discernment. The banter, untiring and tiring, which plays over titles, for instance, is not in itself evidence for or against the possession of a sense of humour; but it does often ring as an unease uncomprehended, and in par-ticular an unease about the understanding of one's own feelings, within literature and in literary studies. The characteristic titles are not jokes, they are jokey. An issue of *Critical Inquiry* (September 1984) had an exchange between Edward Pechter and Christine Froula. Pechter's title was: 'When Pechter Reads Froula Pretending She's Eve Reading Milton; or, New Feminist is But Old Priest Writ Large'. Froula's title was: 'Pechter's Spectre: Milton's Bogey Writ Small; or, Why Is He Afraid of Virginia Woolf?' Here are queasy feelings about self-advertisement and self-respect, about literariness and literary studies. The edgy jokiness is a throwing-up of the hands.

An essay by Frank Kermode in 1980, 'Figures in the carpet: on recent theories of narrative discourse', began with the confidence of the day:

It is commonplace that over the past fifteen years or so we have witnessed extraordinary transformations in literary theory and critical method. Those who hoped to keep quiet, sit it out, and wait for a return to normal must now suppose that they have lost their wager. We have, without question, had some sort of revolution. . . .[7]

Who were those local losers? Were Donald Davie and William Empson and Hugh Kenner among those who hoped to sit it out but then lost a wager? Is there no such thing as honest opposition either to the claim that there *have* truly been 'extraordinary transformations in literary theory and critical method' or to the 'transformations' themselves? This travestying of the unnamed opposition is alive with feelings, but the feelings are not there to be contemplated and so they issue naturally, ten lines later, in the concessive climax of Kermode's introductory history of what he himself calls 'some sort of revolution': 'And by now we may perhaps say that the bandwagon is slowing down a bit; it is easier to climb aboard, or anyway to inspect the goods on offer and make a choice.' What ten lines earlier had been 'some sort of revolution', has reassuringly, ruefully, become a bandwagon. The bantering demeanour or demeaning banter has its polemical power, but at the price of keeping obscured, from the writer as much as from the reader, exactly what is felt, and how much, in the given situation. The irony is in the service of '*in, but not of*'—but the one thing you can't decently be in but not of is the swim. You can't be both aboard the bandwagon and above it.

The second page of Kermode's review of theories of literature was an act of laudatory non-concurrence.

If one asked what motivated the whole Formalist-Structuralist enterprise, one of the answers (not the only one) would have to be that the wish for something like a science of literature is inveterate. 'In order to become, finally, a science, literary history must lay claim to reliability', said Tynjanov (quoted here) in 1927. Fifty years later his successors are still dreaming of a future in which they will have at their disposal a fully developed scientific method, a usable suprasentential grammar for instance; the present

---

[7] *Comparative Criticism Yearbook*, ii (1980), 291.

book[8] also dreams such dreams, taking the view that there are no essential differences between the requirements of research in *science de la littérature* and in the physical sciences, or none that will not yield to a version of Popper's falsification procedures. It is not easy to feel confident about these aspirations. 'Any theory of literature should develop methods to guarantee that the observations and conclusions of the scholar are not obstructed by his personal preferences and values. The very first step in that direction depends on the will to avoid such interference by subjective conditions'. To abolish *interest*, to root out *prejudice*: these are noble aims, but they will not be achieved. Still, there are some gains by the way:

> as no chemic yet the elixir got,
> But glorifies his pregnant pot,
> If by the way to him befall
> Some odoriferous thing, or medicinal. . . .

Kermode does not argue *why* these are noble aims. For me they are not noble at all. His authors' glide from 'preferences' to 'values' is indifferent to truth and to language, and the easy recourse to the word 'subjective', and then to 'prejudice', to which 'values' become assimilated, is implacably hostile to literature. For the assumption that 'personal values' constitute an 'interference', like the longing for a 'guarantee' that all such interferences would be avoided, entails the extirpation not merely of prejudice but of judgement and therefore of literature. It is the peril of literature, but also its glory, that values, convictions, beliefs and profound enduring agreements constitute not only its nature but its medium, language; such is one reason, admittedly, why literature and language are not enough in this life. Far from its being noble to seek to transform the study of literature into 'a science', it is the clerk's highest treason.

. . . these are noble aims, but they will not be achieved. Still, there are some gains by the way:

> as no chemic yet the elixir got,
> But glorifies his pregnant pot,
> If by the way to him befall
> Some odoriferous thing, or medicinal. . . .

Now what are we to feel (not just think) about these lines of Donne? Do they help us to discern, not only what we think but also what we feel, about these matters of both personal and professional

---

[8] Fokkema and Kunne-Ibsch, *Theories of Literature in the Twentieth Century.*

moment? Kermode does not give us the complete first line ('And as no chemic yet the elixir got,' instead of 'as no chemic . . .'), and this for the good reason that Donne's 'And' would invite the previous line. But is it so easy to issue no invitation to the previous line? 'Oh, 'tis imposture all: / And as no chemic yet the elixir got. . . .' Is the reader being tipped a wink ('Oh, 'tis imposture all')? There is no way of knowing, and no way of not wondering. In the very passage in which inappropriate aspirations are prized in the study of literature, an appropriate responsibility is slighted. The quotation from Donne muddies the element, and makes not clearer but obscurer the discernment of exactly what, and how much, is felt. The particular irony is of winks tipped and untipped, but the obstruction of discernment—in this important question of the understanding of feeling—is characteristic of the advocacy of literary theory. The arch charms of Stanley Fish and Geoffrey Hartman are different in timbre but are likewise concerned at once to ease and to obstruct: to ease acquiescence of sentiment and to obstruct discernment of feeling.

The understanding of feeling here has its relation to the understanding of conviction and commitment, and to the continual doubt as to exactly what credit or credence the advocates of theory really place, and invite us to place, either in theory in general or in any one theory in particular. As I heard one of those powerful people say, powerful and (he was insisting) committed, 'I'm a post-structuralist, I guess.' It has been said of D. H. Lawrence's religion that it is all going to church and never getting there; it may be said of the theory revolution that it is all marching to the barricades and never getting there. Here I stand, I can no other, I guess. The thin cry, 'I'm not saying that I agree with it . . .' rises so often that I for one value more than ever those critics who urge writings, whether primary or secondary, upon us because they *do* believe in them—critics like Leavis, Empson, Winters, Trilling, or—from an adjacent discipline— Christopher Hill.

The diffused complaint that theory is not taken seriously is attuned to the largest claim of theory, one which is essentially a claim *to* and not a claim *that*: specifically, a claim to the utmost attention. Insofar as the large claim is made accessible to specific dissent, it turns upon indispensability. The question becomes not legitimate self-defence, whether theorists may do as they choose, but the claim enshrined in 'indispensable' that everybody must do as theorists choose; that is, engage with and in theory. And 'must' is then polemically compounded of two very different things, the one a bolthole when there is trouble for the other: 'must' as 'are inevitably involved in theorizing whether or not they know it and admit it,' and 'must' as 'really ought to face up to their professional obligations'. In his advocacy of theory, Christopher Norris says of William Ray's book *Literary Meaning: From Phenomenology to Deconstruction* that much of its 'great virtue' is its 'refusing to let go of the idea that theory—intelligent theory, if you like—is indispensably a part of the reader's role'. ' "Intelligent theory", if you like': well, even I prefer it, but yet may not like the move that suddenly calls it up. Still, the claim itself is clear: theory is indispensably a part of the reader's role. Not desirable, not even very desirable, but indispensable. But the longing for something indispensable, for a *sine qua non*, is part of the long history of being misguided not only about literary studies but about literature itself. Theory as 'indispensably a part of the reader's role': but *indispensable* when used like this is a blank cheque (like the undiscriminated invoking of 'relevance'). Indispensable in what way to the reader's role exactly? If in every way, the assertion is preposterous; if not in every way, then how? Later in Norris's essay the claim looks as if it is being made more specific, when Norris concurs with J. M. Bernstein's *The Philosophy of the Novel*: 'Theory is indispensably the precondition of enlightened modern thinking, strive as it may to recapture the innocence of communal narrative forms.' But could there not be such a thing as unenlightened or non-enlightened modern thinking? Or does self-appointed enlightenment now enjoy a monopoly of thinking? (The theorist's attack on social complacency is itself then breathtakingly complacent.)

Much of the covert action within such a claim is effected, as so often, by recourse to the myth of the Fall: 'to recapture the innocence of communal narrative forms'; or again, 'post-structuralism has altered our habits of thought beyond hope of a return to the innocence of unreflective origins.' With the same appeal to the same myth, Kermode could say in 1970: 'I had been writing criticism for years without bothering too much about how I did it, but I now find that I am increasingly absorbed with theoretical issues, and foresee no possible reversion to a state of innocence.'[9] In 1984 S. S. Prawer looked down: 'though she once mentions Propp . . . Ms.

---

[9] *New American Review*, ix (1970), 82.

Shaw situates her criticism in a garden of pre-structuralist and pre-deconstructionist innocence.'[10]

Now reports of the innocence of critics prior to the 'revolution', critics such as Coleridge or Eliot or Empson or Trilling, have been much exaggerated, like reports of the death of the author or of God. But the more immediate matter is this indispensable invoking of the Fall. It is manifestly *the* myth or metaphor with which to seek to rebuke the gullibility of any attempt to put the clock back (a metaphor which is itself often gullibly used, since it is not true that you can't put the clock back, and we regularly and rationally do it for travel or for daylight saving). But even if we were to accept the loaded metaphor of the Fall, is it loaded exactly as 'enlightened modern thinking' would wish? For there is something itself 'unreflective', and 'naive', and insufficiently de-constructive about this marked refusal then to interrogate the Fall. For the Fall is not the story of pure gains, but of great gains and great losses. Even by the most hopeful interpretation of the *felix culpa*, fallen man does not enjoy all conceivable felicity. To take seriously the invoking of the Fall (which means not permitting its merely threatening use) is at once to be moved to consider the very matter which the advocates of theory least wish to be raised: that of the losses inseparable from ours being the age, not of (in Prawer's words) 'a garden of pre-structuralist and pre-deconstructionist innocence', but of structuralist and deconstructionist—what? nocence? The loss of innocence must entail not only experience but also nocence, harmfulness. If Prawer and the others wish to invoke Eden's innocence, let them meet their self-chosen obligation to think about their metaphor, and not only to concede but to consider what has been lost and the new harm done. Milton says of the snake, still innocent, 'Nor nocent yet. . . .'

The advocates of theory often declare that we are all theorists whether we realize it and acknowledge it or not. This stratagem has its risks, notably that of eviscerating not just your opponent's argument but the entire argument itself. Of course the declaration can be made invulnerable, by the simple expedient of so defining theory. Coleridge said, 'To think at all is to theorize.'[11] But the trouble with

[10] *TLS*, 17 August 1984.

[11] *The Friend*, Section the First, Essay iv; ed. Barbara E. Rooke (1975), i 189. I owe this to Luther Tyler's witty review of Jerome Christensen; *South Carolina Review*, xvi (1983), 126.

Coleridge's provocation is that there is then, as so often, a need for another word, to make the still-necessary distinction between what used to be called theory and other kinds of thinking. Gerald Graff concedes too much when he says *theory* 'in the sense of a descriptive analysis of the nature of literature', as if any degree of such descriptive analysis constituted theory.

It is a great convenience to maintain or pretend that there is no distinction between thinking at all and theorizing, but it does itself incur its inconvenience. In *Criticism in the Wilderness* Geoffrey Hartman says: 'Leavis's refusal to acknowledge that he was a theoretician *malgré lui* showed how strongly fixed the aversion to theorizing had become'; 'There were English stirrings of theory, nevertheless: in Richards's work especially, even if "principles" sounded more modest and practicable than laws, methods, etc.'[12] But this is the convenience of misrepresentation. Hartman gives no evidence at all that Leavis was refusing to acknowledge something. This is insulting not only to Leavis but also to René Wellek, since the famous exchange in *Scrutiny* between Leavis and Wellek, on the value or indispensability of philosophy and theory in the study of literature, was believed by both Leavis and Wellek to be a substantive disagreement. The adjudication of the dispute in Wellek's favour (as criticism in England had mostly not adjudicated it) would be one thing; but the unargued dissolving of the dispute into a spectral combat between a theoretician and a theoretician *malgré lui* is an act of condescension. Since Hartman refuses to acknowledge that there are such things as principles and that they differ from theory (and not only from 'laws, methods, etc.'), he feels himself under no obligation even to imagine what might count as evidence for his assertion against Leavis. The tactic, throughout Hartman's book, is to divide all criticism into two camps: theory, and practical criticism. If it is acknowledged, just for once, that someone used the word 'principles', he is merely being English and sly, and availing himself of the fact that the word 'principles' sounds modest and practicable. But the strength, say, of William Empson's criticism is always its commitment to principles and not to theory, and this strength is clear in one of his apophthegms, itself a principle about principles: 'Life involves maintaining oneself between contradictions which can't be

[12] (1980), p. 7. Some paragraphs in what follows derive from an article of mine in the *London Review of Books*, 16 April–6 May 1981.

solved by analysis' (Note to 'Bacchus'). It is in philosophy that
something is *stigmatized* as a paradox.

Yet the alternative exists, and a dedication not to literary theory
but to literary principles is neither a self-deception (Hartman's Leavis)
nor a subterfuge (Hartman's young Richards) but a grounded choice.
Theory, if the word is to be required to continue to mean—as it
should—something both more and less than thinking, is characterized by its degree of elaboration, concatenation, completeness, abstraction, self-consciousness, explicitness, regression, recession and
technicality. None of these is unique to theory, and since matters
of degree are involved, there will always be disputed instances. But
to deny that theory is characterized by something—by some such
things—is simply not to win but to nullify the argument. The word
'theory' points towards philosophy, which is why Hartman can speak
repeatedly of 'theoretical or philosophical criticism', and of the
'philosophy or theory'. It would be as debilitating to claim that all
men who think are philosophers as it would be to claim that there
is on every occasion a clear-cut distinction of kind. T. S. Eliot, who
could have held down a job in the philosophy department of Harvard
but fortunately found even better things to do, at once made a
concession to theory and was more or less sceptical of it: 'While we
may of course, and must in fact, make theories more or less, explain
our feelings to ourselves and others: still our theories are, like Mr.
Santayana's "consciousness," only a phosphorescence.' One distinction for Eliot turned on the difference between evading and avoid-
ing: 'To communicate impressions is difficult; to communicate a
co-ordinated system of impressions is more difficult; to theorize demands vast ingenuity, and to avoid theorizing requires vast honesty.'[13] The work of Fish and Hartman demands vast ingenuity, and
they impressively meet this demand; but ingenuity is not only not
all, it is not—as the relative lightness of the word itself allows—one
of the very highest values either in literature or in the study of
literature.

In his vast honesty, Dr Johnson stands as the greatest of English
critics, and his greatness is not distinct from his sustained and rational
opposition to philosophy and to theory. 'The task of criticism' was,
for Johnson, to 'establish principles' (*Rambler*, No. 92), and he everywhere made clear that his refusal to elaborate and concatenate the

---

[13] *The Athenaeum*, 27 June 1919.

needed concepts beyond a certain point (a point reached early) was not a refusal to continue to think, but a decision to think thereafter about the application of the principles and not to elaborate principle into theory.

A fully-fledged theory, taking wing, is a philosophy; a fully compacted principle is rooted as a proverb. Theory is necessarily, and for its purposes honourably, hostile to contradictions; proverbs admit contradictions, and leave us to think not about that but about applicability; we are to decide which of two contradictory truths ('Look before you leap' / 'He who hesitates is lost,' or 'Absence makes the heart grow fonder' / 'Out of sight, out of mind') applies in any given situation. Eliot's use of those last words—'intelligence, of which an important function is the discernment of exactly what, and how much, we feel in any given situation'—points to his here invoking not theory but a principle; for theory, by reason of its proper, though then paradoxically limited, ambitions, seeks exactly to generalize and not to be circumscribed by 'any given situation'. One cannot but be in two minds about Blake's notorious generalization that 'to generalize is to be an idiot', but to generalize is to enter into a new circumscription. Principles, like proverbs, suppose that difficulties are as much worth our attention as are problems; theory, like philosophy, is committed to pressing that once you have said (as Raymond Williams said about these issues) 'What you must do is to admit that a problem exists,' you have an obligation to attend to the problem. But what is the nature of the obligation, especially in relation to other obligations? Assuredly there are theoretical, philosophical, problems about literature; about what are there not? Aggressive advocates of theory are like mountaineering missionary extremists who would claim, not just that they may climb Everest because it is there, or even that they must climb it because it is there, but that we must all climb Everest because it is there.

The antagonism of theory to principles turns on the value and priority of a high degree of elaborated and regressive concatenation. But theorists themselves necessarily do not *complete* elaboration or regression; they too, quite properly except for their often averting their eyes from it, arbitrate a point 'thus far and no further'. For once you insist on regressive or recessive elaborations, not one of your own terms is stable. The death of D. H. Lawrence in 1930 moved E. M. Forster 'to say straight out that he was the greatest imaginative novelist of our generation'. Whereupon T. S. Eliot's recessive philosophical proclivities, which he usually resisted when writing literature or about literature, notoriously encouraged him to speak in the wrong regressive way: 'The virtue of speaking out is somewhat diminished if what one speaks is not sense. And unless we know exactly what Mr. Forster means by *greatest, imaginative* and *novelist,* I submit that this judgement is meaningless.' But the philosophical incitement was disabling, not enabling, and Forster did well to resist it and to turn the tables on it: 'Mr. T. S. Eliot duly entangles me in his web. He asks what exactly I mean by "greatest," "imaginative" and "novelist", and I cannot say. Worse still, I cannot even say what "exactly" means—only that there are occasions when I would rather feel like a fly than a spider, and that the death of D. H. Lawrence is one of these.'[14] For the resistance to the philosophical web was no less dextrous than powerful. Eliot's 'exactly' is just as open to retort as Forster's 'greatest'. Those who stall or forestall the reading of a poem by first asking combatively what it is to *read* can themselves be asked the prior question of what it is to *to*. The existence of a problem need entail no obligation to grapple with it. Every page of literary theory, as of every other discourse, is for instance involved with the question of whether there is freedom of the will, a question that is tacitly set aside.

Hartman says that 'the most peculiar feature of philosophical criticism is indeed the difficult alliance in it between speculation and close reading'.[15] But why is not other literary criticism, non-philosophical criticism, equally characterized by the 'difficult alliance in it between speculation and close reading'? The implication that philosophical criticism has a monopoly of speculation or of the difficult alliance will not bear either speculation or close reading. For such non-philosophical critics as Donald Davie are engaged in speculation and in close reading and in the difficult alliance of the two. For me, the most peculiar feature of Hartman's philosophical criticism is its claiming that the difficult alliance between speculation and close reading is a peculiar feature of philosophical criticism. It is a short step from the risky handy proposition that to think at all is to theorize, to the oppositely risky handy one that only theorists think at all. At this point, admittedly, my resistance to such claims for theory moves into resentment. Hartman again: 'The resistance

---

[14] *Nation and Athenaeum,* 29 March, 5 April, and 12 April 1930.
[15] *Criticism in the Wilderness,* p. 174.

to theory in Anglo-American criticism goes together with a resistance to imported ideas, from non-English countries or from other fields of inquiry, the social sciences, in particular.'[16] But such pre-revolutionary and anti-revolutionary critics, resistant to theory, as Eliot, Trilling, Kenner, and Davie can responsibly be accused of resistance neither to imported ideas from non-English countries nor to imported ideas from other fields of enquiry. Their criticism repeatedly has recourse to both.

Principles permit of counter-principles, as proverbs do. A theory, because its reputability is constituted of elaborated concatenation, cannot accommodate a counter-theory. It claims a much higher degree of comprehensiveness and of sustained cogency ('philosophy or theory'), and it therefore asks to be taken as a whole. There would be something odd about *not* believing both proverb-principles 'Look before you leap' and 'He who hesitates is lost.' Granted, both theories and principles are subscribed to, but the cost of the subscription to a theory is very high, and almost all such subscriptions lapse.

Instances of a principle will matter because of the instances which the principles would themselves illuminate and be illuminated by. Eliot makes a point of principle when he says of wit that 'it involves, probably, a recognition, implicit in the expression of every experience, of other kinds of experience that are possible' ('Andrew Marvell'). This is profound in its economical exactitude, and in the application which Eliot makes of it to metaphysical poetry, and in the living possibilities of further imaginative application which it fecundates. No doubt a theory could be elaborated to accommodate Eliot's principle here; but why exactly should it be? Or why should mustering such a theoretical elaboration have top or high priority? To do this is to not do that. The claims of the applied and experiential are not *prima facie* less worthy than the claims of the generalized and the ideate.

The question is not whether, say, a Wayne C. Booth should be discouraged from theoretical elaborations of irony, but whether William Empson should be stigmatized as innocent, naïve, unreflective, and so on, when he does not elaborate such flexibly suggestive formulations of principle as his saying that 'An irony has no point unless it is true, in some degree, in both senses; for it is

[16] p. 297.

imagined as part of an argument; what is said is made absurd, but
it is what the opponent might say.'[17] I find this a more persuasive
and a more clarificatory way of conceiving of irony—and especially
of distinguishing it from its malignant sibling, sarcasm—than is
available to me in the more theoretically comprehensive accounts
of the matter. It is Empson's principle of irony ('true, in some degree,
in both senses') which helps me to understand the force, for instance, of D. J. Enright's poem 'Streets':

STREETS

The poem was entitled 'The Streets of Hanoi,'
It told of falling bombs and death and destruction
And misery and pain and wastage.
The poem was set to music, which told of death
And destruction and misery and pain and wastage

A hall was found to play it in, a singer to sing it,
An orchestra to accompany the singer, and a printer
To print the programme . . . Whereupon it was felt
(Things being what they happened to be) that
The song had better be called 'The Streets of Saigon.'

It was well sung, well played, and well received.

Truly poetry is international, just like music,
And falling bombs and death and destruction
And misery and pain and wastage,

Truly we only need one poet in the world
Since local references can be inserted by editors,
Theatre managers or clerks in the Culture Ministries.[18]

Indignation is always tempted by sarcasm, but Enright achieves
the more magnanimous (and therefore *more* telling) thing, irony. For
the axis upon which this fine political poem turns, the line which
it is itself obliged to live up to, is one which would be misheard if
it were heard as sarcasm: 'Truly poetry is international, just like
music.' 'True, in some degree, in both senses': truly (and not just
with sorrowful headshaking at the preposterousness of such a thought)
poetry *is* international, but not in the easy empty way which would
suffocate political conscience—such as is true here and now—under
the pseudo-transcendental verities (for Hanoi, read Saigon). Enright's

---

[17] *Some Versions of Pastoral* (1935), p. 56.
[18] *New York Review of Books*, 13 August 1970.

poem validates Empson's principle, and *vice versa*; the principle itself resists ease though it facilitates both understanding and application. Empson himself pointed out that Pope's great couplet 'Now Lapdogs give themselves the rowzing Shake, / And Sleepless Lovers, just at Twelve, awake,' gains its power (as irony, *not* sarcasm, which is inferior in its superiority) from the fact that though the couplet is not credulous about whether 'Sleepless' lovers are really to be believed, it is true to some degree in both senses: for to have been sleepless all night, tossing and turning, is often to fall into a drugged sleep at dawn from which you may wake only at noon. The reader who is awake to Pope's width of mind, at once magnanimous and shrewd, will value Empson's principle and Empson's instance, and will not be obliged to wish that Empson, instead of doing this, had done the other thing, of constituting a theory of the matter. I say 'instead' because it is one ground, for resistance to theory's insistences, that the advocates of theory sound as if no sacrifices ever had to be made, as if all of us could and should do all. Had we but world enough and time. . . . Teachers have particular responsibility to consider 'world enough and time', because the time that they most spend is not their own.

Hopkins, who was a great critic, pre-eminently in his letters, set down an unforgettable and endlessly applicable principle in his unfolding of Tennyson and 'Parnassian'. Hopkins's letter to A. W. M. Baillie moves with beautiful pertinence:

Sept. 10, 1864.

Dear Baillie,

Your letter has been sent to me from Hampstead. It has just come, and I do a rare thing with me, begin at once on an answer. I have just finished *The Philippics* of Cicero and an hour remains before bedtime; no one except Wharton would begin a new book at that time of night, so I was reading *Henry IV*, when your letter was brought in—a great enjoyment.

The letter-writer on principle does not make his letter only an *answer*; it is a work embodying perhaps answers to questions put by his correspondent but that is not its main motive. Therefore it is as a rule not well to write with a received letter fresh on you. I suppose the right way is to let it sink into you, and reply after a day or two. I do not know why I have said all this.

Do you know, a horrible thing has happened to me. I have begun to *doubt* Tennyson. (Baillejus ap. Hopk.) It is a great *argumentum*, a great clue, that our minds jump together even if it be a leap into the dark. I cannot tell you how amused and I must say pleased and comforted by this coincidence I am.[19]

From reading Cicero and *Henry IV*, to reading a letter, to thinking about the principles of writing a letter ('The letter-writer on principle does not make his letter only an *answer*'), to thinking about those principles of poetry and of 'poetical criticism' which are to be the letter's enterprise: the modulation and momentum are superb, and so is Hopkins's finding appropriate amusement, pleasure, and comfort in his being so in sympathy with Baillie about this new qualifying of his sympathy with Tennyson.

Hopkins's letter, famous and inexhaustible, sets out the principles which distinguish 'the language of inspiration' from 'Parnassian', which 'can only be spoken by poets, but is not in the highest sense poetry'. The movement of Hopkins's mind is as naturally a move from a principle to an instance as then from instance back to principle—but never into theory.

Great men, poets I mean, have each their own dialect as it were of Parnassian, formed generally as they go on writing, and at last,—this is the point to be marked,—they can see things in this Parnassian way and describe them in this Parnassian tongue, without further effort of inspiration. In a poet's particular kind of Parnassian lies most of his style, of his manner, of his mannerism if you like. But I must not go farther without giving you instances of Parnassian. I shall take one from Tennyson, and from *Enoch Arden*,[20] from a passage much quoted already and which will be no doubt often quoted, the description of Enoch's tropical island.

> The mountain wooded to the peak, the lawns
> And winding glades high up like ways to Heaven,
> The slender coco's drooping crown of plumes,
> The lightning flash of insect and of bird,
> The lustre of the long convolvuluses
> That coil'd around the stately stems, and ran
> Ev'n to the limit of the land, the glows
> And glories of the broad belt of the world,
> All these he saw.

Now it is a mark of Parnassian that one could conceive oneself writing it if one were the poet. Do not say that *if* you were Shakespeare you can

---

[19] *Further Letters of G. M. Hopkins*, ed. C. C. Abbott (1938), 1956 edn, pp. 215–17.

[20] Published in the previous month, August 1864.

imagine yourself writing Hamlet, because that is just what I think you can*not* conceive.

What makes this statement of principle, with its persuasive instance, so thrilling is its own inspiration, especially in that last leap.

Now it is a mark of Parnassian that one could conceive oneself writing it if one were the poet. Do not say that *if* you were Shakespeare you can imagine yourself writing Hamlet, because that is just what I think you can*not* conceive.

For it is a mark of Hopkins's genius that though I could, I suppose, conceive of myself coming up with some distinction between the inspired and the not inspired, I cannot conceive of myself creating the penetrating terms of this principle itself: 'Now it is a mark of Parnassian that one could conceive oneself writing it if one were the poet.' More, Hopkins's critical feat at once goes beyond critical Parnassianism; do not say that *if* you were Hopkins you can imagine yourself writing these sentences, because that is just what I think you can*not* conceive. Inspiration there is perfectly at one with courtesy, as it was in the opening of this immediately-answering letter, when Hopkins, 'on principle', goes into a letter's needing to be more than an answer; the courtesy within the astonishing, and immediately convincing, appeal to Shakespeare and *Hamlet* is manifest in the sequence, 'because that is just what I think you can*not* conceive'. Not 'just what you can*not* conceive', but 'just what I think you can*not* conceive'. This is the perfection of two kinds of consideration, the co-operation of a considered principle with a considerate tact. Principle and tact are as intimately co-operative in criticism as are comparison and analysis; and it can be a grounded objection to theory that its being reasoned is on occasion no compensation for its being tactless.

Richard Ohmann, with characteristic candour, said at the Center for Literary Studies at Northeastern University: 'I am suggesting that maybe we could profitably, we the people who talk about this kind of thing at all, spend our time better by concentrating on the concept of literature, rather than on literature.' My priorities are obviously the opposite; I cannot conceive of spending my time better than on literature, and, in particular, particular works. If, say, a great song of Bob Dylan's is not literature, that is only because its medium is not words alone. I take 'One Too Many Mornings' to be a work of art, the hearing and pondering of which should be welcome.

ONE TOO MANY MORNINGS

Down the street the dogs are barkin'
And the day is a-gettin' dark
As the night comes in a-fallin'
The dogs'll lose their bark
An' the silent night will shatter
From the sounds inside my mind
For I'm one too many mornings
And a thousand miles behind.

From the crossroads of my doorstep
My eyes they start to fade
As I turn my head back to the room
Where my love and I have laid
An' I gaze back to the street
The sidewalk and the sign
And I'm one too many mornings
An' a thousand miles behind.

It's a restless hungry feeling
That don't mean no one no good
When ev'rything I'm a-sayin'
You can say it just as good
You're right from your side
I'm right from mine
We're both just one too many mornings
An' a thousand miles behind.

Had I but world enough and time, I should wish to bring out that principles, unlike theories, are keen to engage in discriminating, and to apply Hopkins's principle, with patience, so as to understand just what goes wrong and why, throughout the middle stanza of this lovely song. 'From the crossroads of my doorstep / My eyes they start to fade. . . .' This, unlike the first and last stanzas which are inspired, is Parnassian, and—like most Parnassian—it is, in its complaisance, vulnerable to humour, such a worse than unwanted suggestion as 'From the crossroads of my doorstep / My eyes they start to cross.' I can conceive myself writing 'the crossroads of my doorstep' if I were Dylan—and I do not say to myself that if I were Dylan I can imagine myself writing the inspired no-rhyme of 'good' and 'good' in the song's last stanza, at once the fullest and most

conclusive rhyme of all (the word itself repeated) and the emptiest
and least of rhymes at just the point where the previous stanzas
have fully clinched their rhymes:

> It's a restless hungry feeling
> That don't mean no one no good
> When ev'rything I'm a-sayin'
> You can say it just as good . . .

This, in its pained numbness, is something quite other than 'From
the crossroads of my doorstep', which I can conceive myself writing
if I were the artist who wrote, elsewhere, 'through the smoke rings
of my mind'. Do not say that *if* you were Shakespeare you can
imagine yourself writing *Hamlet*; come to that, do not say that *if* you
were Dylan you can imagine yourself writing 'Ophelia, she's 'neath
the window, / For her I feel so afraid. . . .' The point is not that
Hopkins's principle is conclusive, as theory not only may but in
some respects must seek to be, but that such a principle is inaugurative,
and when invoked leaves much still to say.

The claim for principles, as against theory, involves both senses
of the word *application*. Another matter, equally intimate with teaching, is that of discontinuity and continuity, since the intense
specialization that is consummated theory is necessarily, and not
idly, the acceptance of a series of substantial discontinuities where
principles seek to maintain or effect continuities. For the thoroughly
systematic nature of theory induces that dislocation of which
Kierkegaard said: 'In relation to their systems most systematizers
are like a man who builds an enormous castle and lives in a shack
close by; they do not live in their own enormous systematic buildings.' (The authors of books which argue that books are written by
their readers still expect to draw royalties; and others who disclaim
the invoking of intentions claim that their intentions have been misrepresented.) System and theory are not that by which men live or
even really try to live; sometimes this makes for the comedy of
hypocrisy, and always it makes against that continuity which Eliot
incarnated in the word 'principles': 'A literary review should maintain the application, in literature, of principles which have their
consequences also in politics and in private conduct.'

Theory, in its professionalized and systematic intellectuality, widens
the gap between critics and non-professional readers; between critics and writers; between critics and scholars; and—smaller of scale

but professionally germane—between graduates and undergraduates. Hartman, for whom the *only* alternative to theory is 'practical
criticism', says roundly that 'practical criticism is more of a pedagogical and propaedeutic than mature activity' (the word 'propaedeutic' itself being intended to cow the young and immature);
he speaks then of 'the mind of the novice', and of 'the danger in
this undergraduate or undeveloped form of practical criticism'.[21] I
share none of the beliefs which underlie such a way of speaking,
such an estimate of practical criticism in any of its forms, or of
undergraduates, or of the alternatives as Hartman conceives them.
But I am sure that Hartman is right to depict theory, or advanced
thought as they like to think it, as intrinsically inimical to undergraduate teaching.

But when time is almost up, it is time to stress once more that
theory and teaching do not have all the time in the world. Several
great critics have been educators, but only one great critic devoted
his professional lifetime to the profound inspection of education. He
is regularly disparaged these days as having both practised and incited
a resistance to theory, but the resistance itself is related in Matthew
Arnold to a deep understanding of one crucial principle in teaching
and especially in the teaching of literature. Presenting a selection
from the great criticism of his great predecessor Johnson, *The Lives
of the Poets*, Matthew Arnold deplored 'the common notion' that
education is advanced 'by for ever adding fresh matters of instruction'. Arnold instead offered at the start of his preface the essential
educative principle of the limits within which education, like life
itself, needs to acknowledge that it lives:

Life is short, and our faculties of attention and of recollection are limited;
in education we proceed as if our life were endless, and our powers of
attention and recollection inexhaustible. We have not time or strength to
deal with half of the matters which are thrown upon our minds, they prove
a useless load to us. When some one talked to Themistocles of an art of
memory, he answered: 'Teach me rather to forget!'

[21] *Criticism in the Wilderness*, pp. 296, 298.

CRITICISM AT THE PRESENT TIME: TWO NOTES

1. WHAT IS AT STAKE IN THE 'BATTLE OF THE BOOKS'?

A quarter of an hour, on matters of such moment and such complexity, is not long enough to substantiate an argument but it should permit of relating some convictions. The most that such a relating can hope for is that it manifest a readiness for argument unpursued. But the polemics of travesty may be avoided by proposing not *the* but *an* answer to the question 'What is at stake in the battle of the books?' My wish is to identify a prime consideration insufficiently admitted.

What follows is in three parts. First, one person's sense of what is usually and rightly held to be, not at stake exactly, but at issue. Second, my expressing an objection to what is probably the best recent commentary on all this, an objection to the rhetoric in which the argument has been conducted. And third, my questioning not of the rhetoric but of the terms of the argument, to make clear a fundamental reservation about any such solely professional conduct of the debate.

I

But first an acknowledgement of one strong and even perhaps agreed answer to the question of what is at issue. This, which is the link between my three points, is what it has always been: the limited possibility of disinterestedness. 'Critics,' wrote our greatest critic, 'like all the rest of mankind, are very frequently misled by interest.' To proceed as if there were every possibility of disinterestedness— despite what power is and always has been—would be to be a sentimental gull. To proceed as if there were no possibility of disinterestedness would be to be a cynical dog. In this, as in so much else, the words of William Empson might carry our conviction: Life involves maintaining oneself between contradictions that cannot be solved by analysis.

The particular contradictions have long been known. On the one hand, Dr Johnson argues cogently in defence of 'the privilege of established fame and prescriptive veneration'; but on the other hand, Johnson's other hand, there is his acknowledgement that 'approbation, though long continued, may yet be only the approbation of prejudice or fashion'. No one is ever going to be absolved from the necessity of distinguishing responsibly between that which is established because it has been found true and that which is found true because it has become established. Injustices have—cannot but have—occluded or excluded certain writers (though not only for reasons of colour, gender, or class), but it is true too that there are writers, past and present, who are not 'marginalized' but marginal.

For to this ancient siege of contraries there has been added in our day an exacerbated awareness that time, history, and institutions, being powers, have always been open to the abuses of power, and that it will forever suit people of every stripe to claim for what are social arrangements the status of the nature-given or the God-given—or, on the other foot, the guru-given:

> Nature and nature's laws lay hid in night,
> God said 'Let Foucault be,' and all was light.
>
> It could not be—the Devil bawling 'Ho,
> Let Lacan be,' restored the status quo.

So 'relativism' rears its head, at once hydra and chimera. Criticism feels impelled to become meta-criticism, and duly corrugates itself, very like those nineteenth-century agonizers confronting the dreadful possibility that, if God is dead, all is permitted.

'Question authority,' says the health-food T-shirt, making an exception of its own authority. 'She doubts everything,' says Barthes of Kristeva, doubting everything except the desirability of doubting everything. Given the strains, it is not surprising that so much recent criticism has substituted for the stringency of scepticism the complacency of Pyrrhonism.

There is a crucial variant (I have discussed it in *T. S. Eliot and Prejudice*) in the wording of the prefatory note to Mary Douglas's *Rules and Meanings*:

Each person confronted with a system of ends and means (not necessarily a tidy and coherent system) seems to face the order of nature, objective and independent of human wishes. But the moral order and the knowledge which sustains it are created by social conventions. If their man-made origins were not hidden, they would be stripped of some of their authority.

The last two sentences found themselves quoted on the book's jacket—with one small alteration for drama and sales. 'If their man-made origins were not hidden, they would be stripped of much of their authority.' But if 'some' can be silently upped to 'much', why cannot 'much' be upped to 'all'? What is at stake is both the judgement of authority and the authority of judgement, and to say—*tout court*—that knowledge is created by social conventions is to leave no safeguard against the further escalation, after 'some' becomes 'much', to this: If their man-made origins were not hidden, they would be stripped of all of their authority.

II

I now take as an authority on these matters not a straw man but a respected figure, from a respected university, writing recently in a respected journal: John Guillory, and his 1987 essay in *ELH* (*English Literary History*) on 'Canonical and Non-Canonical: A Critique of the Current Debate'. If Guillory is not *representative* exactly, that is mostly because he has taken unusual trouble in the prosecution of these arguments. He is persuasive in his contention that any discussion of 'the canon' has to be placed within the largest context, 'nothing less than the systematic regulation of reading and writing', and that therefore literacy itself must figure saliently. But I must put an objection to his highly professional essay, to suggest why it and its siblings should be resisted. In a word, its words—and I don't mean jargon but rhetoric, a rhetoric both entirely representative of the professionalized 'current debate' and manifesting an insufficient effort at disinterestedness.

For there is a betraying discrepancy between the essay's impetus and its rhetoric. Its impetus, explicitly and not unexpectedly, is to repudiate anybody who might find things, in its indispensable word, 'unproblematic'; and from its first paragraph on, it endorses the obligatory word 'demystifying' and deplores anything 'mystified'. But the trouble is that this bracing programme is everywhere couched in a rhetoric of the massively unproblematic.

Not since Dr F. R. Leavis (no talk of 'problematics' from him) tuned his proems ('It takes no unusual sensitivity to see that . . .', 'It would be of no use to try to argue with anyone who contended that . . .')—not since Leavis has a reader been pressed by so ubiquitously indubitable a rhetoric, about as problematic (except morally) as *peine forte et dure*. 'It would be pointless to . . .'; 'all too easy to demonstrate . . .' (and 'only too easy to demonstrate'); 'It is certainly the case that . . .'; 'It is unquestionably the case that . . .'; 'this is certainly the case . . .'; 'It would not be difficult to prove that this practice of writing is founded on nothing but . . .': these are not from several books by Leavis but from the one essay by Guillory. 'Surely', 'doubtless', 'no doubt', 'undoubtedly', 'must certainly', 'quite evident' . . . 'In fact' must make for good old unproblematics, I'd have thought, and Guillory deploys it all the time (and compounds it: 'In fact, as is well known . . .'; 'the very fact that . . .'; 'This fact is made quite obvious . . .'; 'This fact is quite apparent . . .'). And so he does (of course) with 'of course', and indeed with 'indeed'. Whenever the ranks of his argument are about to waver, he rallies them with 'only' (not in this usage a word compatible with authentic problematics): 'can only be seen through . . .'; 'can only be conceived as . . .'; 'can only be posed when . . .'; 'can only be recovered in relation to . . .'; 'Only as such can . . .'; 'One need only . . .'; 'Only in this way can one explain . . .'; 'One had only to place . . .'; 'can only be defined . . .'; 'It is only to remark the obvious to point out. . . .' And there is the related (and thrice occurring) 'nothing other than. . . .' All these, plus the old-fashioned browbeatings: 'it would not be inaccurate to say . . .'; 'It is important to remember'; 'It is worth emphasizing that. . . .' (That's for us to say, as I am often obliged to write in the margins of the young.) So that when in the penultimate sentence of Guillory's essay I twice read the acclamatory noun 'problematic', I ask myself whether, even apart from the dubiety of so prostrating oneself before the problematic, there *could* be an incitement to a critique of a genuine 'problematic' constituted of such a rhetoric.

Perhaps this would not much matter if the rhetoric were Guillory's own and only his (an *ad hominem* argument, then?); but no, this is the professionally widespread and collusive rhetoric of a hermeneutics of suspicion which never suspects itself of being open to contamination. What is proclaimed as 'the delegitimation of the canon' stands in need of a much greater vigilance about the illegitimacies of its own rhetoric. By their rhetoric shall ye know them. The famous composer refuses, for political reasons, the Legion of Honour. 'Ah, but all his music accepts it.' The authority of the canonical institution may be, as they say, 'refused'; ah, but all their rhetoric accepts it. Authoritarianism, shown the door, sidles back in through the window.

The enveloping pre-emption is sacrosanct, despite the argument's urgings that nothing be so.

For by now, such a word as 'demystification' has become no more exempt from mystificatory manipulation than anything else. So, for instance, Geoffrey Hartman has hearteningly turned to protect the two things closest to his conscience against the very possibility that they might valuably or honourably be demystified. In Wordsworth's great poetry there is 'something which cannot be demystified', a 'quality . . . which resists overconsciousness and demystification'. And in 'the memorial books of Polish Jewry' there is not historiography, the fictive, but history, the real. Such *de*-de-mystification is to be welcomed, and it will certainly be assisted, at the opposite extreme from Hartman's fastidiousness, by the vulgar success of this exploited and exploitative word, a vacant victory evident in the farcical inertia of phrasing with which *The New York Times* announced last month that the sex-shop at Stanford hopes 'to demystify condoms'.

III

'The defense of the non-canonical may justly take as its epigraph,' Guillory pre-emptively strikingly says, 'Walter Benjamin's remark that "there is no document of civilization which is not at the same time a document of barbarism." ' It would be one sign of disinterestedness if those quoting, yet once more, this remark of Benjamin's would be as attentive to the civilization half of it as to the barbarism half; but no, it is from this wing ideologically correct to invoke barbarism but not to invoke civilization. (Guillory, when he approaches 'the "ideals of Western civilization," ' feels obliged to add 'whatever that means'.)

Yet even more central professionally than the rhetoric of the critique is the matter of its terms. The profession of the pedagogue is an honourable one, but the honour of any profession consists in its not arrogating to itself more than a profession should claim. In being a profession, it inevitably suffers indurations and partialities. A profession ceases to be honourable when it makes too little effort to minimize such losses and, complementarily, when it fails to acknowledge them disinterestedly. Guillory's essay is entirely and explicitly bent upon the classroom, upon pedagogic practice, upon 'the whole enunciative apparatus of pedagogy'. Nothing intrinsically wrong with that, provided it is imaginatively granted that this is because of pedagogy's intrinsic interests. The word 'curriculum' is a faithful flat word: it declares an interest. But 'canon' does not. For 'canon' claims, with insinuating misrepresentation, the scriptures' especial authority (which yet did not claim a monopoly of worthy books), and moreover 'canon' at once makes a more than professional claim and yet is an obdurately professional word. Those outside the profession, with good cause too, do not conceive of books as divided into the 'canonical and non-canonical'; and the organic formation which books constitute would be described by them not as a canon but as a literature. See T. S. Eliot's consummate study, 'Was There a Scottish Literature?'

Guillory, like the profession generally, now makes much of, and italicizes, the word *exclusion*. If we in turn ask what or who gets excluded, 'marginalized', or 'disempowered' by the terms of the debate when it is conducted with such solely professional aims, with so narrowed a notion of the disinterested (for professions should acknowledge that they are interested parties), the answer is, first and not surprisingly, all reading other than that conducted under the auspices of pedagogy, and second and no more surprisingly, all *writing* other than that conducted under the auspices of pedagogy. The confidence that there is no reading outside the aegis of the university is misplaced, and it distorts the debate, as if no books were ever—whether justly or unjustly—alive in a literature unless they were part of a curriculum. But the marginalizing of creative writers (or, as they used better to be known, writers) to the point of their exclusion is an even more unworthy hubris of our profession.

Nowhere in such a 'critique of the current debate' is any attention paid to the creation or the creators of works of literature. We hear repeatedly and balefully of 'a hegemonic tradition', 'hegemonic values', 'a hegemonic bourgeoisie', 'hegemonic paradigms', and 'a hegemonic sociolect', but there could not be a more unremitting hegemony than that which is so unmisgivingly circumscribing what is called 'the production of texts' to something in which writers apparently play no part.

David Bromwich pounced recently on some betraying words in the 1989 ACLS manifesto *Speaking for the Humanities*: 'Professionalization makes thought possible. . . .' The previous sentence had urged that we 'assert the value not just of specialization but of professionalization'. But the value of the profession will be in direct proportion to its rising above *folie de grandeur*. The achievements of art put up some valuable resistance to the very words 'profession' and 'professional'; it is clearer, for instance, that Stephen King is a *professional* writer than that Samuel Beckett is. David Bromwich seems to me to despair too promptly, and even too lightheartedly, when he says that 'like any other faith, professionalism cannot be argued with'. I believe that all faiths can and should be argued with; the chances of persuading are not high, but nowhere else are they so either. Giving reasons for the faith that is in one: such was Hazlitt's unprofessionalized conviction.

No one is going to deny that a great many books live, come back to life, and are imaginatively attended to because of their presence in curricula. But the most important and enduring rediscovery or reinvention of a book or of a writer comes when a subsequent creator is inspired by such to an otherwise inexplicable newness of creative apprehension. John Skelton became again a living presence as a poet not because professors and professionals decided that he had been 'marginalized' but because Robert Graves and W. H. Auden showed, in very different ways, what possibilities of new life there were in the old dog yet. The poignant beauty of William Barnes would be unattended to were it not for more than the praises, the creations, of Hardy and Larkin, and Meredith's *Modern Love* if it were not for what Robert Lowell did with and for its mastery of marital misery in his sonnet sequence *The Dolphin*. Ivy Compton-Burnett essentially did more even for so acknowledged a writer as Jane Austen than even Mary Lascelles did.

Such new creation does not lend itself to an attempt such as Guillory's 'to theorize in a new way the question of the canon', but it raises a question of principle, and one which is professionally urgent: that an honourable profession be one which does not vaunt. The crucial constituting of what is tendentiously called the canon is effected not by academics and critics but by creative writers (the obscuring of the distinction having therefore been for some time a professional or trade-union necessity for professors), and the crux is the conviction that works of literature most live, not in the formation of the cunning canon or the candid curriculum, but in their fecundating of later works of literature.

But getting recognition for this truth will not be easy, especially at a time when the profession understandably closes ranks against its external enemies. Hubris harmonizes with whistling to keep our courage up. It is a pity that Harold Bloom, who genuinely loves literature, has countenanced for a serious book this professional aggrandizement: 'Self-styled the "Yiddisher Doctor Johnson," [Bloom's] productivity rivals that of the good doctor' (the good doctor, smiled down upon, like the 'little man' who reads the electricity meter)—but 'Bloom, unlike Johnson, needs no Boswell.' The author of 'The Vanity of Human Wishes' and *Rasselas* did not *need* Boswell. But this is the pass to which things have come, the insecure overclaim of a profession which feels itself, and is in some ways, undervalued. The most signal thing about the fourteen of us speaking on the humanities here today is this: that because of the misguided assumption that a professional occasion should be peopled exclusively by professionals, not one of us is a writer, an artist.

2. WILLIAM EMPSON AND 'THE LOONY HOOTERS'

My title comes from the sonnet by William Empson with which I shall duly end. It is with a different poem by Empson that I shall start. For in considering what has changed in the humanities during the past few decades, one necessary comparison is not that of a present-day practice with something very different that used to be indulged, but that of similar enterprises then and now. And I start with a poem, since the most important, sensitive, and abiding form that criticism can ever take is that of subsequent creation—*not*, then, the humanities, but the arts. Called into being by the grace, not of a profession, however honourable, but of a calling.

Consider the terms, then, and the conduct, the matter and the manners, in which, sixty years ago, the young Empson realized (made real to himself and to others) the age-old congeries of relativism and multiculturalism. Age-old, not, as is now clamoured, brand-newly brought to professional attention.

HOMAGE TO THE BRITISH MUSEUM

There is a Supreme God in the ethnological section;
A hollow toad shape, faced with a blank shield.
He needs his belly to include the Pantheon,
Which is inserted through a hole behind.
At the navel, at the points formally stressed, at the organs
    of sense,
Lice glue themselves, dolls, local deities,
His smooth wood creeps with all the creeds of the world.

Attending there let us absorb the cultures of nations
And dissolve into our judgement all their codes.
Then, being clogged with a natural hesitation
(People are continually asking one the way out),
Let us stand here and admit that we have no road.
Being everything, let us admit that is to be something,
Or give ourselves the benefit of the doubt;
Let us offer our pinch of dust all to this God,
And grant his reign over the entire building.

The patience, humour, honesty, and magnanimity of this poem furnish a touchstone by which to test not only the arguments but the argumentative conduct and tone of our recent and current 'debate'. 'Homage to the British Museum' stands in need of no admonishments as to what it is for things from other lands to be in the *British* Museum. Faced with the inevitable political realities of museum acquisition, the poem (sensitive to the unsettling relation of the political to the *inevitable*) does not lose its Marbles. In being, however ruefully, a homage to the British Museum, it is also a homage to human curiosity wherever found, to human knowledge, to such public service as established in our society's admirable past the great museums and libraries, to the proper study of mankind, and to freedom of mind. The poem's relaxed intelligence is the opposite of any relaxation of intelligence. And its sense—altogether humane and considerate—of how undulating and diverse are the considerations which should inform any thinking about relativism and multiculturalism is one which ought to put to shame what now passes for an advance upon Empson's antiquated 'naïveté'.

A colleague of mine, a couple of years ago, being, as they say, 'empowered' to set the allocations within a mandatory graduate-course which was *called* 'Introduction to Literary Study', specified the first six-sevenths of the course (readings in—natch—Marx, Freud, structuralism, post-structuralism, Lacanianism, and feminism French and American), and then added, not deigning now to specify: 'plus a couple of weeks for the old verities'.

Is this all that everything from Aristotle to Trilling, from Horace and Sidney to Eliot and Empson, amounts to? The old verities? I find this lacking in verity.

Empson's poem is, among so much else, an act of verity. Professionalized contempt for verities, like institutionalized subversion, constitutes an intrinsic absurdity, and all the more so when it is bent upon such art and thought as should keep us in our place; and these current ways of speaking are not an advance in complexity and subtlety of understanding, but a retreat from them.

I start from Empson, clearly, not just because of a conviction that my love of his work is a principled piety, but because—unlike such a member of the same generation as, say, Winters—Empson could with justice be thought of as actively in sympathy with many of the claims or ambitions of subsequent 'developments'. Empson cannot be charged with a cramped notion of what constitutes literature. He cannot be charged with an indifference to other disciplines or to other points of view than that of the liberal humanist (he wrote some of the best Marxist and some of the best Freudian criticism of the century), or charged with subscribing to the narrow insistence that a critic should not stray into areas where he or she is not an expert or an authority. Empson cannot be accused either of ignorance about, or indifference or hostility to, cultures that are not European or Western, having given much of his life to working in Japan and in China and to appreciating their achievements. He cannot be accused of 'complicity' with Christianity, since not only did he argue against the religion with passion and wit, he also studied, with patience, the faces of Buddha. His arguments cannot be brusqued aside as those of a man of the right, since he was a lifelong socialist. He respected such relativism as should be respected. And in terms of the more circumscribed world of literary argument, the author of *Seven Types of Ambiguity* and of *The Structure of Complex Words* cannot be accused of being antagonistic to or unskilled at high speculation and advanced thought. He was not an aesthete. Or a belle lettrist. Or a misogynist or homophobe. Etc., through the grimoire.

For these and many other reasons, Empson constitutes a legitimate *point de repère* when it comes to a comparison of the way we live now with what used to obtain. So take a page of his which engages directly with much of the impetus of our day, a page where Empson—rightly, just because not invariably—turns to consider literature under a political aspect, and even under the now-ubiquitous aspect of class injustice and grievance. Empson's thinking here is a measure, not unfortunately of how far we have come, but of how far our thinking about feeling has manifestly regressed since the days when Empson applied his intelligent conscience to the relations of politics to poetry. ('Intelligence', in Eliot's words, 'of which an important function is the discernment of exactly what, and how much, we feel in any given situation.'[1]) Here is Empson, sixty years ago, in 'Proletarian Literature':

Gray's *Elegy* is an odd case of poetry with latent political ideas:

> Full many a gem of purest ray serene
> The dark, unfathomed caves of ocean bear;
> Full many a flower is born to blush unseen
> And waste its sweetness on the desert air.

[1] *The Egoist*, iv (1917), 151.

What this means, as the context makes clear, is that eighteenth-century England had no scholarship system or *carrière ouverte aux talents*. This is stated as pathetic, but the reader is put into a mood in which one would not try to alter it. (It is true that Gray's society, unlike a possible machine society, was necessarily based on manual labour, but it might have used a man of special ability wherever he was born.) By comparing the social arrangement to Nature he makes it seem inevitable, which it was not, and gives it a dignity which was undeserved. Furthermore, a gem does not mind being in a cave and a flower prefers not to be picked; we feel that the man is like the flower, as short-lived, natural, and valuable, and this tricks us into feeling that he is better off without opportunities. The sexual suggestion of *blush* brings in the Christian idea that virginity is good in itself, and so that any renunciation is good; this may trick us into feeling it is lucky for the poor man that society keeps him unspotted from the World. The tone of melancholy claims that the poet understands the considerations opposed to aristocracy, though he judges against them; the truism of the reflections in the churchyard, the universality and impersonality this gives to the style, claim as if by comparison that we ought to accept the injustice of society as we do the inevitability of death.

Many people, without being communists, have been irritated by the complacence in the massive calm of the poem, and this seems partly because they feel there is a cheat in the implied politics; the 'bourgeois' themselves do not like literature to have too much 'bourgeois ideology'.

And yet what is said is one of the permanent truths; it is only in degree that any improvement of society could prevent wastage of human powers; the waste even in a fortunate life, the isolation even of a life rich in intimacy, cannot but be felt deeply, and is the central feeling of tragedy. And anything of value must accept this because it must not prostitute itself; its strength is to be prepared to waste itself, if it does not get its opportunity. A statement of this is certainly non-political because it is true in any society, and yet nearly all the great poetic statements of it are in a way 'bourgeois' like this one; they suggest to many readers, though they do not say, that for the poor man things cannot be improved even in degree.[2]

There is so much here that deserves and would repay attention. I single out not only the vigilance in concession (which is never merely rhetorical concession, of the 'I'm not saying . . .' kind which is now so convenient) but the insistence that if politics has its needed rights and claims, so too does a tragic sense of life. 'A statement of this is certainly non-political because it is true in any society.' The movement ('And yet . . .') is one of the great returns of the mind on itself, and is itself followed with a further return ('and yet').

[2] *Some Versions of Pastoral* (1935), pp. 4–5.

We may return to an earlier mind than Empson's for a sense of a different veracity weighed. Coleridge has in his Notebooks (Entry 3415, 1808–9):

Full many a flower &c-. Essay. To examine what & whether there be truth in this—Take the present age/Every Boy who strongly wished it, might learn to read—3 out of 4 are now taught reading—it is scarce possible that he might not procure the Bible, & many religious Books, which at all events would give him the best & most natural Language— here quote Dr H. More—probably, Milton, Gray, Thomson, &c/how much more than Pindar ever read!—and yet no great Geniuses start up from the Multitude now more than 100 years back—

Coleridge's pointed doubt about Gray's lines constitutes a reminder that even the widest of particular attentions, such as Empson's, can never be wide enough. Yet how fine is Empson's adherence to Coleridge's principle: 'To examine what & whether there be truth in this'. Not narrowed to 'whether', and not splayed to 'what', but holding the two in happy tension. For Coleridge, too, 'and yet'.

'And yet' . . . 'and yet': in Empson, the thing is so beautifully done that an effort is needed to realize that the humane analysis is—in its attention to how metaphorical likening may insinuate and may belie—deconstruction. In saying this, I don't mean, in the current manner, that what Empson wrote is deserving of our respect because it had the wisdom to anticipate so gratifyingly our present splendid state of enlightenment. Rather the reverse: such criticism as Empson's sets a standard which subsequent indurations, self-advertisements, misrepresentations of that past which Empson went to constitute, fall hideously short of. I heard a colleague of mine aver at a graduate seminar: 'At least since [1968] it has been necessary to *think* about literature.' My challenge to those who set such store by 'recent developments', and who think—or on politically pressing occasions affect to think—that critics like Empson (or Johnson or Coleridge) did not think about literature, would be to produce a recent passage of *political* literary criticism—that is, within exactly the enterprise which is now made so much of—which does as much justice to the issues, is as engaged and engaging, as this of Empson's from the slandered past.

I am reminded of Byron's indignant scrutiny and self-scrutiny when he was pondering the condescension which his time visited upon Pope: 'I took Moore's poems & my own & some others—and

went over them side by side with Pope's—and I was really astonished (I ought not to have been so) and mortified—at the ineffable
distance in point of sense—harmony—effect—and even *Imagination*
Passion—& *Invention*—between the little Queen Anne's Man—& us
of the lower Empire.'[3]

That these days we face a situation new in some or even in most
respects does not mean that what needs to be said, or done, is
anything new. It means the opposite: that the home truths will, not
for the first time, be the old truths. Not—for there is always an
enemy to the right as well as to the left—not that what now needs
to be borne in mind did not need to be borne in mind in the old
days, or was then sufficiently acknowledged or attended to. 'What
is known is rejected, because it is not sufficiently considered, that
men more frequently require to be reminded than informed,' in the
words of Dr Johnson's great reminder.[4]

But there lurks, to adapt Wyndham Lewis, not only *The Demon
of Progress in the Arts* but the demon of progress in criticism of the
arts. I have noticed that my colleagues' sharpness of mind is in
inverse proportion to their recourse to the words 'cutting edge', and
their respect for art in inverse proportion to their invoking the words
'state of the art'—these being the manipulative and capitulative terms
in which many of them praise their peers, seek to shape their
Department, and incite their graduate students.

What are the forces which have increasingly formed or deformed
the humanities in the universities? When Philip Larkin sought to
identify the infernal trinity which had brought death into the world
and all our woe, in the shape (if shape it might be called that shape
had none) of *modern* jazz, *modern* poetry, and *modern* painting, he
resorted to apt alliteration's artful arsenal: Parker, Pound, and Picasso.
Explosively. So: Politicization, Pyrrhonism, and Professionalization.
Not a holy alliance; and a distinctly contrarious, threatening, but
also threatened one.

1. Politicization: which is not at all the same as the claim that,
as Empson understood, all literature, like all else, may on occasion
be seen under a political aspect; instead, we suffer the distorted
insistence that literature has to be seen under this aspect only, and

[3] To John Murray, 15 September 1817; *Letters and Journals*, ed. Leslie A. Marchand,
v (1976), 265.
[4] *The Rambler*, No. 2, 24 March 1750.

this with a very narrow view of the politically honourable and of politics as nobbut power-play.

2. Pyrrhonism: which is, as laxly practised by non-philosophers, scepticism turned self-annulling, complacent, and airy after putting on weightlessness. Pyrrhonism, as in such relativism as forgets Empson's admonition to I. A. Richards in 1949: 'It is a familiar paradox; any serious attempt at establishing a relativity turns out to establish an absolute; in the case of Einstein the velocity of light, and I understand a good deal more by this time.'[5] Pyrrhonism, again, as in deconstruction's elaborate facility, happy to forget T. S. Eliot's reminder in 1933 about deconstruction's parent, *irony*. Every word of Eliot here is pertinent to deconstruction's effortless superiority of pyrrhonism:

What we rebel against is neither the use of irony against definite men, institutions or abuses, nor is it the use (as by Jules Laforgue) to express a *dédoublement* of the personality against which the subject struggles. It is the use of irony to give the appearance of a philosophy of life, as something final and not instrumental, that leaves us now indifferent; it seems to us an evasion of the difficulty of living, where it pretends to be a kind of solution of it. And the work built upon it comes to seem merely superfluous, an encumbrance, a luxury article produced for a public that has disappeared.[6]

3. Professionalization: which needs to acknowledge that it should stand differently to such objects of attention as are intrinsically resistant to the claims of professionalization—for instance, art. 'Professionalization makes thought possible': such were the disgraceful, hubristic, and self-serving words of *Speaking for the Humanities*, an American Council of Learned Societies Occasional Paper, 1989. But the achievements of literature, as of all the arts, put up some resistance—not a simple opposition—to professionalism and professionalization, and this means that the responsibility of the professional scholar to literature (to which he or she owes a responsibility even greater than that owed to any individual or institution) cannot be entirely or briskly assimilated to other professionalisms within the university, such as, say, those very necessary professionalisms of law school or dental school. The virtues of the amateur need to be acknowledged,

[5] *Argufying*, ed. John Haffenden (1987), p. 212.
[6] *The Criterion*, xii (1933), 469.

respected, and incorporated so far as is possible within professional life. Granted, the amateur can slacken into the amateurish, but no more damagingly than can the professional harden into the professionalized.

The professionalizing of literary studies, by which our culture is both the gainer and the loser, has brought with it the sacrifice entailed by all professionalism. That this is inevitable does not mean that there is nothing to be done about it; one thing to do is to strive to maximize the advantages and minimize the disadvantages of the unavoidable plight; another is to live always in the knowledge of such a plight and thereby at least to gain some modesty and be given some pause. Among the most generous things in the world are misgivings.

Since the medium of literature is the same as that of literary studies, there will always be not just the possibility but the likelihood of professional envy and ingratitude. Literary criticism is not only the beneficiary of this continuity of medium but the maleficiary. For every occasion on which literary criticism is thereby enabled to be more precisely applicable and substantiable than, say, criticism of music (which does not manifest itself for most purposes in the medium of music), there will be at least the danger of an occasion on which literary criticism will succumb to the incitements endemic to such continuity. Why have I been talking about Tennyson's poems instead of Tennyson talking about mine? But it is not only a matter of the meeting of the small-minded with the myriad-minded, but of the unavoidable tension, at least, between the two forms—and levels—of word-work.

All this, plus—more plosives—the perennial problem of patronage, now itself a professional pressure.

Literature of any seriousness of ambition and achievement never has been and never will be able to exist without patronage, and the great patron of literature in our society—the university—is no less open to the temptation to coerce and to manipulate than were the other great patrons: the church, a cultivated class, the party. I don't mean the common cry that the university is a mere instrument of the ruling class, an accomplice in hegemony, but simply that a vigilant sense of its own honour would require it to be no less suspicious of its own motives than of others', and not least when congratulating itself on having evolved a 'hermeneutics of suspicion'.

And whereas there is no such thing as philosophical study distinct from philosophy, there is such a thing as literature, which should not be confused with—or by—literary studies. Literary studies, though, are always tempted, and are sometimes eager, to deny or ignore the distinction. Or to admit the distinction but to insist, Better a living dog than a dead lion. For some of us, the most brutal hatred within the acronym DWEM is not the racism of White or the sexism of Male but the embittered provincialism which makes Dead a term of abuse. It was Eliot who saw, as early as 1944, that in our age

there is coming into existence a new kind of provincialism which perhaps deserves a new name. It is a provincialism, not of space, but of time; one for which history is merely the chronicle of human devices which have served their turn and been scrapped, one for which the world is the property solely of the living, a property in which the dead hold no shares.[7]

The sheer desolation of such provincialism, especially when it entails the repudiation of literature under the aspect of life after death, is the lot of those who cannot accede to the truth that Coleridge, white European male, set down. This, a matter not of being marginalized, but of Coleridge's *Marginalia*:

Mem. Among the grounds for recommending the perusal of our elder writers, Hooker, Taylor, Baxter, in short almost any of the Folios composed from Edward VI to Charles II

1. The overcoming the habit of deriving your whole pleasure passively from the Book itself, which can only be effected by excitement of Curiosity or of some Passion. Force yourself to reflect on what you read paragraph by paragraph, and in a short time you will derive your pleasure, an ample portion at least, from the activity of your own mind. All else is Picture Sunshine.

2. The conquest of party and sectarian Prejudices, when you have on the same table the works of a Hammond and a Baxter; and reflect how many & how momentous their points of agreement; how few and almost childish the differences, which estranged and irritated these good men! . . .

3. It will secure you from the narrow Idolatry of the Present Times and Fashions: and create the noblest kind of Imaginative Power in your Soul, that of living in past ages, <wholly devoid of which power a man can neither anticipate the Future, nor even live a truly human life, a life of reason, in the Present.>[8]

---

[7] 'What is a Classic?' (1944); *On Poetry and Poets* (1957), p. 69.
[8] *Marginalia*, ed. George Whalley, i (1980), p. 280.

There is another noble kind of imaginative power, distinguishable from though not divorced from that of living in past ages, and it is that to which, if I were pressed to identify one crucial truth now denied, ridiculed, or ignored in a great deal of recent literary study, I should give the greatest salience. Nothing is more remote from the atmosphere and the proceedings of radical literary theory than one particular truth to which Empson—radical, literary, and a great thinker—gave a central place, and which he knew was anathema to missionaries. Empson wrote of Fielding: 'he does not find relativism alarming, because he feels that to understand codes other than your own is likely to make your judgments better.' But understanding codes other than your own is just what the new presbyters, like the old priests, will not encourage or respect. No orthodoxy, self-righteous and undisturbed, whether the one that Empson was up against or the one that it has now counter-produced, ever pay it more than lip-service.

It strikes me that modern critics, whether as a result of the neo-Christian movement or not, have become oddly resistant to admitting that there is more than one code of morals in the world, whereas the central purpose of reading imaginative literature is to accustom yourself to this basic fact. I do not at all mean that a literary critic ought to avoid making moral judgements; that is useless as well as tiresome, because the reader has enough sense to start guessing round it at once.[9]

It seems to me that the chief function of imaginative literature is to make you realise that other people are very various, many of them quite different from you, with different 'systems of value' as well; but the effect of almost any orthodoxy is to hide this, and pretend that everybody *ought* to be like Homer or Dr Leavis.[10]

The main purpose of reading imaginative literature is to grasp a wide variety of experience, imagining people with codes and customs very unlike our own.[11]

Politically, Empson seldom agreed with Eliot, but each had a large enough sense of this truth for there to be concord between Empson's convictions and those of Eliot when the latter argued for the worth of entertaining beliefs. We all need to be able to entertain beliefs

[9] *Using Biography* (1984), p. 142.
[10] *Argufying*, p. 13, the Introduction, quoting a letter.
[11] (1973); *Argufying*, p. 218.

which we do not now and may perhaps not subsequently find ourselves moved to accept, and literature is one of the great means by which we preserve a respect for the practice of entertaining beliefs (as well as for such beliefs as are not ours) even while not dissolving the indispensable distinction between the entertaining of a belief and the holding of one.

For someone of my beliefs, there is, then, plenty of cause for dismay. There is, first, everything which has not changed in the hundred years since Matthew Arnold issued his warning as to curricular reform:

I have no difficulty in saying that I should like to see standard English authors joined to the standard authors of Greek and Latin literature who have to be taken up for a pass, or for honours, at the Universities. . . . The omission of the mother tongue and its literature in school and University instruction is peculiar, so far as I know, to England. You do a good work in urging us to repair that omission.

But I will not conceal from you that I have no confidence in those who at the Universities regulate studies, degrees, and honours. To regulate these matters great experience of the world, steadiness, simplicity, breadth of view, are desirable; I do not see how those who actually regulate them can well have these qualifications; I am sure that in what they have done in the last forty years they have not shown them. Restlessness, a disposition to try experiments and to multiply studies and schools, are what they have shown, and what they will probably continue to show—and this though personally many of them may be very able and distinguished men. I fear, therefore, that while you are seeking an object altogether good—the completing of the old and great degree in Arts—you may obtain something which will not only not be that, but will be a positive hindrance to it.[12]

There is, next, something which—at least on the scale on which it is now practised—does seem to me to amount to a new cause for dismay: the insolently mendacious misrepresentation not only of the great works of Western literature but of the responses which they received over the centuries. I think, for instance, of a recent paragraph whose rewriting of history could have emanated from a Ministry of Truth, the paragraph which closes the entry on Postmodernism

[12] *The Pall Mall Budget*, 6 January 1887; *The Last Word*, ed. R. H. Super (1977), pp. 379–80.

in *The Johns Hopkins Guide to Literary Theory & Criticism* (1994) and which is bent upon

the future of a Western tradition that now appears more heterogeneous than previously thought even while it appears insufficiently tolerant of (open to) multiplicity. At the very least, postmodernism highlights the multiplication of voices, questions, and conflicts that has shattered what once seemed to be (although it never really was) the placid unanimity of the great tradition and of the West that gloried in it.

But who, outside the world of such politically convenient fantasies (straw men being so much easier to eviscerate), ever posited 'unanimity' in the Western tradition, a unanimity now at last gleefully exposed as non-existent? What tradition of the 'placid' can it be which has had to reckon with Dickens and Carlyle, Milton and Swift, Dante and Racine, Blake and Cobbett? The sleazy prestidigitation of the peroration has to be seen to be disbelieved. And I do not believe that fifty years ago a work of reference, from the university press of a great university, would have been so hospitable to the systematic mendacity which permeates not only the whole of this entry but so much of intellectual life in the humanities.

Cause for dismay, then. But, seeking resolution and independence, one may remember Wordsworth's admonitory rhyming of the line 'And mighty poets in their misery dead' with the line 'And hope that is unwilling to be fed'. We must not be unwilling to feed hope. Sometimes there are more than crumbs of hope, achievements that do more than a little to counteract the dismaying scene.

'Not wrongly moved by this dismaying scene': Empson in his cryptic exultant *Sonnet* managed, even in 1942, to enlist himself weirdly among the hopers, up against the loony hooters, his poem issuing in a vision, once more, of the proper study of mankind, an evocation of the common humanity, for all the human differences, which the arts and their ancillary, the humanities, exist to respect and to restore:

> Not wrongly moved by this dismaying scene
>   The thinkers like the nations getting caught
>   Joined in the organising that they fought
> To scorch all earth of all but one machine.
>
> It can be swung, is what these hopers mean,
>   For all the loony hooters can be bought
>   On the small ball. It can then all be taught
> And reconverted to be kind and clean.

A more heartening fact about the cultures of man
  Is their appalling stubbornness. The sea
Is always calm ten fathoms down. The gigan-
  -tic anthropological circus riotously
Holds open all its booths. The pygmy plan
  Is one note each and the tune goes out free.

ACKNOWLEDGEMENTS

The essays on Gaskell and on literature and fact have been printed only as university lectures; those on Crabbe, Froude, Tennyson, and Empson have not previously been printed.

Doctor Faustus:	the F. W. Bateson Memorial Lecture, *Essays in Criticism*, April 1985
Donne:	*Literature and the Body: Selected Papers from the English Institute, 1986*, ed. Elaine Scarry, 1988
Clarendon:	*Augustan Studies: Essays in Honor of Irvin Ehrenpreis*, ed. D. L. Patey and T. Keegan, 1985
Austen:	the Jane Austen Society, 1982
Gaskell, Froude, Tennyson:	the Clark Lectures, 1991, Trinity College, Cambridge
Gaskell:	the Pratt Lecture, 1994, Memorial University, Newfoundland
George Eliot:	broadcast by the B.B.C., 1980; a shortened version in *The Listener*, 11 December 1980
Hardy:	*The Critical Review*, No. 32, 1992
Lowell:	*Arion*, May 1991
Austin:	*University of Toronto Quarterly*, Spring 1992
Literature and the matter of fact:	the University Lecture, 1990, Boston University
Literary principles:	*Proceedings of the Northeastern University Center for Literary Studies*, 1985
The 'battle of the books':	*The New Criterion*, September 1989, from a symposium at Yale University, April 1989

The author expresses his gratitude:

For Bob Dylan, 'One Too Many Mornings': copyright © 1964, 1966 by Warner Bros. Music, copyright renewed 1992 by Special Rider Music. All rights reserved. International copyright secured. Reprinted by permission.

To Chatto & Windus, for William Empson's 'Camping Out', 'Homage to the British Museum', and 'Sonnet: Not wrongly moved', from *Collected Poems*.

To D. J. Enright, for 'Streets'.

To Gavin Ewart, for 'Discover the Secrets of a Royal Home'.

To Faber and Faber Limited, for W. H. Auden's 'Academic Graffiti', from *Collected Poems* by W. H. Auden edited by Edward Mendelson; T. S. Eliot's 'Sweeney Erect', from *Collected Poems 1909–1962* by T. S. Eliot; Philip Larkin's 'The Literary World: II', from *Collected Poems* by Philip Larkin edited by Anthony Thwaite; Robert Lowell's 'George Eliot', from *History* by Robert Lowell; and excerpts from *Phaedra: A Verse Translation of Racine's Phèdre* by Robert Lowell.

To Farrar, Straus & Giroux, Inc., for Philip Larkin's 'The Literary World: II', from *Collected Poems*; copyright © 1988, 1989 by the Estate of Philip Larkin; and for Robert Lowell's 'George Eliot', from *History*; copyright © 1973 by Robert Lowell, and excerpts from *Phaedra* translated by Robert Lowell; copyright © 1960, 1961 by Robert Lowell, copyright renewed © 1988, 1989 by Caroline Lowell, Harriet Lowell, and Sheridan Lowell.

To Harcourt Brace & Company, for 'Camping Out', 'Homage to the British Museum', and 'Sonnet' from COLLECTED POEMS OF WILLIAM EMPSON, copyright 1949 and renewed 1977 by William Empson. Reprinted by permission.

To the University Press of New England, for James Wright's 'Eisenhower's Visit to Franco, 1959', from *The Branch Will Not Break* © 1963 James Wright, Wesleyan University Press.

To the Rhoda Weyr Agency: © 1976 by Randall Jarrell of the English translation of Goethe's *Faust, Part I*, published by Farrar Straus & Giroux. Permission granted by Rhoda Weyr Agency, New York.

INDEX